4-1-69

Controversy
in the
Twenties

Willard B. Gatewood, Jr.
Editor

Controversy
in the
Twenties ❧ *Fundamentalism,*
Modernism, and Evolution

VANDERBILT UNIVERSITY PRESS *Nashville*

Standard Book Number 8265-1127-9
Library of Congress Catalogue Card Number 69-11279

Printed in the United States of America by
The William Byrd Press, Inc., Richmond, Virginia

The author and publisher gatefully acknowledge permission to reprint from the following copyrighted materials:
Modernism: A Revolt Against Christianity; A Revolt Against Good Government by James M. Gray, copyright 1924, Moody Press, Moody Bible Institute of Chicago. *Christianity and Liberalism* by J. Gresham Machen, copyright 1923, trustees u/W J. Gresham Machen, William B. Eerdmans Publishing Company. "Our Secularized Civilization" by Reinhold Niebuhr, *The Christian Century*, April 22, 1926, copyright 1926, Christian Century Foundation. *Evolution—A Menace* by John W. Porter, copyright 1922, Sunday School Board of the Southern Baptist Convention. *The Famous New York Fundamentalist-Modernist Debates: The Orthodox Side* by John Roach Straton, copyright 1925, George H. Doran Co., renewed 1952, Georgia Hillyer Straton. *The Phantom of Organic Evolution* by George McCready Price, copyright 1924; *Christianity and Progress* by Harry Emerson Fosdick, copyright 1924; *In His Image* by William Jennings Bryan, copyright 1922; Fleming H. Revell Company. *Science: The False Messiah* by C. E. Ayres, copyright 1927, renewed 1954, Bobbs-Merrill Company, Inc. *AAUP Bulletin*, February 1924, January 1925, copyright 1924, 1925, American Association of University Professors. *The New Decalogue of Science* by Albert Edward Wiggam, copyright 1922, 1923, 1925, Bobbs-Merrill Company, Inc., renewed 1953, Albert Edward Wiggam. *The War on Modern Science: A Short History of the Fundamentalist Attacks on Evolution and Modernism* by Maynard Shipley, copyright 1927, Alfred A. Knopf. *Religious Certitude in an Age of Science* by Charles A. Dinsmore, copyright 1924, University of North Carolina Press. *Crossing the Deadline or the Recrucifixion of the Lord Jesus Christ* by H. C. Morrison, copyright 1924, Pentecostal Publishing Company, renewed, Morrison Theological Trust. *American Inquisitors: A Commentary on Dayton and Chicago* by Walter Lippmann, copyright 1928, The Macmillan Company. *The San Francisco Debates on Evolution* by Maynard Shipley, copyright 1925, Pacific Press Publishing Association. *The Gates Open Slowly: A History of Education in Kentucky* by Frank L. McVey, copyright 1949, University of Kentucky Press. *Center of the Storm* by John T. Scopes and James Presley, copyright © 1967 by John T. Scopes and James Presley, by permission of Holt, Rinehart and Winston, Inc. "Why the Dayton Trial Will Resound to the South's Good," *Manufacturers' Record*, August 20, 1925, copyright 1925, Conway Publications. *More Lives Than One: An Autobiography* by Joseph Wood Krutch, copyright © 1962, Joseph Wood Krutch, by permission of William Morrow and Company, Inc. *Teeftallow* by T. S. Stribling, copyright 1926, Doubleday & Company, Inc. *Manse Dwellers* by Luther Little, copyright 1927, Luther Little. "America and Fundamentalism" by S. K. Ratcliffe, *Contemporary Review*, September 1925. *America Comes of Age* by André Siegfried, by permission of Harcourt, Brace & World, Inc. *The Rise of American Civilization* by Charles and Mary Beard, copyright 1933, The Macmillan Company, renewed 1961, William Beard and Miriam Beard Vagts. *The Modern Use of the Bible* by Harry Emerson Fosdick, copyright 1924, The Macmillian Company, renewed 1952, Harry Emerson Fosdick. *The Faith of Modernism* by Shailer Mathews, copyright 1924, The Macmillan Company, renewed, Estate of Shailer Mathews. "Evolution in Education in California" by W. W. Campbell, *Science*, April 3, 1925; "Opposition to Evolution in Minnesota" by George O. Smith, *Science*, December 10, 1922; *Summarized Proceedings of the American Association for the Advancement of Science, 1921-1925;* "Fundamentalism" by Preston Slosson, *Scientific Monthly*, May 1926; copyright 1925, 1922, 1925, 1926, American Association for Advancement of Science. University of North Carolina Papers, Southern Historical Collection, University of North Carolina.

1489698

To my wife

Preface

BOTH lay and church historians have lavished considerable attention upon the disturbance within American Protestantism during the 1920s known as the modernist-fundamentalist conflict. Despite the quantity of historical literature devoted to specific aspects of the subject, few historians have attempted a comprehensive study of the meaning and impact of the conflict. All too frequently the so-called war in the churches during the 1920s has been viewed as merely another aberration of a decade which spawned all manner of cultural curiosities or has been interpreted almost exclusively in the light of its most dramatic phase, the controversy over biological evolution. Actually the modernist-fundamentalist conflict involved far more than either interpretation implies. Its origins lay deep in the history of Protestant thought, and its impact was more pervasive than historians of the 1920s sometimes suggest. The basic purpose of the documents and commentaries which make up this volume is to indicate the nature and dimension of the climactic confrontation between modernists and fundamentalists and to relate their struggle to the cultural and psychological milieu of the post–World War I decade. The place of the evolution controversy is, I hope, sufficiently evident without obscuring the broader phenomenon.

The documentary record of the modernist-fundamentalist disturbance is extraordinarily varied and abundant. It includes literally hundreds of articles, tracts, books, sermons, unpublished letters, and a wide assortment of other relevant materials. Therefore, one of my most perplexing problems involved the selection of a relatively small number of these documents which at once incorporated representative views of the protagonists regarding the basic issues at stake and revealed the diverse implications of the conflict. An effort was also made to include selections which indicated its chronological and geographical scope as well as its pervasive effect upon Protestant denominations in general. The history of the modernist-fundamentalist conflict largely dictated the organization of the documents: at the outset it seemed necessary to present a broad summary of the theological positions of both combatants and to indicate that the fundamentalists were largely responsible for making evolution the focus of the struggle; then, once the general premises and context of the conflict had been established, it appeared appropriate to suggest something about the nature of its impact upon science, education, politics, and literature. Since the Scopes case represented a kind of high point in the drama, it seemed to warrant separate consideration. The closing chapter consists of intelligent assessments of the modernist-fundamentalist dispute by contemporary observers who attempted to probe beneath its more bizarre manifestations.

Numerous individuals have provided valuable assistance in the preparation of this volume. The acquisition of documentary materials was greatly facilitated by the cordial co-operation of librarians and archivists at Duke University, the University of North Carolina at Chapel Hill, the Library of Congress, Emory University, and Columbia Theological Seminary (Atlanta). Among those who so graciously responded to my requests regarding the use of works either written or controlled by them are Harry Elmer Barnes, Kirtley Mather, Hillyer Straton, Mrs. Warner Overton, T. T. Martin, Walter Lippmann, Mrs. Maynard Shipley, and Robert E. Mathews. I am particularly indebted to Mrs. William Franklin Burroughs of the University of Georgia Library for kindnesses too numerous to mention here and to Mrs. Marion Perry for her proficient typing services. My friend and colleague David Edwin Harrell, Jr., read the manuscript and gave me the benefit of his enviable knowledge of American church history. My wife, Lu Brown Gatewood, maintained a constant interest in the project and is actually responsible for its completion.

W. B. G.

Contents

Preface   vii

Introduction   3

1. Contenders for the Faith   49

2. Evolution: Focus of the Fundamentalist Offensive   113

3. Science: A Source of Controversy   147

4. Embattled Academe   217

5. Piety and Politics   285

6. Modernists and Fundamentalists at Armageddon:
   The Scopes Case   331

7. Reflections in the Literary Mirror   369

8. An American Phenomenon: Contemporary Interpretations   409

A Note on Secondary Sources   444

Index   453

Controversy
in the
Twenties

Introduction

A GENERATION familiar with the "God Is Dead" controversy and
C. P. Snow's *Two Cultures* may look back with sympathetic interest
upon the modernist-fundamentalist struggle of the 1920s. Yet the same
generation, accustomed to missiles and moonshots, is likely to dismiss the
most dramatic aspect of that struggle, the disturbance over evolution, as
merely another of the quaint antics so prevalent during the "era of
wonderful nonsense." But behind the more ludicrous episodes spawned
by this disturbance lay the deep-seated fears, anxieties, and frustration of
a people who had come to feel alienated from their past. The old
confidence and optimism often gave way to a sense of uneasiness which
not even the excesses of ballyhoo and "whoopee" could wholly obscure.
This alienation which expressed itself in an infinite variety of ways
helps to explain the ambivalence and irony that characterized the 1920s.

In many respects, World War I was the signal for a series of tremors
that reverberated in American society throughout the postwar decade.
Many agreed with Richard Le Gallienne's observation in 1924 that society was going "through a process of reconstruction, and the process, as
it has always been, is disquieting."[1] More graphic was Willa Cather's
simple pronouncement that "the world broke in two in 1922 or there-

[1] Quoted in *Vanity Fair*, XXI (January, 1924), 94.

3

abouts."[2] The novelist obviously referred to the cumulative impact of a half-century of social, economic, and intellectual changes, as well as the host of new forces unleashed by the war, which collectively created a new America where traditional formulas for the good life seemed strangely inappropriate. Revolutionary developments in science, technology, and psychology substantially altered man's view of himself and his universe as well as his ways of making a living. The easy access of radios, movies, and automobiles in the postwar era had an immeasurable effect upon American culture and contributed significantly to changes in morals, manners, and mobility. Urbanization gathered such new momentum that during the 1920s, for the first time in the nation's history, more people lived in the city than in the country. This shift in population reflected the dramatic growth of industrialism that characterized the period and gained for it the epithet "second industrial revolution." As old ways changed, so did old certainties. A rash of social and cultural innovations threatened traditional concepts and values. Gone was that "ineffable certainty which made God and his plan as real as the lamp-post."[3]

The impact of the "new era" was nowhere more evident than in American religious life. The postwar climate witnessed significant changes in both the institutional and theological positions of the Protestant churches. The decline in church attendance, missionary efforts, and the Social Gospel during the 1920s coincided with an increasing interest in humanism, scientism, and behaviorism. "The agony of a spiritual quest in a world that regarded spiritual matters with indifference," wrote one student of postwar American literature, "was one of the most profound emotional experiences of the 1920's."[4] Many churchmen disturbed by the plight of Protestantism demanded a religious revival. They agreed with Bishop Francis J. McConnell of the Methodist Church who in 1924 declared: "we were told that an upward moral movement was sweeping us in spite of ourselves. The events of the last eight years have pretty well knocked this notion to splinters."[5] Some Americans actually thought they detected the beginning of a "New Reformation." Unable to decide whether religion was in the midst of a reformation or

[2] Quoted in William E. Leuchtenburg, *The Perils of Prosperity, 1914–32* (Chicago: University of Chicago Press, 1958), p. 273.

[3] Walter Lippmann, *A Preface to Morals* (New York: Macmillan, 1929), p. 21.

[4] Frederick J. Hoffman, *The Twenties: American Writing in the Postwar Decade* (New York: Viking Press, 1955), pp. 290–291.

[5] Francis J. McConnell, *Is God Limited?* (New York: Abingdon, 1924), pp. 89–90.

a decline, the distinguished theologian William Pierson Merrill was nonetheless certain that "Protestantism is at the crossroads!"[6] Perceptive foreign observers generally agreed with his assessment. In their view, America's "man-made, not time-made, commonwealth" was in the midst of an awesome "social and moral crisis."[7] In a sense Americans were in the throes of their first major confrontation with the twentieth century.

So direct was the confrontation that Americans could scarcely have failed to recognize that the old order was rapidly disintegrating. Some welcomed the opportunity to overhaul senile institutions and to chart new courses; others were profoundly and geniunely disturbed by what appeared to them to be sheer chaos. All the changes, so it seemed especially to the latter, conspired to dehumanize man, to obliterate areas of certainty in human affairs, and to clear the right-of-way for the triumph of secularism. Such anxiety often induced popular spasms of disorientation characterized by indiscriminate, almost blind, assaults upon all phenomena associated with the new order. One critic, agonized by the irreverence of postwar America, declared:

This is an age of new things. So many new discoveries—so many new inventions—so many combinations that the people are all at sea. In this age we have new thought, new voices, new books, new theology, new psychology, new philosophy, new religion, and everything that hell can suggest and the devil concoct.[8]

Groups and individuals in search of normalcy and the return of certitude often employed the tactic of excluding both ideas and practices which they held responsible for the breakdown of traditional codes and the destruction of eternal verities. Such ideas and practices were considered "subversive," a term used widely in the 1920s in a variety of contexts. Both New York's Lusk Laws of 1921 and the Tennessee antievolution law of 1925 were essentially designed to prevent subversion and to protect the American Way. To a large extent, the Sacco-Vanzetti case and the "Monkey Trial" at Dayton were products of the same exclusionist mood.

6 See William Pierson Merrill, "Protestantism at the Crossroads," *World's Work*, XLVII (February 1924), 418–424.

7 Bernard Faÿ, "Protestant America," *The Living Age*, CCCIV (August 1928), 1193–1201; see also Salvador de Maderiaga, "Americans Are Boys," *Harper's Magazine*, CLVII (July 1928), 239–245.

8 Baxter F. McLendon, *The Story of My Life* and *Other Sermons* (Lynchburg, Va.: Press of Brown-Morrison Co., 1923), p. 38.

The head-on collision between those determined to recapture the past and those desirous of coming to terms with the new conditions filled the air with controversy. Since many were convinced that the battle to preserve American values would be decided on the religious front, it was not surprising that few of these clashes generated more furor than the so-called war in the churches. Throughout most of the decade, theological conservatives or "fundamentalists" waged a militant offensive against religious modernism.[9] The martial language and biblical symbolism employed in their warfare seemed calculated to conjure up the image of an epic struggle between rival contenders for the faith. The martial quality of their combat reached a climax in the controversy over evolution—the most dramatic aspect of a many-sided struggle. A Louisiana clergyman, opposed to all types of modernists, provided some insight into the complexity and pervasiveness of the "enemy" against which many fundamentalists were actually fighting. "I would say," he declared, "that a modernist in government is an anarchist and Bolshevik; in science he is an evolutionist; in business he is a Communist; in art a futurist; in music his name is jazz; and in religion an atheist and infidel."[10] The sustained intensity of the modernist-fundamentalist encounters prompted Professor Richard Hofstadter to describe the 1920s as "the focal decade in the Kulturkampf of American Protestantism."[11]

[9] Obviously there existed in the 1920s numerous American Protestants who could not be classified as either fundamentalists or modernists. Alarmed by the disruptive effect of the modernist-fundamentalist controversy upon the inclusive fellowship of the church, this noncombative element of indeterminate size generally supported the efforts of denominational politicians who worked toward silencing theological debates. Professor Robert T. Handy has grouped American Protestants in the 1920s into five theological categories: (1) modernists; (2) evangelical liberals; (3) conservative evangelicals; (4) strict conservatives; (5) fundamentalists. He also contends that what separated fundamentalists from other theological conservatives "was probably more a matter of mood and spirit than basic theological divergence." For the purposes of this essay the terms "modernists" and "fundamentalists" will be used to designate those at either extreme as well as those who tended to gravitate in one direction or the other when the modernist-fundamentalist conflict climaxed in the 1920s. For an analysis of the five theological parties and an explanation of how Protestants occupying a middle ground "tended to divide in support of one extreme or the other extreme," see Robert T. Handy, "Fundamentalism and Modernism in Perspective," *Religion in Life*, XXIV (Summer 1955), 381–394.

[10] W. E. Dodd, "Three Questions Concerning Modernism," *The Christian Index*, CV (January 22, 1925), 7–8.

[11] Richard Hofstadter, *Anti-Intellectualism in American Life* (New York: Alfred Knopf, 1963), p. 123.

Contemporary accounts of the conflict generally described it in terms of the polarization of Protestantism. Certainly, as it intensified, those who occupied a theological ground between modernism and fundamentalism tended to move to one extreme or the other. Professor Robert T. Handy has noted that in the heat of the battle, when Protestantism seemed bifurcated between modernism and fundamentalism, extremists had their opportunity. Contemporary observers who attempted to explain the origins of the disturbance almost invariably stressed the role of World War I. Some suggested that the shock of war and the "nervous overstrain" that it produced drove prople to extremes, "making liberals more liberal and reactionaries more reactionary." Others saw the war as creating a fighting spirit that outlived the war. And still others held the war primarily responsible for the spread of a "great fear, with a craving for something solid and a return to normalcy." More specifically, the war stimulated discussions of church unity and a demand by liberal churchmen for "deliverance from sectarianism." A church "open free without test or barrier of belief" was essential, declared one modernist, if the church was to "stand the test of our logical and searching years."[12] The relaxation of creedal requirements implicit in such proposals was anathema to the defenders of orthodoxy who generally interpreted the church unity movement as a deceptive tactic by modernists to substitute a commitment to social service for any "declaration of fundamentals." To thwart this "journey into apostasy," the fundamentalists felt compelled to organize an all-out offensive against modernism.

At the same time, the findings of those who investigated the religious beliefs of American servicemen were aggravating the tensions within the churches. Typical was a highly publicized report by the interdenominational Committee on War and Religious Outlook which, in brief, concluded that American men were woefully ignorant of the meaning of Christianity and church membership. For the fundamentalists, such findings confirmed their long-standing contention regarding the inadequacies of the Social Gospel and liberal theology in general and bolstered their determination to remedy the sorry state of American religious life by a revival of the old-time religion with its emphasis on the Bible and individual salvation. Quite to the contrary, liberal Protestants interpreted the committee's report as evidence of the failure of orthodox

[12] Anne K. Tuell, "The House of Unity," *The Open Court*, XXXIV (June 1920), 329.

theology to make the Christian faith relevant to modern man. Leighton
Parks, a distinguished Congregational clergyman whose *The Crisis of
the Church* (1920) reflected this view, protested that the church, under the orthodox formula, would completely obscure the real "meaning
of the Kingdom of God" by identifying "salvation with individual escape from the tortures of hell." After a tour of the American lines in
Western Europe, another well-known liberal theologian, Harry Emerson
Fosdick, reported that the only hope of the church was to proclaim boldly
"social aims worth fighting for, not a mere gospel of safety."[13] Voicing
the rebelliousness of "those wild young people" in 1920, John Carter, Jr.,
castigated the ineffective "religion of our fathers" which his generation
had "been forced to question and in many cases to discard."[14] In 1923
Albert Wiggam's best-selling *The New Decalogue of Science* offered a
formula for salvation through science to replace the Ten Commandments. Such pronouncements served notice upon the defenders of orthodoxy that their creeds and fundamentals were once again imperiled
by the champions of modernity.

Although the resurgent fundamentalism of the post-1918 era was in
part a reaction to the peculiar circumstances created by the war, it was
also the culmination of long-standing tendencies in American society and
culture. In fact, one student of American church history interprets the
modernist-fundamentalist controversy of the 1920s as "one of the consequences of the dichotomy between faith and reason"—between pietism
and rationalism—in American Protestantism. In his view Puritans, as
well as a majority of colonial Protestants, managed to keep faith and
reason in creative tension; but during the eighteenth and nineteenth
centuries the two separated into opposing movements of rationalism and
evangelical pietism. The evangelical liberalism which emerged late in
the nineteenth century was essentially an attempt to restore the creative
interchange between faith and reason, but instead of bridging the gap
"it too easily leapt it and too easily accepted the standards and ideals of
the surrounding culture." Its left wing, the science-oriented modernism,
accentuated the cleavage at the same time that theological conservativ-
ism "went too far" in its reaction against the liberal effort and "saw in

---

13 See Harry Emerson Fosdick, "Then Trenches and the Churches at Home," *The
Atlantic Monthly*, CXXIII (January 1919), 22–33.

14 John Carter, Jr., "These Wild Young People," *Atlantic Monthly*, CXXVI (September 1920), 302.

the new movement only an old enemy." By focusing upon the "excesses" of the radical progeny spawned by evangelical liberalism, the conservatives failed to appreciate the genuine apologetic effort of the liberals.[15] The view that the modernist-fundamentalist controversy of the 1920s was basically "another round in the long struggle between faith and reason" can easily be documented by statements from the discourses of participants in the conflict. For example, in 1923 William Jennings Bryan, a champion of fundamentalism, declared:

Reason versus faith is the great issue to-day as in Eden. Faith says obey; reason asks, Why? The one looks up confidingly to a Power above; the other relies on self and rejects even the authority of Jehovah unless the finite mind can comprehend the plan of the Infinite.[16]

Persistently since the late nineteenth century the supremacy of Protestantism in shaping the life of the nation had been seriously challenged. American Protestantism, according to Professor Winthrop Hudson, became a victim of its own success late in the nineteenth century. Its complacency and "theological erosion" tended to preclude a vigorous response to the demands of the religiously pluralistic society emerging in urban America. The non-Protestant faiths gained strength in the burgeoning cities, while the stronghold of Protestantism, small-town and rural America, declined in relative power and influence. Industrialization continuously posed moral and ethical questions for which orthodoxy appeared to have few relevant answers; the new sciences steadily undermined its supernatural explanation of man and the universe; and higher criticism, supported by the findings in comparative religion, linguistics, and various social sciences, seemed to cast doubt upon the validity of the Bible, the ultimate source of Protestant truth. Steeped in the nonintellectual concerns of traditional evangelicalism, most Protestant churchmen were ill-equipped to deal with the new intellectual phenomena that confronted them. To be sure, some churchmen, particularly within seminaries, boldly tackled the problem of restating the historic faith in terms intellectually defensible and persuasive. Others gravitated to a form of fundamentalism, reaffirmed their orthodoxy and clung tenaciously to the form as well as the substance of the old-time religion. Any alteration, however slight, was likely to be viewed as a

[15] Handy, *loc. cit.*

[16] William Jennings Bryan, *In His Image* (New York: Fleming H. Revell, 1923), p. 67.

compromise with evil and as traitorous defection from the ranks of the true believers. From the late nineteenth century on, fundamentalists intermittently waged a struggle in defense of the historic faith against churchmen who attempted to adjust their religion to the needs of the new age by liberalizing their theology and by emphasizing the social aspects of the gospel.

An acquaintance with the course of fundamentalism from 1865 to 1920, which is often ignored in discussions of the movement after World War I, is necessary to an understanding of the climactic struggle in the 1920s. According to Carroll Harrington's study of the fundamentalist movement from 1870 to 1921,[17] the "first generation of fundamentalists" in the late nineteenth century, led by Dwight L. Moody, specified new methods of operation, created new institutions such as Bible institutes, and clarified the doctrinal position of fundamentalism. The work of this first generation was carried into the twentieth century by a second generation of revivalists and institutional leaders such as William Bell Riley, James M. Gray, Jasper C. Massee, and Amzi C. Dixon. But their efforts after 1900 encountered serious obstacles chiefly because the tenor of the new century was one of dynamic Progressivism and the Social Gospel. By 1912, Harrington maintains, sporadic skirmishes with the advocates of "modern theology" and Christocentric liberalism had induced fundamentalists to abandon all hope of reviving the nation by preaching their Bible-centered theology. Frustrated and embittered, they withdrew to pray for a speedy second coming of Christ. Obviously they could not hold back the tide of modernistic, liberal theology; hence only a swift return of Christ could accomplish the fatherhood of God on earth.

Less interested in fundamentalism as a sociological or psychological phenomenon, Professor Ernest R. Sandeen has concentrated on the origins of its theological affirmations in order to discover what he believed to be the distinctive structure and identity of the movement. In his view fundamentalism "originated in the northeastern part of this continent in metropolitan areas and should not be explained as a part of the populist movement, agrarian protest or the Southern mentality." Fundamentalist leadership was neither ignorant nor ill-informed. Its most notable spokesmen were seminarians and editors of religious periodicals. By 1900

---

[17] See Carroll E. Harrington, "The Fundamentalist Movement in America, 1870–1921," (Unpublished Ph.D. dissertation, University of California, Berkeley, 1959).

fundamentalism was a significant force in American life possessing extraordinary vigor in evangelism and world missions. Following a favorite theme of fundamentalists themselves, historians have generally subscribed to the notion that "theologically and dogmatically fundamentalism was indistinguishable from nineteenth century Christianity." Sandeen vigorously challenged such an interpretation. In fact, his central thesis was that fundamentalism "was comprised of an alliance between two newly-formulated nineteenth century theologies, dispensationalism and the Princeton theology which, though not wholly compatible, managed to maintain a united front against modernism until about 1918."[18] This theological alliance manifested an extraordinary concern for the doctrines of biblical authority, literalism, inspiration, and inerrancy. Although Sandeen and Harrington differ widely in their approach to the history of fundamentalism, both emphasize the place of pre-millennialism in the movement.

By 1923 Rollin Lynde Hartt noted that, despite various shades of opinion among conservatives, they were predominatly pre-millennialists. "One and all," he wrote, "they proclaim the literal, personal, bodily, visible, imminent return to Christ."[19] In fact a substantial number of fundamentalists saw the turbulent period of reconversion following World War I as the fulfillment of biblical prophecies regarding the state of affairs immediately preceding the second coming. Such pre-millennialists, wholly pessimistic about the condition of human society and convinced of the futility of the church's effort to redeem it, concentrated upon saving as many souls as possible before Christ's return. This pre-millennialism helps explain the note of urgency exhibited by fundamentalists.

Whatever the reasons, the aftermath of World War I appeared to fundamentalists as a propitious moment for the launching of a massive revival to lead the nation back to "something solid," to the religion of the fathers. Not only had the war failed to make the world safe for democracy, it seemed also to have destroyed old certainties without providing adequate substitutes. For many Americans it had brought into question some of the basic assumptions of liberal Protestantism: the

18 See Ernest R. Sandeen, "Towards a Historical Interpretation of the Origins of Fundamentalism," *Church History*, XXXVI (March 1967), 66–83.

19 Rollin Lynde Hartt, "The War in the Churches," *World's Work*, XLVI (September 1923), 472.

brutalizing and dehumanizing aspects of the military holocaust tended to discredit the prevailing concept of progress and to reveal "the gigantic power for evil" which science had "put into the hands of modern man." The anti-German hysteria spawned by the wartime propaganda made it easier to identify modernistic theology with the intellectual currents responsible for Germany's "demoniac struggle for power," because modernism owed much to the thought of such German theologians as Schleiermacher and Ritschl. For the fundamentalists, the total impact of the war served to enhance their belief that liberal Protestantism, with its emphasis on the redemption of the earthly city rather than the otherworldly aspect of the gospel, rested on manifestly false premises. Theirs was a movement to return America to a faith shown of the equivocations and vagueness of modernism. Large segments of the populace, troubled by the unsettlement of the postwar period and convinced that America had been wrenched from its moorings, were receptive to the fundamentalist promise of a religion of certitude.

Organized fundamentalism in the 1920s chose to take its battle stand within what was considered the impenetrable fortress of its various doctrines, which were perhaps more significant for their innovations than their preservations. These doctrines, established at prophetic and Bible conferences in the nineteenth century and elaborately expounded in *The Fundamentals,* a series of booklets published between 1909 and 1912, included (1) divinely inspired scriptures which were inerrant in the original writing; (2) Christ's virgin birth and deity; (3) his substitutionary atonement; (4) his resurrection; and (5) his "personal, premillennial and imminent second coming." Fundamentalists' insistence upon the doctrine of an errorless scripture became a front line of defense for their faith and for its challenge to naturalism. Each of the so-called Five Points[20] possessed a special meaning often misunderstood outside,

20 Historians often convey the impression that there was in the 1920s a single creed of five points which all fundamentalists accepted and all modernists rejected. Ernest R. Sandeen, in a recent critique, challenges this view. He holds Stewart Cole's *The History of Fundamentalism* (1931) primarily responsible for the perpetuation of this misconception because of its error regarding the creedal declaration of the Niagara conferences in the late nineteenth century. To be sure, fundamentalist groups subscribed to various doctrinal standards; the Niagara Conference of 1878 adopted a fourteen-point declaration and the World Christian Fundamentals Association in 1919 affirmed a nine-point statement. But even scholars who have relied upon contemporary fundamentalist literature rather than Cole's work could easily fall into the error which Sandeen finds regrettable, because fundamentalists themselves frequently

and even inside, fundamentalist ranks. This misunderstanding resulted in part from oversimplification and downright distortion of fundamentalist theology, particularly at the hands of untutored evangelists and laymen whose dramatic oratory obscured their theological deficiencies.

The views of more sophisticated fundamentalists such as the respected biblical scholar J. Gresham Machen of Princeton Seminary seldom penetrated the din engendered by the noisy zealots. Though cited as proof that fundamentalism had support from the intellectual community, Machen and his *Christianity and Liberalism* (1924) failed to achieve a place in the fundamentalist crusade comparable to that occupied by William Jennings Bryan's *Brother or Brute?*, William B. Riley's *The Menace of Modernism,* or T. T. Martin's *Hell and the High School.* Whatever its place among fundamentalist tracts, his work was generally recognized as a classic defense of the orthodox faith. Machen indicted modernistic theology as an un-Christian and unscientific expression of religious beliefs rooted in naturalism. Its conception of God was altogether at variance with that of Christianity because it refused to recognize "the awful gulf that separates the creature from the Creator." Instead modernists preferred to apply the name "God" to "the mighty world process itself," which was nothing more than a reassertion of pantheism. Equally distressing, according to Machen, was modernism's substitution of "a supreme confidence in human goodness" for the basic Christian concept of man as "a sinner under just condemnation of God." By losing sight of the existence of sin, modernists were destroying the very foundations of Christianity. Without a consciousness of man's sinful nature "the whole of the gospel will seem to be an idle tale." [21]

If Machen was the most erudite theologian in the fundamentalist cause, few laymen offered a more articulate defense of orthodoxy than John Crowe Ransom. A professor at Vanderbilt University, Ransom was

spoke of "the famous Five Points." In 1923 the Presbyterian General Assembly did reaffirm the five-point deliverance of 1910. But whatever the number of points in doctrinal statements issued by fundamentalists, the famous five were common to practically all. Nevertheless, Sandeen's contention is well taken, for fundamentalism obviously cannot be identified solely in terms of the "Five Points." The use of these particular doctrinal declarations to distinguish between modernists and fundamentalists seems to be a case in which historians succumbed to one of the many oversimplifications so prevalent in the rhetoric of the controversy of the 1920s. For Sandeen's extraordinarily provocative reassessment of fundamentalism see the work cited above.

[21] J. Gresham Machen, *Christianity and Liberalism* (Grand Rapids: William B. Eerdmans, 1923), pp. 2–16.

the leader of a coterie of brilliant young southern writers known as the Fugitives. The Scopes trial in 1925 apparently was the one event which did most to engage the Fugitives in religious polemics. For them, the defense of fundamentalism became a part of their defense of the Agrarian South. Writing in 1928, Donald Davidson argued that the re-emergence of fundamentalism, "for all its extravagance," was salutary because it was "at least morally serious in a day when morals are treated with levity."[22] Two years later, after the popular agitation over the modernist-fundamentalist conflict had subsided, Ransom published his "unorthodox defense of orthodoxy," *God Without Thunder*,[23] which was an indictment of the new God proclaimed by modernism and science. Modernism, he insisted, was a "comparatively poor kind of religion." It was "Hamlet without the Prince of Denmark." He insisted that modernists and scientists, despite their talk of "reconciliation," were not reconciling science with the orthodox Christian faith but were in fact expounding a new religion that was naturalistic and secular. But he was inclined to believe that science wanted the "sentimental and aristocratic sanctions of religion just as much as religion wants the industrial and financial prestige of science." Regardless of these sanctions, Ransom insisted that this new religion actually depicted God as "a big scientist behind the scenes, applying the formulas as in the laboratory." And man, being "God-like," was a little scientist himself who could understand God's scientific technique and could apply this technique in the human sphere, "anticipating God and hastening the course of his good works." Ransom's basic quarrel with science and science-oriented modernism was their rejection of myths that he considered essential to satisfy man's need to believe in a supernatural sanction of the natural. He contended that scientists and their theological compatriots the modernists removed God from the realm of the mysterious and made him an abstract "principle" —a beneficient and understandable principle. As a corrective to this naturalistic, secular drift, Ransom called for modern man to insist upon "a virile and concrete God, and accept no Principle as a substitute." "Let him restore to God his thunder," he concluded.

The enemies against whom fundamentalists launched their offen-

22 Donald Davidson, "First Fruits of Dayton: The Intellectual Evolution in Dixie," *The Forum*, LXXIX (June 1928), 898.

23 John Crowe Ransom, *God Without Thunder: An Unorthodox Defense of Orthodoxy* (Hamden, Conn.: Archon Books, 1965).

sive in the 1920s were those who espoused liberalism and modernism, terms equally difficult to define and disassociate. A partial explanation for the difficulties in defining modernism is found in its tenet that religion has always sprung from human needs. Committed to satisfying such needs, modernism was a fluid theology with ever-changing emphases which could scarcely be contained in creedal statements. Clearly modernism made no sharp distinction between the secular and the spiritual; religious truth was found in experience rather than merely in special acts of divine revelation. In general the modernist attempted to restate the substance of Christianity in terms compatible with modern knowledge and refused to base religious belief on authority alone. In contrast to the transcendent God of the fundamentalists, he emphasized an immanent God "present in all that happens and is," a conception which owed much to the influence of science, especially Darwinian evolution. Amid their divergent ideas about divine revelation, modernists generally agreed that man was not solely dependent upon special acts of revelation and that even revelation must be tested by reason and experience. Refusing to rely altogether upon the infallibility of the scriptures, modernists embraced studies in higher criticism which indicated an evolutionary revelation of God reaching its fulfillment in Jesus. They diverged sharply in their concern for the Christian dogmatic traditions. Such radical modernists as Edward Scribner Ames displayed considerably less interest in such traditions than moderates like Shailer Mathews, for whom the doctrine of the incarnation was essential. Despite the diversities of modernist theology and its implications, Ames believed that modernism was so firmly established in the United States by 1918 that he confidently described it as "the new orthodoxy."

Both fundamentalist and nonfundamentalist critics complained of the humanistic orientation and "connivance with naturalism" so evident among the adherents of modernist theology. To be sure, modernists' reverence for science appeared to result at times in a form of scientific literalism and authoritarianism that was scarcely less rigid than orthodoxy's biblicalism. This emphasis on science, in addition to the humanistic tendencies of modernist theology, prompted fundamentalists to include under the label of modernism a potpourri of ideas expounded by humanists, rationalists, secularists, and other advocates of a "new religion" to replace Christianity. Fundamentalists argued that such an association was not deceptive or unfair, as some charged, because modernism was in fact a non-Christian theology derived from secular culture and garbed in the language and symbolism of orthodox Christianity. Fundamentalists calculated that modernists who remained within the church to corrupt it by their "seductive sophistries" were far more dangerous than those who abandoned Christianity altogether for a secular credo or the unabashed atheists represented by the American Association for the Advancement of Atheism.

One of the most comprehensive statements of modernism was provided by Shailer Mathews, a Baptist who served as Dean of the Divinity School of the University of Chicago. Modernism, he said, did not refer to a theology or a philosophy, but to a method. It was "the use of scientific, historical, social method in understanding and applying evangelical Christianity to the needs of living people." The theological affirmations of modernism, therefore, were "the formulations of the results of investigation both of human needs and the Christian religion." The fundamentalist, he argued, started with doctrines and the modernist with the religion that gave rise to the doctrines; the fundamentalist relied on conformity through group authority and the modernist upon inductive method and action in accord with group loyalty.[24]

In an effort to differentiate between modernism and fundamentalism, Mathews began with their differences "as to what constitutes and tests Christian faith." The fundamentalists identified dogmas with the content of religion and made these dogmas, especially the doctrine of an inspired Bible, the test of faith. On the contrary, the modernist found "the norm of Christianity in the person and teaching of Jesus re-expressed in Christian experience." Rather than requiring submission to a final doctrine, modernist theology was functional, "always changing according to the development of social life and the growing understanding of the Christian religion." Therefore, Mathews claimed that, unlike modernism, fundamentalism was not centered in morality and its tests were not spiritual. Since their affirmations concerned the historical or miraculous, fundamentalists moved "Christianity out from the field of life and morals and religious experience and put it in the field of intellectualism." Their tests of loyalty were tests of the intellect. A second difference that Mathews noted between modernism and fundamentalism concerned their use of the Bible. The fundamentalists' reliance upon the-

[24] See Shailer Mathews, *The Faith of Modernism* (New York: Macmillan, 1924), pp. 22–36.

ological authority and biblical inerrancy led them to equate the truth of the Bible with the specific words of the Bible—to literalism. To question any part of the scriptures cast suspicion upon the entire book and left humanity "without a revelation which could be implicitly believed." In contrast, the modernist relied upon "the scientific method" in using the Bible. Hence he viewed the scripture as a record of religious experience and "as of an historical rather than an oracular character." The Bible could contain religious truths without being verbally inspired. Finally, Mathews maintained that fundamentalists and modernists diverged sharply "as to the social content of Christianity." The mission of the church, in the fundamentalist view, was to save individuals from the wrath of God. Fear lay back of the appeal to repentance. Convinced that the gospel was the enemy of fear and that sin was social as well as individual, modernists embraced a social ethic and believed that the achievement of the Kingdom of God on earth required the evangelizing of social institutions and forces. In Mathews's view the issue between modernism and fundamentalism was not merely one of theology; rather it was "a struggle between two types of mind, two attitudes toward culture."[25]

Before 1919 fundamentalists possessed no well-co-ordinated organization from which to wage an offensive against the "new infidelity" preached by Mathews and other modernists who seemed to be extending their control over the major denominational agencies. During the pre–World War I era, fundamentalists were loosely organized into numerous undisciplined and rival societies held together largely by the efforts of energetic individuals. Among the most indefatigable organizers were William Bell Riley of Minneapolis, John Roach Straton of New York, and Paul Rader of Chicago. The discord and divisiveness that characterized organized fundamentalism in the prewar era continued to exist in the 1920s. Fundamentalists took pride in their combativeness as evidence that they were contending earnestly for the faith. "When one quits fighting," a fundamentalist later observed, "it is an indication of either compromise or death."[26] In the 1920s when fundamentalists were not waging war on modernists and other "infidels," they were usually squabbling among themselves. Their internecine battles, especially the

[25] Shailer Mathews, "Fundamentalism and Modernism: An Interpretation," *American Review*, II (January-February 1924), 1–9.

[26] Quoted in Louis Gasper, *The Fundamentalist Movement* (The Hague: Mouton, 1963), p. 15.

power struggles among ambitious spokesmen, helps to explain their organizational difficulties as well as their failure to achieve some of their stated goals.

Not until 1919 was any organizational structure capable of correlating the fundamentalist opposition to modernism created. The formation of the World's Christian Fundamentals Association provided the necessary apparatus. Over 6,500 fundamentalists gathered in Philadelphia for the first annual meeting of the association just as the Paris Peace Conference was concluding its work. Its proceedings and credo, published under the title *God Hath Spoken* and composed largely by older spokesmen long active in the fundamentalist cause, was in effect a militant assault upon all forms of religious modernism and liberalism. William Bell Riley set the tone of the meeting when he declared in his opening address, "The hour has struck for the rise of a new Protestantism." Protestantism, he warned, was "rapidly coming under the leadership of a new infidelity, known as 'Modernism,' the whole attitude of which is inimical both to the church and the Christ of God." The orthodox must wage a mighty crusade against modernism in all its subtle and insidious forms. Therefore, Riley's appeal included not only a demand for a militant defense of the historic creeds but also a bugle call for mobilization against such modernist subversion as "social service" Christianity and church unity movements. Under the direction of Riley, John Roach Straton, and Jasper C. Massee of Boston, the World's Christian Fundamentals Association launched a revivalistic campaign to recapture for orthodoxy its pre-eminent place in American life. Their plan was to disseminate fundamentalism through the distribution of polemical literature, public debates between modernists and fundamentalists, and Bible conferences conducted throughout the United States. In short, the association took its place alongside other organizations bent upon excluding all phenomena which they held responsible for creating the new America. Civic, patriotic, and fraternal orders employed exclusionist tactics again Reds, Catholics, Negroes, immigrants, alcohol, and movies, while the association strove mightily to eliminate religious modernism.

From its inception, the World's Fundamentals Association included Darwinian evolution among the more obvious threats to its orthodox faith. Increasingly fundamentalists called upon modernists to justify their embrace of the scientific theory. In reply some merely stated that evolution, like gravitation, was a fundamental law of science which the modern

Christian had to incorporate into his intellectual apparatus; others characterized evolution as "God's way of doing things," a definition easily reconciled to the modernist view of an immanent deity. But regardless of the explanation, none proved satisfactory to fundamentalists, whose views rapidly hardened into a belief that evolution and the mind it represented constituted the most ominous single menace to the old-time religion. To accept the theory, they argued, was to deny "man's moral responsibility," the "Gospel remedy of sin," and all supernatural elements on Christianity. It denied the virgin birth and deity of Jesus and, in Jasper Massee's phrase, transformed Christ into "the bastard son of illegitimate intercourse between Mary and Joseph."[27] William Jennings Bryan's *In His Image* (1923) expressed an opinion common among fundamentalists when it stated, "Darwinism chills the spiritual nature and quenches the fires of religious enthusiasm." Equally disturbing to fundamentalists was the Darwinian principle of laws which worked through chance variations, apparently independent of the Creator. The product, so it seemed, was not man but man as an animal—a concept that they found difficult to reconcile with their idea of a creature in God's own image.

Obviously another reason why evolution evoked such hostile reaction among fundamentalists was its apparent attack upon their view of revelation. Theirs was a transcendent deity who entered the world in the form of miracles and special acts of revelation such as those recorded in the verbally inspired scriptures. To question any biblical account of these extraordinary events, as indeed higher critics and modernists did, was the first step toward a total denial of the basic premises of Christianity. T. T. Martin, secretary of the Anti-Evolution League, summarized much of the fundamentalist objection to the evolutionary hypothesis when he declared:

Every honest man knows that accepting evolution means giving up the inspiration of Genesis; and if the inspiration of Genesis is given up, the testimony of Jesus to the inspiration of the scriptures goes with it; and if his testimony to the scriptures is given up, his deity goes with it, and with that goes his being a real Redeemer and we are left without a Savior and in the darkness of our sins.[28]

27 Quoted in the *News and Observer* (Raleigh, North Carolina), May 11, 1922.

28 T. T. Martin, "Three Fatal Teachings of President Poteat of Wake Forest College," *Western Recorder* (February 5, 1920), pp. 4–5; for an elaboration of Martin's views on evolution see his *Hell and the High Schools: Christ or Evolution, Which?* (Kansas City: Western Baptist Publishing Company, 1923).

Since such fundamentalist crusaders as Martin made virtually no distinction between organic evolution, Darwinism, and evolutionary philosophy, they found little difficulty in linking evolution with atheism, secularistic trends, "godless education," sexual immorality, disintegration of the family, German militarism, and Communism. In their vocabulary, evolution became a catchall, scare word meaning modern evils in general. One zealot even insisted upon spelling it "devilution."

Even those shocked by the renewal of the nineteenth-century debate over evolution recognized that it was only one ingredient in a many-sided conflict. Watson Davis, the science editor of *Current History,* noted that "evolution and the science of biology seem to have been picked by the fundamentalists as symbols of modernism."[29] "The Darwinian doctrine," W. J. Cash observed, "was indeed no more than the focal point of an attack for a program, explicit or implicit, that went far beyond evolution laws."[30] In fact the disturbance over evolution in the 1920s symbolized a direct confrontation between widely dissimilar mentalities which had previously operated virtually independent of each other at different levels in American culture. But by 1920, advances in education and mass communication largely precluded the continuation of such independence and, according to Richard Hofstadter, "threw the old mentality into direct and unavoidable conflict with the new."[31] A variety of other scientific or psychological theories might well have served as the focus of the conflict; yet the choice of evolution was in many ways a natural one because it was more familiar and less abstract than some of the more recent theories. Perhaps another reason for the fundamentalists' choice was related to the nature of modernism itself. The variety and fluidity of modernist theology tended to make it an elusive enemy. But Darwinian evolution, which was a basic part of the modernist structure, particularly the concept of an immanent deity, provided fundamentalists with a concrete target. To discredit evolution was to destroy the underpinnings of modernism.

By 1921 the fundamentalist crusade, especially as evidenced by the strategy of the World's Christian Fundamentals Association, had aimed its heaviest artillery at Darwinian evolution. The strategic shift in the

29 Watson Davis, "Latest Phase of the Evolution Controversy," *Current History,* XXV (March 1927), 859.

30 Wilbur J. Cash, *The Mind of the South* (New York: Alfred Knopf, 1941), p. 339.

31 Hofstadter, *Anti-Intellectualism in American Life,* pp. 124–125.

campaign first became evident late in 1920 when the association invited William Jennings Bryan to lead a "laymen's movement" against modernism and evolution. At the time Bryan was not prepared to accept the offer. "It was not until the spring of 1921," according to Professor Lawrence Levine, "that Bryan's toleration of the evolution theory, which had been wearing thin gradually, finally came to an end."[32] The folk hero of rural America ultimately decided that he was as unwilling to be crucified on the cross of evolution as on the cross of gold. Convinced that his defense of the old-time religion against evolution was the "greatest" of all his reform efforts, Bryan emerged as one of the most significant spokesmen for militant fundamentalism. Evolution, he claimed, was "the only thing that has seriously menaced religion since the birth of Christ, and it menaces . . . civilization as well as religion."[33] It was responsible for "the destruction of faith" and the modern sin of "mind worship." "But the mind is a mental machine," Bryan insisted, "and needs a heart to direct it. If the heart goes wrong, the mind goes with it."[34] He pursued these themes in numerous speeches, books, pamphlets, and syndicated columns. His personal crusade against evolution was not only a significant part in the fundamentalist effort to achieve restrictive legislation in the various states but also figured prominently in disturbances which rocked the Presbyterian General Assembly and the University of Wisconsin.

The campaign to obliterate modernism by striking at what was considered its chief handmaiden, evolution, was in large part the work of interdenominational fundamentalist groups. Numerous organizations such as the Anti-Evolution League and the Bible Crusaders of America later joined the crusade launched by the World's Christian Fundamentals Association. Collectively these organizations dedicated themselves to the mobilization of public opinion in defense of the orthodox faith and against the "creeping humanism" represented by modernists and evolutionists. William Bell Riley, John Roach Straton, and other fundamentalist leaders stormed the country on forensic tours. Such cities as New York, Philadelphia, and San Francisco, no less than obscure hamlets throughout the nation, were the scenes of their highly publicized

32 Lawrence Levine, *Defender of the Faith: William Jennings Bryan, 1915–1925* (New York: Oxford University Press, 1965), p. 264.

33 William Jennings Bryan, "The Fundamentals," *The Forum*, LXX (July 1923), 1679.

34 William Jennings Bryan, *Orthodox Christianity versus Modernism* (New York: Fleming H. Revell, 1923), p. 29.

debates with evolutionists. At the same time free-lance evangelists contributed to the air of controversy with their flamboyant rhetoric which pinpointed Darwinism as the principal cause for the sorry predicament of modern America. The evolution sermons of Billy Sunday, Mordecai F. Ham, J. Frank Norris, and a host of lesser lights brought into question the fidelity of both denominational and public schools to the historic faith. Testimonials of students whose faith had been wrecked by the teaching of evolution in schools and colleges became standard fare in many tent-revival services.

The antievolution crusaders indicted Darwin's theory on both theological and scientific grounds. Evolutionists, they maintained, substituted a belief in man's ascent from primitive conditions to a fuller life for the Christian concept of the fall of man. This substitution, which contradicted the biblical account of man's origins, invalidated the whole basis of the doctrine of sin and erased all hope of salvation. Lacking a sense of sin, man reverted to the brute morality of his monkey ancestors. Those who espoused the "God-or-gorilla" approach left no room for reservation or equivocation regarding evolution and branded the theistic evolutionist as "the very worst sort of infidel" because his sin included deceit as well as unbelief. But not only was evolution theologically unacceptable, it was also scientifically unacceptable. Fundamentalists insisted that the theory was a "mere guess" first propounded by the pagan Greeks of antiquity. Since evolution was "unproved and unprovable" it should not be taught as science. In 1923 William Jennings Bryan assured the West Virginia legislature that of all the sciences, chemistry most conclusively contradicted evolution because "it proves that degeneration and not progress, disintegration and not construction, is the rule of mankind."[35] Leander S. Keyser, a professor in the Hamma Divinity School and probably the most prominent Lutheran identified with the fundamentalist cause, argued that "the upright posture" of man was itself a denial of biological evolution. The fact that man alone among the animals "naturally stands and walks uprightly" was proof of "the doctrine of special creation in the divine image." "Note," Keyser concluded, "that man can cast his vision toward the transcendent God in no other way than by looking up from the earth."[36] To support their claims that

[35] *Ibid.*, p. 41.
[36] Leander S. Keyser, *The Problem of Origins* (New York: Macmillan, 1926), pp. 220–221.

the evolutionary theory was a "biological absurdity" the fundamentalists marshaled an impressive array of evidence from nineteenth-century scientists who denied the validity of Darwin's hypothesis. They also seized upon any divergence in interpretation regarding evolution within contemporary scientific circles as evidence of its falsity. For example, in 1921, when the noted English scientist William Bateson told the American Association for the Advancement of Science that much about the origins of the species remained "utterly mysterious," antievolutionists cited him as an authority for their contention that evolution was "a hoax." But fundamentalists were not without their "true scientists." One was George McCready Price, a geologist in a Seventh Day Adventist college, whose so-called new geology maintained that scientific evidence confirmed the biblical records of creation. Clearly the content and peculiar form of Price's scientific treatises exempted him from the fundamentalist charge that scientists frequently were "too much absorbed in the things infinitely small to consider the things infinitely great."

Both the free-lance evangelists and spokesmen for national antievolution organizations took advantage of the prejudices and anxieties of the postwar era. The wartime hysteria against all things German made it easier for them to characterize Darwinism as the basic cause of Germany's guilt in bringing about World War I. Oddly enough, Vernon Kellogg, a well-known scientist who served with the American Relief Association in Europe during the war, provided support for such an interpretation in his little volume *Headquarters Nights*, which recorded his conversations with high-ranking German officials. Kellogg concluded that Neo-Darwinism explained Germany's adherence to the "creed of the *Allmacht* of natural selection based on violent and fatal competitive struggle."[37] Germany, so the fundamentalist argument ran, had replaced the standards of Christ with those of the evolution-oriented philosophy of Nietzsche. German universities, gripped by evolutionary heresies, had divested Christianity of its supernatural qualities and moral precepts by embracing higher criticism, rationalism, and modernism. The obvious implication was that America's continued deviation from the orthodox faith would lead to the same catastrophic fate that engulfed Germany.

But the antievolution crusaders not only capitalized on the anti-German sentiment, they also found the mood engendered by the Red

[37] Vernon Kellogg, *Headquarters Nights* (Boston: Atlantic Monthly Press, 1917), p. 28.

Scare useful in the promotion of their cause. In fact, the same highly emotional vocabulary that characterized the Red Scare pervaded the fundamentalist compaign against evolution. They began with the assumption that a belief in evolution, no matter how one attempted to reconcile it with the Protestant faith, led inescapably to atheism. Modernists were, by their reasoning, nothing more than atheists who clothed their infidelity in high-sounding phrases borrowed from Christian theology. Since the Red Scare had pointed up atheism as an important attribute of Communist belief, fundamentalists identified modernism with Communism and evolutionists with Bolsheviks. Albert S. Johnson, a well-known Presbyterian clergyman, assured his congregation that evolution led "to sensuality, carnality, Bolshevism, and the Red Flag."[38] Mordecai F. Ham charged that the teaching of evolution at the University of Oklahoma was financed by "Red money" from Soviet Russia and that the legal war against Tennessee's evolution law was "the work of the anti-Christ Communists."[39] Convinced that evolutionists encouraged all forms of immorality by dispensing with the fall of man and by rationalizing sin out of existence, Amzi C. Dixon concluded: "If Darwin was right and the evolutionists . . . are right, Germany was right and Lenine and Trotsky are right."[40]

A belief in evolution, then, involved more than religious loyalty; it was a threat to American democracy. To accept the biological theory was to risk being accused of un-Americanism. James M. Gray of the Moody Bible Institute insisted that modernism in general and evolution in particular were "bringing into general practice the red doctrine of the Third International of Moscow, and if allowed to grow it can result in only one thing, and that is the overthrow of our government."[41] John Roach Straton was even more explicit in equating the orthodox faith with patriotism:

[38] Quoted in the *Daily Observer* (Charlotte, North Carolina), February 24, 1925.

[39] See Elbert L. Watson, "Oklahoma and the Anti-Evolution Movement of the 1920's," *The Chronicles of Oklahoma*, XLII (Winter, 1964–1965), 396–407.

[40] Raleigh *News and Observer*, December 31, 1922; for an account of Dixon's career see Helen Dixon, *A. C. Dixon: A Romance of Preaching* (New York: G. P. Putnam's Sons, 1931).

[41] James M. Gray, *Modernism: A Revolt Against Christianity; A Revolt Against Good Government* (Chicago: The Moody Bible Institute Colportage Association, 1924), p. 12.

The very foundations of the American Republic were laid down upon the open Bible. The most significant fact, at last, in the history of our country is the fact that the Plymouth fathers, before they ever left the Mayflower and set foot upon these wild shores, opened the Bible in the cabin of the ship and drew up the first charter for their colony in the light of its teachings. The foundation stones in this country's greatness were not laid by men who doubted the Bible, who desecrated the Lord's Day, and who neglected the church. . . . No, the greatness of our country was founded by men and women who held to the old faith, who lived lives of usefulness and service, who walked in the light of God's law, whose sorrows were comforted by the truths of His word, and whose hopes of Heaven were the mainstay and anchorage of their souls.[42]

By relating evolution and modernism to un-Americanism, the fundamentalist crusaders won support from civic and patriotic groups whose primary concern was not ordinarily the protection of religion. Some observers, in fact, suggested that the fundamentalist movement received encouragement from economic conservatives interested in it primarily as an aid in maintaining the politico-economic status quo. "It may well appear to large financial interests," noted Kirsopp Lake of Harvard in 1925, "that industrial stability can be safeguarded by Fundamentalists who can be trusted to teach 'antirevolutionary' doctrines in politics and economics as well as theology." Gerald Johnson claimed that southern cotton manufacturers had long recognized the advantages to be reaped from the work of the fundamentalist evangelist who discouraged strikes by "exhausting the honest workman's capacity for emotion."[43]

Since the fear of conspiracy flourishes in times of anxiety, it is not surprising that the conspiratorial theme appeared so often during the evolution controversy. The defenders of evolution viewed their opposition as a combination of semiliterate elements whose mentality and methods smacked of the Ku Klux Klan. Nowhere was the idea of a fundamentalist conspiracy against education and culture elaborated in greater detail than in the works of Upton Sinclair during the 1920s. Implicit in much of the fundamentalist rhetoric was the idea that a small coterie of intellectuals in colleges and seminaries, constituting a so-called educational soviet, was involved in a clandestine plot to undermine the

[42] John Roach Straton, *The Famous New York Fundamentalist-Modernist Debates: The Orthodox Side* (New York: George H. Doran, 1925), pp. 38–39.

[43] See Kirsopp Lake, *The Religion of Yesterday and To-Morrow* (Boston: Houghton Mifflin, 1925), pp. 162–163; Gerald Johnson, "Saving Souls," *The American Mercury*, I (July 1924), 368.

Christian faith of their students. As evidence that such a conspiracy existed, fundamentalists cited textbooks, personal affidavits of college students, questionnaires, and passages excerpted from scholarly journals. Professional evangelists invariably struck a responsive chord when they lashed out at the small group of arrogant intellectuals who monopolized the control of education financed by Christian taxpayers. In a facetious definition of evolution, Baxter F. McLendon traced man's ancestry from the amoeba to the gorilla, then concluded: "and the gorilla, thank God, begat pin-whiskered professors who draw their breath and salary and use big jaw-breaking words, and talk about the Bible being allegoric, figurative, probable, inferential, and hypothetical."[44] Others such as Billy Sunday, who specialized in attacking the manhood of liberal intellectuals in general, characterized evolutionist professors as "sissies" too cowardly to admit that their aim was to destroy "the faith of our boys and girls." At times the conspiratorial theme assumed overtones of sectionalism, anti-Semitism, and antiforeignism. In the South, for example, antievolutionists blamed "outsiders," notably "Yankee infidels," for undermining the religious beliefs of college students. Fundamentalist zealots were not satisfied merely with exposing the conspiracy; they insisted that all the conspirators be driven from the classrooms and pulpits of institutions whose existence depended upon the support of evangelical Christians. In short, those who deviated from the fundamentalist credo should establish their own schools and churches.

Fundamentalists generally defined their antievolution crusade as an effort to save the children—the future generations of America—from the soul-destroying influence of the Darwinian heresy. In fact, theirs was an attempt to insulate all the family pieties from the "subtle poison" of evolutionary teachings. Billy Sunday described, in his own inimitable way, the theological and moral diet of American school children as a mixture of "this evolution hokum, this gland bunk, this protoplasm chop suey, this ice water religion, this mental-disease crime stuff, this mortal-thought-instead-of-sin blah."[45] A devout mother characterized evolutionist teachers as "German throwbacks" who blighted the lives of her children by "destroying their faith, lowering their ideals, and paralyzing their constructive ability." Teachers who exposed the young to Darwin's

---

[44] Quoted in *The North Carolina Lutheran*, I (September 1923), 4.

[45] Billy Sunday, "Back to the Old-Time Religion," *Collier's*, LXXVI (July 10, 1926), 24.

"slime theory," according to a lady evangelist in Texas, committed a sin greater than murder, because a murderer only destroyed the physical life of his victim while such teachers "crushed the soul."[46]

The fundamentalists' battle against evolution represented, among other things, their reaction to the new ideal of education which was rapidly gaining ascendancy by the 1920s. The new ideal was "not that the child shall acquire the wisdom of his elders, but that he shall revise and surpass it."[47] Such a concept was manifestly unacceptable to those who equated wisdom and righteousness with "the unchanging Word of God." For their children to attempt revisions was to insure moral deterioration rather than improvement. But the fundamentalists faced a difficult dilemma in saving the future generations: the success they desired for their children required an ever-increasing amount of formal education which would almost certainly expose these "impressionable minds" to all the intellectual trends symbolized by evolution. Their problem was to provide their children with the educational requirements of success without alienating them from parental ways and pieties.

In order to guarantee that a "mother's son," reared in the traditional faith and educated at the cost of parental sacrifice, should not return to scoff at her religion, the fundamentalists sought to employ the coercive powers of the state. Their drive for antievolution statutes, launched in Kentucky in 1922, achieved its first victory in Oklahoma the following year. By the end of the decade, bills placing restrictions on the teaching of evolution had been introduced in state legislatures from Maine to California. Some of the restrictions were attached to textbook and appropriation measures; others ranged from mild resolutions which merely recorded legislative opposition to teaching evolution as a fact to stringent proscriptive statutes with penalty clauses. Among the more notable antievolution laws were those passed in Tennessee, Mississippi, and Arkansas. But regardless of their success or failure, the fundamentalist efforts to secure legislative enactments generally followed a similar pattern. A national antievolution organization sent into a given state a battery of crusaders to arouse the people and to enlist the aid of local anti-

[46] Howard K. Beale, *Are American Teachers Free?* (New York: Charles Scribner's Sons, 1936), p. 247; see Woodbridge Riley, "The Fight Against Evolution," *The Bookman*, LXV (May 1927), 282–289.

[47] Walter Lippmann, *American Inquisitors: A Commentary on Dayton and Chicago* (New York: Macmillan, 1928), p. 84.

evolutionists. They in turn pressed the matter upon the legislature and other politically constituted bodies. It would be erroneous, however, to assume that fundamentalists unanimously endorsed the use of legislative power to prohibit the teaching of evolution. Bishop Warren A. Candler of the Southern Methodist Church, a veteran opponent of evolution, stopped short of legal coercion. In refusing Bryan's request to take part in the Scopes trial, Alfred W. McCann, author of the antievolutionist tract *God—or gorilla,* wrote: "Even though we have succeeded in bludgeoning the world with Volsteadism, we can't hope to bottle up the tendencies of men to think for themselves."[48] Many orthodox churchmen, especially among Baptists, who objected to the evolutionary theory, refused to support restrictive legislation on the grounds that it would seriously compromise the principle of separation of church and state.

The fundamentalist effort to use the power of the state in order to forbid the teaching of evolution was by no means extraordinary in the period after World War I. According to fundamentalists, the effective use of legal devices during the war to force conformity in America's crusade to make the world safe for democracy provided sufficient precedent for their own reliance upon legislation to make America safe for Christianity. At any rate, faith in the efficacy of legislation to regulate the mind and morals of the public was manifested throughout the postwar era by the enactment of prohibition and the proliferation of censorship, loyalty oaths, and "morality" bills aimed at outlawing flirting, petting, and gossip. Furthermore, during the two decades prior to 1920, liberal churchmen, imbued with the Social Gospel, had expanded the scope of religious affairs to include a more positive stand on political questions. If the liberal could use the state to fulfill the aims of the Social Gospel, the defenders of orthodoxy reasoned that they could employ the same secular authority to foster their credo. In response to objections that they were violating the principle of separation of church and state, fundamentalists argued that if the state possessed no legal right to teach Christianity, it likewise had no authority to teach anti-Christianity in the form of atheistic evolution. In their view antievolution statutes were altogether consistent with majority rule. Frequently invoking the name of Thomas Jefferson, fundamentalist spokesmen argued that it was tyrannical to compel people "to contribute their money for the purpose of

48 Alfred W. McCann to William J. Bryan, June 30, 1925, William Jennings Bryan Papers. (Manuscript Division, Library of Congress).

teaching conceptions of religious things in which they heartily disbelieve, even though it be done under the guise of teaching science."[49]

William Jennings Bryan perhaps best demonstrated the tendency of fundamentalists to blend populistic democracy and the old-fashioned evangelical faith. The propagation of a scientific interpretation of the Bible in the schools was, in his view, an infringement by the intellectuals upon the rights of Christian taxpayers. Because the heart, not the mind, was more important in religion, the common man was the better judge of what should be taught regarding religion. Subscribing to the "hired man" theory, Bryan often proclaimed that "the hand that writes the paycheck rules the school."[50] In a sense he was still battling monopoly, namely the intellectuals' monopoly over education. His belief that all men would ultimately stand equal before the throne of God was "somehow transmuted into the idea that all men were equally good biologists before the ballot box."[51] Convinced that the voice of the people was the voice of God, Bryan proposed to accept the majority vote of a legislative body to determine scientific and religious truths.

The increasing tempo of the agitation over evolution prompted a vigorous counterattack from those who viewed the fundamentalist crusade as an assault upon modern culture and as a plunge backward into an abyss of obscurantism. Harry Emerson Fosdick stood in the vanguard of a coterie of liberal churchmen, professional scientists, and others determined to prevent a fundamentalist victory. Fosdick contended that as long as God was the creative power, it made little difference whether men arrived by sudden fiat or gradual process. He insisted that the fundamentalist claim that evolution depreciated the dignity of man by linking him with lower animals was absurd in view of their own belief that man came from dust. Although he shared their fear of the rise of a spiritually sterile generation fed only on naturalism and materalistic science, he believed that the crux of the problem was whether man would think of creative reality in spiritual or physical terms and that any particular scientific theory such as Darwin's was practically irrelevant. For him, the fundamentalists' storm over evolution was merely "a red herring

[49] "Aims of the North Carolina Bible League" quoted in Raleigh News and Observer, December 27, 1926.
[50] Levine, Defender of the Faith, p. 278.
[51] Hofstadter, Anti-Intellectualism in American Life, p. 128.

across the real trail."[52] Because of his stand, fundamentalists drove Fosdick from the pulpit of New York's First Presbyterian Church.

But the Fosdick case was only one example of the impact of the fundamentalist crusade upon Protestant denominations. Virtually no major denomination escaped the disruptive influence of the modernist-fundamentalist conflict. The Presbyterian church, especially the northern branch, was plagued by continual strife during most of the decade of the 1920s. A feud, centered at Princeton Theological Seminary and involving J. Gresham Machen, perennially echoed in the annual meetings of the church's governing body, the General Assembly. In 1929 Machen and his colleagues withdrew from Princeton to establish the fundamentalist Westminster Theological Seminary in Philadelphia. Ultimately the schism became complete when Machen's group organized their own denomination, the Presbyterian Church of America. During the same period a sizable and vocal group within the Northern Baptist Convention, led by such well-known fundamentalists as John Roach Straton, Jasper Massee, and Frank M. Fairchild, worked diligently to rout modernists from the denomination. The most powerful fundamentalist agencies among Northern Baptists dedicated to this cause were the Baptist Bible Union and the National Federation of Fundamentalists of the Northern Baptists. The polarization of theology meant that almost every annual meeting of the convention during the 1920s was the occasion for noisy verbal battles and strenuous maneuvering for positions of power between the contenders for the faith. Although modernism undoubtedly had fewer adherents among Southern Baptists, it was nonetheless a persistent source of contention. J. Frank Norris of Fort Worth, Texas, acted as a self-appointed spokesman for extreme fundamentalist Southern Baptists ever ready to rid the church of all except the most rigidly orthodox. Norris and his colleagues waged battles on many fronts, but probably the most widely publicized struggles among Southern Baptists involved their church-related colleges and the teaching of evolution. Of these fracases, none generated more acrimonious debate than Wake Forest College and its president William Louis Poteat who openly defended the teaching of evolution.

[52] Quoted in Gail Kennedy, editor, *Evolution and Religion: The Conflict Between Science and Theology in Modern America* (Boston: D. C. Heath, 1957), p. 33; for Fosdick's views see his *The Modern Use of the Bible* (New York: Macmillan, 1924); *Christianity and Progress* (New York: Fleming H. Revell, 1922).

The internal dissensions which beset the Baptists and Presbyterians as a result of the modernist-fundamentalist conflict were a little less apparent among Episcopalians and Methodists. In both churches, however, the conflict remained close to the surface and occasionally erupted in dramatic incidents. The modernist position of the Episcopal clergyman Percy Stickney Grant of New York prompted a belligerent reaction from conservatives. The prolonged agitation over Grant, which ultimately involved Bishop William T. Manning, ended only with his death at the height of the fundamentalist crusade in 1925. Even more spectacular was the expulsion from the ministry of William Montgomery Brown, the retired bishop of Arkansas, in the first American heresy trial of an Episcopal bishop. No such extraordinary event befell the Methodists; but despite the Methodist emphasis on such questions as denominational unity and prohibition during the 1920s, both the northern and southern branches of the church became concerned to an unusual extent with theological issues. With a few notable exceptions, local skirmishes between modernists and fundamentalists that threatened to disrupt denominational tranquility were contained by bishops adept in the "fine arts of Methodist diplomacy." Despite the intensity of the various intrachurch struggles, especially among Baptists and Presbyterians, there were relatively few permanent scars and schisms as a result.

Because the fundamentalists' antievolution crusade seemed to pose an extraordinary threat to science, distinguished scientists were quick to align themselves against it. Kirtley Mather, Edwin G. Conklin, Henry Fairfield Osborn, Michael Pupin, and Maynard Metcalf were among those who marshaled impressive data in support of evolution and attempted to present it in a form intelligible to the lay mind. Although the decade of the 1920s was "a low point in the scientists' own efforts to understand and verify the process of evolution,"[53] they were convinced that a vigorous defense of evolution was necessary to protect science in general from the fundamentalist assault. Collectively, through such organizations as the prestigious American Association for the Advancement of Science, they took cognizance of the fundamentalist crusade and raised objections to its efforts to force conformity to a "folk science." Individually they waged their offensive through articles in popular magazines and public lectures. A few well-known scientists participated in

[53] Paul A. Carter, *The Twenties in America* (New York: Thomas Y. Crowell, 1968), p. 84.

"evolution dabates" with fundamentalists. In general these scientists insisted that although evolution was a demonstrated fact, confusion in the public mind had resulted from a failure to distinguish between the fact of evolution and the theories, including Darwin's, which had been advanced to explain how it worked. They contended that the antievolutionist, in his attempt to protect the integrity of the Holy Scriptures, had resorted to means neither holy nor scriptural. The fundamentalist effort to equate a scientific theory with a "mere guess" smacked of a deliberate attempt to confuse the issue in the public mind. The defenders of science, in fact, seemed as willing to impugn the sincerity, honesty, and intelligence of the fundamentalists as the latter were to question the validity of scientific hypotheses. Fundamentalists often claimed that scientists demanded of them a humility notoriously lacking in those who proclaimed the laboratory as "the modern Mount Sinai." In his *Science: The False Messiah,* C. E. Ayres, critical of both the fundamentalists and their scientific adversaries, maintained that the latter had transformed science into "folklore in another guise" with a creed as unrelenting as ecclesiastical dogma. More subtle was the critique by Louis T. More entitled *The Dogma of Evolution.* Some fundamentalist crusaders recognized and capitalized on the highly tentative nature of many propositions regarding the evolution of man which were advanced by scientists in the 1920s. In 1965 a distinguished zoologist frankly admitted that he was "impressed by the firm and definite conclusions" about man's ancestry which scientists drew in 1925 on the basis of "scanty fossil evidence" and without the aid of the potassium-argon process or various biochemical tests.[54]

Almost invariably scientists, as well as modernist theologians, contended that evolution in particular and science in general enhanced one's belief in God. In fact, a persistent theme with those who attempted to reconcile science and religion during the 1920s was that the work of the laboratory led to a "more sublime conception of God." A typical approach of these reconcilers was *The New Reformation* by the distinguished physicist Michael Pupin of Columbia University, which depicted God as operating the world on scientific principles for the benefit of man. Pupin maintained that God transformed the universe from a

[54] Lamont C. Cole in *D-Days At Dayton: Reflections on the Scopes Trial,* edited by Jerry R. Tompkins (Baton Rouge: Louisiana State University Press, 1965), pp. 106–107.

chaos of electronic granules into an intelligible order beneficial to man, his highest and most noble creation. This rational orderliness was achieved through such divine "co-ordinators" as the laws of gravitation, thermodynamics, and electromagnetism.

Such attempts at reconciling science and religion aggravated rather than allayed the fears of theological conservatives. Often lost in the violent rhetoric of the most belligerent spokesmen of fundamentalism was orthodox Christianity's concern over what science had done to the traditional conception of God. Hence, the more responsible fundamentalist could say in all sincerity that his objection was not to science per se but to the "New God" which it proclaimed. Modern culture appeared to offer men a choice between the inscrutable God "of our ancient orthodoxy" who worked by fiat and the "new God of Science" who worked only according to rational laws. The fundamentalist was convinced that nothing less than the fate of Christianity was at stake and that all true believers must rally to the historic deity, a stern and awful God who was "the author of evil as well as of good."[55] The faithful must reject not only as unorthodox but as un-Christian the wholly understandable and beneficent God of modern science. In 1925 Justin Wroe Nixon, minister of Brick Presbyterian Church in Rochester, New York, and a nonfundamentalist critic of liberal theology, questioned whether the reconciliation of science and religion was as easy as modernists made it appear. He wrote,

there are many men of a simple and devout faith among scientists, but the main currents of scientific thought reveal no unmistakable movement toward a spiritual interpretation of the universe. The tendency is rather the other way.[56]

Confronted by the choice between the old God of orthodoxy and the new God of modernity, many fundamentalists were inclined to agree with Mordecai F. Ham's declaration, "To hell with science if it is going to damn souls."[57] Whatever its validity, the fundamentalists' attack on evolution forced scientists to assume a defensive position. Although their defensiveness often took the form of pretentious claims and blatant dis-

---

[55] These specific quotations are from Ransom's *God Without Thunder,* but such phrases were used by Straton, Riley, Bryan, and many other fundamentalist spokesmen.

[56] Justin Wroe Nixon, "The Evangelicals' Dilemma," *The Atlantic Monthly,* CXXXVI (September 1925), 369.

[57] Quoted in the Raleigh *News and Observer,* February 20, 1924.

plays of condescension toward religionists, it occasionally prompted introspective analyses regarding science and its place in American culture. The biologist Vernon Kellogg reminded his scientific colleagues of the "limitations of science" and cautioned them against making ridiculous pronouncements about its "all-knowingness and all-mightiness."[58]

Reverberations of the conflict over evolution were nowhere more apparent than in the academic community, where old concepts of education were being rapidly replaced by new ones determined in large part by the influence of science. The antievolutionist clamor alone was often sufficient to intimidate college professors and public school teachers. In states that failed to enact antievolution laws, the aims implicit in such measures were frequently achieved by the actions of college trustees and local school boards. Some teachers other than the few who delighted in flying in the face of orthodoxy were subjected to intimidation or threatened with dismissal. On occasion even the teacher who shied away from what Walter Lippmann called provocative announcements of "strange and unpalatable doctrines"[59] found himself the focus of a local controversy as the result of a garbled version of a classroom discussion or a statement lifted out of context. Amid an atmosphere of suspicion and hostility, ill-founded rumors might well be sufficient to set off charges of "infidelity." Although the National Education Association ultimately registered its opposition to the antievolution crusade, it is not correct to assume that public school teachers presented a solid front of opposition. Undoubtedly many teachers preferred to acquiesce in the wishes of the school patrons rather than risk the loss of their positions. On the other hand, there is evidence to suggest that public school personnel were sometimes in essential agreement with the fundamentalist crusade. In North Carolina, for example, the state teachers' association demonstrated far more enthusiasm for incorporating Bible study into the public school curriculum than in opposing antievolution legislation. The thorough-going manner in which public school administrators and teachers bowed to the fundamentalist pressures suggested that even if the state had passed an antievolution law, it might well have been spared a Scopes trial for the lack of a defendant from the ranks of public school teachers. A study of the American high school curriculum in 1926 offered some insight into

---

[58] Vernon Kellogg, "Some Things Science Doesn't Know," *World's Work*, LI (March 1926), 523.

[59] Lippmann, *American Inquisitors*, p. 94.

the educational repercussions of the antievolution campaign when it revealed that "physics and chemistry received a disproportionate emphasis and that biological sciences were neglected." And even when biology was taught, such topics as evolution and genetics were "practically ignored."[60] 1489698

In college and university circles the opposition to the fundamentalists' crusade was more overt and in some instances resulted in dramatic confrontations. The widening scope of the antievolutionist activity early in the 1920s convinced many academicians that liberal education itself was imperiled. Bryan denounced as agnostics and infidels those college professors opposed to his fundamentalist theology and claimed that through his influence such individuals were joining the ranks of the unemployed. To many educators, Bryan's assertion was no idle boast. Their fears appeared to be confirmed by the suspension of five professors at Kentucky Wesleyan College, the dismissal of Henry Fox, a biologist at Mercer University, the savage attacks on the eminent sociologist Howard W. Odum, the dismissal of C. P. Hojbierg as president of Grand View College (Iowa), and numerous other incidents involving professors unwilling to subscribe to the antievolutionists' credo. The American Association of University Professors assumed an uncompromising stand against what it termed a movement that threatened the very premise of untrammeled inquiry, enlightenment, and education. The five thousand members of the association were warned that fundamentalism was all the more menacing because it was used by various nonreligious interests "to cover their own purposes."[61] Although some faculties were so thoroughly intimidated that sufficient signatures could not be obtained to petition the association to make an investigation, the organization did investigate numerous professorial dismissals to determine whether the principles of academic freedom and tenure had been violated. One of its most widely publicized investigations concerned the firing of Professor Jesse W. Sprowls and six other members of the faculty of the University of Tennessee on grounds that ranged from the use of James Harvey Robinson's *Mind in the Making* to the acceptance of the theory of evolution. The AAUP in some instances actively resisted efforts at the state level to enact antievolution laws. But more significant here were the

---

[60] Quoted in Beale, *Are American Teachers Free?*, p. 238.

[61] Joseph V. Denney in *The Bulletin of the American Association of University Professors*, X (February 1924), 26.

activities of college presidents who risked their own positions as well as the financial support of their institutions. Notable among these were Frank L. McVey of the University of Kentucky, Edward A. Birge of the University of Wisconsin, and Harry W. Chase of the University of North Carolina. Voicing the sentiments of many representatives of the academic community, Chase insisted that legislative restriction on the teaching of evolution was an "abridgement of the freedom of discussion . . . which would go far toward ruining the University because it deals with the vital educational process itself, of which the appropriations and buildings are simply the means to an end." The free competition of ideas, he concluded, was an essential element in the search for truth, for which the passage of a law was no substitute.[62]

Between 1921 and 1929 thirty-seven antievolution measures were introduced in twenty state legislatures. Only five (in Oklahoma, Florida, Tennessee, Mississippi, and Arkansas) won approval.[63] Of these the Tennessee statute became the most famous because of the Scopes case in 1925, which tended to dramatize all the diverse issues at stake in the evolution conflict. The highly publicized spectacle at Dayton had a profound influence upon the future of the controversy. Its damaging effect upon the public image of Tennessee prompted citizens elsewhere to avoid similar showdowns in their own states. Also, Bryan's death shortly after the Dayton trial bestowed an ambiguous legacy upon the crusade: it left a permanent vacancy in the leadership of the movement and at the same time provided antievolutionists with a martyr whose cause they felt obligated to carry to victory. It is not surprising then that the most frenzied phase of the fundamentalist crusade took place between 1925 and 1928, when two states, Mississippi and Arkansas, enacted antievolution statutes.

With the possible exception of Oklahoma, all of the five states which passed such laws were located in the South. And the most unequivocal affirmations of the Genesis account of man's origins by major denominations were those made by the Southern Presbyterians and Southern Baptists. Historians have generally explained these fundamentalist victories in the South in terms of the region's rural character, educational back-

---

[62] H. W. Chase, "Address to the Student Body," February 1925, University of North Carolina Papers (Southern Historical Collection, University of North Carolina at Chapel Hill).

[63] In other states such as California and North Carolina the state boards of education issued rulings regarding the teaching of evolution which undoubtedly achieved the same effects as legislative enactments.

wardness, and religious orthodoxy. As relevant as such factors are, it should be noted that the appeal of fundamentalism was limited neither to rural areas in general nor to the South in particular. Although Professor Winthrop Hudson described fundamentalism as a phase of the urban-rural conflict of the 1920s, he was careful to avoid the idea of a strictly geographical interpretation. Rather he explained it as "a tendency of many who were swept into the new urban environment to cling to the securities of their childhood in rural America."[64] Convinced that the fundamentalist movement was more cultural than religious in orientation, H. Richard Niebuhr claimed that it exhibited "a greater concern for conserving the cosmological and biological notions of older cultures than for the Lordship of Jesus Christ."[65] But, as Professor Paul Carter has suggested, the explanation of fundamentalism requires considerably more than the application of the "culture-lag" theory or the hypothesis of the rural-urban conflict. On the latter point, Carter cautions historians of the dangers in an oversimplified interpretation of the urban-rural polarity which equates fundamentalism with the rural mind. He insists that since "one can be a 'ruralist' by adoption as well as inheritance," fundamentalism gained popularity among people who moved to the city without becoming "urban-minded."[66] Following the Scopes trial in 1925, George Fort Milton asserted that the basic religious views of Tennesseans were no different from those of most Americans. Four years later, the sociological study of "Middletown" by Robert and Helen Lynd lent support to his contention that "the mass of the American people are Fundamentalists."[67]

National in scope, fundamentalism counted Minneapolis, Los Angeles, Philadelphia, and other metropolises among the chief centers of its strength. The mayors of New York and Chicago assured Bryan of their sympathy for his crusade to protect the "plastic minds of the young" from the "seeds of doubt."[68] "Personally," Mayor William S. Dever of

[64] Winthrop S. Hudson, *American Protestantism* (Chicago: University of Chicago Press, 1961), p. 148.

[65] *Ibid.*

[66] Carter, *The Twenties in America*, pp. 80–81; see also Paul A. Carter, *The Decline and Revival of the Social Gospel: Social and Political Liberalism in American Protestant Churches, 1920–1940* (Ithaca: Cornell University Press, 1956), Chapter IV.

[67] George F. Milton, "A Dayton Postscript," *The Outlook*, CXL (August 19, 1925), 550; Robert and Helen Lynd, *Middletown: A Study of Contemporary American Culture* (New York: Harcourt, Brace, 1929), pp. 315–331.

[68] John F. Hylan to William Jennings Bryan, June 21, 1923, Bryan Papers.

Chicago declared, "I rest entirely comfortable in a firm belief in the creation of man as revealed in the Bible."[69] Whether or not "ruralists" by adoption, some of the most flamboyant dispensers of fundamentalist theology centered their activities in large cities. John Roach Straton was pastor of Calvary Baptist Church in New York; William Bell Riley was minister of the First Baptist Church of Minneapolis; Jasper Massee presided over the large congregation of Boston's Tremont Temple; Aimee Semple McPherson preached her Four Square Gospel from the elaborate Angelus Temple in Los Angeles; the Moody Bible Institute, whose staff included such activists as James M. Gray and Paul Rader, broadcast fundamentalist theology from the heart of Chicago; and Edward Young Clarke directed the activities of his profitable, antimodernist Supreme Kingdom from Atlanta.

But fundamentalist legal victories in the predominantly rural states of the South were unquestionably more dramatic and sharply defined; the South wrote into law the prevailing opinion regarding evolution as readily as it had written into law regional racial mores. Reflecting upon the South in 1928 shortly after his departure from the University of North Carolina, Howard Mumford Jones characterized the region as a kind of "extended and rural Chicago" where the absurdities at Dayton scarcely equaled the cruelties of the Sacco-Vanzetti trial.[70] He might also have noted that, however quaint the antics of legislators in Mississippi and Tennessee who succeeded in outlawing Darwin may have been, they were hardly more quaint than actions of the Massachusetts officials responsible for the arrest and trial in 1926 of Anthony Bimba on the charge of violating a seventeenth-century blasphemy law. Many aspects of the Bimba case, including the involvement of such "outsiders" as Dudley Field Malone and the fulminations of a "Holy Roller" preacher outside the courtroom, were remarkably similar to the trial at Dayton.

Obviously the passage of statewide antievolution laws did not provide an adequate index to the impact of the fundamentalist crusade. The aims of the crusaders were accomplished through numerous means far more subtle than legal statutes. Devices which often proved to be as effective as legislative enactments included policies by local school boards, censorship activities of civic and patriotic groups, and pressures

[69] William E. Dever to William Jennings Bryan, July 2, 1923, Bryan Papers.
[70] Howard Mumford Jones, "The Southern Legend," *Scribner's Magazine*, LXXXV (May 1929), 539–540.

of community opinion. In Portland, Oregon, for example, teachers were prohibited from discussing creation or evolution. The township trustees of Lickford and Blackford counties in Indiana announced in July 1925 that "any teacher found imparting the Darwinian doctrine to the students would be summarily discharged."[71] A local school committee in California acted on the assumption that a State Board of Education ruling that evolution could be taught only as theory applied to private conversations between teachers and students. In North Carolina several county boards of education made it a policy to employ no teacher who subscribed to the Darwinian theory. The effectiveness of local regulation and the pressure of public opinion were evident as late as 1941 when a survey by Howard K. Beale revealed that one out of every three teachers was "afraid to express acceptance of evolution."[72]

As early as mid-1927 there was evidence that the modernist-fundamentalist conflict had begun to abate. In that year the Methodist *Christian Advocate* voiced a common sentiment when it declared that the waning of the antievolution agitation was "a happy event for the Christian church."[73] Although Maynard Shipley and his Science League of America continued for several years to publicize the menace of militant fundamentalism and to plead for vigilance against the advocates of "non-science," most veteran combatants in the struggle recognized that the climax had passed. In July 1927 William Bell Riley noted with regret that the activities of the World's Christian Fundamentals Association no longer made the headlines. Shortly afterward, Harry Emerson Fosdick pronounced the demise of "the late controversy between fundamentalists and modernists" and claimed the future for theological liberalism. The struggle which he labeled as merely "a rear guard action" had been, in his opinion, "a lamentable waste of time and energy."[74] He predicted,

After this recent outburst, therefore, will come as usual an epoch during which both conservatives and liberals will recognize that whatever may be the truth about theology, good-will is religion. There will, of course, be diehards in both parties who will wish to keep up their vehemence. In

[71] Beale, *Are American Teachers Free?*, p. 229.

[72] Howard K. Beale, *A History of Freedom of Teaching in American Schools* (New York: Charles Scribner's Sons, 1941), p. 241.

[73] Quoted in *The Literary Digest*, XCIII (June 11, 1927), 33.

[74] Harry Emerson Fosdick, "Recent Gains in Religion," *The World Tomorrow*, X (October 1927), 390–392.

general, however, alike the militant fundamentalist and the supercilious liberal
will meet with scant sympathy from the Christian public.

Fosdick concluded that the restoration of theological peace would witness a renewed emphasis upon the confessional "to help meet the inward
problems of individuals."[75]

As the controversy subsided, both fundamentalists and modernists
were inclined to take stock of their respective achievements. Curtis Lee
Laws, the fundamentalist editor of the *Watchman-Examiner,* maintained
that the crusade in behalf of orthodoxy had forced churchmen to consider doctrinal questions and seminaries "to have a higher regard for
Scriptural teaching." At least liberalism was "no longer having its own
way."[76] Fundamentalists could also claim state and local triumphs which
went far toward achieving their goal of eliminating evolution from public schools. But their victories in other areas, considered within the context of fundamentalist aims, were at best limited and incomplete. They
neither obtained a national constitutional restriction against the teaching of evolution nor succeeded in driving liberals and modernists from
the churches. The most notable fundamentalist experiment in higher
education, undertaken by the Baptist Bible Union in 1927 when it
gained control of Des Moines University, collapsed within three years
because of an internal dispute precipitated by the dictatorial tactics of
the administration.

By the late 1920s the mobilization of the opposition provided a
check to the fundamentalist campaign, while the Scopes trial tended to
corroborate the view expounded in a profusion of novels, essays, and
poetry which identified fundamentalism with bigotry, intolerance, and
ignorance. Following the death of Bryan in 1925, the zealous, highly
combative element within fundamentalism hastened the decline of the
movement by waging power struggles and by exhibiting a growing penchant for sensationalism and vulgarity. The shrill, indiscriminate assaults of various competing splinter groups, as well as their inclination
to tamper with such hallowed principles as religious liberty and separation of church and state, increasingly alienated those noncombative
conservatives who continued to sympathize with the basic goals of the
original compaign but who had become disenchanted with the tactics of

[75] Quoted in *The Literary Digest,* XCV (December 17, 1927), 32.
[76] Quoted *ibid.,* XCVI (February 4, 1928), 32.

the crusaders. By the end of the 1920s the direction of the movement had fallen to men of little experience and even less prominence. Death had claimed such stalwarts as Bryan, Straton, and Dixon, and advanced age had slowed the activities of numerous other veterans.

This is not to say that fundamentalism as a movement fell apart, much less that fundamentalism as a theology disappeared. Such a deduction may at first glance appear reasonable if one considers the fundamentalist crusade as merely another aberration of an era rich in "wonderful nonsense." But neither the premise nor the conclusion is supported by historical evidence. Fundamentalism reached high tide in the post–World War I decade only after a long period of incubation. Though it may well have been theologically and socially reactionary, it was, as Herbert Schneider has noted, a "twentieth century movement of protest and unrest . . . apocalyptic, prophetic, critical . . . reflecting sensitivity to contemporary moral problems."[77] A movement so long in gathering momentum and so vigorous in its climactic thrust did not collapse as suddenly or completely as its modernist opponents suggested. That William Bell Riley in 1929 spoke in good millennial terms about fundamentalists as God's faithful remnant did not mean abject surrender. Though less petulant and noisy, fundamentalism survived and remained firm in its contention that the Christian faith could never allow Darwin's "we may well suppose" to be substituted for God's "Thus saith the Lord." Louis Gasper's study of the fundamentalist movement after 1930 provides an effective antidote to the interpretation that fundamentalism "petered out" following its dramatic encounter with modernism in the 1920s.

The modernists' inventory of their achievements toward the end of the decade often resulted in extravagant claims. Although modernism was triumphant in the sense that it had not been "dethroned" by fundamentalism, its position scarcely warranted Fosdick's contention late in 1927 that "liberalism never felt surer of its standing ground."[78] The prestige of religion in general underwent a decline as a result of the discrediting effects of the more extravagant escapades prompted by the modernist-fundamentalist conflict. As Professor Paul Carter has pointed out, modernists in particular felt the impact of the "deepened gulf

[77] Herbert Schneider, *Religion in 20th Century America* (Cambridge: Harvard University Press, 1952), p. 14.
[78] Fosdick, "Recent Gains in Religion," p. 392.

between the laity and the clergy" and the diminishing influence of the Social Gospel bequeathed by the fundamentalist crusade.[79]

Perhaps one of the most significant results of the modernists' confrontation with fundamentalism was the searching reassessment of their theology. As early as 1925, Justin Wroe Nixon suggested in a perceptive essay on the "dilemma" of evangelical liberalism that the "advanced elements" of Protestantism were "in trouble" for reasons other than the fundamentalist threat. In his view the modernist was so busy combating fundamentalism that he seemed unaware that the humanism and naturalism "developing out of modern science" posed an even greater challenge to his theology. To survive, modernism must "be more daring and yet more livable than the reactionary types of Christianity, on the one hand, and purely humanistic philosophy on the other."[80] Fosdick himself warned his fellow modernists in 1926 that they must move from a merely negative position of criticizing "the fundamentalist assault upon intelligence" to the active construction "of the kind of churches this generation needs." Otherwise their own spiritual aridity would insure the triumph of the very religious obscurantism they were opposing.[81] In the same year an anonymous essay by a disenchanted modernist attracted widespread publicity for its condemnation of modernism as an amorphous theology proposing "god without the devil, an eternal heaven without necessarily an eternal hell." "The problem," the writer concluded, "is whether modernism can find a way to say the word 'God' in a voice of conviction and command."[82] By the close of the 1920s an increasing number of nonfundamentalists who diagnosed "the sickness of liberal religion" described its major symptom as that of an ethically sterile theology.

Among the most incisive critics of modernist religion was Reinhold Niebuhr, a young minister in Detroit who later became a symbol of the shift from liberalism to neo-orthodoxy. A frequent contributor to *The Christian Century* during the 1920s, Niebuhr expressed a growing concern about the moral and ethical inadequacies of modernist theology. Modernism was "weak as a religion," he insisted, because its primary

79 For an elaboration of this point see Chapter IV in Carter, *Decline and Revival of the Social Gospel.*

80 Nixon, "The Evangelicals' Dilemma," p. 373.

81 See Harry Emerson Fosdick, "The Dangers of Modernism," *Harper's Magazine,* CLII (March 1926), 406–410.

82 "Is Modernism a Failure?" *Literary Digest,* XCIV (February 20, 1926), 32–33.

interests were "scientific and metaphysical rather than ethical." The "curse of modern religion" was that it was "so busy adjusting itself to the modern mind that it can find no energy to challenge the modern conscience." What the modernist mistakenly assumed, according to Niebuhr, was that all the moral inadequacies of religion would be "brushed aside with the obscurantism which was indeed responsible for many of the moral limitations of othodoxy." He reminded modernists that although the influence of orthodoxy upon human behavior was not always beneficial, it nevertheless had an effect which was more than could be said for liberalism. Opposed to the fundamentalists' reliance upon dogmatism to obscure doubt, he was no less critical of the "connivance with naturalism" and the "unreal optimism" so evident in modernism. In his opinion liberal theology had succumbed to the "dogma that the world is gradually growing better and that the inevitability of gradualness guarantees our salvation." The dogma had been enthroned in liberal theology "ever since John Fiske and his school made the doctrine of evolution acceptable to the religious mind and heart." For Niebuhr, the ethical interpretation of the doctrine of evolution was responsible for the romantic optimism of liberal theology, which in turn "prevented it from making any realistic estimate of the moral problems of our day." So long as the liberal church held to a romantic view of history and "a Rousseau-istic view of human nature" it provided an inadequate religion.[83] By the end of the 1920s Niebuhr was well under way in his elaboration of a theology in which the place and meaning of reason, myth, revelation, sin, and God were unlike those in either fundamentalism or modernism.

Fundamentalism, then, may well have become "a lost cause," but it had raised issues, often in a crude, unsophisticated manner, on which others would call modernism to account. True to Nixon's prediction in 1925, no sooner had modernists claimed victory over the fundamentalists than they encountered challenges from diverse nonfundamentalist sources whose intellectual prowess and mode of criticism clearly placed modernism on the defensive once again. Perhaps the most immediate threat was the blossoming of a humanist movement in the

[83] See the following works by Niebuhr: *Does Civilization Need Religion?* (New York: Macmillan, 1927); "Can Christianity Survive?" *Atlantic Monthly*, CXXXV (January 1925), 84–88; "Shall We Proclaim Truth or Search for It?" *The Christian Century*, XLII (March 12, 1925), 344–346; "Our Secularized Civilization," *ibid.*, XLIII (April 22, 1926), 508–510; "Would Jesus Be a Modernist Today," *The World Tomorrow*, XII (March 1929), 122–124.

late 1920s. Although the Humanist Manifesto, signed by John Dewey, Harry Elmer Barnes, and thirty other notables, was not issued until 1933, humanism was a lively topic of discussion during the previous decade. In 1928, a nonfundamentalist critic, pursuing a favorite theme of fundamentalism, claimed that modernists were "finding their faith evaporating into the thin air of agnosticism."[84] The humanist, opposed to supernaturalism and committed to human values, claimed that his position was merely the logical end of modernism, an argument persistently used by fundamentalist crusaders. If modernism had made God immanent, so the argument ran, humanism made him completely immanent. God became the world, man, and his dreams; religion became human experience. "Fundamentalism is skeptical of science," a humanist wrote in 1927; "Modernism merely flirts with science; but humanism says that while science may give us inadequate knowledge, it gives us all we have and we must make the most of it."[85] By expressing similar views before the American Association for the Advancement of Science late in 1928, Harry Elmer Barnes of Smith College created a storm of controversy and was severely arraigned by scientists and modernist theologians. According to the proponents of theological orthodoxy, Barnes's forthright declaration of humanism without the paraphernalia of Christian theological terminology was less obnoxious than the deceitful discourses of scientists and modernist theologians. Humanists like Barnes rejected modernism as a "half way reform" and took upon themselves to complete what modernism had begun but had been unwilling to complete.

Obviously modernism was still under siege at the end of the 1920s. What Nixon had described in 1925 as "the flank attack of scientific Naturalism" and the "frontal attack of conservative religion" had in effect been reversed. In the face of assaults from so many directions, a majority of modernists began to adjust their positions without succumbing to humanism. Harry Emerson Fosdick, busily combating humanism as "a tentative makeshift," represented those who gradually shifted their stance in order to keep "the cosmic rootage for truth, goodness, and beauty."[86] Fosdick's sermons offered a rather reliable chart of his chang-

[84] Quoted in *Literary Digest*, XCVII (September 22, 1928), 32.

[85] See Curtis W. Reese, "The Faith of Humanism," *The Open Court*, XLI (May 1927), 270–277.

[86] See Harry Emerson Fosdick, "Religion Without God," *Harper's Magazine*, CLX (December 1929), 50–60.

ing position: his famous "Beyond Modernism" in 1935 was a theological descendant of his "Beyond Reason" in 1928. As one church historian has indicated, the majority of modernist theologians, though still dedicated to reason, an open mind, and the currents of modernity, attempted "to keep the God of Jesus Christ and to keep Jesus as the revelation of God."[87] Even so, their theology continued to elicit criticism from diverse sources.

A recent study of American Protestantism concludes that "Fundamentalism drew a necessary line between historic Christianity and naturalism but it drew the line at the wrong place." With the gradual decline of the modernist-fundamentalist controversy, "the way was open for a more profound and more creative discussion of basic Christian truths."[88] Such a reorientation of Protestant thought, heralded by the translation of treatises by Karl Barth and other Europeans late in the 1920s as well as the maturing of Reinhold Niebuhr's theology, was evident in the emergence of a theocentric neo-orthodoxy and the re-thinking of liberalism. Although neo-orthodoxy diverged sharply from the theological position of fundamentalism, it represented an indictment of modernism and embraced tenets that tended to "dull the cutting edge of the fundamentalists' argument."[89] Despite the influence of such theologians as Niebuhr upon American Protestantism between 1930 and the opening of World War II, the older type of fundamentalism continued to flourish even if it rarely captured the headlines. By 1941 fundamentalism had undergone a considerable transformation in organization, education, scholarship, and sophistication. After World War II, in a sociopsychological climate similar in some respects to that of the 1920s, fundamentalists returned to militant revivalism. The new fundamentalism reached a wide audience through television and other media of mass communication. The popular response was spectacular. Again, evolution was the focus of an insignificant skirmish by combatants "trapped in the stereotypes of previous generations." In the 1950s and 1960s the agitation over Darwin in Arizona, California, and Texas prompted brief notice in the press; in Tennessee it resulted in the repeal of the "monkey

[87] William Hordern, *A Layman's Guide to Protestant Theology* (New York: Macmillan, 1957), p. 98.

[88] H. Shelton Smith, Robert T. Handy, and Lefferts A. Loetscher, *American Christianity: A Historical Interpretation With Representative Documents* 2 vols. (New York: Charles Scribner's Sons, 1963), I, 316–317.

[89] Gasper, *Fundamentalist Movement,* p. 19.

law" of 1925. As Reinhold Niebuhr witnessed the re-emergence of virile fundamentalism after World War II, he undoubtedly had little reason to question the validity of his observation made a quarter of a century earlier:

Frantic orthodoxy is never rooted in faith but in doubt. It is when we are not sure that we are doubly sure. Fundamentalism is, therefore, inevitable in an age which has destroyed so many certainties by which faith once expressed itself and upon which it relied.[90]

But, as Niebuhr also observed in the mid-1920s, neither modernism nor any other theology which took "refuge in various kinds of pantheism" provided a satisfactory alternative. Only a "transcendentally oriented religion" which boldly faced "the moral implications of its faith" would suffice.[91]

[90] Niebuhr, "Shall We Proclaim Truth or Search For It?," p. 345.
[91] Niebuhr, "Can Christianity Survive?," p. 88.

There is in me, as there is in men everywhere to-day, a hunger for a positive faith that will . . . "satisfy the soul of the saint without disgusting the intellect of the scholar." Though neither a saint nor a scholar, I have this hunger because I belong to this generation and this is the modern religious hunger. There is something in me that holds me fascinated at a street corner listening to a Salvation Army exhorter, despite my inner revolt against his inadequate conception of life and religion. I am likewise drawn irresistibly into the liberal camp of religion. But liberalism seems to me not yet to have found itself.

GLENN FRANK, 1923

1. Contenders For the Faith

B Y the end of World War I Americans steeped in the doctrines and individualistic piety of historic Protestantism came to feel that their faith was seriously threatened by theological modernism. Convinced that theirs was the "faith which was once delivered unto the saints," they embarked upon a crusade to maintain their orthodox theology and their system of values founded upon it. But fundamentalism was, for all its aggressiveness, a movement on the run—"a movement that was attempting to defend not only its theology but a complete social and cultural framework which rested squarely upon the foundation of that theology."[1] Fundamentalists charged that modernistic theology, if indeed it was a theology at all, lacked both form and substance. It attempted to replace the historic creedal standards with statements noted primarily for their vague and ambiguous language. So eager were the adherents of modernism to be all things to all men that they were willing to accommodate the Christian faith to virtually every fad and whim of secularism. To continue such dilution of the gospel was, in the fundamentalist view, to leave man with "nothing solid" upon which to build his hopes for salvation.

Few modernists failed to appreciate the difficulty in defining their

---

[1] Lawrence Levine, *Defender of the Faith: William Jennings Bryan, The Last Decade, 1915–1925* (New York: Oxford University Press, 1965), p. 260.

thought, especially for the purpose of comparing it with fundamentalism, which could be succinctly summarized in doctrinal statements. Part
of the problem lay in the dual nature of modernism: it was both a
method and a body of thought. If it meant the use of modern methods
in applying evangelical Christianity to meet the needs of modern life,
then it made for diversity rather than uniformity among its adherents.
Although modernism possessed no uniform precepts comparable to the
fundamentalists' Five Points, it came to be associated with certain ideas
and characteristics. Modernists generally attempted to retain the substance of the historic faith while discarding outworn thought forms and
to make Christianity spacious enough to include modern knowledge. Also
characteristic of their position was a belief in the rationality of the universe, an emphasis upon science, and an optimistic faith in the ultimate
triumph of goodness. Although modernism did not easily lend itself to
concise definition, the brief description provided by one of its most
eloquent spokesmen, Harry Emerson Fosdick, was revealing. Fosdick
explained,

Religious modernism is the endeavor to rationalize religion; it starts with
science and with the new world view which science brings and, taking this
as test and standard, says: We will have nothing in our religion contrary to
that. Says Modernism, you cannot keep your science in one compartment
of your mind and your religion in another. All truth is God's truth and
great discoveries, like evolution and the reign of law, if they are true for
science are true for religion also.[2]

Less friendly observers were inclined to believe that in attempting to
recast the substance of the historic faith, modernists committed the
error of "throwing out the baby with the bath water." A nonfundamentalist critic described modernism as a term destined "ultimately to
cover whatever changes may come over men's thinking." At the moment
it was "understood . . . to imply ways of thinking brought about by the
evolutionary hypothesis."[3]

Following World War I the "reconstruction of religion" was a chief
topic of discussion among lay and clerical groups throughout the United
States. Although most churchmen agreed that postwar America was in

[2] See Harry Emerson Fosdick, "Beyond Reason," *Religious Education*, XXIII (May
1928), 471–477.
[3] See Sherlock Bronson Goss, "Paradox of Modernism," *The Bookman*, LXXII
(January 1931), 458–465.

need of a new religious emphasis and that the hour of "splendid opportunity had struck," the nature of this new emphasis depended largely
upon the social and cultural framework, as well as the theological context, from which one spoke. Modernists in general viewed the postwar
religious reconstruction in terms of establishing a reasonable faith shorn
of the traditional practice of "intellectual frugality" and a unified church
committed to the fulfillment of the social aims of the gospel. Convinced
that the very survival of Protestantism was at stake, they demanded a
bold reassessment of creedal traditions and ecclesiastical policies. "If
we go on stifling the living breath of freedom within walls of ancient
creeds," Robert Leet Patterson remarked in 1920, "then there is scant
hope of swift betterment in the future."[4] The church must revise the
form of its message to make it intelligible to the younger generation and
to make it relevant to the needs of an urban-industrial society.

Essential to the modernist scheme of religious reconstruction in the
postwar era was the unity of Protestantism. In 1918 Charles E. Jefferson,
a well-known Congregational clergyman, predicted that the Great War
would "change the attitude of millions of Christians to church unity
and church union, to the work of coordinating and consolidating the
religious forces of the nation."[5] Various interdenominational enterprises
during the war sponsored by the Federal Council of Churches of Christ
in America and other organizations seemed to indicate a bright future
for Protestant unity. In the immediate postwar period, modernists centered their hopes for such union on the Interchurch World Movement,
an organization designed "to unite all the benevolent and missionary
agencies of American Protestantism in a single campaign for money,
men, and spiritual power."[6] But in spite of the extravagant hopes of
liberal churchmen, the movement collapsed within eighteen months
after its birth in December 1918. Not the least among the varied and
complex causes for its failure was the hostility of fundamentalists within
those denominations which underwrote this "great experiment." Suspicious of union schemes generally, fundamentalists interpreted the Interchurch Movement as another modernist effort to obliterate doctrinal

[4] Robert Leet Patterson, "The Church of To-Morrow," *The Open Court*, XXXIV
(June 1920), 327.

[5] Charles E. Jefferson, *Old Truths and New Facts* (New York: Fleming H. Revell,
1918), p. 151.

[6] See LeRoy Johnson, "The Evolution Controversy During the 1920's," (Ph.D.
dissertation, New York University, 1953), pp. 75–76.

standards and denominational creeds under the guise of unionism. The movement was, in their view, a device by which modernists would obtain money from unsuspecting conservatives for the purpose of propagating their "new infidelity." William Bell Riley expressed a common sentiment among fundamentalists when he denounced schemes for Protestant unity as a clear-cut deviation from biblical teaching. According to him, union movements demoralized and corrupted the church because they sought to include the whole "unregenerate world" rather than limit membership to the "witness-bearing company" of believers.[7] The intensity of the hostile reaction by orthodox Protestants to this aspect of the modernist program for reconstruction suggests that the church unity movement was in large part responsible for the emergence of a militant fundamentalist crusade.

In the era immediately following the war, orthodox clergymen and laymen alike were quick to define, more or less precisely, the credo and aims of the fundamentalist movement. In general they withdrew into what was considered the impenetrable fortress of their doctrinal statements and here waged their war against modernism. Although the doctrines postulated by the various fundamentalist groups were by no means uniform in length or identical in content, commentators often spoke in terms of the Five Points of fundamentalism. Fundamentalists themselves lent credence to the idea of a universally accepted credo by their frequent references to the primacy of the divinely inspired, inerrant scriptures, the virgin birth and deity of Jesus, the substitutionary atonement, the resurrection, and the imminent second coming. These Five Points at least constituted a basic core of theological doctrines on which fundamentalists of widely disparate talents constructed an elaborate defense of their cultural, social, and moral values.

In the 1920s William Jennings Bryan and William Bell Riley were among the most popular spokesmen of fundamentalism. Bryan was a Presbyterian layman whose attempts to become moderator of his church were no more successful than his bids for the presidency of the United States. Riley was a Baptist minister whom many considered as ranking second only to Bryan in the leadership of the fundamentalist crusade. Theologically their positions within the fundamentalist movement might be characterized as middle of the road; they stood somewhere be-

[7] William Bell Riley, "The Great Divide, or Christ and the Present Crisis," *God Hath Spoken* (Philadelphia: n.p., 1919), pp. 40–41.

tween the two extremes represented on the one hand by such seminary professors as J. Gresham Machen and on the other by fire-eating evangelists. Although both Bryan and Riley made Darwinism the focus of much of their discussion, neither rested his case solely upon a "blind acceptance of biblical quotations." Some scholars maintain that Bryan demonstrated his ability to offer rational criticisms of evolution rather than dogmatic denials of it on the basis of proof texts. In Bryan's defense, Professor William Hordern asserts that even scientists have come to accept some of the points made by the Great Commoner.[8] Nor was Riley a "lid-to-lid" literalist who subscribed to many of the quaint notions accepted uncritically by churchmen. But Bryan and Riley were spokesmen of what they considered an embattled theology—indeed a threatened way of life—and in tightening their lines of defense they, like other fundamentalists, tended to exaggerate and overstate their case and to substitute bombast for incisive argument.

The modernist-fundamentalist conflict provoked a steady exchange of criticism between partisans. Fundamentalists described modernism as an un-Christian faith which was all the more dangerous because it used traditional Christian terminology. So bent was the modernist upon accommodating the church to science and secular forces in general that the very essence of the Christian faith had been compromised. Inclined to be more explicit, most fundamentalists claimed that modernism discarded essential doctrines, stripped Christianity of its supernatural elements, and attempted to substitute sociology for the gospel. Succinctly expressing much of the fundamentalist's anxiety was the churchman who lamented: "We are told that the very creeds upon which men have staked their hopes of eternal salvation are crumbling."[9] For the modernist, such a statement merely substantiated his claim that fundamentalists confused the temporary form of the Christian faith with its eternal substance, that a fierce zeal for dogma had replaced "the gospel of love." Modernists interpreted fundamentalism as a re-emergence of an old and popular commitment to creedal orthodoxy and individualistic piety which had long been uncomfortable in the presence of certain intellectual trends of the twentieth century. The widespread disenchantment

8 William Hordern, *A Layman's Guide to Protestant Theology* (New York: Macmillan, 1957), p. 70.
9 W. A. Harper, *Character Building in Colleges* (New York: Abingdon Press, 1928), p. 190.

with such trends, especially those associated with the War and its aftermath, had precipitated an aggressive attack upon modern culture. According to most modernists, the fundamentalists were skilled contro-
versialists whose authoritarian tactics to achieve conformity to rigid
theological creeds at any price posed a serious threat not only to religious
freedom but also to the very existence of democratic society.

   Not all criticism of modernism and fundamentalism emanated from
partisans in the conflict. In fact, some of the most cogent evaluations
of the two theological positions were voiced by those who refused to be
labeled as either modernists or fundamentalists. A substantial portion
of the Protestant community might well be characterized as noncombative during the controversy. For various reasons clergymen in this
category were, as Gerald Johnson pointed out, the "chief sufferers" of the
religious warfare. At any rate, many churchmen attempted to remain
outside a disturbance which they considered likely to distract men from
the more essential task of practicing the teachings of Jesus. In short,
they refused to choose between "the religion *about* Jesus" and "the religion *of* Jesus," phrases often used to distinguish the partisans in the
conflict. Some dissenters undoubtedly agreed with Reinhold Niebuhr's
assessment which characterized fundamentalism as "arbitrary dogmatism" and modernism as "connivance with naturalism." They might also
have agreed with his suggestion that a more pertinent concern of the
Christian ought to be a recognition of the "eternal significance of the
human personality" and the need for an "ethical reconstruction of society." But both modernists and fundamentalists expressed hostility toward outspoken advocates of a thoroughly secular religion dedicated to
the task of constructing a scientifically valid system of ethics. If spokesmen for the humanistic faith believed that orthodox Christianity was a
vestige of a primitive religion that continued to contaminate its adherents with various social and psychological viruses, they were scarcely
more tolerant of modernism which in their opinion represented an unreasonable compromise with fundamentalism.[10] The emergence of a
vocal humanism in the 1920s tended to corroborate the persistent claims
of fundamentalists regarding the "creeping humanism" inherent in modernism. For them, the modernists, having sown the wind, were reaping
the whirlwind.

   [10] See the following selections by Gerald Johnson, Reinhold Niebuhr, and Harry
Elmer Barnes.

The Modernist's Brief

Shailer Mathews and
Harry Emerson Fosdick

Shailer Mathews, Dean of the Divinity School of the University of Chicago, wrote what is unquestionably one of the most comprehensive definitions of the modernists' faith. Modernism, he explained, was neither a theology nor a philosophy. Instead it was an attempt to utilize the method of "the historical and allied sciences" to discover the permanent values in the Christian inheritance. The modernist's affirmations, therefore, rested upon investigations "both of human needs and the Christian religion" rather than creeds and dogmas. Mathews characterized fundamentalists as theological dogmatists who started with doctrines and relied upon conformity through group authority. Modernists, on the contrary, began with the religion which gave rise to the doctrines and relied chiefly upon inductive method and action in accord with group loyalty. In the selection below Mathews attempts to disentangle the real meaning of modernism from the misleading labels pinned on it by its opponents.

What then is modernism? A heresy? An infidelity? A denial of truth? A new religion? So its ecclesiastical opponents have called it. But it is none of these. To describe it is like describing that science which has made our modern intellectual world so creative. It is not a denomination or a theology. *It is the use of the methods of modern science to find, state, and use the permanent and central values of inherited orthodoxy in meeting the needs of a modern world.* The needs themselves point the way to formulas. Modernists endeavor to reach beliefs and their application in the same way that chemists or historians reach and apply their conclusions. They do not vote in conventions and do not enforce beliefs by discipline. Modernism has no confession. Its theological affirmations are the formulation of results of investigation both of human needs and the Christian religion. The dogmatist starts with doctrines, the modernist with the religion that gave rise to doctrines. The dogmatist relies on conformity through group authority; the modernist upon inductive method and action in accord with group loyalty.

An examination of the modernist movement will disclose those distinct aspects of these characteristics.

1. The modernist movement is a phase of the scientific struggle for freedom in thought and belief.

.   .   .   .

The habits of medieval Catholicism and national churches, the appeal to some supernaturally authoritative church or Bible, arguments based neither upon a study of the nature and history of either Bible or church, but upon usage or ecclesiastical action do not satisfy free minds. There is an indubitable struggle between ecclesiastical authority and free scientific method. The two have never been compatible. The modernist, conscious of his loyalty to Jesus Christ, recognizes the value of all theologies, but with him scientific method has replaced the philosophy and the patterns with which the church fathers defended and organized Christian truth as well as the church authority with which their formulas have been enforced. He, too, has propositions for which he would die, but the freedom he asks for himself he would grant to his opponents. If he had the power to enforce his own beliefs on the church, he would not use it. Truth can be trusted to find its own defense in efficiency.

The new movement in evangelical Christianity is, therefore, not to be understood by emphasizing its points of difference with systems of theology. It can be appreciated only as one recognizes that it is the outcome and expression of the Christian life of those who rely upon the inductive method as a way to reality and upon freedom as imperative in religious thought.

2. Modernists are Christians who accept the results of scientific research as data with which to think religiously.

It would, of course, be unsafe to accept every scientific theory as material for theological thinking. But the modernist starts with the assumption that scientists know more about nature and man than did the theologians who drew up the creeds and confessions. He is open-minded in regard to scientific discovery. Believing that all facts, whether they be those of religious experience or those of the laboratory, can fit into the general scheme of things, he welcomes new facts as rapidly as they can be discovered.

When, therefore, he finds experts in all fields of scientific investigation accepting the general principle of evolution, he makes it a part of his intellectual apparatus. He does this not because he has a theology to be supported, but because he accepts modern science. He has no illusions as to the finality of this or that theory, which, like Darwinism, attempts though imperfectly, to describe an evolutionary process, but he is convinced that scientists have discovered that there is continuity of development in the physical world, and that, therefore, such continuity must be recognized by religious thinkers. He is cautious about appropriating philosophies, but he is frankly and hopefully an evolutionist because of facts furnished by experts. In this attitude he is reproducing that of earlier religious thinkers when they abandoned the Ptolemaic system of the universe and adopted the Copernican. When he wants to estimate the worth of dogmatic hostility to such attitudes, he recalls the attacks upon the views of Copernicus by those who had identified Ptolemaic science with religion and waits for good people to show good sense.

Furthermore, in the light of sociological and historical facts, the modernist uses the methods of science in his quest for religious assurance. He knows that the Christian religion developed as a group-possession when men's experience and knowledge grew. He is not content simply to accept a doctrine. He seeks to understand its real purpose and service. He therefore seeks to discover why it arose. He searches for its origin and estimates its efficiency in the light of its conformity with social forces and its capacity to nerve men and women for more courageous living. The beliefs of Christians are less extensive than the loyalties of Christians. A religion is a way of living, and the modernist refuses to think of it as an accumulation of decrees. Attitudes and convictions, he discovers from a study of the Christian movement, are not identical with the language and concepts in which they are expressed.

3. Modernists are Christians who adopt the methods of historical and literary science in the study of the Bible and religion.

From some points of view, this, although not the most fundamental, is their most obvious characteristic. It was the critical study of the Scriptures with which the movement started in the Roman Catholic Church and it has laid the foundation for theological discussion in Protestantism. The modernist is a critic and an historian before he is a theologian. His interest in method precedes his interest in results.

Modernists believe themselves true to the spirit and purpose of Jesus Christ when they emphasize his teachings and the inner faith of a century-long movement rather than the formulas in which aspects of this faith were authoritatively expressed. In this modernists are doing for

Christianity what Americans did for Americanism when they changed
their Constitution in order to give truer application to principles the
Constitution itself expressed. . . .

4. The modernist Christian believes the Christian religion will help
men meet social as well as individual needs.

Any acquaintance with social facts makes plain how responsive the
individual is to social influences. Any intelligent religious program must
take such facts into account. But programs differ. Some emphasize rescue
and others emphasize salvation. The dogmatic mind has always preferred rescue. In practice it has varied from the asceticism of the monk to
the rejection of social idealism.

.   .   .   .

Modernists believe that the Gospel is as significant for social forces
as for individuals. They find little hope in rescue of brands from burning; they want to put out the fire. They believe that the same God who
so loved the world as to give his only begotten Son that those individuals
who believe in him might not perish, also sent his Son into the world that
the world might be saved.

But when the modernist speaks of saving society he does not believe
that society will save itself. He believes that the constant need of God's
gracious help is to be understood as clearly through the laws given him
by the sociologist as the psychologist. He, therefore, hopefully undertakes
to apply the Golden Rule to group action as truly as to the individuals.
He would carry Christian attitudes and convictions into our entire life.
He urges the duty of sacrifice on the part of nations and of classes,
whether they be employers or employees, as truly as on that of individuals. For Jesus Christ to him is more than the savior of isolated individuals. He is the savior of men in society.

This is one reason why the modernist is an object of suspicion. The
dogmatic mind is always to be found among social reactionaries. To no
small degree modernism in theology is opposed because modernists urge
reform in economic matters. In the struggle over economic privilege the
modernist is properly feared as one who takes Jesus seriously and believes
implicitly that his Gospel applies to wages and war as truly as to oaths,
charity and respectability.

5. The modernist is a Christian who believes that the spiritual and
moral needs of the world can be met because they are intellectually con-

vinced that Christian attitudes and faiths are consistent with other realities.

. . . .

6. Modernists as a class are evangelical Christians. That is, they accept Jesus Christ as the revelation of a Savior God.

The modernist movement is, therefore, not identical with liberalism.
With all due respect for the influence of liberalism in clarifying religious
thought, its origin and interest tend toward the emphasis of intellectual
belief and the criticism and repudiation of doctrines per se. The modernist, like any other investigators, has a presumption in favor of the reality of that which he is studying. Both historically and by preference his
religious starting point is inherited orthodoxy of a continuing community of Christians. To this group he belongs. The place of evangelical
Christianity in social and ethical life, the aid it gives to millions of human hearts, the moral impetus it has given social reforms, forbids treat-
ing Christianity as an unborn child of human thought. But if it is to
carry conviction as a way of organizing life, it must be studied and applied according to methods judged effective by those to whom it is recommended. As the early church fathers were Christians who utilized their
Hellenistic training to expound the Christianity brought to them by
Jews; as the Schoolmen were Christians who followed Aristotle; so the
modernists are Christians who use the scientific method to estimate and
apply the values of that evangelical inheritance in which they share. One
might as well expect a student of politics to deny the existence of the
state as to expect the modernist to be disloyal to the Christian church;
to expect a student of medicine to be indifferent to human ills and skeptical as to the use of medicines, as to expect that investigators within the
Christian church should be indifferent or skeptical as to faith.

In brief, then, *the use of scientific, historical, social method in understanding and applying evangelical Christianity to the needs of living
persons, is modernism.* Its interests are not those of theological controversy or appeal to authority. They do not involve the rejection of the
supernatural when rightly defined. Modernists believe that they can discover the ideals and directions needed for Christian living by the application of critical and historical method to the study of the Bible; that they
can discover by similar methods the permanent attitudes and convictions
of Christians constituting a continuous and developing group; and that
these permanent elements will help inspire the intelligent and sympa-

thetic organization of life under modern conditions. Modernists are thus
evangelical Christians who use modern methods to meet modern needs.
Confessionalism is the evangelicalism of the dogmatic mind. Modernism
is the evangelicalism of the scientific mind.

From Shailer Mathews, *The Faith of Modernism* (New York: Macmillan,
1924), pp. 22–23, 28–36.

Harry Emerson Fosdick, a professor at Union Theological Seminary and
a Baptist who served as minister of the First Presbyterian Church of New
York, was one of the most eloquent spokesmen for liberal theology. In the
first selection, taken from the Cole Lectures which he presented at Vanderbilt
University in 1922, Fosdick concentrates upon two questions often debated
by modernists and fundamentalists—the nature of divine revelation and the
place of authority in the Christian religion. He insisted that God's revelation
was progressive rather than static and that any attempt to incorporate it into
"an infallibly settled creed" was futile. In fact, he did not consider creeds
and dogma among the vital necessities of the Christian faith. The second
selection, an excerpt from his lectures in 1924 on the modernist concept
of the Bible, acknowledges the debt which modernism owed to the researches
of higher critics, archeologists, linguists, and others employing "the modern
historic point of view and scientific apparatus." The application of modern
knowledge to the study of the Bible, he maintained, "saves us from the
necessity of apologizing for immature stages in the development of Biblical
revelation," because it reveals "a progressive unfolding of the divine character
and purpose" which culminated in Christ and his Gospel.

————————◦•—————————

Even within the New Testament, therefore, there is no static creed.
For, like a flowing river, the church's thought of her Lord shaped itself
to the intellectual banks of the generation through which it moved, even
while, by its construction and erosion, it transfigured them. Nor did this
movement cease with New Testament days. From the Johannine idea of
the Logos to the Nicene Creed, where our Lord is set in the framework of Greek metaphysics, the development is just as clear as from the
category of Jewish Messiah to the categories of the Fourth Gospel. And
if, in our generation, a conservative scholar like the late Dr. Sanday
pleaded for the necessity of a new Christology, it was not because he
was primarily zealous for a novel philosophy, but because . . . he was

zealous to present Christ to his own generation in terms that his own generation could comprehend.

Undoubtedly such an outlook upon the fluid nature of the Christian movement will demand readjustment in the religious thinking of many people. They miss the old ideas about revelation. This new progressiveness seems to them to be merely the story of man's discovery, finding God, here a little and there a little, as he has found the truths of astronomy. But God's revelation of himself is just as real when it is conceived in progressive as when it is conceived in static terms. Men once thought of God's creation of the world in terms of fiat—it was done on the instant; and when evolution was propounded, men cried that the progressive method shut God out. We see now how false that fear was. The creative activity of God never was so nobly conceived as it has been since we have known the story of his slow unfolding of the universe. We have a grander picture in our minds than even the psalmist had, when we say after him, "The heavens declare the glory of God." So men who have been accustomed to think of revelation in static terms, now that the long leisureliness of man's developing spiritual insight is apparent, fear that this does away with revelation. But in God's unfolding education of his people, recorded in the scriptures, revelation is at its noblest. No man ever found God except when God was seeking to be found. Discovery is the under side of the process; the upper side is revelation.

Indeed, this conception of progressive revelation does not shut out finality. In scientific thought, which continually moves and grows, expands and changes, truths are discovered once for all. The work of Copernicus is in a real sense final. This earth does move; it is not stationary; and the universe is not geocentric. That discovery is final. Many developments start from that, but the truth itself is settled once for all. So, in the spiritual history of man, final revelations come. They will not have to be made over again and they will not have to be given up. Progress does not shut out finality; it only makes each new finality a point of departure for a new adventure, not a terminus ad guem for a conclusive stop. That God was in Christ reconciling the world unto himself is for the Christian a finality, but, from the day the first disciples saw its truth until now, the intellectual formulations in which it has been set and the mental categories by which it has been interpreted have changed with the changes of each age's thought.

While at first, then, a progressive Christianity may seem to plunge us

into unsettlement, the more one studies it the less he would wish it otherwise. Who would accept a snapshot taken at any point on the road of
Christian development as the final and perfect form of Christianity?
Robert Louis Stevenson has drawn for us a picture of a man trying with
cords and pegs to stake out the shadow of an oak tree, expecting that
when he had marked its boundaries the shadow would stay within the
limits of the pegs. Yet all the while the mighty globe was turning around
in space. He could not keep a tree's shadow static on a moving earth.
Nevertheless, multitudes of people in their endeavor to build up an infallibly settled creed have tried just such a hopeless task. They forget
that while a revelation from God might conceivably be final and complete, religion deals with a revelation of God. God, the infinite and
eternal, from everlasting to everlasting, the source and crown and destiny
of all the universe—shall a man whose days are as grass rise up to say
that he has made a statement about him which will not need to be revised? Rather, our prayer should be that the thought of God, the meaning of God, the glory of God, the plans and purpose of God may expand
in our comprehension until we, who now see in a mirror, darkly, may see
face to face. "Le Dieu defini est le Dieu fini."

.   .   .   .

Obviously, the point where this progressive conception of Christianity comes into conflict with many widely accepted ideas is the abandonment which it involves of an external and inerrant authority in matters of religion. The marvel is that the idea of authority, which is one
of the historic curses of religion, should be regarded by so many as one
of the vital necessities of the faith. The fact is that religion by its very
nature is one of the realms to which external authority is least applicable.
In science people commonly suppose that they do not take truth on any
one's authority; they prove it. In business they do not accept methods
on authority; they work them out. In statesmanship they no longer believe in the divine right of kings, nor do they accept infallible dicta
handed down from above. But they think that religion is delivered to
them by authority and that they believe what they do believe because a
divine church or a divine book or a divine man told them.

In this common mode of thinking, popular ideas have the truth
turned upside down. The fact is that science, not religion, is the realm
where most of all we use external authority. They tell us that there are
millions of solar systems scattered through the fields of space. Is that

true? How do we know? We never counted them. We know only what the authorities say. They tell us that the next great problem in science is breaking up the atom to discover the incalculable resources of power there waiting to be harnessed by our skill. Is that true? Most of us do not understand what an atom is, and what it means to break one up passes the farthest reach of our imaginations; all we know is what the authorities say. They tell us that electricity is a mode of motion in ether. Is that true? Most of us have no first hand knowledge about electricity. The motorman calls it "juice" and that means as much to us as to call it a mode of motion in ether; we must rely on the authorities. They tell us that sometime we are going to talk through wireless telephones across thousands of miles, so that no man need ever be out of vocal communication with his family and friends. Is that true? It seems to us an incredible miracle, but we suppose that it is so, as the authorities say. In a word, the idea that we do not use authority in science is absurd. Science is precisely the place where nine hundred and ninety-nine men out of a thousand use authority the most. The chemistry, biology, geology, astronomy which the authorities teach is the only science which most of us possess.

There is another realm, however, where we never think of taking such an attitude. They tell us that friendship is beautiful. Is that true? Would we ever think of saying that we do not know, ourselves, but that we rely on the authorities? Far better to say that our experience with friendship has been unhappy and that we personally question its utility! That, at least, would have an accent of personal, original experience in it. For here we are facing a realm where we never can enter at all until we enter, each man for himself.

Two realms exist, therefore, in each of which first-hand experience is desirable, but in only one of which it is absolutely indispensable. We can live on what the authorities in physics say, but there are no proxies for the soul. Love, friendship, delight in music and in nature, parental affection—these things are like eating and breathing; no one can do them for us; we must enter the experience for ourselves. Religion, too, belongs in this last realm. The one vital thing in religion is first-hand, personal experience. Religion is the most intimate, inward, incommunicable fellowship of the human soul. . . .

This does not mean, of course, that there are no authorities in religion. There are authorities in everything, but the function of an

authority in religion, as in every other vital realm, is not to take the place
of our eyes, seeing in our stead and inerrantly declaring to us what it sees;
the function of an authority is to bring to us the insight of the world's
accumulated wisdom and the revelations of God's seers, and so to open
our eyes that we may see, each man for himself. So an authority in literature does not say to his students: The Merchant of Venice is a great
drama; you may accept my judgment on that—I know. Upon the contrary, he opens their eyes; he makes them see; he makes their hearts
sensitive so that the genius which made Shylock and Portia live captivates
and subdues them, until like the Samaritans they say, "Now we believe,
not because of thy speaking: for we have heard for ourselves, and know."
That is the only use of authority in a vital realm. It can lead us up to the
threshold of a great experience where we must enter, each man for himself, and that service to the spiritual life is the Bible's inestimable gift.

At the beginning, Christianity was just such a first-hand experience
as we have described. The Christian fellowship consisted of a group of
men keeping company with Jesus and learning how to live. They had no
creeds to recite when they met together; what they believed was still an
unstereotyped passion in their hearts. They had no sacraments to distinguish their faith: baptism had been a Jewish rite and even the Lord's
Supper was an informal use of bread and wine, the common elements
of their daily meal. They had no organizations to join; they never
dreamed that the Christian Gospel would build a church outside the
synagogue. Christianity in the beginning was an intensely personal experience.

Then the Master went away and the tremendous forces of human
life and history laid hold on the movement which so vitally he had begun. His followers began building churches. Just as the Wesleyans had
to leave the Church of England, not because they wanted to, but because
the Anglicans would not keep them, so the Christians, not because they
planned to, but because the synagogue was not large enough to hold
them, had to leave the synagogue. They began building creeds; they had
to. Every one of the first Christian creeds was written in sheer self-de-
fense. If we had been Christians in those first centuries, when a powerful
movement was under way called Gnosticism, which denied that God, the
Father Almighty, had made both the heaven and the earth, which said
that God had made heaven indeed but that a demigod had made the
world, and which denied that Jesus had been born in the flesh and in
the flesh had died, we would have done what the first Christians did: we

would have defined in a creed what it was the Christians did believe as against that wild conglomeration of Oriental mythology that Gnosticism was, and we would have shouted the creed as a war cry against the Gnostics. That is what the so-called Apostles' Creed was—the first Christian battle chant, a militant proclamation of the historic faith against the heretics; and every one of its declarations met with a head-on collision some claim of Gnosticism. Then, too, the early Christians drew up rituals; they had to. We cannot keep any spiritual thing in human life, even the spirit of courtesy, as a disembodied wraith. We ritualize it: we bow, we take off our hats, we shake hands, we rise when a lady enters. . . .

So historic Christianity grew, organized, creedalized, ritualized. And ever as it grew, a peril grew with it, for there were multitudes of people who joined these organizations, recited these creeds, observed these rituals, took all the secondary and derived elements of Christianity, but often forgot that vital thing which all this was meant in the first place to express: a first-hand, personal experience of God in Christ. That alone is vital in Christianity; all the rest is once or twice or thrice removed from life. For Christianity is not a creed, nor an organization, nor a ritual. These are important, but they are secondary. They are the leaves, not the roots; they are the wires, not the message. Christianity itself is a life.

If, however, Christianity is thus a life, we cannot stereotype its expressions in set and final forms. If it is a life in fellowship with the living God, it will think new thoughts, build new organizations, expand into new symbolic expressions. We cannot at any given time write "finis" after its development. We can no more "keep the faith" by stopping its growth than we can keep a son by insisting on his being forever a child. The progressiveness of Christianity is not simply its response to a progressive age; the progressiveness of Christianity springs from its own inherent vitality.

.   .   .   .

Stagnation in thought or enterprise means death for Christianity as certainly as it does for any other vital movement. Stagnation, not change, is Christianity's most deadly enemy, for this is a progressive world, and in a progressive world no doom is more certain than that which awaits whatever is belated, obscurantist, and reactionary.

From Harry Emerson Fosdick, *Christianity and Progress* (New York: Fleming H. Revell, 1922), pp. 156, 157–164, 165.

The total consequence of all the work of the Higher Criticism is that at last we are able to see the Bible a good deal as a geologist sees the strata of the earth; we can tell when and in what order the deposits were laid down whose accumulated results constitute our scriptures. Was there ever such an unfortunate label put upon an entirely legitimate procedure as the name "Higher Criticism"? Were one to search the dictionary for two words suggestive of superciliousness, condescension, and destructiveness, one could hardly find any to surpass these. Yet the Higher Criticism simply asks about the books of the Bible: who wrote them, when and why they were written, and to whom. Every efficient Sunday school teacher, according to his own ability, has always been a higher critic. This process, however, armed with our modern instruments of literary, historical, and archeological research, pushed with unremitting zeal and tireless labor, after following many false trails and landing in many cul-de-sacs, has gotten a result, at least in its outlines, well assured. We can arrange the documents of the Bible in their approximately chronological order. Endless minor uncertainties, difficulties, and unanswered questions remain; but, for all that, it is possible now for Dr. Harlan Creelman to give us his volume in which the strata of the Old Testament are chronologically distinguished, and for Dr. Julius Bewer to give us his continued story of Hebrew literature from its first emergence to its canonization.

From the purely scientific point of view this is an absorbingly interesting matter, but even more from the standpoint of practical results its importance is difficult to exaggerate. It means that we can trace the great ideas of scripture in their development from their simple and elementary forms, when they first appear in the earliest writings, until they come to their full maturity in the latest books. Indeed, the general soundness of the critical results is tested by this fact that as one moves up from the earlier writings toward the later he can observe the development of any idea he chooses to select, such as God, man, duty, sin, worship. Plainly we are dealing with ideas that enlarge their scope, deepen their meaning, are played upon by changing circumstance and maturing thought, so that from its lowliest beginning in the earliest writings of the Hebrews any religious or ethical idea of the Bible can now be traced, traveling an often uneven but ascending roadway to its climax in the teaching of Jesus.

.   .   .   .

Moreover, the new approach to the Bible saves us from the necessity of apologizing for immature stages in the development of the biblical revelation. From the beginning of the church many things in the early documents have been a stumbling block to the faithful. Indeed, before the church began, Philo of Alexandria with great candor faced difficulties that have troubled modern minds. He was a passionate believer in Judaism and gave his life to the task of commending it to the acceptance of the Greek world. But he says that it would be a sign of great simplicity to think that the world was created in six days; that the literal statement that woman was made out of a man's rib is fabulous; that to suppose Cain actually built a city is "not only extraordinary, but contrary to all reason"; that to picture God literally planting a garden in Eden is "impiety" and "fabulous nonsense." In general Philo would regard it as utterly missing the Old Testament's real meaning to take any of the anthropomorphic representations of God in the Old Testament as representing literal fact.

Now, the older Hebrew and Christian interpreters, lacking the modern historic point of view and scientific apparatus, had one resource in their difficulties. They allegorized away the things they did not like. They read out the literal sense and read in the sense they wished to find. They ascribed to ancient writers a mystical knowledge of all later learning and made the early stories of a childlike age the parables and symbols of the Greek philosophy or of Christian theology. Such a resource is no longer possible to us. We know that the early writings of the Bible meant what they said. But we do not need to apologize for their crudities. They are early stages in a great development. Their lack is the lack of immaturity, not of perversion. They are as acorns to the oak, fountains to the river, and as such they require no defending as though they were impertinences in the revelation of God. They are the infancy of a progressive unfolding of the divine character and purpose, and they are to be judged, as all things are to be judged, by what they came to in the end. And what they came to in the end was Christ and his Gospel.

.   .   .   .

If this difficulty of naturalizing the Bible in the modern world concerned only stories like those about Jezebel, it might be comfortably arranged. The real problem lies deeper. When one moves back to the scripture with a mind accustomed to work in modern ways, he finds himself in a strange world. The people who walk through its pages often do not speak his language, nor use his intellectual viewpoints, nor explain occurrences by his categories. Knowing modern astronomy he turns to the Bible to find the sun and moon standing still or the shadow retreating on Ahaz's dial. Knowing modern biology he hears that when Elisha had been so long dead that only his bones were left, another dead body, thrown into the cave where he was buried, touched his skeleton and sprang to life again, or that after our Lord's resurrection many of the saints long deceased arose and appeared in Jerusalem. . . .

Here is the perplexity which more than any other afflicts the minds of educated men. They honor the Bible. They know that in it are the springs of the noblest elements in our civilization. They stand uncovered before Jesus Christ. But they are honestly bothered by many things in scripture. They do not know what to make of them. They find it hard to use one set of mental presuppositions and categories in every other realm of life and another set in religion. They have to shift their mental gear too suddenly when they turn from their ordinary intellectual processes to the strange ways of thinking that the Bible contains.

If this practical difficulty in using the old Book in the new world so confuses many minds today, it is important to understand the process that has caused the problem. What has happened can be briefly put: historical knowledge has given us a vivid understanding of the old world from which the scriptures came until we see the Bible's original, native meanings in terms of the time when it was written; and, on the other side, the new world in which we live has become very new, with ways of thinking that never were on earth before; and these two worlds stand over against each other alien at a multitude of points. What once was said of Jehovah can in a different sense be said of the Book—its thoughts are not our thoughts, neither are its ways our ways. . . .

The ultimate cause of this problem is to be found in the ambition of all biblical scholarship to get at the original meaning of scripture, to discover in terms of historic significance just what any passage meant to the folk who first wrote it and first read it. Surely, this is not only an innocent ambition; it is an indispensable goal for any interpreter of ancient literature to seek. Nor is it new in the church's attitude toward the Bible. Go back to the Syrian school of interpretation with Theodore of Mopsuestia for its scholar and John Chrysostom for its preacher, a school that is alike the glory and despair of the early church because it rose so splendidly and then was so soon quenched by ignorance, and you find an honest, earnest, and energetic endeavor to get at the original historic sense of scripture. Those first great exegetes, in spite of the prevalent allegorizing of their time, sought to know what the Bible meant to say in terms of the time when it was written. This, too, is the strength of Calvin's work, which causes one modern admirer to call him "the first scientific interpreter in the history of the Christian Church."

If, then, those older interpreters, with an eager desire to get at the historic sense of the Bible, did not fully achieve their end, it was not for lack of will but for lack of means. Though they hungered and thirsted for the original connotation of the Book, they did not yet have the apparatus, historical, documentary, linguistic, archeological, which could put them in possession of the setting out of which the Bible came, the ways men used to think, their social customs, intellectual categories, and prevalent beliefs. What is new in our situation is the achievement of new instruments. As never was true before in the church's history, the scientific desire to get at the historic sense of scripture has scientific machinery with which to work. Now we are able, as our fathers were not, vitally to enter into the understanding of older civilizations, their mental habits and social institutions, and in particular by many new avenues to get at the world out of which the Bible came. We can understand the original meaning of its words and ways of thinking until, for those who know, that old world lives again with picturesque vividness.

Consider the various disciplines that enter into biblical scholarship today and see how they all contribute to one aim: to make luminous and clear the historic meaning of the texts. First of all, knowledge of the ancient languages has supplied an indispensable instrument for the understanding of what the Bible originally meant to say. In 1800 not a word of the inscriptions of Egypt had been deciphered. In 1802 the Rosetta Stone began to surrender its secret. By 1832 decipherment of Egyptian inscriptions had been put upon a secure basis. . . . In 1849 not a word of all the Assyrian inscriptions had been translated except the names of Nebuchadnezzar and his father. In 1851 Major Rawlinson published, with grammatical notes, a translation of a trilingual inscription of Darius. Since that time we have seen the rediscovery and reconstruction of a great civilization of almost incalculable antiquity which was once immensely influential on Hebrew religion and which now is indispensable to its full understanding. Even the linguistic relationship of Hebrew, Aramaic, Arabic, Ethiopic, and Amharic, as dialects of one original language, was not securely established before 1800; and since then students of the Book have had put into their hands not only an organized knowledge of Hebrew, but of all the allied Semitic tongues and the different languages of Egypt, to say nothing of a greatly improved knowledge of the Hellenistic Greek in which the New Testament was written.

For another thing, the discovery and translation of contemporary literatures have thrown a luminous light upon the historic meanings of the scripture. To be sure, the church has always known Josephus and Philo, and certain apocalyptic books, notably Enoch, have been used from the days of Origen and Jerome. Yet, in a way no longer true, the Bible once stood out sharply from antiquity, and the thought and life of man that had lain around it remained in the shadow, largely unregarded. Now the light spreads as current books which sprang out of the same situations come within our den and, with others long known, are subjected to careful scrutiny, and what in our knowledge of Biblical times was incomplete is, by the new information, often rounded out and fulfilled. So the Jewish apocalypses have been brought to light in these last few years, their importance has been vividly realized, and the study of them has illumined the development of apocalyptic hopes in Judaism. So the work of Cumont, Reitzenstein, and others is making clearer the meaning of those Hellenistic mystery religions which surrounded and rivaled Christianity and which affected some of the thought and phraseology of the New Testament.

All this added knowledge of language and literature has made textual criticism a powerful help in correcting obscure and perverted renderings and in getting back as nearly as we can to the original autograph copies of the scriptures. How many people do not know that the most ancient extant manuscript of the Old Testament dates from the ninth century A.D. and the most ancient extant Greek manuscript of the New Testament from the fourth century; that the versions are variant at so many points that one could say of them what Jerome said of the Latin translations of his day, that there are almost as many forms of texts as there are copies? The clearing up of the texts, therefore, the selection of the more ancient or more sensible renderings, the correction of obviously mistaken copying, have in all cases been useful and in some cases, as with Jeremiah, have rescued a book from obscurity.

To this same end of lighting up the original meaning of the Bible, history makes an important contribution. Nobly and rightly distinguished are those fathers of history whose writings are still unexhausted quarries of information, Herodotus, Thucydides, Livy, and Tacitus; yet Professor Shotwell is justified when he exclaims "By what miracle has the long lost past been at last recovered, in our own day, so that we are checking up Herodotus by his own antiquity, correcting the narrative of Livy or Tacitus by the very refuse deposited beneath the streets upon which they walked?" No longer the story of dynasties alone, but of peoples, their customs, laws, domestic habits, mental categories, religious faiths, their folklore and folkways, history, with its many modern auxiliaries, has done for old civilizations whose influence lay around and permeated the Bible what the spade has done for Pompeii. Once more we can walk the ancient streets, and, while life is gone, the memorials of its presence are so clear that in imagination we can reconstruct the humanity that once toiled, dreamed, thought, and suffered there.

Add to the list archeology, and no long comment is needed to make clear the incalculable service which has been rendered by modern research to the understanding of the Bible. At innumerable points the scriptures have been corroborated, illumined, supplemented by the manifold results that have come from the "romance of the spade." It was only in 1872 that George Smith, working over some clay tablets from the library of Asshurbanipal, found the first parallels of the deluge story. . . . Every new discovery binds the Book more closely to the life out of which it sprang and reveals more clearly what its narratives, laws, rituals, doctrines, and customs meant in terms of the generations when they arose.

Last but not least, comparative religion has made an immense contribution to our understanding of the original meanings of the Bible. Once the Hebrew religion and its Christian fulfillment stood alone and the religious life of the world outside was either shrouded in obscurity or else was lumped in one general condemnation as heathenism. Gone was the noble catholicity of the early church's greater minds, when on the basis of the doctrine of the Logos "which lighteth every man," cosmopolitan Christians recognized all the world's wisdom and goodness as part of the divine revelation. Gone was the breadth of vision which had stirred Paul on Mars Hill and which had made Clement of Alexandria say that philosophy was given by God to the Greeks as "a schoolmaster to bring the Hellenic mind . . . to Christ." The older cosmopolitanism of the Graeco-Roman world was finally lost when the Empire fell, when the Turks shut off the Orient from the Occident and the shadows of the medieval age closed in.

But the new world of broken boundaries and open avenues has brought back to us interest in other religions than our own, and with that interest, made effective by the diligent study of the legends, cosmologies, rituals, doctrines of other people, new light has come upon our sacred books. Supreme they may be, but they are not, in their typical ways of conceiving the world and describing events, isolated and alone. Primitive cosmology, animal sacrifice, offering of first fruits, circumcision, clean and unclean foods, shrines on high places, priestly garments of linen, sacred trees like the oak of Shechem, sacred chests like the holy Ark, instruments for obtaining divine oracles like the Urim or Thummim, ordeals to determine guilt or innocence, angelic or demonic visitations, and all manner of miracles, are familiar elements of man's religious life wherever its records reveal the past or its present practices and beliefs preserve unchanged an older heritage. Often, lecturing on some ancient idea or custom indicated in our Bible, I hear from a missionary student a perfect parallel out of the religious life of the people among whom he works.

This, then, is the result which follows from all these disciplines of modern scholarship converging on one point: the world in which the Bible first was written lives again in our thought. We can enter into its mind, understand its problems, catch the native connotation of its words. Historic imagination has well-accredited data on which to work and can picture how men lived, thought, talked, and hoped in scriptural times. Perhaps what has been gained is as nothing in comparison with the light that yet shall come, but, for all that, it is true that when we read the Book today we read it with increasing clearness in terms of its contemporary meanings. In a way never true in Christian history before, we stand face to face with the historic sense of the scriptures.

In the meantime, while this old world of the Bible has been growing more vivid in our apprehension, the new world in which we actually live has been growing very new. Science has remade from top to bottom our outlook on the physical universe; philosophy has restated its problems, reformed its methods, and, when discussing old questions or new ones, uses suppositions and structural ideas of which the ancient world never heard; the inductive method of scientific investigation has revolutionized man's ways of discovering and using truth; the idea of evolution in biology has blossomed out into the idea of progress in human life, a conception as far as possible removed from the static view which controlled the ancient world's ethical problems have so changed that polygamy, chattel slavery, imperialistic government, and war are rightly recognized as sins to be hated and overcome, although all of them are taken for granted in large areas of the Bible without reproof, and in some of the older documents are inculcated and encouraged; democracy has arrived and has introduced ideas to which older theories of the state were utter strangers; the machine has remade our industry, and our whole economic life, alike in its extent, its methods, and its problems, is far removed from the economic background of the Bible. We live in a new world, we picture with increasing clearness the contemporary meanings of an old world, and we feel the incompatibility between them— that is the difficulty which multitudes of modern folk are having with the Bible.

From Harry Emerson Fosdick, *The Modern Use of the Bible* (New York: Macmillan, 1924), pp. 7–8, 27, 34–44.

The Fundamentalist Credo
William Bell Riley
James M. Gray
J. Gresham Machen

William Bell Riley, pastor of the First Baptist Church in Minneapolis and head of the Northwestern Bible and Missionary Training School, was probably the most persistently active clerical spokesman for fundamentalism during the 1920s. As early as 1919, he summoned all orthodox believers to rally to the standard of their embattled theology and to combat the spread of the new infidelity, modernism. An indefatigable organizer and campaigner, Riley figured prominently in the activities of the World's Christian Fundamentals Association and numerous other fundamentalist societies. He also staged "Bible conferences" throughout the United States, engaged evolutionists and modernists in public debates, wrote several widely distributed books, and attempted unsuccessfully to persuade the Minnesota legislature to enact an antievolution statute. The following selection by Riley, written almost a decade after he launched his militant crusade, is a succinct statement of the fundamentalist faith which reveals the persistence of a fighting spirit in one convinced that "liberal bandits" threatened to rob fundamentalists of the last vestige of their theological inheritance and institutional handiwork.

———◆◆◆———

Fundamentalism undertakes to reaffirm the greater Christian doctrines. Mark this phrase, "the greater Christian doctrines." It does not attempt to set forth every Christian doctrine. It has never known the elaboration that characterizes the great denominational confessions. But it did lay them side by side, and, out of their extensive statements, elect nine points upon which to rest its claims to Christian attention. They were and are as follows:

1. We believe in the scriptures of the Old and New Testaments as verbally inspired by God, and inerrant in the original writings, and that they are of supreme and final authority in faith and life.

2. We believe in one God, eternally existing in three persons, Father, Son, and Holy Spirit.

3. We believe that Jesus Christ was begotten by the Holy Spirit, and born of the Virgin Mary, and is true God and true man.

4. We believe that man was created in the image of God, that he sinned and thereby incurred not only physical death, but also that spiritual death which is from God; and that all human beings are born with a sinful nature, and, in the case of those who reach moral responsibility, become sinners in thought, word, and deed.

5. We believe that the Lord Jesus Christ died for our sins according to the scriptures as a representative and substitutionary sacrifice; and that all that believe in him are justified on the ground of his shed blood.

6. We believe in the resurrection of the crucified body of our Lord, in his ascension into Heaven, and in his present life there for us, as High Priest and Advocate.

7. We believe in "that blessed hope," the personal, premillennial, and imminent return of our Lord and Savior Jesus Christ.

8. We believe that all who receive by faith the Lord Jesus Christ are born again of the Holy Spirit and thereby become children of God.

9. We believe in the bodily resurrection of the just and the unjust, the everlasting felicity of the saved, and the everlasting conscious suffering of the lost.

It would seem absolutely clear, therefore, that many of the liberal writers of recent years have never taken the pains to ask for the basis of our belief. Had it been so, an Old World writer could not have said of us that we held to "a flat earth," to "an immovable world," . . . to "a canopy of roof overhead"; and some New World textbook producers would not have been willing to assail immature student minds with similar absurd sentences. This charge of ignorance in realms of science against the leaders of fundamentalism has about as much basis of truth as had the statement from the university professor that the author of the Tennessee antievolution bill had, upon learning that the Bible was not made in heaven and dropped down, expressed his regret that he ever wrote or advocated the passing of the bill. Modernism when it comes to deal with the fundamentalist movement is suddenly possessed with a strange imagination. If you want to know what the movement is *not* and who its leaders are *not*, read their descriptions of both. Certainly as to what we believe, the above declaration leaves no doubt, and only the man ignorant of the Bible or utterly indifferent to its teachings, could ever call into question that these nine points constitute the greater essentials in the New Testament doctrinal system.

Fundamentalism insists upon the plain intent of scripture-speech.

The members of this movement have no sympathy whatever for that weasel method of sucking the meaning out of words and then presenting the empty shells in an attempt to palm them off as giving the Christian faith a new and another interpretation. The absurdities to which such a spiritualizing method may lead are fully revealed in the writings of Mary Baker Eddy and modernists in general. When one is permitted to discard established and scientific definitions and to create at will his own glossary, language fails to be longer a vehicle of thought, and inspiration itself may mean anything or nothing, according to the preference of its employer.

.   .   .   .

There are men who would join us tomorrow if we omitted the seventh point from our doctrinal statement, and they marvel that we permit it to remain in our declaration, knowing its divisive effect. Our answer is: Fundamentalism insists upon the plain intent of scripture-speech and knows no method by which it can logically receive the multiplied and harmonious teachings of the Book concerning one doctrine and reject them concerning another. The greater doctrines are not individual opinions that can be handled about at pleasure. In the judgment of the fundamentalist they are "forever settled in heaven." "Holy men of God, who spake as they were borne along by the Holy Ghost," have told us the truth—God's truth—and truth is as unchangeable as imperishable. "Scripture cannot be broken." The "truth of the Lord endureth forever." "The empire of the Caesars is gone; the legions of Rome are moldering in the dust; the avalanches that Napoleon hurled upon Europe have melted away; the pride of the Pharaohs is fallen; the pyramids they raised to be their tombs are sinking every day in the desert sands; Tyre is a rock for bleaching fishermen's nets; Sidon has scarcely left a rock behind; but the Word of God still survives." And it not only endures forever, but it remains forever the same—the same words, the same in meaning, the same in spiritual intent. God's work is incapable of improvement. The sun is old, but the world needs no new or improved one!

Fundamentalism is forever the antithesis of modernist critical theology. It is made up of another and an opposing school. Modernism submits all scripture to the judgment of man. According to its method he may reject any portion of the Book as uninspired, unprofitable, and even undesirable, and accept another portion as from God because its sentences suit him, or its teachings inspire him. Fundamentalism, on the contrary, makes the Bible "the supreme and final authority in faith and life." Its teachings determine every question upon which they have spoken with some degree of fullness, and its mandates are only disregarded by the unbelieving, the materialistic, and the immoral. Fundamentalists hold that the world is illumined and the church is instructed and even science itself is confirmed, when true, and condemned when false, by the clear teachings of the open Book, while liberalism . . . "pretends to preach the higher criticism by interpreting the sacred writings as esoteric fables." In other words, the two have nothing in common save church membership; and all the world wonders that they do or can remain together, and the thinking world knows that but one tie holds them, and that is the billions of dollars invested.

Nine of ten of those dollars, if not ninety-nine out of every hundred of them, spent to construct the great denominational universities, colleges, schools of second grade, theological seminaries, great denominational mission stations, the multiplied hospitals that bear denominational names, the immense publication societies, and the expensive magazines, were given by fundamentalists and filched by modernists. It took hundreds of years to collect this money and construct these institutions. It has taken only a quarter of a century for the liberal bandits to capture them, and the only fellowship that remains to bind modernists and fundamentalists in one body, or a score of bodies, is the Irish fellowship of a free fight—fundamentalists fighting to retain what they have founded, and modernists fighting to keep their hold on what they have filched. It is a spectacle to grieve angels and amuse devils; but we doubt not that even the devils know where justice lies, and the angels from heaven sympathize with the fight and trust that faithful men will carry on.

From William Bell Riley, "The Faith of the Fundamentalists," *Current History*, XXVI (June 1927), 434–436.

James M. Gray, the president of Moody Bible Institute of Chicago, was closely identified with the fundamentalist leadership during the 1920s. The school which he directed had been an important agency for the propagation of orthodox Christianity ever since its establishment in 1886. By 1923 the Institute possessed an impressive physical plant and enrolled a thousand students in its regular curriculum. But it exerted influence upon many thousands more through its correspondence department, monthly magazine, and colportage association. Jasper C. Massee, a prominent fundamentalist crusader, declared in 1923 that "the constituency that has gone out from the Moody Bible Institute during the last ten years has saved the evangelical churches of this country." Gray dedicated his school to the task of combating the "diluted gospel" preached by his "fellow-townsman" Shailer Mathews, whom he described as an apostate and infidel. In the following excerpt from his address to the graduating class of the institute in 1923, Gray summarized his indictment of modernism as a revolt against historic Christianity.

(1) Modernism is a revolt against the God of Christianity. Who is the God of Christianity? For answer one might pick up almost at random any creedal statement of either Protestantism or Catholicism. They are all one in their teaching as to the nature of Deity. The statement of the Apostles' Creed is sufficient—"I believe in God the Father Almighty; Maker of heaven and earth."

The God of Christianity is a transcendent God. He is higher than, and independent of, the universe he has made. In the supreme sense he controls and directs its affairs. His intelligent creatures are under his authority and accountable to his government. All this seems primary to the average Christian, the A B C of his faith.

But modernism will have none of this. I do not now refer to individual modernists among whom, of course, there are many differences and degrees of thinking, but I refer to modernism itself as a system of religion or philosophy.

In the teaching of modernism the transcendence has given place to the immanence of God. And this means, as modernism holds it, that God is merely the ultimate principle of the universe in a sense hard to distinguish from stark pantheism. . . .

(2) But, secondly, it is a revolt against the Bible of Christianity.

Now, what is the Bible of Christianity? Again, one might pick up almost any of the historic creeds for answer. Hodge, in his great work on theology, puts it thus: "The Scriptures of the Old and New Testaments having been given by inspiration of God, are the all-sufficient and only rule of faith and practice, and judge of controversies."

But modernism will have none of this. Professor Gerald Birney Smith of the University of Chicago tells us that "we are becoming accustomed to the use of the Bible as a book of religious experience, rather than a supernaturally-produced literature. . . ."

(3) In the third place, it is a revolt against the Christ of Christianity. Who is the Christ of Christianity? He is Jesus Christ, the only begotten

Son of God, our Lord; "who was conceived by the Holy Ghost, born of the Virgin Mary; suffered under Pontius Pilate, was crucified, dead, and buried; the third day He arose again from the dead; He ascended into heaven, and sitteth on the right hand of God the Father Almighty; from thence He shall come to judge the quick and the dead."

But modernism will have none of this. Its representatives speak of some kind of an incarnation of God in Christ, but that which they mean is an incarnation that is nothing else than the incarnation of God in all men carried to a superlative degree in Christ.

"Divine immanence means that we look for Christ's divinity in his humanity, not outside of it," says one.

"Christ is essentially no more divine than we are or than nature is," says another.

"God is continually incarnating himself in human life; all human history represents the incarnation or manifestation of the eternal Son or Christ of God," says a third.

We thus see, . . . that, according to modernism, Christ was the product of the world, not a Savior come to us from outside of the world. An entirely new picture of Christ is thus offered to us by modernism. "The bond of union among us all," says a Unitarian professor, "is the fight against the deity of Jesus Christ."

But I hasten to consider another feature of the subject—if anything, still more serious. I refer to the deceitful methods by which modernism has gained its present influence in the visible church and over human thinking.

During the World War, a detachment of German troops was being moved along a road one part of which was plainly exposed to the enemy. Therefore, the plan was conceived to roof over the exposed part with wooden planking and board up the side. The boarded side was then painted in imitation of trees and shrubbery to give the effect of an innocent country land. To further heighten the illusion, some heavy dray horses harnessed to slow moving vans were introduced on the wooden planking. All this time the watching foe was unaware that underneath and out of sight, the German troops were steadily advancing to their objective. The French called this camouflage, and it illustrates the modernistic way of doing things. . . .

Albrecht Ritschl, the German theologian credited as the father of modernism, defended the principle that it is right and proper, in order to allay the fears of conservatives, to express the new theological opinions in the old familiar words. And ever since Ritschl's day, theological counterfeiting or two-facedness has been in fashion among his followers. . . .

I am not a fundamentalist in the sense that I have joined that association, but of course, I stand for the essential doctrines for which that movement stands, and so do you. Therefore, you may expect to be called unpleasant names as well as I. But we shall not be ashamed if we do. There was a great revival in the 17th century, and they, through whom it came, were called "Pietists." There was another in the 18th century, and they through whom it came were called "Methodists." Those names, and others like them, have become dear in the history of the Christian church, but they were odious in their generation. It may be true of fundamentalism now, but for all that, fundamentalism represents a revival of our holy religion.

From James M. Gray, *Modernism: A Revolt Against Christianity; A Revolt Against Good Government* (Chicago: The Moody Bible Institute Colportage Association, 1924), pp. 5–10.

J. Gresham Machen, a recognized biblical scholar at Princeton Theological Seminary, in 1923 produced a closely reasoned defense of orthodox Christianity which even nonfundamentalists described as a significant work. The following selection from the introduction to his famous critique of modernism does little more than indicate the general nature of his major indictments. Machen not only described modernism as "un-Christian" and unscientific, but he also pinned on it such labels as "anti-intellectual" and "irrational," terms more commonly associated with fundamentalism. He argued that the modernists were the real obscurantists because of their disdain for theology, especially theological doctrines, and their tendency to read into the scriptures whatever they wished to find there. The result was a hodgepodge of vague ideas incorrectly called modernistic Christianity. Despite modernism's use of traditional Christian terminology, Machen insisted that it was a nonredemptive religion rooted in naturalism.

<hr>

In the sphere of religion, in particular, the present time is a time of conflict; the great redemptive religion which has always been known as Christianity is battling against a totally diverse type of religious belief, which is only the more destructive of the Christian faith because it makes use of traditional Christian terminology. This modern nonredemptive religion is called "modernism" or "liberalism." Both names are unsatisfactory; the latter, in particular, is question-begging. The movement designated as "liberalism" is regarded as "liberal" only by its friends; to its opponents it seems to involve a narrow ignoring of many relevant facts. And indeed the movement is so various in its manifestations that one may almost despair of finding any common name which will apply to all its forms. But manifold as are the forms in which the movement appears, the root of the movement is one; the many varieties of modern liberal religion are rooted in naturalism—that is, in the denial of any entrance of the creative power of God (as distinguished from the ordinary course of nature) in connection with the origin of Christianity. The word "naturalism" is here used in a sense somewhat different from its philosophical meaning. In this nonphilosophical sense it describes with fair accuracy the real root of what is called, by what may turn out to be a degradation of an originally noble word, "liberal" religion.

The rise of this modern naturalistic liberalism has not come by chance, but has been occasioned by important changes which have recently taken place in the conditions of life. The past one hundred years has witnessed the beginning of a new era in human history, which may conceivably be regretted, but certainly cannot be ignored, by the most obstinate conservatism. The change is not something that lies beneath the surface and might be visible only to the discerning eye; on the contrary it forces itself upon the attention of the plain man at a hundred points. Modern inventions and the industrialism that has been built upon them have given us in many respects a new world to live in; we can no more remove ourselves from that world than we can escape from the atmosphere that we breathe.

But such changes in the material conditions of life do not stand alone; they have been produced by mighty changes in the human mind, as in their turn they themselves give rise to further spiritual changes. The industrial world of today has been produced not by blind forces of nature but by the conscious activity of the human spirit; it has been produced by the achievements of science. The outstanding feature of recent history is an enormous widening of human knowledge, which has gone hand in hand with such perfecting of the instrument of investigation that scarcely any limits can be assigned to future progress in the material realm.

The application of modern scientific methods is almost as broad as the universe in which we live. Though the most palpable achievements are in the sphere of physics and chemistry, the sphere of human life cannot be isolated from the rest, and with the other sciences there has appeared, for example, a modern science of history, which with psychology and sociology and the like, claims, even if it does not deserve, full equality with its sister sciences. No department of knowledge can maintain its isolation from the modern lust of scientific conquest; treaties of inviolability, though hallowed by all the sanctions of age-long tradition, are being flung ruthlessly to the winds.

In such an age, it is obvious that every inheritance from the past must be subject to searching criticism; and as a matter of fact some convictions of the human race have crumbled to pieces in the test. Indeed, dependence of any institution upon the past is now sometimes even regarded as furnishing a presumption, not in favor of it, but against it. So many convictions have had to be abandoned that men have sometimes come to believe that all convictions must go.

If such an attitude be justifiable, then no institution is faced by a stronger hostile presumption than the institution of the Christian religion, for no institution has based itself more squarely upon the authority of a bygone age. We are not now inquiring whether such policy is wise or historically justifiable; in any case the fact itself is plain, that Christianity during many centuries has consistently appealed for the truth of its claims, not merely and not even primarily to current experience, but to certain ancient books the most recent of which was written some nineteen hundred years ago. It is no wonder that that appeal is being criticized today; for the writers of the books in question were no doubt men of their own age, whose outlook upon the material world, judged by modern standards, must have been of the crudest and most elementary kind. Inevitably the question arises whether the opinions of such men can ever be normative for men of the present day; in other words, whether first-century religion can ever stand in company with twentieth-century science.

However the question may be answered, it presents a serious problem to the modern church. Attempts are indeed sometimes made to make the answer easier than at first sight it appears to be. Religion, it is said, is so entirely separate from science, that the two, rightly defined, cannot possibly come into conflict. This attempt at separation, as it is hoped the following pages may show, is open to objections of the most serious kind. But what must now be observed is that even if the separation is justifiable, it cannot be effected without effort; the removal of the problem of religion and science itself constitutes a problem. For, rightly or wrongly, religion during the centuries has as a matter of fact connected itself with a host of convictions, especially in the sphere of history, which may form the subject of scientific investigation; just as scientific investigators, on the other hand, have sometimes attached themselves, again rightly or wrongly, to conclusions which impinge upon the innermost domain of philosophy and of religion. For example, if any simple Christian of one hundred years ago, or even today, were asked what would become of his religion if history should prove indubitably that no man called Jesus ever lived and died in the first century of our era, he would undoubtedly answer that his religion would fall away. Yet the investigation of events in the first century in Judaea, just as much as in Italy or in Greece, belongs to the sphere of scientific history. In other words, our simple Christian, whether rightly or wrongly, whether wisely or unwisely, has as a matter of fact connected his religion, in a way that to him seems indissoluble, with convictions about which science also has a right to speak. If, then, those convictions, ostensibly religious, which belong to the sphere of science, are not really religious at all, the demonstration of that fact is itself no trifling task. Even if the problem of science and religion reduces itself to the problem of disentangling religion from pseudo-scientific accretions, the seriousness of the problem is not thereby diminished. From every point of view, therefore, the problem in question is the most serious concern of the Church. What is the relation between Christianity and modern culture; may Christianity be maintained in a scientific age?

It is this problem which modern liberalism attempts to solve. Admitting that scientific objections may arise against the particularities of the Christian religion—against the Christian doctrines of the person of Christ, and of redemption through His death and resurrection—the liberal theologian seeks to rescue certain of the general principles of religion, of which these particularities are thought to be mere temporary symbols, and these general principles he regards as constituting "the essence of Christianity."

It may well be questioned, however, whether this method of defense will really prove to be efficacious; for after the apologist has abandoned his outer defenses to the enemy and withdrawn into some inner citadel, he will probably discover that the enemy pursues him even there. Modern materialism, especially in the realm of psychology, is not content with occupying the lower quarters of the Christian city, but pushed its way into all the higher reaches of life; it is just as much opposed to the philosophical idealism of the liberal preacher as to the biblical doctrines that the liberal preacher has abandoned in the interests of peace. Mere concessiveness, therefore, will never succeed in avoiding the intellectual conflict. In the intellectual battle of the present day there can be no "peace without victory"; one side or the other must win.

As a matter of fact, however, it may appear that the figure which has just been used is altogether misleading; it may appear that what the liberal theologian has retained after abandoning to the enemy one Christian doctrine after another is not Christianity at all, but a religion which is so entirely different from Christianity as to belong in a distinct category. It may appear further that the fears of the modern man as to Christianity were entirely ungrounded, and that in abandoning the embattled walls of the city of God he has fled in needless panic into the open plains of a vague natural religion only to fall an easy victim to the enemy who ever lies in ambush there.

Two lines of criticism, then, are possible with respect to the liberal attempt at reconciling science and Christianity. Modern liberalism may be criticized (1) on the ground that it is un-Christian and (2) on the ground that it is unscientific. We shall concern ourselves here chiefly with the former line of criticism; we shall be interested in showing that despite the liberal use of traditional phraseology modern liberalism not only is a different religion from Christianity but belongs in a totally different class of religions. But in showing that the liberal attempt at rescuing Christianity is false, we are not showing that there is no way of rescuing Christianity at all; on the contrary, it may appear incidentally, even in the present little book, that it is not the Christianity of the New Testament which is in conflict with science, but the supposed Christianity of the modern liberal church, and that the real city of God, and that city alone, has defenses which are capable of warding off the assaults of modern unbelief. However, our immediate concern is with the other side of the problem; our principal concern just now is to show that the liberal attempt at reconciling Christianity with modern science has really relinquished everything distinctive of Christianity, so that what remains is in essentials only that same indefinite type of religious aspiration which was in the world before Christianity came upon the scene. In trying to remove from Christianity everything that could possibly be objected to in the name of science, in trying to bribe off the enemy by those concessions which the enemy most desires, the apologist has really abandoned what he started out to defend. Here as in many other departments of life it appears that the things that are sometimes thought to be hardest to defend are also the things that are most worth defending.

In maintaining that liberalism in the modern church represents a return to an un-Christian and sub-Christian form of the religious life, we are particularly anxious not to be misunderstood. "Un-Christian" in such a connection is sometimes taken as a term of opprobrium. We do not mean it at all as such. Socrates was not a Christian, neither was Goethe; yet we share to the full the respect with which their names are regarded. They tower immeasurably above the common run of men; if he that is least in the Kingdom of Heaven is greater than they, he is certainly greater not by an inherent superiority, but by virtue of an undeserved privilege which ought to make him humble rather than contemptuous.

Such considerations, however, should not be allowed to obscure the vital importance of the question at issue. If a condition could be conceived in which all the preaching of the church should be controlled by the liberalism which in many quarters has already become preponderant, then, we believe, Christianity would at last have perished from the earth and the gospel would have sounded forth for the last time. If so, it follows that the inquiry with which we are now concerned is immeasurably the most important of all those with which the church has to deal. Vastly more important than all questions with regard to methods of preaching is the root question as to what it is that shall be preached.

Many, no doubt, will turn in impatience from the inquiry—all those, namely, who have settled the question in such a way that they cannot even conceive of its being reopened. Such, for example, are the pietists, of whom there are still many. "What," they say, "is the need of argument in defense of the Bible? Is it not the Word of God, and does it not carry with it an immediate certitude of its truth which could only be obscured by defense? If science comes into contradiction with the

Bible so much the worse for science!" For these persons we have the highest respect, for we believe that they are right in the main point; they have arrived by a direct and easy road at a conviction which for other men is attained only through intellectual struggle. But we cannot reasonably expect them to be interested in what we have to say.

Another class of uninterested persons is much more numerous. It consists of those who have definitely settled the question in the opposite way. By them this little book, if it ever comes into their hands, will soon be flung aside as only another attempt at defense of a position already hopelessly lost. There are still individuals, they will say, who believe that the earth is flat; there are also individuals who defend the Christianity of the church, miracles and atonement and all. In either case, it will be said, the phenomenon is interesting as a curious example of arrested development, but it is nothing more.

Such a closing of the question, however, whether it approve itself finally or no, is in its present form based upon a very imperfect view of the situation; it is based upon a grossly exaggerated estimate of the achievements of modern science. Scientific investigation, as has already been observed, has certainly accomplished much; it has in many respects produced a new world. But there is another aspect of the picture which should not be ignored. The modern world represents in some respects an enormous improvement over the world in which our ancestors lived; but in other respects it exhibits a lamentable decline. The improvement appears in the physical conditions of life, but in the spiritual realm there is a corresponding loss. The loss is clearest, perhaps, in the realm of art. Despite the mighty revolution which has been produced in the external conditions of life, no great poet is now living to celebrate the change; humanity has suddenly become dumb. Gone, too, are the great painters and the great musicians and the great sculptors. The art that still subsists is largely imitative, and where it is not imitative it is usually bizarre. Even the appreciation of the glories of the past is gradually being lost, under the influence of a utilitarian education that concerns itself only with the production of physical well-being. The "Outline of History" of Mr. H. G. Wells, with its contemptuous neglect of all the higher ranges of human life, is a thoroughly modern book.

This unprecedented decline in literature and art is only one manifestation of a more far-reaching phenomenon; it is only one instance of that narrowing of the range of personality which has been going on in the modern world. The whole development of modern society has tended mightily toward the limitation of the realm of freedom for the individual man. The tendency is most clearly seen in socialism; a socialistic state would mean the reduction to a minimum of the sphere of individual choice. Labor and recreation under a socialistic government would both be prescribed, and individual liberty would be gone. But the same tendency exhibits itself today even in those communities where the name of socialism is most abhorred. When once the majority has determined that a certain régime is beneficial, that régime without further hesitation is forced ruthlessly upon the individual man. It never seems to occur to modern legislatures that although "welfare" is good, forced welfare may be bad. In other words, utilitarianism is being carried out to its logical conclusions; in the interests of physical well-being the great principles of liberty are being thrown ruthlessly to the winds.

From J. Gresham Machen, *Christianity and Liberalism* (Grand Rapids: William B. Eerdmans, 1923), pp. 2–12.

Neither Fundamentalism Nor Modernism
Gerald W. Johnson
Reinhold Niebuhr

Gerald W. Johnson, as a young, highly perceptive journalist whose family had long occupied a prominent place in the Southern Baptist church, viewed the modernist-fundamentalist conflict of the 1920s from a peculiar vantage point. Although the ecclesiastic described in the following essay undoubtedly represents a type rather than a specific individual, his qualities are remarkably similar to those of identifiable Baptist spokesmen with whom Johnson was personally acquainted. In fact, the author's own father, Archibald Johnson, was an intelligent and tolerant Baptist editor who refused to march under either the banner of fundamentalism or modernism. Johnson's chief concern in this essay is for the enlightened clergyman "with a streak of the mystic in him" whose very nature compels him to remain a noncombatant within the arena of theological artillerymen. Such individuals are the "chief sufferers" during the heat of battle when they are scorned by zealous warriors on both sides. But Johnson is inclined to consider them the real heroes in the long run. Their mystical "spirituality" will survive and enable them to clean up "the mess the demolition squads have made."

***

It is my pleasure to number among my acquaintances several academic gentlemen who are regarded by large numbers of their fellow-citizens as something in the nature of regrettable incidents that must not be allowed to happen again. These gentlemen are teachers of various branches of science that have to do with paleontology. Earnest efforts are being made to deprive them of their professional positions and to strip them of all authority, dignity, and prestige in the academic world. In a word, formidable powers seek their ruin. Yet they are, without exception, blithe spirits, intellectual sword-blades, if you please, bright and keen.

I have the honor also of the acquaintance of certain leaders of the movement to cast into the ignominy of outer darkness all biologists, geologists, behavioristic psychologists, and the like. These leaders see visions that seem to me sufficiently appalling. From their private as well as public utterances I gather that they contemplate the possibility, if not the probability, of the total destruction of religious faith, which, in their opinion, involves the repeal of the moral law. They envisage the dissolution of all the bonds that hold the social structure together. Yet if no one would venture to describe them as gay dogs, still they are not melancholiacs. They customarily go into action with the grim resolution that must have characterized Cromwell's Ironsides and that certainly characterizes a southern police squad raiding a Negro crap game. One is left with the impression that, like the Ironsides and the patrolmen, they find a stern but tremendous joy in the impact when they crash through and scatter the devil's myrmidons.

Thus the great religious war of the twentieth century goes on, as far as the active combatants are concerned, right merrily, as wars usually go among the men who fill the trenches. The modernist professor who sees ruin rising before him feels every emotion except sorrow. The fundamentalist clergyman who sees hell opening at his children's feet is not acquainted with grief. As it was in the beginning, is now, and ever shall be, the warhorse saith among the trumpets, "Ha, ha!"

But this generation's unusually complete schooling in tragedy has taught it where to look for woe when war breaks out. We all know that the profoundest suffering is not to be found in a shell-whipped field where the infantrymen are dropping faster than one can count, or even in the hospitals where the wreckage of the battle is swept up. The most hopeless misery is to be found along roads bordered with clocks and cradles and bundles tied up in quilts. There the vacant-faced refugees trudge endlessly from the wrath behind toward a cold and hopeless vacuity ahead. From the first shot it matters not who wins the war; they are certain to lose it. They march forever and never fight. They bear all hardships and no medals. They die in huge numbers but without glory. Surely their fate is worthy of a passing word of pity, even in war's alarms.

But they seldom get even that. Dr. Jacques Loeb and Mr. William J. Bryan are bewailed by countless thousands. To be sure, the obsequies of each gave intense and widespread satisfaction, also; but each had mourners to beat their breasts and dolefully proclaim that a prince and a great man had fallen. The dust that thickens over the arena has not blotted them out. On the contrary, looming through it indistinctly, their figures already assume a superhuman stature. They verge upon the legendary. But the man who is neither modernist nor fundamentalist, but merely religious, may be trampled underfoot, and few will realize that he is gone.

Yet one who has come into personal contact with the refugees remembers them when the lines of guns and caissons and lorries and marching men have almost faded from his mind. It is my fortune—whether good or ill I am not sure—to be acquainted also with some of the refugees of this war; and there is nothing else in the modernist-fundamentalist controversy quite so moving as their suffering. It is high time that at least one dispatch from the front should take note of it.

For instance, I could name a certain ecclesiastic who is typical. It has become somewhat the fashion to speak lightly of ecclesiastics; because some of them have shown themselves so light that they bring the average weight of the whole class close to the imponderable. Still, I have the temerity to ask serious consideration of the present state of an ecclesiastic. The man is an intelligent clergyman, which, in the South at least, is not yet a contradiction in terms. He has a streak of the mystic in him. That, notwithstanding the contrary opinion of certain scientists, is by no means incompatible with a high degree of intelligence, but insofar as the present religious combat is concerned it is the equivalent of flat feet. It renders the man so afflicted unfit for service.

For a mystic obviously cannot qualify as any sort of materialist, and in the tremendously active and arduous campaign now in progress none but able-bodied materialists are fit to march under either banner. The behavioristic psychologist, who makes John Calvin resemble a twin brother of Arminius as regards predestination, is all right. His doctrine that his whole physical, mental, and moral future was long since predestined by the mating or mismating of chromosomes is materialistic enough to carry him through the hottest theological encounter. The literalist, with his conception that the whole world might be damned by a printer's error, is materialistic enough to meet the psychologist on even terms. Whether one stakes his hope of salvation on baptism or on metabolism, he stakes it on a physical process and he is not in any wise handicapped by spirituality. He can fight unimpeded.

But my friend the ecclesiastic gags at both doctrines. His mysticism humbles him. He conceives that it is possible for him to be mistaken. He is acutely aware of the truth of Guedalla's assertion that any stigma will do to beat a dogma, and therefore eschews dogma, scientific or theolog-

ical. I have no doubt that if one were to present to him tomorrow irrefutable proof that the pavement of heaven does not consist of a metal-
lic element bearing the chemical symbol Au, having a specific gravity of
19.2 and an atomic weight of 197, he would, far from being appalled,
not even be much interested. If one brought him Mrs. Lot's forefinger
and demonstrated by laboratory tests that it did not consist and never
had consisted of sodium chloride, he would consider it merely an irrelevant detail. How, then, is it possible for him to become excited over
the fact that modern biology texts accept the Darwinian hypothesis of
organic evolution as the best guess made to date?

This same mysticism has always caused him to cherish a certain distrust of the more ruthless manifestations of Calvinism. I suspect him of
harboring a secret belief that old John was a good bit of an idiot anyhow, and Calvinism seems to him no less idiotic when it is presented under the name of behavioristic psychology. About the future life he may
hesitate to venture an opinion, but he clings to the fixed idea that
neither God nor chemistry has condemned many men to destruction in
this life. He will not be shaken from the belief that the average man has
within him the capacity to choose between good and evil, because God
has not willed that he shall go to hell, and neither has chemistry de-
creed that he shall go to the electric chair for a murder done on account
of inscrutable reactions within his body cells.

Obviously my friend is a noncombatant in the present conflict. But
he happens to be an ecclesiastic, which is to say he lives within the war
zone. To his charge have been committed certain interests of his
church. With his inveterate mysticism, he persists in regarding that
charge as a sacred one. As the shell-fire increases, and the interests he
cherishes are progressively knocked to pieces, his state becomes forlorn
indeed. He cannot fall back upon behaviorism and trace the whole
situation to some unknowable and unpredictable mechanistic accident
which he could not prevent and therefore might as well regard philosophically. All that he can remember is that it is he who was given the
responsibility of taking care of this little plot of earth through which
the high-explosive shells are ripping, and he cannot avoid the belief that
it is his duty to salvage all that can be saved.

The particular part of the work of his church over which he has
supervision has been going to pot for two years. Nobody any longer
pays attention to his appeals, not that anyone denies their justice, but

because the crescendo thunder of the guns drowns his voice completely. Who can be interested in pruning and cultivating the vineyard of the Lord while the doctors of divinity and the doctors of philosophy are bayoneting and dynamiting each other all over the place? Even if the workmen do not take sides, the show is too stupendous to expect them to wield their tools vigorously while it goes on. So my friend the ecclesiastic looks on, frantic but helpless, while collections dwindle, attendance dwindles, interest in the work of the church dwindles steadily toward the vanishing-point.

In the long range of the absolute, measured by the criterion of ultimate truth, it may well enough be that the shooting up of this farmstead is wholly inconsequential. But that point of view is absolutely unattainable by the distracted owner as he watches the roof go up and the walls come down. He was engaged, a few years ago, in building hospitals, in endowing schools, in establishing and maintaining churches in remote and poverty-stricken communities. Delusion or not, it is his firm belief that when the physically lame walk, the mentally blind receive their sight, and the poor have the gospel preached to them, the work is both good and important. At present he is engaged in stopping prospective enlargements of hospitals, in narrowing and reducing the curricula of schools, in closing churches in fields that have been fruitful, all in order to bring his expenditures within his narrowing income. Even since this war waxed furious some have continued faithful, which means that some hospitals can be kept open, some schools can be maintained, some missionary preachers can be kept at their posts. In a desperate endeavor to save the largest possible proportion of the work, my friend is working at a pace that means hardened arteries and frayed nerves. His sleep decreases and his gray hairs increase. At any moment he may become a casualty on the field.

As it happens, the militant members of this cleric's sect are largely enlisted under the fundamentalist banner, and they have scant sympathy to waste on him. He stands by the side of the road, guarding his clock and his cradle and his quiltful of pitiful odds and ends, wringing his hands as the troops march by. Perhaps they do not actually jeer him, but they certainly do not cheer him. Their thoughts are tinged with scorn. He has little to do, they think, to be fussing about collections when the army is on the march to make the world safe for theocracy. Great events are impending. Every wood and ravine is filled with artillery standing wheel to wheel. Every road is choked with marching columns as division on division deploys for the assault that presently will shake the world. And all that he can think about is his wretched little field and farmstead, all that he can do is struggle to drag some valuables out of danger. The gross materialist!

If a modernist detachment passed, it would be no better. This fellow, they would say, claims to be an orthodox Christian, but he will not even stand up and fight us. All he can think of is the effect of the war on the worldly affairs of his church, and the disaster to his finances and his organization fills his mind to the complete exclusion of higher considerations. A priestly politician. A sanctified opportunist. A spiritual father without as much spirituality as a bacteriologist or a psychiatrist. Faugh!

So there my friend the ecclesiastic stands, target for the contempt of both sides. Stronger is the contempt of the complete cynic, who understands what is in his mind and acquits him readily enough of sordid aims, but sees in him only a pathetic imbecile, suffering horribly in his effort to preserve something for the benefit of war-crazed fools who, if they ever come back, will never give him a word of thanks for his trouble.

He is not a materialist, but is he an imbecile? It must be taken into consideration that, after all, refugees do come back. When the armies have warred to exhaustion, when one has been defeated and the other disbanded, then the flood of the dispossessed streams in again. In the long run the artillery cannot compete with them for possession of the land any more successfully than it can compete with the grass. A single season's cultivation of the most hotly contested field will wipe out or conceal the deepest scars of battle.

In this simple truth the mystic sees his parable and will not be persuaded that it is a false analogy, because he believes that the same voice that said, "Let the earth bring forth grass," speaks to him, not indeed, in words printed or spoken, and not in stained slides under a microscope, but in ways too subtle for him to understand, much less explain. If parados and parapet along the hills of Picardy have become mere grassy hummocks, if cattle pasture in the gun-emplacements of Verdun, the Power that wrought this work is certainly greater than the wrath of man, so why set any boundary to it? It operated before there were either Bibles or microscopes. It would continue to operate were both swept from the earth. When theological warriors are all gone, all dead or scattered, will not the Power that sends grass back to the blasted earth, renew the green fields and vineyards in which its servants labored?

What is to be done with such men? You may rend the very earth under their feet, but they are as persistent as the grass, and they come back with it. They defy the analysis of the laboratory. They defy the exegesis of the literalists. They obviously have something that is absent from the makeup of the more furious combatants on both sides. It must be spirituality.

It is great fun to be an idealist and keep a rendezvous with death at some disputed barricade, or, in Mr. Pickwick's less thrilling phrase, to shout with the crowd, and if there are two crowds, shout with the largest. But as I see my friend the ecclesiastic standing by the roadside desolate, idealism somehow loses its glamour and assumes an uncomfortably convincing resemblance to idiocy.

For the future of idealism is uncertain, but the future of this materialist is as sure as anything human can be. A year, or two years, or five years hence, when the captains and the kings depart, he will be back in his old field, cleaning up the mess the demolition squads have made. His clock will be on the mantel, and his quilt will be on the bed. By that time Moses may have been shot against a brick wall, or Darwin may have abdicated and fled to Holland, but in either case the field over which my friend has been given charge will be green and the harvest promising. The vineyard will be pruned and tended.

My friend will be growing old then, with little money, less fame in the world, and apparently no honor at all. He will still be occupied with the worldly affairs of his church, still concerned over finances and organization, still regarded by militant spirits as a dull fellow whose soul is incapable of firing to a great crusade. Of the earth earthy—so will he be regarded as he potters among the young vines and cares for the walks and hedges of his small enclosure. No man will go there to do him honor.

Yet I, for one, am afraid to set him down as a person of no consequence. Being neither a theologian nor a scientist, I am not informed of what Deity may do next. Therefore I cannot sniff at this man. After all, he might be right in his conviction that as the sun of his life goes down, God will walk in his garden in the cool of the day.

From Gerald W. Johnson, "The Religious Refugee," *The Century Magazine,* CXI (February 1926), 399–404.

Reinhold Niebuhr by the mid-twentieth century was regarded as a dominant voice in American religious thought. But when he wrote the following critique,

he was still minister of a small Evangelical and Reformed church in a working class district of Detroit. From this vantage point he observed at close range the complexities and injustices of the working man's predicament in a metropolitan community and drew some rather pessimistic conclusions about the state of religion in urban, industrial society. He interpreted the contemporary theological struggle as largely irrelevant to the needs of such a society because it tended to ignore what he considered the most critical task confronting religion—"the ethical reconstruction of modern society." The following selections by Niebuhr point up the inadequacy of both religious liberalism and orthodoxy to redeem modern man. In his view only a transcendentally oriented Christianity, committed to the moral implications of its faith, could save the world.

It is quite clear that the world can be saved only by a spiritual ethics which will inspire men to trust human nature as essentially good, and which will make economic and political institutions subservient to human welfare. The church has such an ethics in the Gospel of one whom it reveres as Master. In the original Gospel, which the church ostensibly regards as revealed finality, the moral implications of a transcendental conception of the universe are made unmistakably explicit. We are bidden to love even our enemies and to trust our fellow men beyond their immediate ability to validate our trust. But the Gospel of Jesus became diluted with Greek philosophy, and the church, which was sworn to teach it, became involved with social groups and nations whose interests and instincts ran counter to its ideals; so that in time an emaciated ethics of mere respectability was substituted for real Christian morality. This failure of the church to insist on its own religion has been disastrous to civilization and to the church itself. Having become impotent before or in actual league with the forces of economic greed and racial passion which have destroyed our civilization, it must face the scorn of the millions who suffer from the sins of modern society and are beginning to understand the causes of their misery.

There are indications that organized religion is awakening to the challenge which the sorry plight of modern civilization offers to it. The tendency of liberal Christians is to substitute the authority of Jesus for the authority of the Bible and thus to deliver the church from the futile quietism which it derived from Paul and the barren Puritanism which had its roots in the Old Testament. That is a tremendous gain. Yet

Christian liberalism would do well not to be too sure that it is the force which is to vitalize religion and redeem civilization. It lacks the necessary passion for that task. Its position is weak because it was reached by a retreat and not by an advance. Liberalism rediscovered the religion of Jesus because it found the authority of the Bible untenable in the modern day. It was captivated by the theological simplicity rather than by the moral splendor of His Gospel. It was the impatience of our age with theological subtleties and dogmatic absurdities, rather than its sense of moral need, which prompted this development. Having arrived at the religion of Jesus by a strategic retreat, liberalism has lacked the spiritual passion to make a bold advance upon the positions of economic and political paganism which imperil our civilization. In its hands the heroic vigor of the Gospel has frequently been reduced to a few amiable ethical precepts which have no power to match the social iniquities of our day. If it believes that men ought to be loved and trusted, it has gained that appreciation of human nature more from the Renaissance than from the genius of its own religion. It consequently fails to understand how evil essentially good men can be. That is why Christian liberalism, particularly in America, is corrupted and vitiated by a facile optimism. It deludes itself in the belief that the monstrous sins which lurk in our economic and political traditions may be overcome by a few well-meaning church resolutions, generally judiciously qualified to soften their rigor.

Spiritually the orthodox pessimism, which thinks the world too evil to be saved and waits for redemption upon a divine receivership for a bankrupt civilization, has many advantages over the fatuous optimism of most current religious liberalism. In Europe, where the forces which are destroying our civilization are less obscured and better understood than among us, a marked asceticism characterizes much religious thought. Even this asceticism, which offers the sensitive soul some way of escape from the sins of the world, is in some respects superior to religions which obscure rather than define the task which confronts modern civilization. Religions which despair of the world or persuade us to flee from it will of course make no great contribution to its redemption; but they have at least the merit of correctly measuring the strength of the forces against which the best in men must contend.

If religion is to be restored as a force in modern life, it must be able to gauge the evil in human life and yet maintain its faith in the spiritual potentialities of human nature. It must be able to deal with the problems of economic and political life in the spirit of scientific realism and offer for their solution the dynamic of a faith that is incurably romantic. Nothing less than a transcendentally oriented religion is equal to this task, but it must be a religion which fearlessly faces the moral implications of its faith.

From Reinhold Niebuhr, "Can Christianity Survive?," *Atlantic Monthly*, CXXV (January 1925), 87–88.

The secularization of modern civilization is partly due to our inability to adjust the ethical and spiritual interests of mankind to the rapid advance of the physical sciences. However much optimists may insist that science cannot ultimately destroy religion, the fact remains that the general tendency of scientific discovery has been to weaken not only religious but ethical values. Humanism as well as religion has been engulfed in the naturalism of our day. Our obsession with the physical sciences and with the physical world has enthroned the brute and blind forces of nature, and we follow the God of the earthquake and the fire rather than the God of the still small voice. The morals of the man in the street, who may not be able to catch the full implications of pure science, are corrupted by the ethical consequences of the civilization which applied science has built. While pure science enthroned nature in the imagination, applied science armed nature in fact.

It is a part of the moral obfuscation of our day to imagine that we have conquered nature when in reality applied science has done little more than debase one part of humanity to become purely physical instruments of secular purpose and to cause the other part to be obsessed with pride in the physical instruments of life. The physical sciences armed nature—the nature in us—and lured us into a state where physical comfort is confused with true happiness and tempted us to indulge our lust for power at the expense of our desire for spiritual peace. We imagine we can escape life's moral problems merely because machines have enlarged our bodies, sublimated our physical forces, and given us a sense of mastery. The mastery of nature is vainly believed to be an adequate substitute for self-mastery. So a generation of men is being bred who in their youth subsist on physical thrills, in their maturity glory in physical power, and in their age desire nothing more than physical comfort.

Vaguely conscious of the moral inadequacy of such an existence, men try to sublimate it by restraining their individual lusts in favor of the community in which they live. Thus nationalism becomes the dominant religion of the day, and individual lusts are restrained only to issue in group lusts more grievous and more destructive than those of individuals. Nationalism is simply one of the effective ways in which the modern man escapes life's ethical problems. Delegating his vices to larger and larger groups, he imagines himself virtuous; the larger the group the more difficult it is to fix moral responsibility for unethical action.

It would have been too much to expect of religion that it find an immediate antidote for the naturalism and secularism which the modern scientific world view has created. It was inevitable that the natural world, neglected for centuries, should take vengeance upon the human spirit by making itself an obsession of the human mind. But it cannot be said that religion has been particularly wise in the strategy it developed in opposition to naturalism. Religion tried to save itself by the simple expedient of insisting that evolution was not mechanistic but creative, by discovering God in the evolutionary process. Insofar as this means that there is room for freedom and purpose in the evolutionary process, no quarrel is possible with the defenders of the faith. But there is after all little freedom or purpose in the evolutionary process, in short little morality; so that if we can find God only as he is revealed in nature, we have no moral God.

It would be foolish to claim that the defense of a morally adequate theism in the modern world is an easy task; but it is not an impossible one. Yet most modernists have evaded it. Modernism on the whole has taken refuge in various kinds of pantheism, and pantheism is always destructive of moral values. To identify God with automatic processes is to destroy the God of conscience; the God of the real is never the God of the ideal. One of the vainest delusions to which religionists give themselves is to suppose that religion is inevitably a support of morality. There are both supramoral and submoral factors in religion. Professor Santayana makes the discrimination between two instincts in religion, the instinct of piety and the instinct of spirituality, the one seeking to hallow the necessary limitations of life and the other seeking to overcome them. Pantheism inevitably strengthens those forces in religion which tend to sanctify the real rather than to inspire the ideal.

That is why modernism, which has sloughed off many of religion's antimoral tendencies, but which involved itself in philosophic monism and religious pantheism more grievously than orthodoxy ever did, has been so slight a moral gain for mankind. Liberal religion is symbolizing a totality of facts under the term God which orthodoxy, with a truer moral instinct, could comprehend under no less than two terms, God and the devil. It would be better to defy nature's immoralities in the name of a robust humanism than to take the path which most modern religion has chosen and play truant to the distinctive needs of the human spirit by reading humanity into the essentially inhuman processes of nature. There is little to choose between the despair to which pure naturalism tempts us when we survey the human scene and the easy optimism which most modern religion encourages. What we need is both the spirit of repentance and the spirit of hope which can be inspired only by a theism which knows how to discover sin by subjecting man to absolute standards and to save him from despair by its trust in absolute values.

The secularization of modern life is partly due to the advance of science, but also to the moral inadequacies of Protestantism. If liberal Protestantism is too pantheistic, traditional Protestantism is too quietistic to meet the moral problems of a socially complex age. Protestantism . . . has no understanding of the social forces and factors which impinge on and condition human personality. It believes that righteousness can be treated in a vacuum. It produces no sense of tension between the soul and its environment. The conversions of which it boasts may create moral purpose, but that moral purpose is applied to a very limited field of motives where application is more or less automatic. It helps men to master those sins which are easily discovered because they represent divergence from accepted moral customs, that is, the sins of dishonesty, sexual incontinence, and intemperance. It does not help men to discover the sins lurking in their social customs and moral traditions.

No religion is more ineffective than Protestantism against the major social sins of our day, economic greed and race hatred. In a recent trial of Negroes growing out of a race riot in one of our metropolitan centers, the defense lawyer shrewdly manipulated the selection of the jury so that there would be at least a minority of Jews and Catholics in the jury box, and it is reported that their votes were for the defense when the jury failed to reach a decision. No real progress can be made against the secularization of modern life until Protestantism overcomes its pride and complacency and realizes that it has itself connived with the secularists.

By giving men a sense of moral victory because they have mastered one or two lusts, while their lust for power and their lust for gain remains undisciplined, it is simply aggravating those lusts which are the primary perils of modern civilization.

Protestantism reacted against the dualism in Roman Catholic ethics which produces asceticism on the one hand and an easy-going connivance with human weakness on the other. . . . But Protestantism has a dualism equally grievous, which produces . . . a pagan and a puritan in one person, whose puritanism becomes an effective anodyne for a conscience not altogether easy in the sins of paganism. If a choice has to be made between monastic and quietistic ethics, surely monastic ethics must be termed the most Christian for it is better that the world shall be feared than that it be embraced with a good conscience.

From Reinhold Niebuhr, "Our Secularized Civilization," *Christian Century,* XLIII (April 22, 1926), 508–509.

A Demand for a Secular Religion
Harry Elmer Barnes

Among those who demanded a "new God" resting upon a thoroughly secular and humanistic basis was Harry Elmer Barnes, professor of sociology at Smith College. Throughout the 1920s his criticism of the supernatural orientation of orthodox Christianity sparked lively debates. One of his articles which appeared in the *Journal of Social Forces,* a sociological journal published at the University of North Carolina, provoked a bitter controversy in which its editor, Howard W. Odum, and the university were subjected to a barrage of criticism from fundamentalists opposed to such "anti-Christian sociology." Even more controversial was an address which Barnes presented at the meeting of the American Association for the Advancement of Science in 1928. His indictment of religious orthodoxy as well as modernism which acquiesced in orthodoxy's code of morality prompted rebukes from well-known scientists and liberal theologians. The following selection is an expanded version of that address, the basic theme of which was the need for a new conception of God in keeping with modern science and culture. The "Yahweh complex" and all its harmful implications including the notions of sin, immortality, and other untenable vestiges of a theology founded upon the thought of a "primitive-minded people in an age devoid of science" should be replaced by a code of conduct based on science and aesthetics "which will be wholly devoted to producing a better life for man here on earth." Despite the fact that modernist churchmen were quick to condemn Barnes's humanism and to disassociate their theology from it, the defenders of orthodoxy refused to make any such distinction. Rather they were convinced that Barnes merely exhibited greater candor in expressing what they considered the essence of modernism.

———————— ✦ ————————

Our fundamentalist friends have furnished us with a concise epitome of what they regard as the essence of contemporary orthodoxy. The writer will attempt to formulate in equally brief and specific form what appear to him to be the vital arguments of modern scholarship against orthodox supernatural religion. These arguments—and it seems that the modernists will have to concede them if they expect modernism to receive the benediction of informed and educated persons in the second quarter of the twentieth century—are the following:

1. That the question of a new conception of God is of vital social

significance, because upon it hinges our whole philosophy of the good life and our attitude toward a multitude of social and cultural issues.

2. That the biblical God, Yahweh of the Hebrews, has been thoroughly undermined and discredited by the progress of natural science, biblical scholarship, and cultural history.

3. That the conventional orthodox view of Jesus Christ as the literal "only begotten son of God" and a peerless and unique religious teacher is undermined as certainly and completely by the state of contemporary knowledge as is the Hebrew God Yahweh.

4. That the task of constructing, in the disciplined human imagination, a conception of God compatible with the framework and perspective of modern knowledge is so difficult and baffling as to be, for all practical purposes, futile.

5. That any conception of God compatible with modern knowledge would be so vague and indefinite as to be of no direct utility with reference to a personal religion for man here on earth.

6. That we must surrender any belief in literal immortality, whether physical or spiritual.

7. That the basic categories of the old theology relative to spiritual entities—the soul, sin, and the like—must be surrendered and replaced by determinate secular concepts.

8. That the cause of modernism will be unnecessarily damaged, if not, indeed, fatally discredited, by clinging to vulnerable and untenable vestiges of the old theology.

9. That religion is probably essential in any complete scheme of social idealism and social control; but in order to possess any validity and permanence in the present order, it must rest upon a thoroughly secular basis and found its attitudes and policies upon the discoveries of the natural and social sciences and aesthetics.

The question of a new conception of God is important, in the first place, because it has a direct relationship to our philosophy of life and our resulting social practices. In the orthodox scheme of things man is looked upon as essentially a theological or spiritual entity, who should be concerned primarily with saving his immortal soul and securing an eternal life in the world to come. Society is viewed as the earthly equipment essential for testing . . . man for this future salvation. Social codes and institutions are believed to be divinely revealed, and hence, above legitimate criticism by man. Human deeds are judged primarily in relation to the supposed will of God, rather than with reference to their effect upon man's condition here on earth. The good life is not regarded as that which will make man more happy here and now, but that form of conduct which will make future salvation more certain.

Modern science and secularism repudiate all this. From now on we must realize that human problems are the only valid concern of man, and that the increase of his earthly happiness is the only important issue which confronts him. We may survey the heavens and thereby cultivate terrestrial humility and cosmic reverence, but in our life aspirations and achievements we are thrown back exclusively upon our earthly habitat. Society cannot continue to be regarded as the testing ground for the scheme of salvation; it must be viewed as the means whereby man may, through co-operative endeavor, work out institutions and cultural traits designed to make his mundane existence ever more efficient, decent, happy, and beautiful. The criteria of the good life must be sought in the relative contribution of every human act and policy toward the realization of this mundane and human ideal. In the new outlook there can be no good but human desires and their satisfaction, though we must recognize that the satisfaction of desires may well express itself in ever higher forms of manifestation and may be guided ever more perfectly by science and aesthetics.

Once this secular and humanistic approach is adopted, the trained observer in modern society cannot fail to discern a multitude of ways in which orthodox religion obstructs the free play of human intelligence and decreases human happiness. Indeed, it may be held . . . that no other single factor is so comprehensive in its disastrous influence upon mankind.

The secular scientist looks upon the great volume of religious fears and superstitions and sees that they have not the slightest scientific validity; nevertheless, they continue to terrorize millions. He notes the great wealth accumulated by those ecclesiastical organizations devoted to exploiting superstitions and imaginary fears and must reflect upon what might be done with such resources of money and potential intelligence in advancing the secular welfare of mankind—indeed, in promoting a sane, secular religion. He considers the unhealthy and unhappy mental states which afflict millions in America today, because of false theories of life and conduct which were inculcated in earlier ages when man was concerned solely with salvation, and when he had no scientific means of understanding what constitutes a healthy and happy life here on earth.

The secular commentator discovers families in dire poverty and the world approaching the saturation point in population growth, which, by accentuating the bare struggle for brute existence, may well turn humanity back into barbarism—all because of an archaic religious prejudice against birth control. He observes unscrupulous employers exploiting supernatural religion as a socio-economic anesthetic, thus enabling them to escape their decent and just obligation to pay fair wages and grant a humane working day. By aiding the priesthood in their effort to perpetuate belief in supernaturalism and other-worldliness, these employers are reasonably successful in inducing laborers to accept their harsh and miserable life here on earth in the hope of better things in heaven.

The candid observer of present conditions must further note our barbarous divorce laws, which degrade the institution of marriage and rob hundreds of thousands of families of freedom, sentiment, and independence. They make it necessary to deal with the family as a theological entity rather than a social institution. Likewise, he cannot ignore a fanatical prohibition scheme, parading under the guise of "a noble experiment," but actually debauching American morals and political loyalty, stimulating crime, and paralyzing our system of criminal justice. . . . If, in addition to scientific knowledge and acumen, the scientists possess some degree of aesthetic appreciation, he must also deplore the ugliness, brutality, and wastes which are the inevitable and inseparable accompaniment and byproduct of the superstitions, prejudices, and solemnity of orthodox, supernatural religion and its puritanical proclivities.

For these reasons it is apparent that the orthodox conception of God and its associated attitudes and practices is not a mere metaphysical and academic question; it raises the most fundamental issue which has ever faced man from the pre-Lucretian days to the post-Ingersoll epoch.

Modern astronomy and astrophysical concepts have completely and finally undermined the pretensions of Yahweh, the biblical God, who was conceived and elaborated by primitive-minded peoples in an age devoid of scientific knowledge, and at a time when geocentric views everywhere prevailed. In our age, in which the cosmos is conceived by scientists in terms of billions of light years, there is no place, other than historical, for a deity who was invented at a time when this earth was looked upon as a small bit of flat turf around the eastern end of the

Mediterranean Sea, and the heavens were regarded as an inverted blue bowl . . . a few miles from the earth.

Even more disconcerting have been the results of biblical criticism and cultural history. These have shown that there is nothing basically unique in the Jewish religion, which was a branch of the Semitic cults; and that Yahweh was taken by Moses from the Kenites along with his wife, the daughter of Jethro the Kenite. Crude pastoral deities like the Old Testament Yahweh have existed by the score, and Yahweh owed his remarkable reputation to the dramatic history of the Jewish people who had adopted him.

Biblical criticism has thoroughly discredited the orthodox view of the Bible as a unique religious book, directly and literally dictated by Yahweh to Moses and other faithful scribes. We now know that it was written by scores of human authors at different times and for different purposes, and that it cannot be regarded as divinely inspired to any greater degree than any other literary product of the ages which produced it. Therefore, the history of religions and textual scholarship sweep away the pretensions of Yahweh to being the "Lord of Hosts" as effectively as astrophysics dismantles his claim to being the creative and directive principle of the cosmos.

It is difficult to see how any informed, logical, and courageous person can doubt that astrophysics, history, and biblical criticism wreak equal havoc with the orthodox view of Jesus as the "only begotten son of God" and a religious teacher of unique authority and relevance for all subsequent ages of man. The writer advances this assertion for the following reasons: (1) The whole notion of Jesus as the "only begotten son of God" is completely foreign to, and incompatible with, the perspective of the cosmos now well established by modern astronomy, and the thesis of the virgin birth is contradicted by every tenet of modern genetics. (2) The historical background of Jesus' mission—the Messianic hope of the Jews—was directly linked up with Yahweh and biblical lore. (3) Jesus owed his original reputation and status very literally to the fact that he was regarded by his believers as the son of Yahweh, his followers having no comprehension whatever of a cosmic deity. (4) When viewed in a secular sense, there is nothing unique in the teachings assigned to Jesus, while the cosmology of Lucretius, the moral conceptions of Plato, and the ethics of Aristotle far transcend the doctrines of Jesus in precision of statement, in grandeur of design, and in solidity of substance.

(5) We have but the most fragmentary knowledge of the teachings of Jesus, even if we accept as authentic every word attributed to him in the Synoptic Gospels. (6) The opinions and doctrines attributed to Jesus by the orthodox are often indeterminate and contradictory on the most vital issues, such as whether he had in mind the establishment of a secular utopia here on earth or a spiritual assemblage of saints in the world to come. (7) He was an uneducated man who lived a very simple and restricted life in a backward and provincial economy two thousand years ago; hence he was totally unfamiliar with modern social and economic conditions, and with the natural and social science of today. (8) Therefore, he was in no sense prepared to give out competent opinions to guide mankind in the twentieth century.

.   .   .   .

It would appear, therefore, that any well-informed modernist can speak upon any relevant contemporary subject with far more authority than Jesus. For a modernist to invoke Yahweh in his sermons and to base his preaching upon the Synoptic Gospels is as absurd as it would be if a physician in the year after 1929 prescribed insulin for diabetes only after offering an earnest incantation to Aesculapius and then reading at length from Hippocrates or Galen. The modernist cannot logically taunt Mr. Bryan or Dr. Straton for their views on Yahweh and then himself cling to the conventional view that Jesus was unique as a religious and moral teacher. Yahweh and Jesus are a theological couplet and a cultural complex that stand or fall together.

The prospect of man's being able to reconstruct God in the light of modern science is slight indeed. The whole enterprise is fundamentally nothing but a rationalized vestige of the Yahweh complex. It rests upon the wholly mundane and anthropomorphic conception that all things in the cosmos must have a maker and a directive principle—an assumption the truth of which we have no means of demonstrating. The categories and methods with which we approach the problem are only human improvisations—limited instruments with which we hope to fathom issues and problems of an altogether different order and nature. We assume that the cerebral power in the human cortex is equal to isolating, observing, and estimating the infinite. The very facts of the extent and complexity of the cosmos, in the light of which the new conception of God must be established, are ever becoming more and more baffling to the human mind, if, indeed, they have not already passed the point where they can be intelligently assimilated and interpreted by man.

Yet, recent discoveries indicate that we are only in the infancy of our potential discoveries as to the scope and content of the cosmos. The intricacy of physical matter and modern theories of the atom and electron are as impressive as the cosmos; but, as Professor Eddington has well reminded us, they throw no direct light upon the question of God. Einstein has shown that energy is the physical ultimate of science and has suggested that time and space are only manifestations of energy; but this is no aid to precise theism.

Whether or not man will ever be able intelligently to conceive of God in terms of the new cosmology and physical chemistry, it is certain that any conception which could emerge from such postulates and such a quest would be far too remote, indefinite, and impersonal to serve as the basis for any practical, personal, and social religion. It would, at best, be nothing more than the basis for generalized cosmic reverence— which may be secured and conceded without any specific conception of God.

In short, the conception of God savors so much of the older anthropomorphic theism, carries with it so many archaic and unpleasant associations, and is so incapable of definite formulation in the light of contemporary knowledge, that we may probably agree . . . that it is best for a modernized religion to drop the God-conception altogether. Yet the quest for God is a noble venture . . . and we can cast no aspersions upon those who desire to carry on this type of exploration. It will doubtless captivate many superior intellects as long as man exists on the earth. Manifestly, insofar as the quest for the new cosmic God helps on the abandonment of Yahweh, it will be a great gain for civilization and humanity.

Not only is God apparently indeterminate and irrelevant to religion in the new perspective, but it is also evident that a sense of the reality of God and a conviction of our ability to lean upon Him for cosmic support is not an inherent necessity of human nature. The sense of dependence upon God is a conditioned response. . . . No child brought up independent of the God-complex would have any sense of dependence upon God, and an ever-increasing number of people are coming to be able to live happily and adequately without any sense of cosmic support from God. Even more, people are becoming capable of supporting vital religious movements entirely divorced from any belief in God.

Many contend that the God question is practically subordinate to the problem of acquiring a new and adequate religion. The writer heartily concedes this contention, but he maintains that no adequate secular religion can be secured until we have disposed once and for all of the biblical God and the supernatural orientation associated with Yahweh and all his works.

The belief in immortality cannot be squared with modern scientific facts. The conception arose in the undisciplined imagination of primitives. The Christian view of heaven and hell was derived from the Persians and has no more standing than any other aspect of the folklore and superstitions of ancient Persian culture. Modern physiological chemistry and physiological psychology have shown the sheer impossibility of perpetuating psychic life after the intervention of the chemical change known as death. If we have any immortality, it can be only the immortality of the germ-plasm and the immortality of our earthly achievements. If this is true, then it is worse than futile to govern our conduct by considerations designed to help us escape hell and attain heaven.

The natural and social scientist would also insist upon relinquishing still another ancient animistic conception—namely, the category of "sin." Sin connotes a supernatural situation—a violation of the specifically revealed will of God. Today, when there is no means of proving the very existence of God, to say nothing of His nature and express will, it is obvious that we do not possess the prerequisites of sinning. This outworn term should be abolished and all forms of antisocial action should be determined and classified according to their mundane nature and consequences. No act can be regarded as bad or harmful, no matter how ancient or deep-seated the religious taboo against it, which does not diminish human happiness and the beauty of life. Socially harmful acts should be rechristened with wholly secular terms such as crime and immorality.

The notion of sin and the supernatural origin of morality only confuses, complicates, and obstructs clear and honest thinking in the premises. Psychiatrists have long since shown that the sense of sin is but a commonplace conditioned-response—the product of post-adolescent emotional development. It is even less necessary to comment upon the legend that man is a base, vile, and sinful being because of the "fall of man" in Paradise. This is one of the most primitive strains in Bible lore, with less scientific and historical standing than the Yahweh myth. Man may not rank high compared with some hypothetical inhabitants of other celestial bodies, but he is the best exhibit that has thus far appeared on our planet, and it behooves us to make the most of our heritage instead of vilifying our traits.

If modernism is to save religion, it must surrender such of its present tenets as do not square with those scientific discoveries and scholarly researches which are not open to challenge. If it compromises and wavers, it is bound to lose its most intelligent and indispensable supporters; for those who might constitute the core of its forces will be driven out of the churches to seek intellectual freedom and consistency elsewhere. It profits modernism nothing to abandon one sinking craft to take refuge on another that is just as certainly foundering.

Moreover, and this is fundamental, theological modernism is of no value unless it carries with it sociological modernism. It avails a modernist clergyman nothing to reject Yahweh and yet cling desperately to the moral code which owes its validity and sanctity to the fact that it was supposed to have been revealed and dictated by Yahweh. There are today three major socio-religious groups in America: (1) Fundamentalists, who accept the Yahweh-complex and logically control their conduct with reference to the hope of attaining heaven and avoiding hell; (2) The great majority of modernists, who reject Yahweh and eschatology, but support the fundamentalist code of life and behave exactly as though they accepted fundamentalist theology; (3) The secular modernists and the nonreligious groups, who reject the Yahweh-complex and all its associations and implications and are attempting to construct a code of conduct on the basis of science and aesthetics which will be wholly devoted to producing a better life for man here on earth.

The writer believes that if humanity and civilization are to be preserved we must have collaboration between science and a dynamic secular religion. He readily concedes that Bertrand Russell, John B. Watson, James Harvey Robinson, Clarence Darrow, and George Dorsey have no need of God or religion in order to behave in a seemly fashion; but with half of the American population falling below the intellectual level of the dull-normal type, we shall certainly require some form of social control beyond the appeal to pure intelligence. Further, there are many capable persons more sensitive to aesthetic considerations than to matters of cold intelligence. For these two types, a social institution which could exploit human emotions and enlist them in support of just and decent causes will prove indispensable. Such a secular religion would, of course, obtain its factual guidance from science—natural and social; but it would aid science in the social application of such facts. In short, the new religion, if sound and practicable, must rest upon a thoroughly secular basis, must secure its facts from science, and must conceive its ideals in terms of sociology and aesthetics. It must join forces with the new queen of the sciences—that is to say, mental hygiene.

Some exponents of religion might hold that this scheme only makes allowance for man as man, and they would contend that religion endeavors to make us something "more than man." The writer would join issue directly on this point. In the light of the facts about our inherent nature, no rational person can hope to make man more than he is. It is a sufficient challenge and task to be able to bring out the best that is in man. This is an achievement which has never been attained thus far in human history. Further, if orthodox religion has actually endeavored to "make us something more than ourselves," it has failed signally, and, in reality, has almost invariably made us far less than ourselves.

Religion must abandon its hopeless effort to adapt ancient categories and concepts to new knowledge of entirely different nature and connotation. Rather, it must base its reconstruction upon the facts of the cosmos, of the world, and of man as we now know them, and then determine what valid religious concepts and practices can be worked out in harmony with the new knowlege and perspective. Never has there been a more pertinent example of the futility of attempting to force new wine into old bottles than we find in the conservative modernist apologetic.

From Harry Elmer Barnes, "The Passing of Supernaturalism," *The Forum,* LXXI (April 1929), 204–210.

The theory of evolution is the only menace to religion that has appeared in the last 1900 years.

WILLIAM JENNINGS BRYAN, 1923

2. Evolution: Focus of the Fundamentalist Offensive

THE theory of biological evolution became the focus of much of the debate between modernists and fundamentalists during the 1920s. In the course of their exchanges, protagonists tended to obliterate distinctions between evolution and theories explaining its operation, between organic evolution and evolutionary philosophy. Even those discussions designed to deal strictly with the scientific aspects of evolution strayed into philosophical and theological realms. The result was a confusion of tongues ostensibly dealing with a single topic but in actuality concerned with a conglomeration of issues involving a broad spectrum of American values and morals. In effect, evolution became the symbol of many aspects of modern culture which fundamentalists considered undesirable. It served as a focus for their protest against the naturalistic, secular tenor of twentieth-century life.

Critics claimed that their focus upon the evolution theory was itself a commentary on their backwardness and ignorance. Edmund D. Soper, a well-known liberal theologian, described evolution as "last year's bird nest" and suggested that fundamentalists might well find psychology a more fertile ground for protest than biology.[1] Although the defenders of orthodoxy were disturbed by the encroachment of the nat-

[1] See Willard B. Gatewood, *Preachers, Pedagogues and Politicians: The Evolution Controversy in North Carolina 1920–1927* (Chapel Hill: University of North Carolina Press, 1966) p. 193.

ural upon the supernatural represented by the more recent psychological and scientific theories, their choice of evolution as the focus of their campaign was in many ways a natural one. It was not only more familiar and less abstract than some of the more recent scientific propositions, but it also constituted a more fundamental and pervasive part of the modern intellectual structure. Even opponents of fundamentalism were quick to admit that evolution was one of the touchstones of modern thought. Regardless of the degree to which the theological implications of evolution had been "resolved" within the intellectual community, fundamentalists had never become reconciled to the theory. According to Professor Kenneth K. Bailey, "the contradictions between fundamentalism and the theory of evolution were as real and irreconcilable as religious conservatives imagined them to be." The contradictions continued to exist "even though scientists did not in fact classify man as a descendant of the monkey, and even after the harsh survival of the fittest doctrine was mitigated by the findings of Mendel, de Vries, and others."[2]

The experience of World War I strengthened the fundamentalists' misgivings about evolution and other ideas associated with Darwin. The war not only tended to discredit the prevailing concept of progress which owed much to the evolutionary concept, but it also prompted the public mind to relate Darwin's theory with what was called "Germany's demoniac struggle for power." The anti-German hysteria during the war contributed to the notion that Germany was "the scourge of God to show the nations the evil of their ways." According to the fundamentalists, German "paganism" was founded upon "the brute philosophy of Nietzsche," whose ideas were borrowed from Darwin. Thus, the Nietzschean form of Darwinism was responsible for such facets of Germany's "pagan civilization" as theological modernism, higher criticism, and "materialistic science."[3] But anti-Christian Darwinism failed to disappear with the defeat of Germany; rather a new scourge of God, also rooted in the Darwinian principle that "might is right," reappeared in the form of atheistic Communism. For the fundamentalists, the lessons of Prussian-

2 Kenneth K. Bailey, *Southern White Protestantism in the Twentieth Century* (New York: Harper and Row, 1964), pp. 73–74.

3 Charles A. Ellwood, *The Reconstruction of Religion: A Sociological View* (New York: Macmillan, 1922), p. 103; see also L. H. Gray, "Prussian Frightfulness and the Savage Mind," *Scribner's Magazine*, XLIII (March 1918), 308–314.

ism and Bolshevism were obvious: the preservation of Christian America required nothing less than the obliteration of that complex of ideas associated with Darwin and labeled evolution.

The fundamentalists' assault upon evolution was largely an effort to preserve their theology and the system of values it undergirded. Evolution and the mind it represented were regarded as deadly enemies of virtually all basic tenets of the fundamentalist credo. Many fundamentalists agreed with Jasper Massee's declaration: "The scientific mind cannot pray. The scientific mind cannot approximate God."[4] Of all the products of the scientific mind the most dangerous, in the fundamentalist view, was evolution. Not only did it challenge the authority of the Bible by contradicting the divinely inspired account of man's origin, it also substituted a belief in the ascent of man from a primitive condition to a fuller life for the biblical concept of man's fall from a state of innocence. As if by a single stroke, evolution shattered the theory of an inerrant Bible, invalidated the whole premise of original sin, and eliminated the hope of salvation. Jesus the Redeemer became a mere "Jewish bastard" whose ancestry could be traced to the same simian origin as that of all other men. One fundamentalist pamphleteer claimed that anyone who accepted "the logic of evolution" automatically relinquished his belief in seven "fundamental doctrines of the Church": (1) inspiration of the Bible; (2) fall of man; (3) sin; (4) deity and virgin birth of Christ; (5) atonement by substitution; (6) regeneration; (7) holiness of God.[5] Any attempt to reconcile evolution and the Christian faith, he concluded, was futile. It invariably resulted in a form of pantheism.

The fundamentalists were particularly disturbed by what they viewed as the Darwinian emphasis upon chance variations which operated wholly independent of a Creator. "The real issue . . . ," declared John Roach Straton, "is whether the earth and man originated, or came, by *design* through the creative power of God, or by *chance* through the haphazard operation of evolution."[6] It appeared to Straton and other fundamentalist spokesmen that evolution flatly denied the biblical description of man as a creature in God's own image. The notion that

[4] Quoted in the *News and Observer* (Raleigh, North Carolina), May 11, 1922.

[5] See J. E. Conant, *The Church, The Schools and Evolution* (Chicago: Moody Bible Institute Colportage Association, 1922), pp. 23–40.

[6] John Roach Straton, *The Famous New York Fundamentalist-Modernist Debates: The Orthodox Side* (New York: George H. Doran, 1925), p. 62.

man was "first cousin to the ape" robbed him of his dignity and relieved him of his moral responsibility. It encouraged him to assume the attributes of his brutish ancestors. The moral shabbiness which fundamentalists detected in the post–World War era seemed to justify their declarations about the pernicious influence of evolution. Among the modern "evils" which they traced to this single source were secularism, heresy, adultery, busy divorce courts, disintegration of the family, Prussianism, and Bolshevism. For such fundamentalists as Billy Sunday, evolution was an assault upon all those things—"decency, patriotism and manliness"—which they equated with salvation.

Although their objections to evolution were primarily theological in nature, fundamentalists were also quick to challenge its scientific validity. They characterized the theory as a "mere guess" borrowed from the pagan Greeks of antiquity by Charles Darwin, whose own life ended in the atheist's grave. Efforts by scientists to point out differences between the "demonstrated fact" of evolution and the various theories advanced to explain this fact were scorned as obvious devices to beg "the real issue." Fundamentalists allowed neither reservations nor equivocations; they labeled those who called themselves "theistic evolutionists" infidels of the worst variety whose position of unbelief was hidden by a veil of deceit and hypocrisy. The scientific evidence marshaled in defense of fundamentalism was, with few exceptions, drawn from nineteenth-century authors. The exceptions included contemporary scientists whose writings challenged theories explaining the process of evolution rather than "the fact of evolution." One twentieth-century "scientist" widely quoted by the opponents of evolution was George McCready Price, who claimed that his geological research offered conclusive proof of the biblical account of creation. In fact, Price succinctly summarized the fundamentalists' chief objections to evolution when he stated: "No Adam, no fall; no fall, no atonement; no atonement, no Savior."[7]

[7] Quoted in Norman Furniss, *The Fundamentalist Controversy, 1918–1931* (New Haven: Yale University Press, 1954), p. 16.

The Root of Modern Evils
Amzi Clarence Dixon

Amzi Clarence Dixon, brother of the novelist Thomas Dixon, was an internationally famous fundamentalist preacher and an editor of *The Fundamentals* published in 1910. He was a member of the original group which sponsored the organization of the World's Christian Fundamentals Association. As early as 1919 he urged the association to view evolution as the equal of modernism in causing unbelief. In the following sermon delivered at the Baptist Tabernacle in Raleigh, North Carolina, Dixon demonstrates the tendency of antievolutionists to hold Darwin's theory responsible for virtually all "modern evils," including World War I, Communism, and the disintegration of the family. He reiterated these antievolution arguments in pulpits throughout the United States and Great Britain.

Many unbelievers claim that they are dominated by the scientific spirit of the age and cannot, therefore, be Christian. But what is science? The best dictionaries agree in this definition: "Science is knowledge gained and verified by exact observation and correct thinking," and within the circle of this definition I am a Christian, because I am a scientist. Before the time of Lord Bacon, scientists had their theories and sought to make nature recognize them. As a result the scientific world was divided into two contending factions. Bacon insisted that we sit at the feet of nature and accept what she teaches. First learn the facts; then draw your deductions from them. There seems to be a trend now in the scientific world back toward the pre-Bacon period. Some scientists have accepted a theory of evolution and they spend their time seeking proof of their theory instead of confining themselves to "knowledge gained and verified by exact observation and correct thinking."

Within this sphere of "knowledge gained and verified by exact observation and correct thinking," we find that germinal, embryonic life develops gradually into the mature product. "First the blade, then the ear and after that the full corn ear," Mark 4:28. And we find that this development is governed by certain fixed laws. One of them is that germinal embryonic life is never reproductive. Only the mature product can reproduce a germ or embryo. Embryos do not multiply into embryos.

Eggs do not hatch eggs. Apples do not multiply into apples. It takes a tree to produce an apple. Even babies do not bear babies, though they have passed far beyond the embryonic stage. Now, when you leave the realm of "knowledge gained and verified by exact observation," and go into the abysmal past and insist that germinal embryonic life, without the power of reproduction, shall evolve through millions of years into the mature product, my scientific spirit revolts against the absurdity. It is not a question as to whether God created first an egg capable of hatching into an eagle under certain conditions of heat. That is not evolution but direct creation. Evolution demands that the egg shall have been created millions of years ago and shall gradually evolve through those millions of years into the eagle. It is unscientific to believe that this can take place without the power of reproduction. The knowledge that I have gained by exact observation and correct thinking forbids my believing this biological absurdity.

I find again in the scientific realm of "knowledge gained and verified by exact observation and correct thinking" that germinal, embryonic life is unimprovable except through the mature product. If you would have better apples, you must make better trees. You cannot improve the quality of an apple by working directly upon it. You are apt to mar, if not destroy, it. If you have better eggs, you must make better hens. To attempt to improve the quality of an egg by working directly upon it is almost certain to vitiate its quality, if not destroy its life. Darwin experimented much with pigeons but if he ever experimented with pigeon eggs, he almost certainly had on his hands a basket of addled eggs in a few days. If you claim that germinal, embryonic life came into existence without the mature product and evolved through millions of years into the mature product without the power of improvement, you multiply my difficulties, if I am to be governed by the scientific spirit. How can I believe that germinal, embryonic life came into existence in the abysmal past and continued to exist through millions of years without the power of reproduction and continued to improve without the power of improvement? It strikes me as utterly unscientific to accept this twofold biological absurdity. I find, also, in the realm of "knowledge gained and verified by exact observation and correct thinking" that germinal, embryonic life is not preservable except under favorable conditions for a limited time. Nature provides for such preservation during a brief period, but under unfavorable conditions germinal, embryonic life is easily destroyed. A British scientist said to the British Association, that, if embryonic life had come into existence in the chaotic conditions under which we claim that it did, it could not have existed two weeks. It would certainly have been destroyed immediately. It has not, in itself, the power of resistance against unfavorable conditions, and the conditions must be unfavorable when there is no mature product with the fostering care of motherhood.

If, now, you claim that germinal, embryonic life came into existence millions of years ago and continued through long successive ages without the power of reproduction, continued to improve without the power of improvement, and continued to be preserved without the power of preservation, you have multiplied my difficulties still more. I do not see how a scientific spirit can accept this threefold biological absurdity.

I find, further, that in the realm of "knowledge gained and verified by exact observation and correct thinking" one species does not evolve into another species. When two species cross, the result is a hybrid, as in the mule. Not one reputable scientist claims that one species has ever evolved into another species. Propagation after its kind as revealed in the first chapter of Genesis is, universal law. And when you invite me to imagine with you in the abysmal past this law has somehow been violated by the evolution of one species into another, my scientific spirit revolts against this unscientific procedure. If in the realm of imagination you insist that germinal, embryonic life continued to exist through long stretches of time without the power of reproduction, continued to be preserved without the power of preservation and that one species is evolved into another without proof of any such evolution, you have multiplied biological absurdities which my scientific spirit finds it difficult to accept.

Tracing this evolution to its fountainhead, I find that it originated in an unscientific speculative age. Between 700 and 300 B.C. there were several schools of evolutionists among the Greek philosophers. Thales of Miletus taught that water was the primordial germ. Heraclitus taught that fire was the primordial germ. Pythagoras, the mathematician, taught that numbers was the primordial germ. Plato, greatest of them all, disagreed with his compeers and insisted that man began equal with the gods and that beasts were degenerate men.

Charles Darwin in his university course caught the vision of the Greek philosophers and, rejecting the theory of Plato, became an ardent advocate of the hypothesis that everything has evolved from beneath; that life originated with germinal embryonic beginnings; that in nature there is perpetual war which he called "the struggle for existence," the strong and fit destroying the weak and unfit, and thus causing everything to move upward. Darwin did not get his idea of perpetual warfare in nature from the Greek philosophers, who were more benevolent in their thinking. They believed that all life and form were evolved from beneath by quiet forces; but they did not give the strong the scientific right to destroy the weak. Darwin confesses in his autobiography that he received the suggestion from Rev. Thomas Robert Malthus, an Anglican clergyman who died in 1834, when Darwin was twenty-five years old. I do not know that Darwin met Malthus, but he was a careful reader of his books and in his autobiography acknowledges that he received the suggestion from Malthus who taught that man increased with geometrical ratio, while the food supply increased with arithmetical ratio. Therefore, wars and pestilences are necessary, that the surplus population may be killed off, in order that the remainder may survive.

A little careful thinking makes it clear that Malthus was wrong. Man does not increase with geometrical ratio while food supply does increase "from 30, from 60, and from an hundredfold." But Darwin was deceived by the plausible reasoning of Malthus and made this mistake one of the foundation stones of his scientific system. It is a libel upon a benevolent God, who has provided enough for man and beasts without demanding that the strong shall kill the weak. The fact that dolphins should eat flying fish for food and that some animals are intended for the food of others does not prove that in nature there is perpetual warfare, but rather the contrary. It is a benevolent provision that some animals should be intended as food for others so that the strong may subsist without a struggle with their equals for existence. Read George Paulin's book, "No Struggle for Existence, No Natural Selection" and you will see proof enough that there is no struggle for existence even among carnivorous animals, a benevolent God having provided a kinder method of preventing a dangerous increase.

One of the most pathetic bits of biography in existence is the effect of this pagan teaching and the atmosphere it produced upon Darwin himself. In early life Darwin was a believer in the Bible as the Word of God, and he believed that God answered prayer. In his later life he confessed with regret that he had lost all taste for poetry, music, painting, and religion. But he wrote the best book on worms ever penned. He glorifies the little creatures as benefactors of mankind none too much. It is all true. But what I insist upon is that any theory or atmosphere which effaces all taste for music, poetry, painting, and religion, while it makes one revel while studying the habits of worms, has something the matter with it; and when we observe that the effect of the theory in others is to drag them down from the spiritual to the material, from the realm of music, poetry, painting, and religion to the realm of the worm as it works in the dirt and dark, we are driven to the conclusion that there is something in this pagan theory which drags us down into the mud and robs us of the clearer vision and purer atmosphere of the higher spiritual realm.

Evolution with its "struggle for existence" and "survival of the fittest," which gives the strong and fit the scientific right to destroy the weak and unfit, is responsible for the oppression and destruction of the weak and unfit. It has fostered the autocratic class distinctions and is no friend to those who stand for the protection of the weak against the oppression of the strong. The greatest war in history, which has drenched the world with blood and covered it with human bones, can be traced to this source. If the strong and fit have the scientific right to destroy the weak and unfit that human progress may be promoted, then might is right, and Germany should not be criticized for acting upon this principle.

Nietzsche, the neurotic German philosopher, hypnotized the German mind with his pagan brute philosophy. "The weak and botched," said he, "shall perish; first principle of humanity." And they ought to be helped to perish. What is more harmful than any vice? Practical sympathy with the botched and weak Christianity. "If what I publish be true," he wrote to an invalid women, "a feeble woman like you would have no right to exist."

"Christianity," he said, "is the greatest of all conceivable corruptions, the one immortal blemish of mankind." And he hated it because of its sympathy for the botched and weak. He glorified his own ideal "blond beast" and gave to the world a "superman," one third brute, one third man, one third philosopher. Under the spell of his daring brutality, Germany adopted the motto, "Corsica has conquered Galilee." Nietzsche's philosophy of beastliness has its roots in the evolutionary assumption that the strong and fit, in the struggle for existence, have the scientific right to destroy the weak and unfit.

Under the spell of Nietzsche's "superman" there came into the heads of the German politicians and militarists the vision of a super nation with the scientific right to destroy the weaker nations and build its throne upon their ruins.

One Sunday morning, four months after the war began, I spoke something like this from the Metropolitan Tabernacle pulpit, London, and after the service a gentleman with military bearing appeared in the vestry and said:

I am a German and a Christian. I love Jesus Christ and believe the Bible, but my wife and daughter have had their faith wrecked by Nietzsche and his pagan gang. You have said that this terrible war was due to Darwinian evolution and I believe it. But what I want to say to you is that we Germans got Darwinism from England. We took it from you and worked it out to its legitimate consequences. So, when you mention it again, speak softly, for you are really getting back what you sent.

I could not deny it. Back of this war and responsibility for it is Darwin's pagan teaching that the strong and fit have the scientific right to destroy the weak and unfit.

This suggests the fact that England gave to Germany her first lesson in the destructive higher criticism of the Bible. It was Jean Astruc, a learned dissolute French physician, of Marseilles, who first suggested that Genesis had two authors. Dr. Eichhorn of Germany took Astruc's suggestion as a clue and announced that he had discovered many authors. Thus, began a movement which has done much to discredit the Bible. The scientists of Germany took Darwinism from England with its struggle for existence, giving the strong and fit the scientific right to destroy the weak and unfit, and gave to the politicians the dictum that might is right, while the German theologians took from Jean Astruc his composite authorship of Genesis theory and worked it out to the discrediting of the Bible as the revelation from God. Through Darwin and Astruc England and France let loose a flock of scientific and theological vultures which put their talons into the vitals of academic thinking and ethics in Germany, destroying faith in the Bible and vitiating the spiritual life of the people. Strengthened by their feast upon Germany's vitals, these ferocious birds returned to England to wreck the Christianity founded upon the Bible, which has been the glory of English history and which broke the fetters of papal superstitions that for centuries retarded the progress of France.

It was hoped that the World War, with its unutterable horrors, would open the eyes of the educators of England and France to the wreck of faith and character which their scientific and theological dreamers had wrought; but instead of that, the religious liberal leaders of England and France, realizing that their rationalistic theories and their books based upon them are in danger, are reasserting with nervous haste their destructive teachings. While victory on the side of liberty and humanity has checked, if not destroyed, German militarism, it remains for those who believe and love the Bible to mobilize and fight the battle for the truth which has given to the world its passion for liberty and humanity.

I tremble for the future of the world if the millions of China are to be molded and dominated by a philosophy which gives to the strong and fit the scientific right to destroy the strong and unfit. It is easy for the patriotism of any nation to make its people believe that they are the fittest nation in the world; only, if China with the conviction should become conscious of her strength, she could become, under masterful military leadership, a menace of the future. Any nation that teaches this pernicious delusion to its youth is now a menace to the peace of the world; and if all nations teach it, war will be the normal method of settling all disputes. Universal peace can never come until nations turn from this voice of the jungle to the song of the angel floating from the skies above the plain of Bethlehem, "peace on earth among men of good will."

If the home is to be preserved as a sacred institution, the Bible which teaches that marriage came down from God and not up from the beast must be believed. The jungle theory as to the origin of marriage is today keeping busy the divorce courts of the civilized world. If government came down from God, so that "the powers that be are ordained of God," law will rule in righteousness and courts will mete out justice, but if the basis of government came from the jungle where brute force prevails, the Bolshevik rule by bullet and bayonet is scientific and the scientific mind ought to accept it. This jungle origin of government is a worldwide peril. If the Bible is a revelation from God through inspired men, its teaching is authoritative and its truths have in them an irresistible dynamic, but if the Bible is the mere record of human experience as men have struggled upward from their jungle origins, its teaching has no authority and its saying ought to be accepted or rejected by the inner consciousness of man, which is itself a product of the jungle theory.

If man came down from God, created in his image, and has been wrecked by sin, the sin is an intrusion, an enemy that ought to be expelled; but, if man came up from the beast through the jungle, sin is "embryonic goodness," "righteousness in process of formation," even a search after good; of course such sin has no guilt and may be condoned, if not coddled. Such a delusion makes it easy to believe that sin has no existence and all things, even theft, falsehood, and murder are good because there is no evil in the world.

If the church came down from God in the sense that its members are "born from above," we have on this world a unique spiritual organism, of which Jesus Christ is the head imbued with an irresistible dynamic, "power from on high." But if the church came up from the beast through the jungle and is the expression of man's struggle out of beastliness into spirituality, we have simply one earthborn institution among many and cannot be optimistic regarding its destiny.

If Christ came down from Heaven as he said he did, "the only begotten son of God," in the sense that he is the only one in the universe begotten of God in a virgin's womb, "God manifest in the flesh," "the Word made flesh and dwelling among men," we have in him a unique personality; God who is a spirit made concrete, thinkable, approachable, and lovable; God, lowering himself to our level, that he may lift us to his level. But if Christ is the expression of humanity's struggle up from the beast through the jungle, we have in him a combination and culmination of jungle life in body, soul and spirit, detached from heaven, on the same plan with others, with little power to lift or to transfigure.

The beast jungle theory of evolution robs a man of his dignity, marriage of its sanctity, government of its authority, and the church of her power and Christ of his glory.

From the *News and Observer* (Raleigh, North Carolina), December 31, 1922.

The Great Menace: Evolution
John W. Porter

John W. Porter, the editor of the Baptist *Western Recorder,* was a leader in
the campaign to outlaw the teaching of evolution in the public schools of
Kentucky. So successful was the crusade that the legislature barely defeated
an antievolution bill in 1922. Two years later, Porter became president of the
Anti-Evolution League of America which he had helped to organize. The
following excerpts from one of his widely circulated tracts include many of
the standard arguments against evolution.

No evolutionist can consistently accept the Bible as the fully inspired Word of God, directly revealed by God to man. Evolution implies
a process and a growth, while the Bible claims to be a direct revelation
and a finished product. The Bible is not the result of "resident forces"
in man, but is from God. The history of creation, as given in Genesis, is
flatly contradicted by every known hypothesis of evolution. It is for this
very reason that evolution and destructive criticism go hand in hand.
Like the Siamese twins, they are one and inseparable. If evolution is
true, the Bible, or at least portions of it, are absolutely false. Evolution
subjects the Bible to its theory, and not its theory to the Bible.

The Christian religion is fundamentally and essentially a supernatural religion. Evolution emphatically denies any supernatural factor in
the development of life. It denies the existence of a miracle in the life-
process. Or as Haeckel defines it, "the non-miraculous origin and progress of life." The moment the supernatural, or miraculous, is admitted
in the scheme of development, the whole structure of evolution must
collapse.

Uniformity is simply the assumption that things have always happened and, of necessity, must continue to happen as they now occur.
Such a statement is incapable of proof, involves a universal negative,
and implies a universal knowledge of natural law.

It should be said, in justice to all concerned, that there are those
who proclaim to be theistic evolutionists. This, if not a "new species,"
is certainly a peculiar one, and deserves, perhaps, more than passing

notice. This particular brand of evolution tries to reconcile the Bible with the false assumptions of so-called science. There can never be a conflict between real science and true religion. Evolution is not a science and is incapable of scientific demonstration. At most it is an unproved and unprovable hypothesis. The phrase "theistic evolution" was coined to overcome the odium of atheistic evolution. The meaning sought to be conveyed is that one may believe in God and also in evolution. It is significant that they choose to designate themselves "theistic" rather than "Christian." Tom Paine was a theist, and so are Jews and Unitarians. It is but just to assume that theistic evolutionists, with their boasted wisdom, have rightly named themselves. It is possible to conceive of a theistic evolutionist, but impossible to conceive of a Christian evolutionist of the Darwinian type. Every known scheme of evolution implies uniformity, variation by natural selection, and progress by "resident forces." All theories of evolution are restricted to natural processes, and therefore must reject the miraculous. Christianity is predicated upon the fact that Jesus was the Son of God, and not a Superman developed by "natural selection and scientific eugenics." It is absolutely impossible to reconcile the fact of the bodily resurrection of our Lord with the natural process of the theory of evolution. The virgin birth is also contrary to the demands of evolution.

The coining of this phrase has not been in vain, however, since it has enabled not a few to draw good salaries from institutions supported by Christian denominations while undermining the very foundations of the Christian faith.

.   .   .   .

For a season, we heard much about our present horse being a descendant of the "five-toed horse." Later investigation has successfully demonstrated that this five-toed animal was not a horse of any kind. The structural arrangement is essentially different, to say nothing of the difference between the hoof and toes. With equal propriety, it might have claimed that the cow sprang from the five-toed horse. . . .

Certainly one should know more of his own family history than of others in no way related to him. It is, perhaps, a delicate matter to contradict one concerning his ancestry, even when he solemnly affirms that his progenitors were apes, beasts, birds, and reptiles. Suppose then, for the sake of argument, we grant the ancestral claims of the evolutionists concerning themselves. Should they not accord the same right to others?

The great rank and file of God's people claim that they were created by God, and in his image, and are not at all anxious to claim kin with the evolutionists, or their forebears. Should they, then, get angry because our ancestry was divine, and theirs, according to their own confession, inhuman reptiles and beasts? If one wishes to believe that his great-great-great-grandparents roosted in trees with their tails wrapped around a limb, they are clearly entitled to all the comfort that comes with their belief. Just how a man can look into the face of his noble conse-crated mother and believe she descended through the wild ferocious wolf is to the average mind unthinkable.

.   .   .   .

The real test of any philosophy—and evolution is at most a phi-losophy which attempts to explain the development of the world—is to carefully note the effects or the fruits of it. Let us therefore glance at some of the fruits of this unproved and unprovable theory of evolution.

1. The theory of evolution denies man's moral responsibility. Le-Conte, who classed himself a theistic evolutionist, and who was well qualified to speak in this regard says: "What we call evil is not a unique phenomenon confined to men. It is a great fact pervading all nature and a part of its very constitution." According to him, this sin, or "what we call evil," existed in nature long before it existed in man and came up through brute creation to man. A Russian author recently wrote an article in which he said: "When I kill a hen or rat, no one says anything. Why do you say anthing when I kill a man, for he is only an animal with a little higher reasoning." Was he not right, if the claims of evolution be true?

2. The theory of evolution denies the gospel remedy for sin. Ac-cording to the life-succession theory, man would, apart from supernat-ural help, achieve his own redemption. This would be particularly true of the survival of the fittest in the "struggle for existence." If evolution be true, the only fall man ever had was a fall upward from the brute. In its very nature, evolution can recognize no atonement. In its scheme, there is no place for one to die for another, but to the contrary, the stronger kills the weaker in order that the stronger may survive. The only redemption that evolution offers is heredity and environment. Vi-carious sacrifice is contrary to the very genius of evolution. According to the doctrine of the "survival of the fittest," Christ perished in a "strug-gle for existence," because the Pharisees were the fittest.

3. It destroys belief in the Bible and thus takes away from the people the greatest civilizing force known to the world. The evolutionist is quite right in saying that geology, as interpreted by him, is contrary to the account of Creation. Every evolutionist must believe the account of the Creation given in Genesis is either figurative or false.

.   .   .   .

According to the evolutionists the command to keep the Sabbath was entirely useless, since creation was not completed as affirmed by the Bible. The Sabbath is the memorial of a finished creation.

Evolutionists did not discover a process of creation, but invented one. There is abundant evidence that the teachings of these textbooks is unsettling the faith of thousands of students. Many of these, through respect for their parents' faith, say but little, while many others are outspoken in their rejection of the Bible account of Creation. In a recent meeting . . . a prominent businessman wept as he told of the damage done his daughter's faith by this teaching. This is not an unusual, but an almost everyday, occurrence.

4. It is wrecking the faith of many students in all our state institutions and not a few in denominational schools.

.   .   .   .

5. It undermines all the fundamentals of Christianity. It denies the supernatural in the scheme and process of life. It finds no place for a miracle, or a miracle-working God. It exalts "resident forces" and makes God a pantheistic force in nature only. Of necessity it must deny the deity of Christ. According to the evolutionist, Christ came up through the insect, reptile, fowl, bird, and beast. It denies the incarnation, virgin birth, and resurrection. In spite of this, it is a fact that every nation worthwhile in the whole world achieved its greatness by belief in the Bible.

6. It robs man of his spiritual nature and makes him a developed beast. An evolutionist considers himself the offspring of the beast and hence with brute blood in his veins. Why should not the descendant of the brute be brutal? Nietzsche refers to his own countrymen as the "blond beasts." In his brutality he would only prove true to his type and perpetuate the nature of his species. The spiritual nature of man is rarely referred to in any work on evolution.

7. It exalts the law of the jungle. If this brutal theory be true,

in the "struggle for existence" the weak must be killed that the strong may survive. It places a premium on murder and glorifies the demon of destruction. It builds its hope of life on the graves of others. That evolution may have recourse and may run and be glorified, there should be no physicians or hospitals. The weak and sick and unfit should be allowed to perish that the strong and fit may survive. Evolution knows neither God nor mercy, but only "variation" and brute strength.

8. Evolution logically and inevitably leads to war. Nietzsche's philosophy was a legitimate product of Darwinian evolution. In full accord with the inevitable logic of "survival of the fittest," he crowned the Superman, glorified war, expressed contempt for Christ, and decried all rule of right and right living. To his philosophical treatises, more perhaps than all other causes, was due the late cruel war. Nietzsche claimed that Darwin was one of the three greatest men of his century. If the survival of the fittest is the supreme law of life in the struggle for existence, then war is the ideal agency for carrying out this brutal theory. Pseudo-scientists have sowed the seed, and they have brought forth "after their kind."

From John W. Porter, *Evolution—A Menace* (Nashville, Tennessee: Sunday School Board of the Southern Baptist Convention, 1922), pp. 5, 26–29, 48–50, 82–89.

Evolution and Supernaturalism
John Roach Straton

Four "fundamentalist-modernist debates," between Charles Francis Potter and John Roach Straton, were held in New York during April 1924. That the protagonists were themselves storm centers of controversy only heightened public interest in this match of wits, which was broadcast over radio. Potter was a Unitarian minister whose militant advocacy of modernism and evolution prompted some fundamentalists to label him a "rank infidel." Straton, a flamboyant dispenser of orthodox theology, was minister of Calvary Baptist Church in New York and a significant figure in several fundamentalist, anti-evolutionist organizations. In fact, so diverse were his activities and powers that some referred to him as the "fundamentalist pope." The topics of the four debates between Potter and Straton were the infallibility of the scriptures, the validity of biological evolution, the virgin birth, and the deity of Jesus. The following selection is a portion of Straton's argument against evolution.

———◆◆◆———

RESOLVED, THAT THE EARTH AND MAN CAME BY EVOLUTION.

There are but two theories concerning the origin of the earth and of man—one is creation by a living God; the other is evolution by dead force.

Evolution is not a fact of science, but a dogma of philosophy. Both its history and its essential nature prove that it belongs primarily to the realm of subjective speculation and not to the field of demonstrated fact. . . .

Those of us who deny the theory of evolution, therefore, have no antagonism to true science. We only object to having that which is merely an hypothesis proclaimed dogmatically as though it were really fact. So far as I am personally concerned I am ready to accept evolution if it can really be proved true. Every man ought to be willing to accept truth from any quarter, however destructive it may be of former convictions. It is significant, however, that many who at first are fascinated by the plausible generalizations of evolution turn from it after fuller examination of its alleged evidence and more mature consideration of its claims.

The great scientist Prof. George Romanes of Oxford had such an experience. For a period of his life he was an infidel and extreme evolutionist; and it is highly significant that during that time he wrote and spoke strongly against the Bible teaching of Creation, and against supernaturalism in all its forms. But later in life, through the letters of a Japanese missionary friend, dealing with experimental and practical religion, he changed his views entirely, accepted the Bible, and died in 1894, confessing his faith in God and in the full deity of Jesus Christ. . . .

I, also, have had a similar experience. For quite a period of my life—extending into a part of the time that I have been a preacher—I was an evolutionist . . . and accepted that view of the universe and of man; but fuller study, both in the field of science and philosophy, not only convinced me that evolution is a colossal error, but that when logically followed out it is utterly incompatible with the Christian religion.

My honorable opponent, before the first debate of this series, remarked that he had some advantage over me because before he became a Unitarian he was a Baptist, and therefore he thought he knew about what my arguments would be in the debate on the Bible.

I now profess the same advantage over him. I was once an evolutionist and skeptic, but I have come back to the truth of Creation by a living God rather than evolution by blind chance. Therefore, I can speak with a deeper degree of conviction than if I had not passed through such an experience. We have agreed to accept LeConte's concise definition, namely that evolution is "continuous progressive change, according to fixed laws, and by resident forces." We have the privilege, however, of turning the light of other and fuller definitions from authoritative sources upon the question, that we may see clearly just what evolution really is and what it leads to.

It is highly significant that the idea of evolution originated in pagan and heathen minds and was not a native product of the Christian intellect. The Greek philosophers speculated about the origin of the world in a fire mist, and Aristotle developed some of the main ideas of evolution long before Lamarck of Darwin or Spencer lived.

. . . .

My opponent, therefore, cannot claim God as the "resident force" under our definition. . . . Unless, indeed, he is willing to admit himself a pantheist, and say that God is wholly locked up in nature. If we admit any god outside of nature, then we must say with Genesis: "In the beginning, God." A living God, therefore, must be before the material world which he made. Hence, he cannot be wholly in that material world. A living God must be transcendent as well as immanent. He is before and above the world, and yet in it through his providential control and directing care. The engineer cannot be in his engine. He is the maker and driver of the engine, and his skill and controlling power are in it, but the engineer himself cannot be in the fire and the steam that drive the engine. The idea of any sort of "spirit" of living God locked up in the earth as it passed through stages of gaseous nebulosity and then of molten fire, etc., is simply unthinkable. It is an absurdity. The only possible god of evolution is the god of pantheism, not a *living* being at all, but merely the "principle" or "law" of nature.

Now since the only god possible to evolution is pantheism—god in nature as a mere "principle" or "law" or "eternal energy," as Spencer put it—it is proper that we should point out that pantheism always has and always will lead to ruinous moral and social results when it is accepted by men.

For one thing, it leads to the worship of nature—principally the sun. And the awful immorality and the social decay of ancient Egypt and other countries through the worship of the sun and of nature, should be a sufficient warning to us. Another inevitable and immediate result to pantheism is that it leads to the deification of man, and hence to self-worship, with all the vanity and moral and social decay that inevitably follow such colossal error.

Therefore, the issue in this debate is not only an issue between creation and evolution, but between God and no God.

Furthermore, it is evident that there is no possible compromise between these two systems of thought. There is no middle ground. Either Creation is true and evolution is false, or else evolution is true and Creation is false. Either we must accept the revelation of a living God, and his creative and redemptive activities as given in the Bible, or we must utterly reject this and turn to the infidel philosophy of chance and materialism.

In other words, there is no such thing as so-called theistic or Christian evolution. Such terms are misnomers. Christianity is a religion founded on definite historical facts. These facts—including the creation of the world, and the creation, fall, and salvation of man—are recorded in the Bible. If, therefore, the Bible is rejected, Christianity itself is rejected. In the face of the essential nature of evolution, and in the light of definitions of it already given, the terms "Christianity" and "evolution" are mutually exclusive and self-contradictory. If it is Christianity, then it is not evolution; and if it is evolution, then it is not Christianity. The mixed teachings of such men as Henry Drummond, Lyman Abbott, and others prove that they did not think these evolutionary theories through to their logical and inevitable conclusion in unbelief. Such men either do not know what real Christianity is, or else they do not know what real evolution is. They are manifestly self-deceived if they try to hold on to both evolution and Christianity.

The question for debate is not, therefore, primarily a question of method. It is primarily a question of origins. Method cannot begin to work until something has originated for the method to work in or on. Hence a beginning must precede any evolution. The very name of such a book as Darwin's "Origin of Species" shows that. The real issue in the debate is whether the earth and man originated, or came, by *design* through the creative power of God, or by *chance* through the haphazard operation of evolution. It is the issue between naturalism and supernaturalism; between calculated planning and mere fortuitous circumstance.

From John Roach Straton, *The Famous New York Fundamentalist-Modernist Debates: The Orthodox Side* (New York: George H. Doran, 1925), pp. 56–58, 59–61.

"Darwin's Christ was Nobody"
William Jennings Bryan

William Jennings Bryan entered upon his last crusade in the spring of 1921 when he issued a series of attacks upon Darwin's theory of evolution. As early as 1904 he had voiced objections to it which were basically the same as those he propounded so militantly during the last four years of his life. "What had changed," according to Professor Lawrence Levine, a recent Bryan biographer, "was not Bryan's conception of evolution but his toleration of it. By 1921 he had become convinced that the evolutionary thesis was no longer a potential danger but an immediate threat." Scarcely had the Commoner cast his lot with fundamentalism than he emerged as its most popular spokesman. The impact of his diverse activities as the "defender of the faith" soon became evident in legislative halls, school rooms, the press, and solemn assemblies of churchmen. In 1923 Bryan figured prominently in the struggle that erupted between modernists and fundamentalists within his own denomination, the Northern Presbyterian church. Shortly after the tumultuous session of the Presbyterian General Assembly that year over the famous Five Points, Bryan published an article, at the request of the editors of *The Forum*, to explain his position. The following excerpt from his essay suggests the extent to which the fundamentalist crusade had come to focus on evolution as "the root cause of nearly all of the dissension in the church."

But what is it that dost progressively whittle away the Word of God and destroys its vitality? I venture to assert that the unproven hypothesis of evolution is the root cause of nearly all the dissension in the church over the five points under discussion. "Liberalism," however you define it, is built upon the guess to which the euphonious name "evolution" has been given. Not all evolutionists are dissenters, but all dissenters are evolutionists,—some theistic evolutionists and some atheistic evolutionists. Those who call themselves theistic evolutionists indignantly deny that evolution is inconsistent with Christianity,—but what are the facts?

First, Darwin began life as a Christian, but, following the hypothesis that bears his name, he rejected, one after another, the vital principles of the Christian religion. Just before he died he wrote a letter (it is reproduced in his "Life and Letters") in which he describes his departure from the orthodox faith. He says as a young man when he made his famous trip south on the "Beadle" he was called "orthodox and heartily laughed at by some of the officers for quoting the Bible as an unanswerable authority on some point of morality." Expressing his opinion at the time he wrote his letter, he says, *I do not believe there ever has been any revelation.* In the same letter he says that about the time he wrote the "Origin of the Species" he deserved to be called a theist because he felt "compelled to look for a First Cause, having an intelligent mind, in some degree analogous to man." But after that this belief, he says, became weaker "very gradually with many fluctuations." He concludes by saying, "The mystery of the beginning of all things is insoluble by us, and I for one must be content to remain an agnostic." If that is what Darwinism did for Darwin, what is it likely to do for immature students who are throwing off parental authority and who gladly accept any hypothesis that will justify them in throwing off the authority of God also?

That Darwin's experience was not exceptional but the natural and logical results of the evolutionary hypothesis is proved by the investigations of Professor James H. Leuba, teacher of psychology at Bryn Mawr College. Some eight years ago he wrote a book on "Belief in God and Immortality." He starts out by saying that belief in God and immortality is dying out among the educated in the United States. To prove his proposition, he submitted questions to the leading scientists of the country. . . . On the answers received, he declared that over half of these scientists told him that they did not believe in a personal God or personal immortality. He then selected nine representative colleges and universities and wrote to the students. On their answers, he declared that 15 percent of the freshmen had discarded Christianity, 30 percent of the juniors, and from 40 to 45 percent of the men who graduated. This change was, in his opinion, due to the influence of the "cultured men" under whose instruction the students passed.

Is not this testimony sufficient to challenge the attention of Christians? Will the Christian church admit that there is anything in education that naturally or necessarily weakens faith? This cannot be admitted. The church has been the greatest patron of learning,—the greatest friend that education has ever had. What is there, then, in our colleges that undermines faith and paralyzes religion? Only one thing: namely, an hypothesis that links man in blood relationship with every other form of life, and makes him cousin to brute and bird and fish and reptile,— the flower and fruit, vegetable and weed. Even in the Christian colleges the student is asked to substitute the hypothesis of evolution for the Bible record of creation, although not one species has ever been traced to another species. The "missing links" between a million species,— Darwin estimated the number at from two to three millions, are yet to be found; not one has been produced. And yet, it is a common thing for evolutionists—theistic evolutionists—to declare that evolution is as firmly established as the law of gravitation or the roundness of the earth.

. . . .

But theistic evolution is even more demoralizing than atheistic evolution. Atheistic evolution denies the existence of God and thus arouses indignation. Theistic evolution, on the other hand, lulls the young Christian to sleep with the assurance that evolution recognizes God and offers a more sublime method of creation than the Bible records. Recently forty prominent Americans, among whom were two cabinet officers, one ex-cabinet officer, several bishops, and several college presidents, joined in a statement containing this language: "It is a sublime conception of God which is furnished by science," etc. Then follows the statement about God "revealing Himself through countless ages in the development of the earth as an abode for man and in the age-long inbreathing of life into its constituent matter culminating in man with his spiritual nature and all his god-like powers." This high-flown language compliments the ape theory at the expense of the Bible record of man's creation. Theistic evolution is an anesthetic; it deadens the pain while the Christian religion is being removed. There are all shades of belief among theistic evolutionists, according to the hold that the hypothesis has upon them, according to the religious momentum they have applied to it. Some stop when they have traced their ancestry to the jungle and established the kinship with the animal world below us. Exhausted by the effort, they are inconsistent enough to stop there and to accept all the Bible except Genesis. Some follow the path of evolution a little farther and reject some of the miracles, retaining the theory of atonement, the virgin birth, and the resurrection, in spite of the fact that they all involve the miraculous. Others go still farther, differing in the place at which they stop; while some, like a Presbyterian preacher in New York, boldly announce that they do not accept any of the propositions declared by the General Assembly to be "essential" as well as true.

Theistic evolution and atheistic evolution travel together until they reach the origin of life; at this point the theistic evolution embraces the atheist, tolerantly if not affectionately, and says, "I beg your pardon, but here I must assume a Creator." Some put the beginning of life at 25,000,000 years ago; some, like Darwin, put it at 200,000 years ago; others add all the ciphers that they have to spare. Some theistic evolutionists like Canon Barnes of Westminster Abbey, commence with the universe filled with "stuff" and imagine electrons coming out of "stuff" and forming atoms, atoms forming matter, matter forming life, life forming mind, and mind forming spirit, with infinite ages since God's creative power was permitted to act. Their faraway God does not invite prayer or give the comforting assurance of His presence,—what coercive power has the sense of responsibility if it must be strained through the blood of all animal life which, according to the evolutionists, forms man's ancestry? There is no place in evolution for the cry of the penitent soul; it knows no such transformation as being born again or having sins forgiven. As Romanes confessed even when an agnostic, it substitutes the "lonely mystery of existence" for the "hallowed glory" of the creed of orthodox Christianity.

. . . The evolutionary hypothesis is the only thing that has seriously menaced religion since the birth of Christ; and it menaces all other religions as well as the Christian religion, and civilization as well as religion,—at least this is the conviction of a multitude who regard belief in God as the most fundamental of all beliefs and see in Christ the hope of the future.

The world is just emerging from the bloodiest war known to history; thirty millions of human beings lost their lives directly or indirectly because of the war; three hundred billion dollars worth of property was destroyed, and the debts of the world are more than six times as when the first gun was fired. This war cannot be blamed upon ignorance; the governments of the civilized nations have been in the hands of educated men. The battleships, the dreadnaughts, and the superdreadnaughts were built by college graduates; and college graduates trained the armies of the world. Scientists mixed the poisonous gases and manufactured liquid fire. Intellect guided the nations, and learning without heart made war so hellish that civilization itself was about to commit suicide.

It is evident that nothing but universal peace can save the world from universal bankruptcy, and nothing but universal disarmament can bring universal peace. Not until the armies and navies are so reduced as to eliminate all thoughts of contests and merely provide domestic police protection can the world begin again the upbuilding of society. To whom can the world turn? To whom, except to the Prince of Peace. If the gigantic task of world rehabilitation must rest upon One reared in a carpenter shop, we must not divest Him of the strength that the task requires. Darwin's God was nowhere, he could not find Him; Darwin's Bible was nothing,—it had lost its inspiration; Darwin's Christ was nobody,—he had a brute for his ancestor on both his father's and his mother's side. Evolution, carried to its logical conclusion, robs Christ of the glory of his virgin birth, of the majesty of his deity, and of the triumph of his resurrection; such a Christ is impotent to save. If love is to be substituted for force and co-operation for combat, religion must lead the way.

From William Jennings Bryan, "The Fundamentals," *The Forum*, LXX (July 1923), 1675–1680.

A Five-Point Indictment
J. J. Sims

Among the antievolution societies organized in 1925 to carry on the work of William Jennings Bryan, "the fallen Elijah," was the Bryan Bible League with headquarters in Turlock, California. Its founder was Paul W. Rood, an evangelist of Scandinavian origins, who first became alarmed over the "scientific heresies" emanating from American colleges while he was preaching at a tabernacle located near the University of Washington in Seattle. Rood and his organization figured prominently in the unsuccessful movement to enact an antievolution statute in California. Later, he created another fundamentalist society known as the Defenders of the Christian Faith and established a Bible college committed to the ideals of orthodox theology and antievolutionism. As the evolution controversy entered its most frenzied phase late in 1925, the Bryan Bible League, like similar organizations, stated its objections to biological evolution with a precision which had earlier characterized the Five Points of the fundamentalists' theological affirmations. In the following selection J. J. Sims, Field Secretary of the League, presents a five-point indictment of the theory.

————————◄•►————————

There are five reasons why a Christian rejects the theory of evolution:

1. Because it is a pagan theory born in the dense darkness of Greek materialism.

2. Because in its modern form, it was largely sponsored by atheists and agnostics, who rejected the Bible. Huxley declared the story of the Deluge and of Creation were pure fiction. He said also it was impossible to believe in evolution and believe in the Bible, which is true.

3. Because it is not supported nor confirmed by a single fact of science. The natural growth of an egg to a chicken, or a nut to a tree, is always "after its kind." Development into variations is always restricted to that species, that is, "after its kind." Discovery and development of the forces latent in nature have produced the aeroplane, the automobile, the radio, but the kite didn't "evolute" into an aeroplane, nor the wheelbarrow into an automobile. The very essence of evolution is that it proceeds by resident force, without any *outside interference*.

4. Because it is essentially opposed to Christianity. To the consistent evolutionist, as the late John Burroughs has expressed it, "Christianity is a whimpering, winning [sic] sentimental religion." Evolution has no atonement, no Savior. If there is a God, He is far off, "unknown and unknowable." There is no hope for the future. Man came from the beast and dies like the beast. . . .

5. Because of the evil results that follow its acceptance. Nietzsche's evolutionary propaganda, which captured the German people, is largely responsible for the "Great War," with its German atrocities, and worldwide misery. Recently, communities have been shocked and horrified at the immoralities that have come to light, connected with high schools and colleges. This is to be expected. If you take away the Bible from the young people, telling them that what the Bible calls sin is only a fragment of the bestial nature still remaining in them, and there is no future for them, either of reward or punishment, what is there to restrain them? Their conscience has been drugged. So, two students murder another student to get a new sensation. A promising student at a modernist university commits suicide, because he had been wrecked, body and soul, by the moral conditions that he obtained there. Many of these modernist colleges are hotbeds of infidelity. God help the young men and women that come under their influence! Evolution has never saved a soul. It has ruined thousands. Christianity has lifted up millions. The difference between Christianity and evolution is—Christianity regenerates, evolution degenerates.

From J. J. Sims, "Why a Christian Rejects Evolution," *Bryan Broadcaster*, I (November 1925), 12–13.

Fundamentalist Geology and Evolution
George McCready Price

Well-known scientists were almost universally hostile to the fundamentalist crusade against biological evolution. But George McCready Price, a Canadian-born, Seventh Day Adventist professor of geology and prolific writer of books and tracts, was the one scientific authority most frequently cited by anti-evolutionists. He had been an instructor in various small colleges in California and Nebraska until 1925 when he moved to England. He created considerable excitement among the British by his antievolution speeches and publications. Among his numerous works were *The New Geology, Q.E.D. or New Light on the Doctrine of Creation* and *The Predicament of Evolution.* The following excerpts from a "popular work" published in 1924 summarized Price's thesis that geological evidence supported the biblical view of creation and the biblical record of a universal deluge.

——————•◦•——————

The fact is, geology furnished no true evidence for the theory of organic evolution. On the contrary, if we look at the fossil world in a broad way, it is impossible to avoid the conviction of a catastrophic death and burial of the vast majority of the animals and plants found as fossils in the strata. Lyell and his followers have always tried to blunt the force of this evidence by formulating an alleged chronological scheme of the geological deposits all over the globe, so as to have these burials take place a few at a time, on a sort of installment plan. But the methods employed to formulate this alleged chronology have always been regarded by the keenest and most logical thinkers as a burlesque on true scientific methods; and as I have shown in my special works on this subject, these methods must be abandoned, and a truer and more scientific theory of the science must be allowed to give us the bare facts, without their being overlaid so completely by evolutionary theory. A true and impartial science of geology tells us of the ruins of a world, not of its growth and development.

The voluminous materials which have so long been taught to the world under the name of geology, constitute a vast mixture of facts and grotesque speculations; and the average student of this science has hitherto been quite unable to discriminate between the statements made in the name of this science and tell how much is real fact and how much is only mere hypothesis or theory. But this differentiation is now beginning to be made. And it is now becoming very evident that, if the mere speculative parts of geology be cast aside, there are no real indisputable facts regarding the rocks or the fossils which could not be readily accounted for by the hypothesis of a world cataclysm. Accordingly, this hypothesis now stands before the world as at least a possible explanation of the facts, and indeed as much the most reasonable explanation of these facts.

But all this is fully in accord with that sublime record of the early days of our earth, which tells us that the world "that then was, being overflowed with water, perished."

And if this record be taken at its face value, either from nature or from revelation, the theory of organic evolution becomes indeed a phantom.

. . . .

Certain it is that the deniers of organic evolution, who are also the believers in the New Catastrophism in geology, are the ones who are taking the scientifically safe attitude. They are the ones who are now maintaining the magnificent tradition of a natural science which repudiates fantastic speculations and rests upon facts and facts alone. They are the ones who are now carrying on to maintain the spirit of non-dogmatic science. The evolutionary theory showed its true character of intolerant dogmatism under the leadership of such men as Buffon, Oken, Lamarck, and Haeckel; and the modern leaders of the doctrine are also living up to their old tradition, in the face of rapidly accumulating adverse facts. The latter are the real obscurantists, the reactionaries. The true progressives and the best friends of modern science are the ones who are trying to hold to facts alone; but they can not be blamed for recognizing that the new discoveries are tending so remarkably to confirm the Bible record about the early days of the world. It is the stand-patters in science who are complaining about these new lines of discovery, that each of these new revelations of the secret ways of nature is merely leading them up a blind alley, into a cul-de-sac, to an impasse, and is not contributing in any way to the further development of the evolution theory.

From George McCready Price, *The Phantom of Organic Evolution* (New York: Fleming H. Revell, 1924), pp. 64–65, 89.

Local Guardians of the Faith
Resolutions by Minnesota Clergymen

Throughout the United States, interdenominational gatherings of ministers and laymen resulted in co-operative efforts to preserve orthodoxy at the local level. Such a group which assembled in North Carolina under the name of the Committee of One Hundred in 1926 evolved into the crusading North Carolina Bible League. A similar gathering of antievolutionists in Spokane, Washington, in 1927 organized the Fundamentalists' Federation. In Minnesota, a prime target of William Bell Riley's fundamentalist crusade, a large gathering of Protestant clergymen convened in Saint Paul in October 1922 to protest against the dissemination of infidelity under the guise of science. Cited below are the resolutions adopted by the Minnesota clergymen. Their form and content were typical of pronouncements issuing from such assemblies.

———◦●◦———

Preamble—As American citizens we believe in the complete separation of church and state, and are opposed to religious teaching in public schools—higher or lower.

As those who wish to teach Christianity must support their private schools, we believe it but just that those who wish to teach anti-Christian theories should be forbidden the use of tax-supported schools for propagating their opinions.

Whereas, The evolutionary hypothesis has come to be accepted by many American teachers and is increasingly taught in the public schools of Minnesota, including high schools, our state normals, and state university, and

Whereas, This hypothesis, after sixty-three years of study, remains wholly unproven and has increasingly shown itself to be a foe to the Christian faith, denying as it does the veracity of the Scriptures,

Therefore be it resolved, That we, citizens of Minnesota, representing thousands of our fellow citizens, hereby utter our protest against this propaganda of infidelity, palmed off in the name of science, and we call upon the trustees of state institutions to demand of teachers a cessation of such teaching and the removal from our schools of such textbooks as favorably present the same.

143

We do this in the interest of true science vs. science falsely so-called; and in the interest of fair dealing.

We hold that the first amendment to the Constitution of the United States, "Congress shall make no law respecting an establishment of religion," was never intended to be interpreted that the state should become sponsor for irreligion; and that it is manifestly unfair to impose taxes upon Christian taxpayers to inculcate teaching inimical to the Bible and destructive of civilization itself.

We have waited patiently for this hypothesis to either prove a truth or to pass from public instruction. Having now no prospect of either, we demand that the state shall prove its impartiality toward its citizens by dispensing with a subject that is utterly divisive; and is, in the judgment of thousands of its taxpayers, utterly false.

And we declare that if the school authorities prove derelict in the enforcement of the law relating to the teaching of religion or of theories subversive of the Christian faith, we will appeal to the legislature for the enactment of such laws as shall eliminate from our tax-supported school system this antiscientific and antiscriptural theory of the origin of man and the universe.

From George O. Smith, "Opposition to Evolution in Minnesota," *Science,* LVI (November 10, 1922), 530.

Science will greatly modify our theories and speculations; she will never disturb the deeper interests of the soul.

CHARLES ALLEN DINSMORE, 1922

. . . to hell with your science if it is going to damn souls.

MORDECAI F. HAM, 1924

. . . our salvation lies wholly with science and not at all with religion.

JAMES F. PORTER, 1927

3. Science: A Source of Controversy

So steadily had the prestige of science risen since the late nineteenth century that there seemed to be no limits to what Americans expected of it by the outbreak of World War I. Such optimistic faith in the potentialities of science was not surprising in view of its influence upon American life during the previous half-century. It had not only radically altered man's way of living by providing the basis of the machine age but had also affected man's view of himself and his universe. The scientific spirit which prompted men to "re-examine their beliefs and the process by which they arrived at them" had occasionally triggered intellectual tremors at the elite level.[1] The theories of Charles Darwin, for example, had produced such a disturbance late in the nineteenth century. But by the 1920s the spirit and method of science had become part of popular culture largely as a result of the democratization of education and knowledge. Americans were impressed too with the practical contributions of science in winning the war, combating disease and providing such material wonders as radios and Ford automobiles. According to one observer, science had been raised to the level of a national cult in the United States. Indeed, it appeared as if the new national criterion had become "is it scientific?" This preoccupation with science was re-

[1] See William Adams Brown, *The Church in America* (New York: Macmillan, 1922), pp. 140–145.

147

flected in what Americans read and what they went to hear. J. Arthur Thomson's *Outline of Science* (1922) remained a best-seller throughout the decade. Scarcely less popular were the lectures and writings of Michael Pupin, a famous physicist and inventor, who viewed science as a religious endeavor in which man could understand the workings of a "directing Intelligence." The public, awed by the achievements of science and technology, was inclined to look to scientists for counsel in the nonscientific matters. The scientific reputations of Luther Burbank and Thomas A. Edison appeared to enhance the validity of their discourses on the soul and immortality. Only Burbank's doubts about immortality prompted anyone to question whether his accomplishments in botany equipped him to speak with any special authority on the nature and destiny of the soul.[2]

"No department of knowledge," remarked the orthodox theologian J. Gresham Machen in 1923, "can maintain its isolation from the modern lust of scientific conquest; treaties of inviolability, though hallowed by all the sanctions of age-long tradition, are being flung ruthlessly to the wind."[3] Although few doubted the accuracy of Machen's observation, churchmen displayed little unanimity in their responses to the challenges which science seemed to pose for traditional Christianity. Many who recognized only too well the validity of his statement trembled at its implications. Particularly disturbing for orthodox churchmen was the disparity between the scientific and biblical views of man. Liberal theologians, concerned with reconciling such disparities, seemed willing on occasion to settle for an illusionary peace between science and religion. Conservatives rejected this reconciliation as an unwarranted acquiescence by theology in the demands of science. At any rate, the conflict between modernists and fundamentalists, especially as evidenced in the disturbance over evolution, involved a collision of widely divergent views regarding science and its relationship to the Protestant faith.

Those who subscribed to modernism accepted science as "a dominating fact in modern civilization" and assumed that the adjustment of religion to science was a prime prerequisite for the adaptation of re-

---

[2] "Luther Burbank's Religion," *Christian Century*, XLIII (February 25, 1926), 243; "Edison on Immortality," *Literary Digest*, XCI (November 6, 1926), 30.

[3] J. Gresham Machen, *Christianity and Liberalism* (Grand Rapids: William B. Eerdmans, 1923) p. 3.

ligion to the requirements of modern life.[4] Modernists placed their faith
not so much in the achievements of science as in the scientific method
and its use in their quest for religious assurance. Shailer Mathews, for
example, maintained that the use of such a method, especially in historical study, made it possible for the modern Christian "to find, state,
and use the permanent and central values of inherited orthodoxy" shorn
of their supernaturalism and dualism, which at best were implausible.
The modernist, he declared, "starts with the assumption that the scientists know more about nature and man than the theologians who drew
up creeds and confessions. He is open-minded in regard to scientific discovery."[5] Modernism, therefore, was a religious expression which merged
the spiritual with the secular. Reinhold Niebuhr maintained that herein
lay the "curse of modernism," that is modernism "was so busy adjusting
itself to the modern mind that it can find no energy to challenge the
modern conscience."[6] According to Professor John C. Greene, the modernist theology of Mathews, whether Christian or not, "certainly did not
present a biblical view" because its "leading ideas were derived from
biology and comparative religion, not scripture."[7]

Underlying much of the fundamentalists' hostility to the science-
oriented modernist theology was their identification of science with
naturalism, materialism, and other intellectual trends which challenged
the orthodox faith that undergirded their system of values and morals.
Such a view gained wider acceptance in the era immediately after World
War I. The experience of the war, coupled with the general mood of
disillusionment that followed, tended to raise questions about the utopian prospects of science and confirm the convictions of some pious
Americans of "its essentially irreligious character." The devastation
wreaked upon humanity during the war revealed "the gigantic power
for evil" inherent in science. William Jennings Bryan often reminded
his audiences that the science demanding absolute freedom in the 1920s

4 For a straightforward statement of this theme see Charles A. Ellwood, *The Reconstruction of Religion: A Sociological View* (New York: Macmillan, 1922).

5 Shailer Mathews, *The Faith of Modernism* (New York: Macmillan, 1924), pp.
22–24; see also Stow Persons, *American Minds: A History of Ideas* (New York: Holt,
Rinehart, and Winston, 1958), pp. 417–421.

6 Reinhold Niebuhr, "Would Jesus Be a Modernist Today," *The World Tomorrow*,
XII (March 1929), 122–124.

7 John C. Greene, *Darwin and the Modern World View* (Baton Rouge: Louisiana
State University Press, 1961), p. 52.

was the same science which "manufactured poisonous gases to suffocate soldiers" during the war.[8] Although science furnished man with all kinds of power, it failed to provide the ingredients for the control of that awesome power. Since science was amoral, Bryan concluded, such control could be derived only from a morality based upon the historic precepts of the Christian faith. Any compromise of the theological foundations of Christian morality in the name of science was an invitation to disaster.

The frequent use of the term "godless science" by fundamentalists led many to conclude that they were hostile to science itself. Such phrases can perhaps be more appropriately interpreted as an expression of their opposition to a theological viewpoint derived from a source which, according to Bryan, "has no morality." The fundamentalists spurned such labels as "anti-science" and repeatedly insisted that they "had no antagonism to true science."[9] But they did not hesitate to denounce the notion of "science as the only guide of mankind." The object of their crusade, they proclaimed, was not to depreciate science per se but to preserve the integrity of the biblical religion which had been compromised by scientific criteria of judgment. Fundamentalists, no less than modernists, recognized that they lived in an age of science; in fact, the aim of their struggle was to achieve religious certitude in an age of science. But they were unwilling to accept the formula of reconciliation prescribed by such liberal theologians as Charles A. Dinsmore of the Yale Divinity School because it appeared to sacrifice too many essentials of biblical religion for the sake of accommodating the affimations of science.

In the fundamentalist view the seeds of destruction were already present in modernist theology because it had replaced "an atmosphere of unquestioning trust" with "the scientific spirit of critical inquiry."[10] Such a substitution seemed to grant license to men who invoked the name of science to attack the validity of the miracles, the virgin birth, and the divine origin of man. Even when those imbued with the ideals and apparatus of science attempted to formulate new standards of faith and morality, their efforts proved to be wholly unacceptable to funda-

[8] Lawrence Levine, *Defender of the Faith: William Jennings Bryan, The Last Decade, 1915-1925* (New York: Oxford University Press, 1965), p. 280.
[9] *Ibid.*, pp. 279–280.
[10] Brown, *The Church in America,* p. 140.

mentalists because they either rejected or submerged the supernatural elements of Christianity. Fundamentalists objected to modernism precisely at this point, i.e., it was merely a form of naturalism. John Roach Straton, the New York fundamentalist leader, consistently maintained that the central issue at stake in the modernist-fundamentalist dispute was the issue between "naturalism and supernaturalism."[11]

Although the fundamentalists' challenge of naturalism in the name of historic Christianity may well have been necessary, their approach obviously had serious shortcomings. In support of the contention that the fundamentalists drew the line between historic faith and naturalism at the wrong place, the authors of a recent multi-volume study of American Christianity wrote:

The doctrine of the incarnation is central for historic Christianity. But this was not properly formulated or adequately defended by fundamentalism's emphasis on the virgin birth of Christ. The conception of revelation from God is basic to Christianity, but insistence on the inerrancy of the Bible in no sense takes measure of the problem. The question of the relation of God to the physical universe had been a central problem in western thought since the rise of natural science three centuries ago, but it is not properly dealt with by insisting on the historicity of physical miracles.[12]

Whatever its inadequacies, the fundamentalist challenge to naturalism signaled another bout in the so-called warfare between science and religion.

In response to this challenge, professional scientists and modernist theologians rallied to the support of modern science. Those who had assumed it to be an unassailable fortress found themselves combating the charge that science was essentially irreligious. In 1923 Robert A. Millikan, a prominent physicist, drafted a statement on the relationship of science and religion, which was signed by thirty-five distinguished scientists, theologians, and "men of affairs." The purpose of the statement was to allay popular fears that science and religion actually occupied "irreconcilable and antagonistic domains of thought." Millikan's statement read:

[11] John Roach Straton, *The Famous New York Fundamentalist-Modernist Debates: The Orthodox Side* (New York: George H. Doran, 1925), p. 62.

[12] H. Shelton Smith, Robert T. Handy, and Lefferts A. Loetscher, *American Christianity: An Historical Interpretation With Documents* (2 vols.; New York: Charles Scribner's Sons, 1963), II, 316.

The purpose of science is to develop, without prejudice or preconception of any kind, a knowledge of the facts, the laws, and the processes of nature. The even more important task of religion, on the other hand, is to develop the conscience, the ideals, and the aspirations of mankind. Each of these two activities represents a deep and vital function of the soul of man, and both are necessary for the life, the progress, and the happiness of the human race.

It is a sublime conception of God which is furnished by science, and wholly consonant with the highest ideals of religion, when it represents Him as revealing Himself through countless ages in the development of the earth as an abode for man and in the age-long inbreathing of life into its constant matter, culminating in man with his spiritual nature and all his God-like powers.[13]

Nothing revealed so clearly the defensive position of scientists and their theological allies as their explanations of the evolution theory which the American Association for the Advancement of Science pronounced "one of the most potent influences for good that has thus far entered into the human experience."[14] Some maintained that evolution dealt only with processes and did not touch the question of ultimate causation; others characterized the theory as a staunch ally of Christianity. Still others, such as Albert E. Wiggam, the author of *The New Decalogue of Science* (1923), and Maynard Shipley, the founder of the Science League of America, were unwilling to make any concessions to fundamentalism. Shipley characterized fundamentalists as obscurantists whose quaint notions of truth as something "revealed from on high" were wholly unacceptable in an age that embraced the scientific method.[15] Sharply critical of the position displayed by Shipley and other defenders of science were Clarence E. Ayres, a respected philosopher, and Vernon Kellogg, a well-known biologist. Kellogg was disturbed by the "sweeping and positive utterances regarding the all-knowingness and all-mightiness of science" uttered by his scientific colleagues. "It is in the realm of what science doesn't know," he declared, "that lie all these human capacities which really distinguish and define the very thing that humanness is."[10]

The dialogue regarding the place of science, so much in evidence during the controversy over evolution, not only pointed up the widely

13 Quoted in New York *Times,* May 27, 1923.

14 See the following selection from *The Summarized Proceedings of the American Association for the Advancement of Science, 1921–1925.*

15 Maynard Shipley, *The War on Modern Science: A Short History of the Fundamentalist Attacks on Evolution and Modernism* (New York: Alfred A. Knopf, 1927), p. 5.

16 See the selection below from Kellogg's, "Some Things Science Doesn't Know," *World's Work,* LI (March 1926).

different context from which the protagonists spoke but also demonstrated the difficulties in communication between pulpit and laboratory. Content as well as semantics posed problems. Even debates which proposed to consider only the scientific validity of evolution included extensive excursions into such theological matters as the infallibility of the Bible and the deity of Jesus. Fundamentalists quickly disposed of evolution as a "mere guess" and concentrated upon explaining how it undermined faith in the Bible and its moral teachings. By his own admission William Jennings Bryan was less interested in whether evolution was true or false than he was in its effect upon morality. Although scientists marshaled data to support their contention that evolution was a *demonstrated* fact of science, they were quick to explain that it in no way cast discredit upon the Christian faith. Such explanations often revealed that they possessed little more proficiency in theology than the fundamentalists displayed in their handling of scientific questions. Testimony by a scientist that he was an active layman in some evangelical church and at the same time a believer in evolution scarcely constituted an irrefutable argument in support of the compatibility of evolution and the Christian faith. It suggested that the egotism which Kirtley Mather credited to antievolutionists was perhaps shared by their opponents. As Harry Emerson Fosdick later admitted, modernists in the 1920s often "talked as though the highest compliment that could be paid to Almighty God was that a few scientists believed in him."[17]

Precisely what was accomplished by the dialogue over science is difficult to assess. Undoubtedly it aroused interest in the question of the relationship between natural science and the biblical faith. It exposed the inadequacies of fundamentalism as a theology acceptable to modern Americans and served to point up the limitations of science. It raised serious questions about the adequacy of a nonbiblical, science-oriented theology such as modernism. Perhaps the debate of the 1920s was a necessary step in paving the way for a more profound and creative discussion about the relationship of God, man, and the universe.

[17] Quoted in Herbert Schneider, *Religion in 20th Century America* (Cambridge: Harvard University Press, 1952), pp. 107–108.

The Arrogance of Science
Arthur I. Brown

Arthur I. Brown, a physician born in Michigan and educated in Canada and Europe, practiced medicine in Vancouver, British Columbia, for a dozen years before joining the fundamentalist crusade in the United States during the 1920s. A Fellow in the Royal College of Surgeons of Edinburgh who abandoned the medical profession to become an evangelist, Brown first achieved prominence in fundamentalist circles in 1924 as a member of the staff of *The Conflict*, organ of the Anti-Evolution League of America. Later, he held the position of "National Scientist" in the elaborate hierarchy of the Bible Crusaders of America. As a Crusader, he made numerous speech-making tours in which he was invariably billed as a world-renowned scientist whose research had led him to repudiate biological evolution. The following excerpt from his column in the Bible Crusaders' magazine includes arguments which he employed on many occasions to demonstrate the arrogance of scientists who, for all their claims to objectivity, dogmatically proclaimed the validity of evolution by means contrary to common sense and reason as well as to the scientific method. At best theirs was a pseudo-science.

———————— •◦• ————————

Many modern scientific leaders deliver their dogmatic fiats with an arrogant air of finality and even omniscience. In measured terms they denounce those of quite equal intelligence who refuse to accept their conclusions.

They ridicule them as "ignorant obscurantists," or "apostles of systematized ignorance." They would have us believe that they are actuated by a sincere determination to know and be guided by the truth, at all costs. They only have the mental equipment to make accurate observations and draw logical deductions.

But fundamentalists refuse to accept the lowly position allotted them by the evolutionary scientists. They claim to possess intellectual powers of equal grade, at least, and positively decline to accept grotesque interpretations of the facts of nature—interpretations which are manifestly illogical and denied by all the evidence.

The only reason why evolution has any following today seems to be that the creation record of Genesis must be repudiated, no matter what happens, even if that repudiation demands the dethronement of common sense and the assassination of reason.

The evolutionist claims a monopoly of the facts, but in reality, he starts with nothing and ends nowhere. He deals in nonexistent phantoms which he causes to undergo imaginary and impossible processes until finally, with the assistance of hypothetical and unworkable factors, operating on mythical material, he produces the crowning glory, a complex, sentient being—Man!

The modernist rejects miracles and the supernatural, but in the light of these facts, who, we ask, exhibits the greater degree of credulous simplicity and immeasurable faith in the miraculous?

We are told that the method of Science—always spelled with a capital "S"—is objective, while that of religion is subjective. As if Science deals only with the tangible, proven facts, and religion with ephemeral, emotional fancies.

This obviously absurd assumption is usually accompanied by sweeping, ponderous, and grandiloquent generalizations in regard to the "irrefutable mass" of corroborative evolutionary evidence. True, when asked to produce it, we are informed, somewhat petulantly, that it is not yet available, but the alluring hope is dangled before our yearning and weary eyes, that someday, somewhere, in the hidden profundities of earth or sea, we shall come upon this well-filled storehouse of sorely needed evidence.

We have waited long—are waiting yet—How long, O Lord, how long?

Any aggregation of facts must be interpreted according to some previously established principle and by assignment to a known category. Science is much subject to the vicissitudes of fashion and is influenced by the ebb and flow of intellectual currents, impelling a certain kind of influence which dogmatically accepts or rejects particular theories.

The modern intellectual current bears the stamp of uniformity and negation. The moral emasculation which characterizes this twentieth century induces a temper to which the miraculous is repugnant. It is the correct thing to deny all that our fathers believed and, at any price, to welcome innovations.

It would be well for the evolutionists to remember occasionally that the live fish swim strongly against the stream, while the dead ones drift with the current. To believe what the majority believe is not, of necessity, to be right. To allow other men's opinions to float in and occupy our brains is to surrender one of the most valued possessions.

. . . .

Creation has satisfied the intellect of the greatest men who have lived in every age. A belief in it subjects our faith and our reason to no excessive strain. To postulate a Creator able to design and fashion all inanimate and animate nature requires no great stretch of imagination.

We believe in an omnipresent, ominiscient, and omnipotent Creator, invisible, incorporeal, spiritual, eternal, personal. We are created in his mental and spiritual image and, in an infinitesimal degree, we share some of his attributes.

We believe such a Creator had the power to control the transmission of an accurate record of his method of creation. This record is in Genesis and in it there is no room for evolution. Moreover, all the factual evidence supports the written Word.

The scriptures have foretold such a time as this, when God's arch-enemy would make his final, most fierce and subtle attempt to overthrow the Kingdom of Heaven. And also, it was foretold that "learning falsely so-called" would be the weapon that should be used to batter down the strongholds of Christianity and destroy the faith of men in the only Book which reveals to them the way back to God. But this hammer of a pseudo-scholarship is inevitably doomed to be shattered to atoms on the impregnable anvil of God's truth.

This Book, which has resisted numberless assaults in the past, stands and will stand, unmoved and imperishable. Its ramparts are invincible and unscalable by enemy hordes; its walls invulnerable to the attacks of hatred and agnosticism. Those who have found refuge within the sheltering folds are safe from all alarm and will be untouched in the fearful and impending cataclysm which shall rock and wreck the foundations of a world rapidly approaching chaos and destruction.

From Arthur I. Brown, "The Limitations of Science," *The Crusaders' Champion*, I (December 25, 1925), 19.

A Cleric and A Scientist Debate

William Bell Riley v.
Zeno P. Metcalf

The following selection is a journalistic account of a debate over the validity of evolution held in 1922 on the campus of North Carolina State
College in Raleigh. The protagonists were Professor Zeno P. Metcalf of the
college's biology department and William Bell Riley, the well-known antievolution crusader from Minneapolis who was in the city to conduct a
Bible conference under the auspices of the World's Christian Fundamentals
Association. Observers generally agreed that the debate was "quite without
parallel in the annals of polemics hereabouts."

To the accompaniment of vociferated demonstrations that often
attained the volume and heat of bitter political partisanship, scientist
and theologian met in wordy combat in Pullen Hall yesterday afternoon;
and each came off victor in the eyes of his own sympathizers when Dr.
Z. P. Metcalf, professor of biology, and Rev. Dr. W. B. Riley joined in
debate on the validity of evolution as science.

On the one hand, Dr. Metcalf upheld evolution as a recognized
science, proved by the findings of honest men's inquiry for a century and
not out of sympathy with the teaching of Christianity. On the other
hand, Dr. Riley held up to ridicule all that the scientist can offer and
harked back to the Mosaic account of the creation of the world as the
only explanation of existence.

For a full hour and a half, the crowd that jammed the hall to the
last foot of its capacity to hold humanity, seemingly equally divided in
their sympathies, yelled and whistled, clapped their hands and pounded
the floor with their feet, often interrupting the speakers and forcing them
to suspend their speaking until the demonstration would wear itself out.
It was quite without parallel in the annals of polemics hereabouts.

There were no judges. Every man and every woman and every child
was left to make up his own mind about the relative merits of evolution
as supported by Dr. Metcalf and as derided by Dr. Riley. To the neutrals,
of which there were but few present, it appeared that everybody came

in and went out with the same set of opinions. Everybody was good humored about it, perhaps wrung dry of any other feeling in the general tumult of applause.

Not many people were turned away for want of room within the building. Those who went carried with them sufficient interest to make the hardship of standing up and even of allowing somebody else to stand on their feet of relatively small consequence. The building was full, quite the fullest that anybody remembers ever having seen it. The applause might have been louder had there been more elbow room.

Students of the college largely partisan to their biology teacher, took to the galleries, hanging on to the railings by any hold they could get, however insecure. Townspeople for the most part filled the lower floors to the very doors and halfway down the steps. Anything like a census of the crowd is patiently impossible, but a full 2,000 people must have packed within.

It was with no little difficulty that Dr. Riley, the first of the speakers to arrive, made his way down the aisle two minutes before four o'clock. Halfway down to the platform, the crowd recognized him, and thunderous applause greeted him. He smiled slightly and continued his way to the platform where another burst of ovation greeted him. The crowd settled back to regard the man.

Tall, distinguished in his manner, he had, with a somewhat thin face, a big, well-formed nose. His eyes are a brown that have a snap in them. His lips are full, and sometimes one gets the impression of scorn in the twist of them, but most of the time it is a kindly smile. His hair is thick and stands out from his large, well-formed head. He is a handsome figure.

A stir of greeting from the rear of the hall interrupted the scrutiny of Dr. Riley. A small man, bespectacled, leaning to the inconspicuous, made his way out of the crowd that packed the rear. A roar came down from the gallery and spread out among the hundreds that crowded the lower floor. There was more noise than greeted Dr. Riley, but then it was made by younger and more adaptable makers of noise. It was Dr. Metcalf. With never a flicker of a smile on his face, he came down to the rostrum, greeted Dr. Riley, and the speakers took their places on the platform.

Preliminaries occupied but a few brief moments. R. L. McMillan came forward as the presiding officer, and with him John A. Park and

W. T. Bost who were announced as time keepers. Half an hour for each speaker, ten minutes rebuttal for Dr. Metcalf, a quarter of an hour for Dr. Riley, and five minutes more for the scientist. Dr. Metcalf rose to speak, and never yet did he become conscious of the rush of applause that swept up to meet him. He read but without effort.

The speech was carefully prepared, balanced with cool scientific precision and delivered without effort at oratorical effect. At the outset he regretted the insufficiency of time to present the entire case that science has collected and concluded his introduction with the simple statement: "I am a Christian. I have accepted in its entirety the fact of evolution. I have never found anything in evolution to shake my fundamental Christian religion."

. . . "By evolution we mean the demonstrated fact that living things have changed in geological times and are changing now from simple to complex forms," Dr. Metcalf declared. From that he began with examples of changes in living organisms, the blindfish in Kentucky caves which have eyes under their skin, the coalescing of the eyes of the flounder, the eyes of the mole that are atrophied by its habits, the field of agriculture and the development of plants and animals from lower to higher forms. Geological evidence was next marshaled by the professor, with the story of the strata, going back over long geological eons to the coal era, where only nonflowering plants and fish fossils are shown. Today there are mammals in the kingdom and 125,000 known species of plants in the place of the few found in the coal age.

In the development of the human species, nature has clearly made use of organs that are not now used in the functions of the body, he declared, the vestige is the scientific name for them, the appendix and 186 other such organs that are gradually being discarded from the human system. In concluding he presented Dr. Riley with four questions. They, with the answers, follow:

METCALF—Why do living organisms present themselves in such marvelous graded series, protozoan to man, bacterium to dandelion?

RILEY—That is the order of God's creation. He began with grass and ended with man.

METCALF—Why do the higher organisms develop the nonuseful structures known as vestiges?

RILEY—Who said they were nonuseful? God may have a function for

them that you have not found out. I have still got my appendix and
I'm going to keep it. Those other 186 I never did have.

METCALF—Why should individual organisms in their development go
through the wasteful process of forming ancestral structure, merely
to have them disappear before the organism is full grown?

RILEY—Answering this question Dr. Riley applied the same reasoning
developed in his answer to the second question, elaborating it with
incident and sarcastic comment.

METCALF—Why among the vast array of simple animals and simple
plants known to have lived in the coal age not one flowering plant
nor one mammal has been found?

RILEY—That is down where God began.

Here Dr. Riley went into some discussion of the validity of the stratic
theory, setting up the claim that it is by no means certain that strata
are left in the original order in which they occurred but may have been
shifted and mixed in cataclysmic changes in the crust of the earth.

Dr. Riley suffered from the handicap of having no set speech, but
whatever lack he felt on that score, he evened the balance with his
ability as a ready speaker, experienced in the values of phrases, in the
weight of ridicule, even sparingly used. His answers to the questions were
categorical and delivered with the utmost assurance and conviction. He
was always at ease, always smiling, always the perfect master of himself.

Matter and energy are at a standstill in the universe, and creation has
done nothing new since God formed man out of the dust, and breathed
the spirit of life into him, he declared. He turned with ridicule upon
the claim that Harvey had discovered the circulation of the blood and
declared that Moses had made the discovery 3,000 years before. He
ignored Luther and Copernicus.

Darwin had been discredited years ago, he declared. Throughout
his first half hour, Dr. Riley shifted the attack with bewildering movement, at one moment reciting an anecdote that left his supporters howl-
ing, and bringing smiles to the supporters of Dr. Metcalf, and the next
delivering cryptic indictment with sharp, incisive sentences.

At one point he picked up a volume on evolution, and turned to
some pictures of prehistoric men. He made a to-do about pronouncing
their names, ridiculed them, with side trips into Darwin's survival of
the fittest. "Come up here after the debate and look at these pictures,

and I am sure you will see somebody who looks just like them when you get downtown. I am glad that the weak don't die. Some of you folks may develop into something yet if you stick around here for 500,000,000 years."

Darwin's theory is not evolution and has nothing to do with it, declared Dr. Metcalf in rejoinder. Evolution has nothing to do with the creation of life. "And no scientist would declare that there is no life without blood. Go look for blood in yonder green maple tree."

Dr. Riley returned to the attack in kind, and back to the blood in the maple tree. "Go in the spring and cut a ring around it, and see it bleed to death." And when Dr. Metcalf was up for the final word in the debate, he said that there are as many creeds that interpret the Bible as there are interpretations of the Darwinian theory. Dr. Riley was so enthused when his time was up that it was a full minute before he heard the pounding of the time keepers.

The crowd surged out. It was satisfied. Each had won a victory, and each had opportunity to let off the steam that had been generated within the week of discussion that had reached from the highest to the lowest. Neither speaker had quite got the range of the other, nor had they come to close grips; but to the supporters of each there was imminent satisfaction with the outcome of it.

From the *News and Observer* (Raleigh, North Carolina), May 18, 1922.

The Folklore of Science
Clarence E. Ayres

If fundamentalism was associated with the forces of obscurantism, modernism was identified with the contemporary faith in science. Among those who took issue with this new faith was Clarence E. Ayres, a professor of philosophy at Amherst College and sometime associate editor of the *New Republic*. In his *Science: The False Messiah*, Ayres compared what he called the folklore of religion to the folklore of science and pointed up some of the dilemmas of the modernists. With the notable exception of H. L. Mencken, reviewers hailed the work as a "refreshing piece of intellectual emancipation." The following excerpts from this book indicate the nature of Ayres's dissent.

———•◦•———

SCIENCE—so we have been constrained to think—is true. All its major propositions have been definitely established to our complete satisfaction. This is what makes it so hard to think about. Only with the greatest reluctance do we ever seriously reflect upon what we have already decided to believe, or inquire in retrospect how we came to believe in it and just what there is about it that has so completely captured our assent. Because science is true, we omit to inquire what the limitations of its truth may be. Because the truths of science have been established, we lose interest in how they were established. Indeed, we do not wholly admire the type of mind which insists always upon poring over limitations and shortcomings instead of accepting all blessings with a thankful heart and a happily sated imagination. To doubt any accepted belief is of course impiety, a thing which we all righteously abhor. It even verges upon impiety to make such inquiries as might lead to doubt. This is pretty generally our feeling about science, and a very significant frame of mind it is. It suggests, by direct and forcible comparison, that science has attained the state of an established creed.

To be sure, science does not represent itself as folklore. But then neither did the folklore of our superstitious past. Folklore never does. We must not imagine Moses coming down from Mount Sinai and urging Joshua and Aaron to bear in mind that his various narratives are folklore. It was enough that they were marvelous. Joshua and Aaron understood them so and no doubt interpreted them as accurately as we interpret our neighbor's stories of the voices he has heard over his radio, coming out of a thick cloud of static. It is a mistake to think that Joshua and Aaron thought them any stranger than that. But it should also be a mistake to suppose that the Israelites were as surprised by Moses' story as we should be, or as surprised as they would have been to hear him say that he had been borne through the clouds at one hundred twenty miles to the hour and accompanied by the sound of an awful roaring. Sufficient unto the day is the folklore thereof. In Moses' time direct communion with the Lord was uncommon, but by no means unknown. His miracles were of the same order as those performed by all the contemporary prophets. So are ours.

The proper parallel to the miracles of ancient prophets is, however, not the commonplace adventures of ordinary citizens, but the accomplishments of our own prophets, the men who have had direct communication, not with the Jehovah of the Israelites, but with the atoms and electrons, with stars so far off that their distance is measured in the number of years it takes their glimmer to arrive, with dried-up oceans and glaciers before the dawn of history, with the gorgons and chimeras that inhabited the earth before those glaciers came, with animalculae so small that they pass through the finest filter and so powerful that they will strike down a man in a few hours. These men tell tales of the creation of all living things from primoridal ooze, of the origin of the earth from spouts of incandescent gas from the sun, of rays that penetrate the solidest-seeming stuff, of the electron-stuff of which all things are composed. They sing of matter which is not matter but energy . . . which changes places from moment to moment, and of different moments which are simultaneous in different locations. These are the real marvels of the age of science. We must not dismiss them lightly because we believe that they are true. After all, the Israelites believed Moses. That is how they can help us to understand the character of folklore.

Moreover, these modern tales of the creation and composition and regulations of the universe provide another clue to the folklore: they imply vast mysterious forces in the background, sublime powers at which they can only hint. They are the powers which rule our lives. Ordinary men cannot come nigh them. They can be approached only by the prophets, and even by them only at appointed spots and through the invocations appropriate to whatever powers they be. Such, always, is the meaning of the legends.

We must not be misled by our belief that folklore of our time has been "proved," and so is not lore at all but fact. This, also, is the nature of folklore. The legends of creation can always be proved, each in its own appropriate way. Every time a woman feels the pain of childbirth, she proves the truth of the Hebrew legend of creation. After the Fall, Jehovah said: "In sorrow thou shalt bring forth children." And so it is. The obvious objection to this demonstration of the legend is that although, if we assume the legend to be true, we find the current facts bearing it out, we must grant that if we assume the legend to be false, these facts may be explained by some other legend even better—for example, by the legend of evolution, according to which we suppose that the difficulties of parturition are due to the effect of our erect posture. But what we overlook when we urge objections like this against other people's legends is that the same objections can be urged against ours. The theory of evolution is a case in point. No doubt we possess an enormous number of facts concerning the resemblances between the structure of our bodies and that of anthropoid apes, and back of them the mammals generally, and back of them vertebrates generally, and so on. The theory of evolution "fits" these facts beautifully, so we say; and it is true. But the legend of the Fall fits the pains of childbirth beautifully. In neither case does the legend do any more than fit. The facts are what they are; and rather more so: there are always more facts which do not fit the theories, and about which we do not hear so much—until a new theory has been invented into which those erring facts do fit. No fact ever obliges anyone to invent a theory, or to believe one theory and not another. People believe theories and legends and all sorts of folklore for other reasons.

The leading reason is that they are accustomed to it, so that it sounds perfectly natural, and therefore plausible. A folklore does not spring into existence overnight, nor even during forty days and forty nights. At the end of such a period, legend has it, Moses emerged from Mount Sinai with an extraordinary code of public law and divine etiquette. But even if we accept this legend at face value, we must still allow that the Commandments and all their corollaries, running through the Book of Exodus and most of the Book of Leviticus, form only a portion of the folklore of the people. Moses did not invent Jehovah with all his functions as tutelary deity of the Israelites. All this was prepared for him. Consequently he could claim little originality for the circumstances surrounding the revelation of the tables of the laws: granted Genesis and earlier portions of Exodus, the episodes upon Mount Sinai were not only prepared for; they were inevitable. While if we take a later point of view and regard the Sinaic legends with a critical eye, it becomes extremely probable that so extensive a code as the Mosaic one must have developed gradually, becoming established bit by bit after the manner of the folkways, and only becoming the subject of a legend after the event. The Mosaic folklore thus appears as a codification of a much more extensive body of folklore of which it was a free translation.

All this, too, is perfectly illustrated and illuminated by science. Our scientific lore is decidedly extensive—vastly more extensive than the legendary history of the Israelites. But it has been a very gradual growth. No major hypothesis has ever emerged fully formed from the brain of a single inspired prophet. The prophets have always built upon the familiar and the accepted in large part. Such a miracle as Einstein's relativity is sometimes spoken of as "revolutionary." But anyone who cares to look into that admirable edition of Poincaré's *Foundations of Science,* to which Josiah Royce wrote an introduction, will see that the philosophical and mathematical basis of relativity had been gathering for several decades. . . . Evolution, another "revolutionary" conception, which completely "reorganized" biology, was also a gradual accretion of ideas which had already become traditional before the revelations of Charles Darwin. Darwin's relation to evolution is quite similar to Moses' relation to ancient Hebrew lore: it is associated by tradition with his name.

The authority of these names is very great. We must allow that Darwin is a name to conjure with; and this helps us to understand the attitude of the Israelites and the later inheritors of their folklore towards Moses. But it is an equivocal authority. If we say that evolution is not legendary but true and cite the authority of Darwin for the justification of our belief, we fall at once into a predicament, should anyone require us to explain the authority of Darwin. Darwin's greatness is established by the same folklore that established evolution. We can hardly say that evolution is true because Darwin discovered it, and then say that Darwin is reliable because he discovered evolution. We do say exactly that, however; and this further illuminates the character of folklore. That is precisely what we find in the case of Moses. According to his own story, the Commandments are to be accepted on his authority;

while his authority is vouched for by the fact that to him alone were the Commandments thus revealed.

A great deal has been said, first and last, upon the subject of authority. The defenders of the faith of science have been at considerable pains to expose the weakness of authority as the basis of a folklore. In all this they have been quite right. Their only mistake has been their naive belief that all other folklores except their own rest only upon authority; whereas the truth of the matter is that no folklore does so. But it is one of the rules of the game that the other fellow's legends are supported by no other prop than the credit of their legendary heroes. Elijah considered that he had only to discredit Baal to discredit all his followers, and Elijah used for the purpose a test of his own devising. Scientists do the same. Holding that the folklore of a church is established only upon that authority of the legend authors, they have in many cases discredited those authors quite completely—according to tests that are accepted among scientists. This is like discrediting physics by denying that Newton was the discoverer of gravitation.

In a delightful little essay on certainty in science and theology, first published some years ago in the *Hibbert Journal*, Professor Charles Cobb, a mathematician, made an interesting point. Like science, he said, folklore is founded upon axioms. The truth and authority of each depend entirely upon the axioms. If its axioms are true, the rest of the body of theory or legend which is derived from them is true also. This does not seem at first to be much of a point. The devout believers in any folklore are quite likely to accept it, but with a reservation. "Ah," they will say, "but those axioms! There is just the difference between our knowledge and the false theories of believers." But so far as science is concerned, there is nothing to be said for the axioms except that they are what we are accustomed to believe. This is the authority upon which we receive the initial axioms of geometry. "Let us suppose what is only reasonable, as follows: that a straight line is a line such that if any part of it be cut off and laid along any other part, so that the ends of the first part lie upon the second part, the two parts will coincide throughout and be one and the same straight line." This seems reasonable because we are accustomed to sighting. Our most familiar imagery on the subject is the straight edge of a board along which we sight. If, when we sight from one end to the other, all the intervening edge lies directly in the line of vision, we consider the edge straight. The axiom only defines this process, somewhat laboriously. The upshot of it is that a straight line is the path of light. But if we define a straight line directly as the path of light, and if Einstein is right about the path of light in a gravitational field, then surprising things follow—not at all such as we should expect from a perusal of the elementary propositions of plane geometry. And there is no reason whatever for preferring one definition to another, except that it is what we are accustomed to.

The nether part of the argument requires no explanation. Few folklores expose their axioms to view as nakedly as mathematical assumptions. But it is comparatively easy to see that other folklores are nevertheless based on assumption in very much the same way. And if Judaism did not list its axioms, neither does biology.

If anything is lacking to complete the picture, it is the awe in which we hold the truth of science and the prophets to whom we attribute these revelations. We say, of course, that we stand in awe before the awful truth, and that we venerate the saints of science because of what they have done for humanity in giving it the truth. If we ever notice the passion for canonization by which so many scientists are fired, we set it down to a laudable zeal for the welfare of mankind. This, again, is precisely the state of mind of every loyal believer. However primitive his folklore, no one ever stands in awe of what he does not credit, or reverence men whom he considers humbugs. Our attitude toward science is the last perfection of unreason, the final genuflection of the faithful, as our explanation of it makes amply evident. We honor because we believe; we believe because we honor. The lore giveth and the lore taketh away; blessed be the name of the lore. Folklore becomes holy by the same process by which the mores become holy: because the folklore makes it so. Folklore is a body of truth verified by repetition and sanctified by faith. This proposition includes science.

. . . .

The question remains whether any appeal of reason to modern civilization can be effective. Has the modern world as yet developed a civilization—a positive scheme of institutions and ideas, a stable power-unit centered in science or democracy or something of the kind? Or do we live only in a process of transition, itself a progressive dilution and distillation of ancient European civilization, making way for another as yet unrealized order of which the only positive hint thus far is machine technology? Is modernism what it is because civilization is what it is, the blind leading the blind? The actual substance of our modernized religion should throw some light on these questions. Most of us feel inordinately proud of our reasonable pieties. But this may be a delusion on our part. We may be proud of a laborious achievement because of the effort it has cost. It still remains to show that the result was worth the effort.

Strangely enough, none of us is precisely satisfied with our achievements in this field. We are the prey of enervating doubts. Fundamentalists—worse luck!—are not beset with doubts. They are as liable to quarrel as the rest of humankind; but however much they quarrel, there still remain to them an established church and a consecrated dogma. The church pronounces the dogmas, and the dogmas stabilize the church. But modernists discover to their sorrow that a reformed church weakens the authority of its own creed, while a renovated creed saps the foundations of its own ecclesiastical establishment.

The contemporary leaders of reform do not appear to be aware of this dilemma. Some are caught upon one horn, some on the other. Theologians, like for example Professor Kirsopp Lake of Harvard, are extremely sensitive to practical problems. The intellectuals ask, "How can the church pretend any longer to depend upon such attenuated beliefs as even reasonably well-informed people can now hold?" And as if giving the antiphony of a chant, the practical men respond, "How can we make such attenuated beliefs the basis of the church's appeal?" Reformed superstitions are no beliefs at all. A disestablished church is no church at all. When both occur together, how can they appeal to each other for relief? Enlightened unbelief is not a very powerful slogan for the promotion of a church, and a church membership that is wholly optional and voluntary is not a potent buttress to belief. Such is the dilemma of the modernists.

This dilemma, in which the reform of our religion has come to its uneasy end, is characteristic of modern civilization. We have undertaken to become at the same time enlightened and free. Confusion is the inevitable result. It is a hopeless confusion because the whole process of reform is negative. No doubt something will take the place of the pieties we have reformed. But it will be another piety, a belief in something else, a respect for authority of another kind.

From C. E. Ayres, *Science: The False Messiah* (Indianapolis: Bobbs-Merrill, 1927), pp. 21–30, 183–185.

Scientists Mobilize
The American Association
for the Advancement of Science

The American Association for the Advancement of Science, one of the largest and most respected scientific groups in America, expressed its opposition to the antievolution crusade in a series of resolutions passed in 1922. At the association's meeting in 1921 the English biologist William Bateson had read a paper in which he stated that it was impossible for scientists "to agree with Darwin's theory of the origin of the species." The antievolutionists seized upon this statement and utilized it to "prove" that all reputable scientists had abandoned the theory of evolution. The following resolutions were passed by the Council of the American Association for the Advancement of Science largely in an effort to refute this impression.

———◆●———

Inasmuch as the attempt has been made in several states to prohibit in tax-supported institutions the teaching of evolution as applied to man, and

Since it has been asserted that there is not a fact in the universe in support of this theory, that it is a "mere guess" which leading scientists are now abandoning, and that even the American Association for the Advancement of Science at its last meeting in Toronto, Canada, approved this revolt against evolution, and

Inasmuch as such statements have been given wide publicity through the press and are misleading public opinion on this subject;

Therefore, the Council of the American Association for the Advancement of Science has thought it advisable to take formal action upon this matter, in order that there may be no ground for a misunderstanding of the attitude of the Association, which is one of the largest scientific bodies in the world, with a membership of more than 11,000 persons, including the American authorities in all branches of science. The following statements represent the position of the Council with regard to the theory of evolution:—

(1) The Council of the Association affirms that, so far as the scientific evidences of evolution of plants and animals and man are concerned,

there is no ground whatever for the assertion that these evidences constitute a "mere guess."

(2) The Council of the Association affirms that the evidences in favor of the evolution of man are sufficient to convince every scientist of note in the world, and that these evidences are increasing in number and importance every year.

(3) The Council of the Association also affirms that the theory of evolution is one of the most potent influences for good that have thus far entered into human experience; it has promoted the progress of knowledge, it has fostered unprejudiced inquiry, and it has served as an invaluable aid in humanity's search for truth in many fields.

(4) The Council of the Association is convinced that any legislation attempting to limit the teaching of any scientific doctrine so well established and so widely accepted by specialists as the doctrine of evolution would be a profound mistake, which could not fail to injure and retard the advancement of knowledge and of human welfare, by denying the freedom of teaching and inquiry which is essential to all progress.

From *The Summarized Proceedings of the American Association for the Advancement of Science, 1921–1925* (Washington, 1925), pp. 66–67.

The New Decalogue of Science
Albert Edward Wiggam

One of the most popular nonfiction books published in the 1920s was *The New Decalogue of Science* by Albert Edward Wiggam. A well-known lecturer and a member of the editorial staff on the *American Magazine,* Wiggam figured prominently in several "scientific bodies" including the American Eugenics Society and Maynard Shipley's antifundamentalist Science League of America. Disturbed by the march of fundamentalism and by the attempt of the Kentucky legislature in 1922 to outlaw the teaching of evolution, he concluded that the time had arrived for a bold announcement of a new decalogue, "with none of the absolutism of the old," which would enable man to do God's "scientific will." The commandments of his new scientific decalogue were listed under the following headings: eugenics, scientific research, measuring man, humanizing industry, preferential reproduction, trusting intelligence, art, internationalism, and philosophical reconstruction. Wiggam believed that the obvious failure of the old decalogue to teach men how "to be good" necessitated a new code, based upon findings of modern science which guaranteed man "a true technique of righteousness." In many respects *The New Decalogue of Science* was a bizarre volume for a best-seller. It was a curious blend of science and eugenics employing much of the terminology and symbolism of Christian theology. The following brief excerpts from Wiggam's book indicate its general tenor. His claims for science, especially in the realm of ethics and morality, were of the kind that prompted religious fundamentalists to denounce "the presumptions of scientists."

It is, therefore, no extravagant assumption but the surest deduction from science itself that science only can supply mankind with the true technology of the will of God. If his will is ever to be done on earth as it is in Heaven, it will have to be done through the instrumentalities of science, that is through the use of intelligence. Conscience will have to look through the microscope if it ever sees its duty aright. The most earnest sense of duty will not supply men with the true objectives of that duty. The "spirit of Christ," which we are glibly told will suffice for salvation, is majestic in its impulse and in its objective, but sadly lacking in any technique for connecting the two. It points truly the "steep and thorny path to Heaven," but it supplies no engineering details for making the ascent.

.   .   .   .

Obviously, then, science, a knowledge of how the universe works, lies at the basis of all morals. You can not be truly righteous until you find out how. Science alone can teach you how. So far you have explored nature, first, out of sheer curiosity, and second, because it gave you money, pleasure, and power. You must now explore nature because it brings you more righteousness, more capacity to make correct adjustments, first, to the universe, and second, to your fellows.

Science is the effort to find out what to do with the universe and what to do in the universe. So far you have used your science only to get rich; you must now use it to become righteous. Righteousness, correct conduct, is the true aim of evolution. The amoeba that made correct adjustments that gave it better structure, more chance of survival, more abundant life was a good amoeba. The one that failed in this organic duty was a bad amoeba. One developed evolutionary morals, the other evolutionary wickedness. Amoeban morals and human morals are in the same cosmic category. "From the muscles of an ox to the morals of an empire" the moral problem runs the same. And from this day on when biology, psychology, chemistry, and physics have all pointed out your evolutionary immorality, you just bend them to your service to develop a true evolutionary morality that will minister directly to the continued evolution of man. In short, your morals so far have stopped progressive evolution. You must now through science set evolution going forward again.

In achieving true evolutionary, biological righteousness, the search for bringing it about has scarcely begun. Man is millions of years old, but science is but a babe in arms. We are still in dense ignorance as to the causes of evolution itself. We have, so far, only learned better how to manage it. As Charles Darwin said, "Our ignorance of the cause of variations, is profound." After sixty years of study we are compelled still to say our ignorance in this direction is profound. We know almost nothing about social psychology. The psychology of religion remains well-nigh an untouched field. Political psychology is still on the knees of the gods. Just yesterday we began to learn a little about intellectual education, but moral education is still largely in the realm of the occult. We have made immense isolated discoveries, but we do not know yet how to synthesize them into that right social conduct that will minister to organic progress and social progress at the same time. To synthesize and synchronize the "ethical process" and the evolutionary process, which so puzzled Huxley, is the next great social task of man.

But all this need not appall us, because we have learned two things, first the aim to be achieved, and second, how to study. As a friend of mine puts it very bluntly but truthfully, "We have learned how to put salt on the tail of the occult and see what happens." We have learned to experiment. We have learned how to compare, and we have got over being afraid. We are no longer afraid of God. The scientist has accepted both him and his universe and has quit trying, as the fundamentalist does, to put him outside of his universe and build one of his own. True, we make mistakes. "Science goes forward by zigzag. And we never can tell whether it is a zig or a zag." But the thing is that it always goes forward.

The significant and beautiful thing is that we *know* at last that we are working in utter harmony with "that high, unknown purpose of the world which we call God." Whatever God is, we know he is the immanent genius of things. That man is the most religious who learns the most about him, who questions him the most wisely and fearlessly, who experiments both with the universe and with life the most daringly. It is only in the laboratory of science that knowledge, morals, religion, and the world wisdom of the poet, preacher, sociologist, statesman, and philosopher all meet. It is only here that they can all be synthesized into the final great ethic religion of man.

In this great synthesis you, the statesman who controls life more than any of us, must play an immense part. For two thousand years you have read the injunction, "Seek ye after God if haply ye might find him." And the scientist gazing through his microscope, his telescope, his spectroscope, and into his test tube can say with a faith born of a knowledge which the old prophets did not have, "I have sought after God and I have *begun* to find him." The man who has not seen the scientist as he calculates the speed of an electron as being as true an apostle of righteousness as was Moses, Jesus, St. Paul, has missed the whole round expanse of the modern moral opportunity, and all the rich, deep excellence of a new and untried companionship with God. Herein lies his own command to scientific research, that it is just this eternal search for fresh knowledge which always means fresh obligations and new fields of duty—the search for new means of conquest over life and circumstance and new controls over moral effort, lifts the soul to new religious contacts, furnishes the finest adventures of the mind, and gives undying lilt and joy to the moral struggle.

For the scientist has at last taught us to experiment fearlessly, lovingly, exaltingly with life and with God. It is only thus that we can find out what life is and what God is. I have said we do not know the cause of variations, we do not know what makes a new spot on a rabbit, a new perfume in a primrose, or a new trait in a genius. But the moment science began, the primrose ceased to be a mere "primrose by the river's brim," and became an object of experiment. And in the same moment God ceased to be a mere "object of worship" and became a living God worthy of study. He had urged us by every inner call of the mind to seek after him, if haply we might find him. But we were afraid to experiment and merely worshiped. You burned at the stake every brave mind that sought to find him. You have now become passive and in the main leave the free thinker alone. You must also become active and aid him. If you do, someday, it may be soon—the scientist will find out for you the cause of variations, the cause of evolution. And then we shall know how God created at least the organic world. Only then can we become his loving and obedient children and know what to do to aid him in creating a still better world.

Science, then, I repeat, has alone made true righteousness possible. When some unknown genius of the past mixed nine parts of copper with one part of tin and made bronze, he not only lifted all mankind from the Stone to the Metal Age, but he began a new era of morals, because he began experimentally to seek after God.

From Albert Edward Wiggam, *The New Decalogue of Science* (Indianapolis: Bobbs-Merrill, 1923), pp. 19, 115–119.

The Superiority of Science
Maynard Shipley

Maynard Shipley, a former newspaper editor who described himself as a writer and lecturer on astronomy, evolution, and economics, organized the Science League of America early in the 1920s specifically for the purpose of protecting the freedom of teachers and scientists. The organization waged a militant campaign against the fundamentalist effort to enact antievolution laws. Shipley was an indefatigable crusader who engaged antievolutionists in public debates and wrote numerous articles and tracts in defense of science. The following excerpt is from the introduction to his "short history of the fundamentalist attacks on evolution" of the 1920s. The work, significantly entitled *The War on Modern Science*, provides an example of what fundamentalists often depicted as the arrogance of science and its defenders. Shipley expressed complete confidence in the methods of science as the most reliable means of ascertaining truth, which he equated with knowledge; and he looked with scorn upon those who sought truth by what he called the "traditional method" of divine revelation. Despite the fundamentalists' crusade against evolution, Shipley contended that it was "not so much the doctrine of evolution which the fundamentalist fears as it is the scientific method." He characterized the fundamentalist movement as "organized ignorance" and reaction engaged in a mighty struggle against science and other forces of enlightenment and progress.

———◆◆———

The forces of obscurantism in the United States are in open revolt!

More than twenty-five millions of men and women, with ballot in hand, have declared war on modern science. Ostensibly a "war on the teaching of evolution in our tax-supported schools," the real issue is much broader and deeper, much more comprehensive in its scope.

The deplorable fact must be recognized that in the United States today there exist, side by side, two opposing cultures, one or the other of which must eventually dominate our public institutions, political, legal, educational, and social. On the one side we see arrayed the forces of progress and enlightenment, on the other the forces of reaction, the apostles of traditionalism. There can be no compromise between these diametrically opposed armies. If the self-styled fundamentalists can gain control over our state and national governments—which is one of their avowed objectives—much of the best that has been gained in American culture will be suppressed or banned, and we shall be headed backwards toward the pall of a new Dark Age.

Centering their attacks for the moment on evolution, the keystone in the arch of our modern educational edifice, the armies of ignorance are being organized, literally by the millions, for a combined political assault upon modern science. . . .

It is imperative that it be fully recognized that a fight to the finish between science and dogma is now in progress throughout the United States. The fundamentalists are well organized; they are in deadly earnest, believing as they do that their particular brand of religion cannot survive and flourish together with the teachings of religious liberalism and modern science. For the first time in our history, organized knowledge has come into open conflict with organized ignorance.

. . . .

To the fundamentalist, the validity of scientific conclusions, or the soundness of a theory based upon discovery and the systematization of knowledge, rests not upon ascertained facts and reasoned inferences, but upon the harmony of the conclusions of science with the theological dogmas of fundamentalism. To the traditionalist, the stability and welfare of governments, along with the edifices of scientific research, rest upon theological "truths," not discovered, but revealed from on high. It is blandly affirmed in *Signs of the Times* (a Seventh Day Adventist paper . . .), that "there is never any doubt about any great problem when people look to God's Word for the solution, and not to history or science."

To the scientific mind, knowledge—"truth"—is something to be gained by patient, laborious study and research. To the fundamentalist mind, knowledge concerning the origin of the earth and the life upon it is something to be gained, not by research, but by means of ancient Hebrew writings, which the fundamentalists assume to be literally "the word of God." The fundamentalist is already in possession of the solution of every "great problem," and no account need be taken of the lessons of "history or science." Knowledge results from the will to believe, not from the will to find things out for oneself.

. . . .

It is quite clear . . . that the present conflict between science and fundamentalism is the inevitable result of a clash between the method of science, which is discovery, and the method of fundamentalism, which is the theological or traditional method known as revelation. In other words, it is a conflict between two directly opposed theories of the source and meaning of knowledge and of its value, and therefore an irreconcilable conflict between two opposing conceptions of what constitutes the proper (and lawful) method to be used in attaining knowledge and truth.

If the scientific and historical method is correct, then the fundamentalist or traditional method is false and fruitless. Hence, say the fundamentalists, scientific methods and results must not be taught in our schools and colleges; since, being in conflict with the method and results of revelation, the findings of scientific research must be false: that is, "contrary to the Word of God," which is literally in the possession of the fundamentalists.

All that need be or can be known about the origin, nature, and early history of man having already been revealed, research becomes unnecessary; the savant may put away his instruments, pack up his books, and go to—well, let us say, a "revival meeting." If he should persist in his researches and insist upon making known the results of his patient labor and study, he must be fined or jailed as a criminal. This is the method of revelation, reinforced by the policeman's club, as opposed to the method of science, reinforced by what man is daily finding out.

While it is well known that no one living scientist of recognized standing in his profession doubts that things came to be what they are found to be by a process of evolution or orderly change, nevertheless, what the friends of science are really supporting, or trying to protect, is not so much a unanimous conclusion of the scientists as the validity of the method of science and the moral right and duty of the scientists to make known to the students in our tax-supported schools the results of their researches.

Scientists, either individually or as a body, may be mistaken as to a matter of fact or as to a question of theory. But they cannot today be mistaken as to the question of method. It is not so much the doctrine of evolution that the fundamentalist fears as it is the scientific method.

The superiority of the scientific method, then, as against the "revelation" of those afflicted with the disease of traditionalism (or, rather, of arrested development), lies not in the fact that science has attained true conclusions in so many cases, but in the fact that scientists have adopted the system of analyzing and formulating their assumptions on the basis of discovery—on ascertained facts. They have laboriously developed a technique for testing the validity not only of their theories and hypotheses, but even of their tentative "beliefs."

From Maynard Shipley, *The War on Modern Science: A Short History of the Fundamentalist Attacks on Evolution and Modernism* (New York: Alfred A. Knopf, 1927), pp. 3–8.

Science: "The Highest Form of Human Theology"
Michael Pupin

During the 1920s few professional scientists were more concerned with publicizing the religious implications of science than Michael Idvorsky Pupin, a distinguished professor of electro-mechanics at Columbia University. An immigrant from Hungary whose career had all the ingredients of a Horatio Alger tale in a scientific setting, Pupin persistently argued that not only could science and religion be reconciled, but that science brought man "into a closer relationship with God." The most complete statement of his argument appeared in a lengthy volume entitled *The New Reformation: From Physical to Spiritual Realities.* The following selection is a portion of an interview with Pupin regarding the relationship of science and Christianity arranged by Albert E. Wiggam of *American Magazine.* In this interview, as in his lectures and writings, Pupin makes clear his conception of God as a law-abiding, intelligible deity whose "busy little worker," the electron, is designed to serve mankind. Equally noteworthy is his belief in the scientific plausibility of the soul and immortality. Despite his claim that science made man "a better Christian," fundamentalists found little consolation in his efforts as a "reconciler." His references to a "Divine intelligence, that we, as intelligent beings, can depend on" was far removed from their conception of an inscrutable God whom man must serve unselfishly. In their view Pupin's reconciliation was merely a variety of pantheism that was essentially un-Christian in its premises and results.

———◆—◆———

"These big hot stars are only the beginning of God's creative energy, the beginning of cosmic history. But the human soul, insofar as science can penetrate, is the last chapter of this history as far as it has been written.

"And, furthermore, it is in the soul of man, in that great world within us, that Divinity resides. And when we think of that, we are not so small. Nay, we are very important. Science has found nothing in the universe which even compares in importance with the life of man. Compared to the human soul, everything else sinks into insignificance.

"The stars had to condense and become fluid, and then solidify and cool to a low temperature, before a planet such as our earth was possible, upon which life could exist. Of course there may be other planets like ours. If there are, there may be other souls, other organic lives. But science has forced us to believe that wherever the soul of man exists, that soul represents the highest product of cosmic creation.

"We have felt all this intuitively. Even the savage feels that he is the most important thing in the universe. But to this faith science has added *knowledge,* which means a higher faith. Science shows us more clearly the meaning of it all, and what is our relationship to the Creator.

"Wherever science has explored the universe, it has found it to be a manifestation of a co-ordinating principle. It leaves us no escape from the conclusion that back of everything there is a definite guiding principle, which leads from chaos to cosmos. We are faced with two alternatives: We can either believe that cosmos, the beautiful law and order, is simply the result of haphazard happenings, or that it is the result of a definite intelligence. Now, which are you, as an intelligent being, going to choose?

"Personally, I choose to believe in the co-ordinating principle, the Divine Intelligence. Why? Because it is simpler. It is more intelligible. It harmonizes with my whole experience.

"The theory that intelligent beings like ourselves, or intelligent processes like the movements of the stars, are the outcome of unintelligent haphazard happenings, is beyond my understanding. And why should I accept such a theory when I observe the evidence of a directing intelligence every day?

.   .   .   .

"Of course, you cannot produce a mathematical demonstration about the Divine Being, in the same sense that you can demonstrate the laws that govern the motions of physical bodies. The Divine Being is far too complex to permit of that kind of proof. But from time immemorial we have felt that our own intelligence is part of something higher. And we have not discovered in the material universe anything higher than the human soul, which manifests itself through our intelligence. And as the soul of man has developed, this intuition of Divine Intelligence has grown stronger. And now, in our day, have come most of our scientific discoveries about the universe. And not a single discovery that science has made tends in the least to contradict this innate feeling that a definite intelligence is back of everything. Indeed, the more deeply science penetrates into the laws of the universe, the more it leads us to a belief in an intelligent divinity.

"So, you see that science, instead of taking God out of the world, as some have feared, brings men into a closer spiritual relationship with Him.

"Today the average man understands the structure of the universe imcomparably better than did the prophets of three thousands years ago. We scientists, therefore, ought to be able to teach him more about the Divinity which, to a spiritually-developed scientist, seems so obviously present everywhere in the universe.

"I believe I can illustrate what I think science has revealed for man's higher spiritual and religious life by taking a text from St. Paul. You remember the apostle said: 'We all, with open face beholding as in a glass the glory of the Lord, are changed into the same image from glory to glory. . . .'

"During the past three hundred years, since the Pilgrim Fathers landed at Plymouth Rock, science has revealed four distinct physical realities of the universe. Before that time men did not dream that these four realities existed. And these four realities, these four discoveries about the structure and nature of the universe, are, in my judgment, true glories of the Lord. Each one has brought man's soul just that much closer to beholding with open face the final Divine Glory behind everything.

"The first physical reality, the first glory revealed by science, was when Galileo discovered the meaning of *matter in motion*. He was the first to formulate the law of the acceleration in the motion of material bodies. This was the beginning of modern physical science.

"A hundred years later, Newton crowned Galileo's discovery with his discovery of the law of gravitation. Nothing exhibits the beauty of this physical reality so well as the motion of the planets around the sun. Here we have a cosmic system of bodies in which each part moves along its own prescribed path with a precision impossible to attain in any mechanism constructed by the hand of man. Yet the only guiding force is gravitation. All matter everywhere is ceaseless motion, yet everything reduced down to a simple law—a simplicity such as the world never saw before.

"Then came the second revelation of a physical reality—a new glory. This was the discovery of electricity in motion. Benjamin Franklin and Michael Faraday must be mentioned first among the founders of this physical reality. Franklin discovered that lightning is electricity in motion. This revealed to mankind a new source of power. Then later

Volta and Faraday and Clerk-Maxwell explained the laws in accordance with which electricity moves.

"These proved to be just as simple as the laws which Newton and Galileo discovered, which govern the motion of material bodies on the earth or of the celestial bodies in the heavens.

"Then came the revelation of a third physical reality, a third glory, namely radiant energy in motion. By that I mean that the whole universe is filled with the radiation of light and heat.

.   .   .   .

"And, sixty years ago, Clerk-Maxwell, the great electrical mathematician, spoke like a prophet when he made the startling announcement that this radiation of light is a manifestation of moving electricity. The most precious among the fruits of this discovery of Maxwell is that the origin of all light radiation is in the motion of the tiny electrons, which are, as far as we know today, the unchangeable, primordial building stones of the material universe.

"Everything that moves seems to be deriving its breath of existence from the electrical forces which have their origin in these tiny electrons. These little workers, infinitely small but infinitely numerous, by their combined activities make up the larger activities of that stupendous thing we call the universe.

"And this busy little worker the electron is the most law-abiding creature in the universe. It loves, honors, and obeys the laws, and its eternal mission is to serve. God employed the heavenly host of electronic workers to build the atoms, the molecules, and the galaxies of burning stars. These celestial furnaces, throbbing with the blazing energy of the electronic host, are molding all kinds of planetary castings and tempering them so as to be just right for organic life.

"One of these planetary castings is our Mother Earth: it is a mere dust speck in the universe, but this dust speck is the home of the soul of man, and this lifts our tiny earth to a place of honor near the throne of God. The soul's very breath of life is the beautiful electronic music, and to be thrilled by the melody of that cosmic song is the highest aim in our study of electrical science.

"And now the biologists are revealing a fourth reality—a fourth glory of the Lord. This glory is the science of organic life. It is the latest reality of the universe which science has given us. And, again, this living reality is found to be so very simple, so beautiful, so inspiring, so intelligent!

"The spiritually inspiring thing which the biologists have shown us is that all life has progressed from the lowest toward the highest. If one does not believe that life has been a progressive development, step by step, under the guidance of a co-ordinating principle, then he has a very poor idea of Divinity. For, if life has progressed from small beginnings up to man in, say, ten million years, where will it be ten million years from now? Man is revealed by science as a being who is constantly progressing from glory to glory, changing more and more toward the spiritual image of his Creator.

"You see that the realities of both physical science and organic science reveal a God, a divine intelligence that we, as intelligent beings, can depend on. We cannot place our faith in haphazard happenings, but we can place the utmost faith in Divine Intelligence. There is dependability, continuity, everywhere. Science finds that everything is a continuously developing and intelligent process. It reveals man as a being with a soul which is progressing more and more toward Divinity in a universe of unbroken continuity."

At this point, I said to Doctor Pupin: "You say the law of the universe is continuity, that there is no break anywhere. Do you believe that death itself does not break the continuity of the life of the soul?"

"In order to answer that question," replied Doctor Pupin, "we shall have to look back just a moment, and ask another question: What is the only mystery today in electrical science? It is this: Where, when, and how did the electron come into existence?

"The sensible man will answer, God created the electron, and, therefore, only God knows, where, when, and how. This eliminates the mystery at once. The rest we can see for ourselves. God created a host of electrons to be his assistants in building the universe. And when science discovered the electrons and learned to use them in man's service, it was our first glimpse of the divine method of creative operation. Consequently, when we light our houses or send a telegram, we are using the electrons—we are merely imitating the creative method of God.

"Let us see what happened after God had made the stars out of electrons: One of the celestial bodies, the earth, for example, got denser, gradually cooled, and became habitable for living things. Life began. We do not know where, when, or how. St. John said: 'In the beginning was the Word and the Word was with God. . . .' Today a spiritual scientist's translation of the phrase would be: 'In the beginning was the Guiding Intelligence, and the Guiding Intelligence was with God.'

"Let us follow the story a little further through the infinite years, until finally we have man—the soul of man—as far as we know, the highest product of God's creative handiwork.

"Now, after God has spent untold time in creating man and endowing him with a soul—which is a reflection of His image, is it reasonable to suppose that man lives here on earth a short span of life—and then is quite extinguished by death? Is the soul going to perish when the physical body dies? Is the soul going to have existed in vain?

"It does not seem reasonable to me that a creation which has been going on for billions and billions of years, insofar as we can tell, for the very purpose of producing that wonderful soul, should cause the soul—your soul and my soul—to exist only as long as our physical bodies exist. Although science does not offer mathematical proof of the immortality of the soul, it gives us plenty of food for thought and belief, plenty of grounds for intelligent hope. And it adds to our conviction that our physical life is only a stage in the existence of the soul.

"You can certainly say that in my opinion, all scientific evidence tends to show—not to prove, but to point toward the belief—that it is very unlikely the soul of man is going to cease its existence when the body perishes. The law of continuity and the general scientific view of the universe tend, I think, to strengthen our belief that the human soul goes on existing, and *developing,* after death.

"You see science is constantly revealing Divinity and man's relationship to Divinity. Science is, therefore, the highest form of human theology, the highest form of reasoning about God. Science leads us straight to a belief in God, and this is the foundation of religion.

"Science does not prevent a man from being a Christian but makes him a better Christian. It has made me a better Christian. For the next year I am going to talk to the students of various colleges on this higher spiritual meaning of science. My personal belief is that everything that happens in this great universe is for a purpose; and that purpose is the development of the human soul. That is where science and religion touch. Science adds immeasurably to the foundations of religious faith. Science will strengthen religion. It has strengthened mine—strengthened it very greatly."

From Albert Edward Wiggam, "Science Is Leading Us Closer to God: An Interview with Michael Pupin, the Distinguished Scientist," *The American Magazine,* CIV (September 1927), 194, 196.

"Science and the Faith of the Modern"
Edwin Grant Conklin

Few scientists were more active or articulate in defense of evolution than Edwin Grant Conklin, an eminent professor of biology at Princeton University. His treatment of the subject in magazines, books, and public lectures revealed his facility for translating highly technical data into terms understandable to the layman. Conklin rarely restricted his discussions to the scientific aspects of evolution but challenged the antievolutionists' arguments on theological grounds as well. His famous collection of lectures, published in 1921 under the title *The Direction of Human Evolution,* included a definition of the basic principles of biological evolution and an analysis of their relationship to the biblical account of creation. Evolution, he maintained, "deals only with processes and does not profess to touch the question of ultimate causation." Evidence for the existence of God stood "quite apart from the truth or falsity of evolution." Like many scientists, Conklin made his defense of evolution a point of departure for a defense of science in general, which he believed the fundamentalist crusade threatened. In the following excerpt from an essay published six years after his *Direction of Human Evolution,* he attempts to refute the notion that science had "destroyed the foundations of ethics and religion." His emphasis is upon three critical areas in which science has made significant contributions to these foundations. Opposed to the idea of any basic antagonism between religion and science, Conklin conceived of truth as embracing "scientific reality" as well as "religious ideality," both of which were "necessary to normal, happy, useful living."

———————

Fundamentalism, if logical, would demand the abolition of the teaching of all science and scientific methods, for science in general and not merely the theory of evolution is responsible for the loss of faith in the old traditions. It is folly to attempt to promote education and science and at the same time to forbid the teaching of the principal methods and results of science. The only sensible course would be to abolish altogether the teaching of science and scientific methods and to return to ecclesiasticism. The church once told scientists what they could think and teach, and now state legislatures propose to do it. Such methods of resisting change have always failed in the past and are foredoomed to failure now.

The real problem that confronts us, and it is a great problem, is how to adjust religion to science, faith to knowledge, ideality to reality, for adjustment in the reverse direction will never happen. Facts cannot be eliminated by ideals, and it is too late in the history of the world to attempt to refute the findings of science by sentimental objections or supposed theological difficulties. If science makes mistakes, science must furnish the cure; it can never be done by church councils, state legislatures, nor even by popular vote.

The only possible remedy for the present deplorable condition is not less, but more and better, science and education; science that recognizes that the search for truth is not the whole of life, that both scientific reality and religious ideality are necessary to normal, happy, useful living. We must keep our feet on the ground of fact and science, but lift our heads into the atmosphere of ideals. "To the solid ground of Nature trusts the mind that builds for aye." Education from the earliest years must teach love rather than hate, human brotherhood rather than war, service rather than selfishness; it must develop good habits of body and mind; it must instill reverence, not only for truth but also for beauty and righteousness.

"Where there is no vision, the people perish." Man cannot live by bread alone; he must have ideals and aspirations, faith and hope and love. In short, he must have a religion. The world never needed a religion of high ideals and aspirations more than it needs it now. But the old religion of literalism and of slavish regard to the authority of church or book, while well suited to some minds, cannot serve the needs of those who have breathed the air of science. Must all such be deprived of the benefits of a religion which they need and be forced into a false position of antagonism to religion as a whole because they cannot accept all the literalism, infantilism, and incidentalism of so-called fundamentalism? The fundamentalists, rather than the scientists, are helping to make this an irreligious age.

Science has destroyed many old traditions but it has not destroyed the foundations of ethics or religion. In some respects it has contributed greatly to these foundations:

1. The universality of natural law has not destroyed faith in God, though it has modified many primitive conceptions of deity. This is a universe of ends as well as of means, of teleology as well as of mechanism. Mechanism is universal but so also is finalism. It is incredible that the

system and order of nature, the evolution of matter and worlds and life, of man and consciousness and spiritual ideals are all the results of chance. The greatest exponents of evolution, such as Darwin, Huxley, Asa Gray, and Weismann, have maintained that there is evidence of some governance and plan in nature. This is the fundamental article of all religious faith. If there is no purpose in the universe, or in evolution, or in man, then indeed there is no God and no good. But if there is purpose in nature and in human life, it is only the imperfection of our mental vision that leads us sometimes to cry in despair: "Vanitas vanitatum, all is vanity." No one can furnish scientific proof of the existence or nature of God; but atheism leads to pessimism and despair, while theism leads to faith and hope. "By their fruits ye shall know them."

2. Science leaves us faith in the worth and dignity of man. In spite of weakness and imperfection, man is the highest product of a billion years of evolution. We are still children in the morning of time, but we are attaining reason, freedom, spirituality. The ethics of mankind is not the ethics of the jungle or the barnyard. In the new dispensation men will no longer be restrained from evil by fear of hell or hope of heaven, but by their decent instincts and their high ideals. When love of truth, beauty, goodness, of wife, children, humanity, dies in us, our doom will be sealed. But it will not die in all men; the long-past course of progressive evolution proves that it will live on, somewhere and somehow.

3. Science leaves us hope for the future. Present conditions often seem desperate; pessimists tell us that society is disintegrating, that there will never be a League of Nations, that wars will never cease, that the human race is degenerating, and that our civilization is going the way of ancient Egypt, Assyria, Greece, and Rome. But though nations have risen and fallen, and cultures have waxed and waned, the major movements of human history have been forward. After civilization had once been attained, it never completely disappeared from the earth. The torch of culture was handed on from Egypt to Greece and from Greece to Rome, and from all of these to us. One often hears of lost arts and civilizations of the past, but the best elements of any culture are immortal.

The test of biological variations and mutations is whether they lead to increasing fitness, and the test of all social and moral mutations and revolutions, such as those of today, is whether they lead to increasing perfection and progress. The great principle of the survival of the fit has guided evolution from amoeba to man, from tropisms and reflexes to intelligence and consciousness, from solitary individuals to social organizations, from instincts to ethics, and this great principle will not be abrogated today or tomorrow. It is the "power, not ourselves, that makes for righteousness." Man can consciously hasten or hinder this process, but he cannot permanently destroy it. He can refuse to take part in it and can choose to be eliminated, but the past course of evolution for millions of years indicates that somewhere and somehow this process will go on.

The evolutionist is an incorrigible optimist; he reviews a billion years of evolution in the past and looks forward to perhaps another billion years of evolution in the future. He knows that evolution has not always been progressive; that there have been many eddies and back currents, and that the main current has sometimes meandered in many directions; and yet he knows that, on the whole, it has moved forward. Through all the ages evolution has been leading toward the wider intellectual horizons, the broader social outlooks, the more invigorating moral atmosphere of the great sea of truth.

What progress in body, mind, and society; what inventions, institutions, even relations with other worlds, the future may hold in store, it hath not entered into the heart of man to conceive. What does it matter if some men refuse to join this great march onward, what does it matter if even our species should become extinct if only it give place to a better species! Our deepest instincts are for growth; the joy of life is progress. Only this would make immortality endurable. Human progress depends upon the increase and diffusion among men of both knowledge and ethics, reality and ideality, science and religion. Now for the first time in the history of life on this planet, a species can consciously and rationally take part in its own evolution. To us the inestimable privilege is given to co-operate in this greatest work of time, to have part in the triumphs of future ages. What other aim is so worthy of high endeavor and great endowment?

From Edwin Grant Conklin, "Science and the Faith of the Modern," *Scribner's Magazine*, LXXVIII (November 1925), 451–458.

Christianity's Staunchest Ally
Kirtley F. Mather

Kirtley F. Mather, an "ardent Baptist" and a distinguished professor of geology at Harvard University, was active in the cause of science throughout the fundamentalist-modernist controversy. He engaged William Bell Riley in a public debate on evolution, wrote numerous articles and essays in an attempt to reconcile science and religion, and traveled to Dayton, Tennessee, in 1925 to appear as a defense witness in the Scopes trial. Among his most provocative lectures "concerning Science and Religion" were those he delivered at the Institute on World Unity, Green Acre, Maine, in 1927, which were later published under the title of *Science in Search of God*. The following selection, which he described as an attempt to probe "the mind of the antievolutionist," is equally revealing regarding the mind of the modern scientist. Mather explained the antievolutionist psychology in terms of three elements: popular ignorance and confusion over the meaning of evolution; a potpourri of "unnecessary fears and faulty logic"; and the "superb egotism" of the human species regarding its ancestry. By combining a misuse of the Bible with a misconception of science, the antievolutionist concocted an argument noted for its oversimplifications and inconsistencies and often employed the tactics of the demagogue in preaching a distrust of science. Professor Mather refused to accept the view that the "survival of fittest" was a justification for greed and selfishness: instead he interpreted it to mean "the survival of those who serve others most unselfishly." Hence, evolution was Christianity's "staunchest ally."

To the man of science the modern revival of the old warfare between science and religion is extremely puzzling. It intrigues his interest chiefly because it demands an explanation. He finds it difficult to understand why many devout men of religion spend so much energy and time laying a barrage against the doctrine of evolution; he cannot help wondering at the mental process of those who today seem determined to sunder two great fields of thought in each of which so much remains to be learned. There must be some basic reason for the current attack upon the results of scientific research; its discovery may assist in clearing the atmosphere.

Disputes are never settled by casting reflections upon the mental

189

acumen of the gentlemen of the opposition, no matter whether such aspersions are phrased in the dignified and erudite language of pulpit and textbook or in the blunt and ofttimes crude terms of the soapbox orator and politician. Where there is so much smoke there must be some fire. If the smoke is to be dissipated, the fire must be discovered and quenched.

.   .   .   .

To many persons the thought of human evolution from the "lower animals" seems to be repugnant if not almost shocking. The timeworn question "Was your grandmother a monkey?" is an indication not only of the ignorance of the questioner concerning the scientific conception of man's origin but also of his large residue of the superb egotism which seems to characterize the human species. The same self-satisfaction which led Linnaeus to classify man as "Primate" in his subdivisions of the animal kingdom has long been fostered in many quarters. Collectively, it is man's mission, we are told, to subdue the earth, to rule among the creatures whose only excuse for existence is that they may minister to his comfort; while enjoying the fruits of the earth, he is preparing for a heavenly home which he merits because he is only a little less than the gods. Individually, he has been taught to revere his ancestors, to set as his goal of perfection the good old days and the good old ways of a past more or less remote. How can these things be, if his origin is the same as that of the beasts of the field, if in every fiber of his being there is that which makes him kin to the animals destined to contribute even their lives to his welfare? No wonder the smug philosophy of self-centered mankind is rudely disturbed by the evolutionary doctrine.

And yet, the antievolutionist is generally quick to deny that egotism is a motive impelling his attack upon modern biology. Possibly this is because of the easy rebuttal which the man of science may make. It is now definitely known that the human species "Homo sapiens" has been in existence on the earth for more than 30,000 years. Our truly human ancestry, therefore, runs back for at least a thousand generations. To find an ancestor common to man and any other living creature, one must go back at least to that mid-Tertiary geologic epoch known as the Miocene, when horses had three toes instead of one and elephants had little more than made a start toward the development of trunk and tusks: the time, two or three million years ago, when in anthropoid evolution the strain that led to man was differentiated from those that led to the chimpanzee, the gorilla, and the other apes. Or if one is really interested in the degree of his consanguinity with the monkey, it may be comforting to know that the most modern creature which could by any possibility have been a common ancestor to the monkeys in the one line, and the apes and man in the other, lived and died before the Oligocene epoch of geologic history—perhaps five million years ago.

To me, however, such facts are immaterial and irrelevant. I had a college chum who used to say "It isn't where a fellow came from, it's what he brought with him that counts." I trust he will pardon me if I apply the important truth contained in that sophomoric statement to the question in hand. Personally, I take just as much pride in my lineage from an unknown semibrute who "flaked a flint to a cutting edge," as I acquire on account of an ambitious ancestor who aspired to know the difference between right and wrong and therefore was driven from a garden of contentment into a world of problems.

Possibly also the antievolutionist's denial that egotism is a motive for his animosity toward evolution is a tribute to his desire to display the jewel consistency. Surely those who insist that the African Bushmen or the South Sea Negritos are their "brothers" need not feel any repugnance at accepting the apes or even the monkeys as their remote "cousins." The essential unity of the human family is but an application of the evolutionary principle of kinship throughout the entire organic world.

Should we uncharitably harbor a suspicion that, in spite of the antievolutionist's denial, human egotism is even now—as it certainly has been in the past—a prime motive for opposition to the biologist's conclusions concerning man's heredity, we can but charge it to those unscientific habits of mind which all of us find it hard to overcome. To the man of science, "Truth is truth, if it sears the eyeballs." He follows "wherever and to whatever abyss truth leads him"; for he knows that "truth shall make him free."

It is a favorite remark of the antievolutionists that evolution is just a theory, one among an endless series of scientific hypotheses, born today and changed or killed tomorrow. Wait, say they, until it is a proven fact and then we will be ready to consider its acceptance; in the meantime it is unworthy of our trust. It is obvious that this is an excuse rather than a reason for the attack waged against evolution; but it is, nevertheless, an angle of our field which needs surveying. The charge

that evolution is only an unsubstantiated theory—an educated guess perhaps—is not surprising. To the untutored mind the fiat of a "revealed
book," or a mysterious tablet of stone or bronze, or the dogmatic assertion of someone who for any reason occupies a position of prominence, bears greater weight than the carefully considered statement of a
man of science. Few appreciate the fact that all of modern science, with
its remarkable contributions to human welfare and comfort, rests upon
a foundation of theories none of which is more susceptible of "proof"
than is the theory of evolution.

The majority of antievolutionists unwittingly make "Darwinism"
or "the Darwinian theory" a synonym for evolution. As a matter of fact,
Darwin's contribution in this field of knowledge was a dual one. First, he
amassed so great a series of observed facts which led toward the conclusion that all animate nature was the product of evolutionary development, that men of science almost with one accord abandoned the theory
of separate creation of each species, quite generally held before 1849, in
favor of some theory of evolution, which of course Darwin was by no
means the first to suggest. Second, he proposed a particular hypothesis
which attempted to explain how evolution had taken place. He suggested that natural selection is the mainspring of evolution, continually
fitting plants and animals with great nicety to their fluctuating surroundings. This is what men of science call the Darwinian theory of
evolution. It is altogether independent of Darwin's demonstration that
evolution is the method by which the world has been peopled with living
creatures.

The modern biologist does not for a moment question the veracity
of the first of these two ideas which Darwin advanced. The fact that all
living creatures are products of some sort of evolutionary process is accepted by all reputable biologists as proven and no longer open to argument. That "theory" has their confidence for exactly the same sort of
reasons as impels all astronomers to accept the Copernican "theory" of
the organization of the solar system—all known facts of nature, and
there are literally millions of them, are in accord with it and explained
by it.

Darwin's second contribution, however, is on a very different basis.
His suggestion as to how evolution may have occurred has not with-
stood the tests applied by critical students. It is apparent now that the
hypothesis which he presented along this line must be radically changed
if not completely abandoned when the final statement of evolutionary

methods is at last constructed. And this statement cannot now be made. There are at present several "theories" of evolution, perhaps none of which will stand the tests of time. Each of them is under consideration; each has its supporters and each its opponents. Additional data concerning the processes of evolution are continually being amassed. Facts newly discovered serve to discredit or to support one or the other of these theories. Gradually the truth is being learned.

It is not surprising, therefore, that the layman, finding in scientific literature a record of these discussions and especially noting the current criticism of Darwin's ideas, should conclude that the "Darwinian theory," and with it the whole concept of evolution, is tottering toward its fall. He fails to appreciate the distinction which I have attempted to set forth in the preceding paragraphs. Current discussions about evolution, in which biologists today engage, are concerned with methods and processes; none of them even suggest the slightest doubt that all species have come into existence through evolution which in scientific circles everywhere is believed to be a basic law of nature.

In branding the evolutionary concept of life as "just a theory," many antievolutionists take a most extraordinary and peculiarly unstable position. They accept the theory as a sound one and adequately substantiated by facts, insofar as it pertains to plants and the lower animals; all these may have originated by evolution from simpler forms of life. But between them and man a great gulf is fixed; the human species alone is exempt from the evolutionary process and was created in some other way. Obviously, one who takes that view is not worried very much about evolution per se, but only about evolution as applied to man. Again, we get the clue that the objection to evolution is really based on some moral delinquency supposed to be inherent in its laws. . . .

Apparently one of the most widely held reasons for the modern distrust of science is the idea that evolution displaces God. Even though the evolutionist stoutly affirms that he believes in God, he is told that something is wrong with his mental processes and he should promptly and inevitably be an agnostic or an atheist. The psychology of the antievolutionist is such that he is almost unshaken in his certitude that acceptance of the evolutionary principle leads necessarily to the denial of God's presence in the world. To many, the title of Bergson's masterpiece "Creative Evolution" means that evolution is a power which men of science wish to enthrone in the place of God. In Carruth's well-known poem . . . there is the implication that God and Evolution are synonyms. . . . Obviously, from such suggestions, it is very easy to reach the conclusion that there is not room for both God and evolution in one's philosophy and that one must go.

But there is a tremendously significant fallacy in such reasoning. Evolution is not a power nor a force; it is a process, a method. God is a power, a force; he necessarily uses processes and methods in displaying his power and exerting force. Many of us believe that science is truly discovering in evolution the processes and methods which God, the spiritual power and eternal force, has used and is using now to effect his will in nature. We believe that the more we know about these processes and methods the more accurate knowledge we possess of the nature of God and of his will concerning man. It is in that sense that the scientist "thinks God's thoughts after him."

.   .   .   .

At least two of the avenues of thought we have followed in the attempt to gain the citadel of the anievolutionist's mind led to the suggestion that evolution when applied to man in some way involved a serious moral delinquency. Many have looked with great suspicion upon the doctrine of evolution for fear that it would lead them into an ethical dilemma. Christ's answer to the fundamental questions of life is phrased in terms of love and fellowship and self-sacrifice. For him the whole meaning of life is found in service to others. His philosophy was summarized in the command "that ye love one another." To many people, evolution means "the survival of the fittest in the struggle for existence." That is taken to imply that the selfish triumph, the most cruel and bloodthirsty are exalted, those who disregard others win. Obviously that would be the very antithesis of Christianity. Both principles cannot be true; one must be false. The Christian needs not to be told which of the two it is.

Here is a widespread concept which serves as a real reason for opposition to evolution. Men are not driven from it by the fear of discovering that their bodies are structurally like those of apes and monkeys. It does not bother us to discover that we are mammals. It would bother us to find such an implication that the law of progress as discovered by science is thus in opposition to the fundamental spirit of Christian doctrine.

It is of course evident to any honest thinker that even though the moral implications of evolution were in this regard opposed to Christian ethics, the Christian should not object to knowledge of them if they are sound deductions from demonstrable facts. Truth, unpleasant as well as pleasant, needs to be known if man is to be free. But before we decide that the only way to save civilization is to destroy it, let us investigate the facts to see if such conclusions are sound.

Historical geology surveys the road that leads from the unfathomable past to man and his present environment. As the forerunners of mankind have trod that road, successive milestones have been left behind. Survival values have differed at different crises in life development. One milestone was passed by vertebrates selected because they possessed the best apparatus for breathing air and thus were most fit to leave the aquatic environment of their ancestors and their comrades to advance upon the land. A little later, survival values were for a time measured in terms of armament, brute strength, and massive bulk; a host of cold-blooded reptiles dominated land and sea and sky during the Age of Reptiles. For the most part these were small-brained and large-bodied creatures who placed their trust in strength of talon and claw rather than in mentality and agility. Observing the earth at that time, one could not help but think that no good could possibly come from that welter of bloodthirstiness and cruelty. Yet there was present a small minority of ancestral mammals, physically puny and comparatively weak, who were specializing in care of offspring and in intelligent co-operation with each other. Weighed in the balance with the majority of powerful but witless reptiles, the mammals thus endowed with specific virtues were selected as fit to pass the milestone in earth history which marked the close of that geologic age.

Especially in the strain that leads to man has there been a progressive increase in breadth and depth of the spirit of co-operation and fellowship. The dawn of parental love occurred in comparatively recent geologic time; the classes of animals characterized by it are today dominant on the land and in the sky. Early in human history the spirit of the clan dominated the life of the individual. Gradually the co-operative units have increased in size until national solidarity has been achieved. The trend in human evolution is unmistakably toward Christ's ideal of brotherhood.

Animal organisms are distinguished from the unconscious crystal or rock by their consciousness; their actions are largely governed by instinct. Man is characterized by self-consciousness; his actions are largely governed by reason. The next upward step will achieve world-consciousness; reason will be replaced by love. The next milestone in the progress of life will be safely passed only by those who are skilled in the art of brotherliness. Survival values will be measured in terms of love and service.

The survival of the fittest does not necessarily mean the survival of the "fightingest." It has meant in the past, and I believe it means today and tomorrow, the survival of those who serve others most unselfishly. Even in evolution is it true that he who would save his life must lose it? Once more the man of science may stand shoulder to shoulder with the man of religion, working in co-operation toward the realization of the Christian hope.

The conclusion is inevitable. Opposition to the acceptance by the Christian of the evolutionary principle is based partly on misuse of the Bible, partly on misconceptions of what evolution really means, partly on unnecessary fears and faulty logic. There are probably only two real reasons which lead the antievolutionist to take his present position, and neither of these justifies the current attack upon all evolutionary science. It is possible to construct a strictly materialistic and mechanistic philosophy of evolution, but this is only one of several different evolutionary philosophies. Theologians should join forces with the believers in theistic evolution in the attempt to prove the latter more logical and more practical than any atheistic philosophy of life; the scientists need re-enforcement here just as much as the religious leaders need scientific methods and information when they seek to solve the problems of modern life. The fact that some evolutionists are materialists is no excuse for an attack upon all evolutionists; evolution is much less to blame for the spread of atheism than are the preachers whose sole aim is to preserve a tradition rather than to search for truth.

Similarly, it is true that evolution has been cited by some as justification for ruthless extermination of the weak and has been used as an excuse for untrammeled selfishness. But such use is unfair to evolution as it would be to Christianity. On the contrary, a true understanding of the role of service, the importance of co-operation, and the significance of love in the development of life during geologic history gives to evolution moral values of the finest Christian type. Instead of being an enemy to religion, evolution is really its staunchest ally.

From Kirtley F. Mather, "The Psychology of the Anti-Evolutionist," *The Harvard Graduates' Magazine,* XXV (September 1926), 8–20.

The Limitations of Science
Vernon Kellogg

In 1919 Vernon L. Kellogg, a professor of zoology at Stanford University
and a well-known author of treatises on evolution and Darwinism, became
secretary of the National Research Council in Washington. In the following
selection Kellogg applauds the achievements of modern science but cautions
his scientific colleagues about their tendency to make pronouncements regarding its "all-knowingness and all-mightiness." He reminded them of "some
of the things that science doesn't know" and characterized as bigots those
"narrow-minded devotees" who claimed that science "knows more than it does."
For all their sophistication, he concluded, scientists failed to explain satisfactorily either the origin of the species or the controlling causes of evolution.
And they were even less enlightening about such concerns of homo sapiens
as consciousness, conscience, and immortality. Disturbed by the implications
of the Scopes trial, Kellogg suggested that science and religion should be
complementary rather than antagonistic. Both were "realities of human life"
with legitimate claims upon truth. His essay, however, is noteworthy primarily as an effort by a professional scientist to deal candidly with the
limitations of science and the presumptuousness of its lay as well as professional friends. In the polemical atmosphere of the 1920s such efforts were
rare.

Occasionally I hear from some of my scientific colleagues, and even
more often from various enthusiastic lay friends of science, sweeping
and positive utterances regarding the all-knowingness and all-mightiness of modern science. I am even not unaccustomed to hearing myself
say something to the same effect.

. . . .

Truly, science is great and Einstein is its prophet. This is the
age of science, of scientific research and discovery, of homo scientificus.
I am glad to be living in it and proud of the amazing achievements of
my scientific colleagues. Only I sometimes wonder if we do not overlook—
when we have the opportunity to tell of the rapidly succeeding triumphs
of science and to show how very wide and inclusive scientific knowledge
is today—the fact that some groups of natural phenomena, and especially
some very important attributes of life, and particularly of human life,

have so far strenuously and successfully resisted the elucidating efforts
of scientific men, and hence cannot yet be included in our catalogue of
scientifically understood and explained things. It is to this fact that I
invite your attention.

As my experience in science is that of a biologist, a professed student
of living things, I have not hesitated to cast an inquiring eye on various
important attributes and certain significant behavior of human beings.
For to the thoroughgoing biologist human life is, nominally, just the
life of another living thing, larger than the grasshopper, smaller than
the elephant, related to the ape, although admittedly more complex
psychologically than any of these. So without attending at all to those
phenomena in the fields of physics and chemistry, of astronomy and
geology, which science has not explained—and they are very many and
very important—I shall limit my scrutiny and reference to certain phenomena in the field of biology, and especially the field of human biology,
which have so far been a puzzle to the explaining scientist.

We may begin with the puzzle of organic evolution. For despite all
the biologists know about evolution—and that is really a great deal—it
is, after all, still much of a puzzle. Certain interesting recent events
have recalled, in a seizing way, the matter of evolution to the attention
of all of us. For all of us read newspapers, and for the first time, perhaps,
since the days of Darwin, evolution has been on the front page of the
newspapers.

The events in Tennessee did not come to pass because of any special
interest in or enmity toward evolution in general, but because of evolution in particular, namely, the evolution of man. Aye, there's the rub!
The mere thought of man's cousinship to the apes leads, with many
people, to a temperature. But that is merely an item in the catalogue
of all those genealogical branches and twigs arising one from another
which make up the tree of organic evolution. There is evolution. Biologists know much of its course. There are little puzzles all along the
way of this course, but the big puzzle is not a genealogical one. It
is the fundamental one of how, of cause, of method. We are less confident today that we know the causal explanation of each of the two
co-ordinate major problems of evolution—to wit, the origin of species
and the adaptation of these species to their environment—than we were
fifty or sixty years ago.

In every decade since those days we have accumulated more proof of evolution, including more proof of the evolution of man, but we have also accumulated knowledge, especially some regarding the nature and behavior of heredity and variations, which tends to show that the old explanations of evolution do not explain it. The plausible and fascinating explanation of Lamarck, based on the assumed inheritance by offspring of changes acquired by the parents during the development and lifetime, is found to be insecurely based. Acquired characters, in the Lamarckian sense, are not inherited. Hence, new species and perfected adaptation do not come that way.

Similarly, the more widely accepted and apparently rigorously logical explanation of Darwin, based on the assumption of a life- or death-determining value of the actually occurring many small congenital variations, and of the hereditary transmission of these variations by the parents naturally selected on their basis, in the struggle for existence, is also seen to be more logical than real. Most of the "Darwinian variations" are neither of selective value nor are they inherited by their offspring. They are simply normal fluctuations, according to the law of probabilities, around a mean—fluctuations too small to determine individual fate, and not inherited in the degree of their departure from this mean.

Unfortunately, during this recent period of the undermining of the Lamarckian and Darwinian explanations of evolution we have not developed any convincing new explanation to take the place of the old ones. The most important new explanation offered is that of the so-called mutations theory, given some place in the sun chiefly through the work of De Vries, a Dutch botanist of great achievement. He observed the occurrence of congenital variations among the offspring of evening primrose parents growing side by side under similar environmental conditions, these variations not being the usual Darwinian fluctuations, but of more marked and radical character, and directly and continuously heritable. Other botanists have found similar mutations in other plants, and zoologists have found them among some animal species.

There seems to be no doubt that mutations can and do give rise to fixed new forms. But up to the present time they have been noted to occur in no such wholesale way as to make them satisfactory as a full explanation of species-forming. If they constituted the only, or even the principal, basis of the origin of species we ought to see thousands more of them among thousands of more kinds of animals and plants. This we do not see.

And when we try to explain adaptation—that equally important part of the whole evolution problem—by them, we simply get nowhere at all. Mutations, in order to produce gradual and finally complete adaptation, would have to move in right directions—which is equivalent to saying that there would have to be something to determine them to appear in just such a way as to lead to a cumulation of modification in precisely the direction necessary to produce adaptation. When one recalls the amazing comprehensiveness, complexity, and preciseness of many adaptations, one realizes that mutations, unaided, or even aided by natural selection, are out of the question as the producers of adaptation. Think only of the extraordinary reciprocal relations between many flowering plants and their cross-pollinating insect friends, and between hosts and their parasitic enemies, let alone all the marvels of other kinds of shifts for a living, protection, food-getting, reproducing, and what not else. Some directive factor is needed in any causal explanation of adaptation.

Face to face with this situation, then, namely, a present inability to explain satisfactorily either the origin of species or adaptation, by the inheritance of acquired characters or by natural selection or by mutations, biologists and natural philosophers have inevitably turned to conjecture, to speculation. Some of these conjectures have a more scientific seeming than others.

The paleontologists, for example, who have been greatly impressed by what may be called "straight lines" in the chronologic succession of plants and animals through geologic periods, are inclined—at least many of them are so inclined—to assume the occurrence of orthogenetic or determinate variation, itself determined either by special extrinsic or intrinsic influences working on successive generations of groups of organisms.

But they find it hard to reconcile their general disbelief in the inheritance of acquired characters with any assumption of the power of extrinsic, that is, environmental, influences, to explain straight-line variation and movement. Because for extrinsic influences to be able to do this, some mechanism must be discovered which will introduce their effects into inheritance.

Various biologists, students of present-day life, also accept the existence of determinate variation and try to find some explanation of its cause that does not land them in the objectionable—to them—situation of admitting the existence of some intrinsic power in living things—in fact, in the very life-stuff itself—which directs organic evolution in a definite path or paths. For to postulate any such cause is to assume a mystery.

However, some biologists, and more natural philosophers, have boldly assumed the existence of some intrinsic causing and directing force compelling evolution, and, indeed, evolution forward along definite lines, and upward toward ever more specialized, more perfected, higher forms of life. Indeed, when one faces the extraordinary development of adaptation, its amazing complexity and preciseness, and the inconceivability of its ever having come about through miscellaneous variation, one is almost irresistibly inclined to feel that some power wholly a mystery to us now has compelled and directed this development.

The rigorous-minded scientific man does not like the word mystery because of its popular connotation of permanent inexplicability, of being beyond human understandings. But if by mystery is to be meant something at present not understood but something to be investigated and sometime to be promoted, or degraded, into the realm of things understood, he accepts the word and even uses it. The origin of life is now a mystery, but the mechanist-biologists, who study life from the physico-chemical point of view, expect to elucidate it. They may never do it. This mystery may, indeed, be forever beyond human understanding. But human attempts to understand it will never be given up.

The biologists face, then, as we have noted, two major biological mysteries: one is the origin of life, the other the controlling causes of evolution. They do not know—science does not explain—how either comes to be.

Then there is that other great biological—and human—problem, which has had much attention for many years, and must have more attention for probably many years to come before, if ever, its solution will be in our hands. Once in our hands, however, we shall be able to make immediate use of it in directing our individual and societal behavior to most important ends. I refer to the problem of the relative influence of hereditary and environmental (including educational) conditions in determining individual and societal fate.

But with all this new knowledge of heredity, and the fillip it has

given to the claims made for the dominance of heredity over environment in determining individual outcome, we do not yet really know
enough to estimate justly the relative influence of these two great factors
in individual development. We do know only that each plays an important role in this all-important matter, and we do see more clearly than
we used to see that the role played by heredity must no longer be
overlooked, as it has sometimes been, in connection with attempts to
better the societal treatment and conditions of human beings. But we
certainly do not know anything that permits us to study heredity as a
factor in human fate independent of other factors. There is simply
no heredity without environment, and the disassociation in any study
of human biology or sociology of these two factors of evolution and
individual development can result only in a contribution to ignorance.

But the biologists face still other major phenomena associated with
life, especially with human life, of which there are at present no scientific explanations. The consciousness of human beings, their altruistic
emotions and actions going beyond all biological advantage, their imagination, and above all their spirit or soul—all are at present mysteries
of human biology. The identity, or at least close similarity, of human
structure, human physiology, and certain human instincts, with those
of lower animals, must be admitted. The evolutionist sees humankind
the resultant of the natural processes which have brought into existence
the many kinds of animals and plants, yet he sees this humankind reveal
certain attributes and capacities the possession of which he does not
dare to claim is scientifically explained. At best he may only dare to
declare that it will be scientifically explained. Well, that is an expression
of opinion. Another's opinion may be the opposite.

In connection with these phenomena let us glance at the biologist
and evolutionist in two places: in his laboratory, and in his home and
community. We have all given some attention to the scientific man in
his laboratory. We know his behavior there, and the point of view, the
natural philosophy, which determines this behavior. But have we given
as much attention to him in his home, as a member of a family, of a
church, perhaps, of human society in its various organized and unor-
ganized forms? Or, if we have given him attention here, have we
thought of the significance of what we observe?

If we do give some close attention to him in this latter setting we
shall be rather amazed. He reveals himself, usually, as a bundle of

interesting inconsistencies. How readily he sloughs off his rigorous laboratory manner. How easily he accepts the reality and the guidance, in his behavior, of human attributes whose existence no scientific knowledge explains or rationalizes. He does not merely mate: he finds some woman to adore. He regards his children with a love far transcending in its manifestation that rational care of them indicated by instinct or by reason as necessary to maintain the human species. He adds to his instinct for gregariousness a reasoned organization of family, society, and nation. To any instinctive pleasure in pleasant sounds, or any biologically advantageous use of them, he adds a highly technical development of music; he possesses not only a marvelous capacity for its creation but a marvelous spiritual appreciation of it. He does not stop with a biologically useful development of speech and writing and picture-making, but he produces a great literature of prose and poetry, and interminable galleries of paintings and sculpture. He goes far beyond the biological demands of protection and comfort in building houses; he erects cathedrals and architectural memorials to satisfy a dominating desire to worship a God in heaven and to glorify human demigods on earth.

How little, how restricted, seem the explanations of the mechanist-biologists and the behavioristic psychologists of some of the simpler phases of human physiology and psychology, in the face of the glorified capacities of mankind in the fields of societal organization, of art and literature and mathematics and logic and religion! It is in the realm of what science doesn't know that lie all these human capacities which really distinguish and define the very thing that humanness is. It is not being a vertebrate and a mammal and a primate: it is not his zoological characteristics and classification, known to science, that define man—they tell where he came from and who or what are his animal cousins—but it is his attributes that science doesn't know about that really make man man.

This is not to decry what science does know about man—his structure, his physiology, his psychology. This is not to withhold due recognition of the interest and importance of the discoveries the mechanist-biologists have made with regard to the part that physics and chemistry play in vital processes. It is not to underrate, in any degree, the highly important things that the biological student has found out about variation, development, heredity, the effects of environmental influence, selection, evolution—all of them fundamental factors in human as well as in plant and animal life. Great progress has been made in the last three quarters of a century, and especially in the last quarter century, in increasing knowledge along all these lines.

And equally great progress has been made in developing applications of biological knowledge for the benefit of human welfare. Think of the startling advances in recent years of the applied biological sciences of medicine, sanitation, agriculture, forestry, and applied psychology with its powerful new light on problems of education, criminology, vocational selection. The scientific men who are stressing today in speech and writing the importance of the new information that the science of human biology has to offer the sociologist, the teacher, the jurist, and the statesman are fully justified in their insistence that this new information must not be disregarded. They are not justified only at those times when they give the impression, as some of them do, that science knows more than it really does about human life; that science alone can guide us in our individual and societal behavior.

In a recent magazine article about a well-known scientific friend of mine the author quotes this friend as explaining, in answer to the question "What is science doing for you and me?" that "Science has enabled man to travel fifty times as fast, accomplish a hundred times as much work in a day, lift a weight a thousand times as heavy, and make his voice heard ten thousand times as far as he could without science." Which is all very exciting and interesting. But another answer of a different sort, but also true, could be given. It might run like this:

> Science has not enlightened me to any satisfactory degree about my consciousness or my conscience; has not told me why I can compose or play or deeply enjoy music—except that it says part of the reason is that my father or mother or other ancestors could, that is, that I inherit this capacity, which is only pushing the original question back to be asked about the musical ancestor. Science has not told me why I love my little girl so extravagantly; nor why I can write poetry—if I can; nor, and perhaps this is the question I put to it most often and most insistently and most want answered, whether I have an immortal soul or not.

What does science, what does the student of human biology, have to say to us about immortality? The answer is, in effect, nothing. Science describes to us the fact of bodily death. It follows the fate of the lifeless body in distressing detail. But whether this ends the human—or for that matter the plant or animal individuality—science does not know. While some hardy scientific men declare that it does, science as a whole takes the agnostic position. Ignoramus.

Certainly science does not—although a few scientific men do—accept the various alleged proofs that the spiritists have offered of life or soul-persistence after death. But while science has no proofs that enable it to declare that there is spirit-persistence after death, it would be an unscientific scientist who would declare that there is not, nor can be, such persistence. To do that would be for the scientist to make a foolish assumption; no less an assumption than that he is acquainted with the whole order of nature—which he is not—and that immortality is not a part of this order.

Science does not assume that it knows—despite the great deal that it does know—more than a very small part of the order of nature. The constant effort of science is to know more. Research—one hears the word everywhere and all the time now—research in the universities, research in special research institutes, research patronized by scientific societies and academies and by the great philanthropic foundations, research fellowships and research professorships. All this feverish activity of research, and all this wide and generous support of it, mean a recognition by scientific men, and by the public as well, of the high importance of scientific knowledge, but also mean a recognition of the present limitations of scientific knowledge. It means that there is a great deal to find out, a great deal that science doesn't know and that all of us want known.

Research is making great conquests. We are cumulating knowledge rapidly. And all such cumulation, passed on by social inheritance to successive generations, makes possible further cumulation more rapidly and more comprehensively. No wonder scientific men, as they survey the conquests already made over ignorance, and those now making, proudly make large claims of final victory over all the still unknown. And the general public, already greatly impressed—and rightly so—by the actual large achievements of science, inclines a sympathetic ear to these claims.

But as a scientific man, and one proud of the achievements of science so far and certain of further and perhaps even more striking achievement by it in the future, I want to express a scientific doubt about the probability of science's some day knowing everything. It would, indeed, be a sad day for science if such a day were to come, because the joy of science is not in knowing, but in finding out. There is much joy, then, ahead for scientific workers, for there is so very much that science doesn't know now.

The only thing we know now about many things in human life is that they are attributes of human beings and of human beings alone. By such attributes are we really distinguished from other creatures. We are arisen from other creatures, but we are different from them. We are like them in structure and physiology and share with them certain psychological possessions. But we are different from them in possessing capacities unique with us. And these unique capacities are the greatest things in life. I believe that most scientific men recognize them as such, recognize them as greater than that very great thing, science itself.

Outside of science is religious belief. Science has been often pictured as intolerant of religion, even subversive of religion. It should not be. There are bigots both among scientists and among those of religious faith. These bigots make dogmatic and irritating declarations. They condemn each other to purgatory. One group would keep the home fires of the Inquisition burning; the other would gladly try the effects of experimentally submitting a Bryan to the temperature of absolute zero. Neither group helps anybody to any understanding.

Scientific men may be ardent apostles of Jesus or Mohammed; some are. Religious leaders may welcome every new advance of science; some do. Science may be truth and so may religion. Science and religion coexist. Both are realities in human life. They should not be looked on as antagonistic or as displacing each other. They should be looked on as complementary. A full human life includes both, depends on both.

The cause of things may be called God; the manner of things, science. Science has never explained ultimate causes. It doesn't know ultimate causes. It explains much of the course of things, whose existence it accepts because it sees them exist. It is gratifying that science knows as much as it does. It is unfortunate when its too narrow-minded devotees claim that it knows more than it does. And it is wholly unnecessary for the glorification of science, and entirely unconvincing, for any such devotee to claim that it will sometime know everything.

Science steadily gains more knowledge of the ways of nature; it as persistently knows no more about the ultimate cause of nature than it did when the Greeks and Egyptians, Cro-Magnon or Neanderthal men, made their beginnings of scientific knowing. Primal being and ultimate becoming are beyond the purview of science. They are truly something that science doesn't know, and I very much doubt will ever know.

From Vernon F. Kellogg, "Some Things Science Doesn't Know," *World's Work*, LI (March 1926), 523–529.

Two Kinds of Knowledge
Charles A. Dinsmore

Charles Allen Dinsmore was pastor of the First Congregational Church in Waterbury, Connecticut, for fifteen years prior to his professorial appointment in the Yale Divinity School in 1920. Two years after his appointment, he delivered the McNair Lectures at the University of North Carolina where he discussed the general topic of "religious certitude in an age of science." The following selections from two of his lectures indicate that he, like other liberal theologians of the era, believed religion was indebted to science and the scientific spirit "working upon the documents of our faith." Dinsmore was critical of dogmatism in both science and religion and urged religionists to respect the contributions of science. But he refused to admit that science had a monopolistic claim on knowledge. "The contrast between science and religion," he concluded, "is not a contrast between knowledge and belief, but between two different kinds of knowledge." Undoubtedly many individuals troubled by the apparent conflict between science and religion saw in Dinsmore's position the basis for a reconciliation between the claims of the two. Zealous fundamentalists, however, vehemently protested the lectures as a wholesale capitulation by a theologian to the demands of science.

———◆•◆———

The spirit of science working upon the documents of our faith has given us a new Bible, immeasurably more human, significant, and real than that which the first settlers brought to these shores. In no irreverent spirit, but actuated by the most earnest desire to find out the truth, the most competent men in historical research—and they are earnestly Christian men—tell us that the former theory of plenary inspiration of the scriptures is no longer tenable. These scholars find that God has not left himself without a witness among any people, but to the Jews he gave a special insight into the things of the spirit. Their great men were not generals or philosophers, but prophets. They interpreted God through nature indeed, but pre-eminently through the moral and spiritual nature of man. They conceived of an ethical deity, a righteous and merciful God, Lord of the whole earth, who was using the nations in the interest of a redeemed humanity. The Bible is the record of the growing insight, and the accumulated experiences with the Eternal, of a uniquely endowed people. The Koran gives the point of

208

view of one man, occupying a moment only in the process of history. The Analects of Confucius give the moral judgments of a single genius, at a definite period of time. The sacred books of India and Persia contain much noble philosophy and many penetrating intuitions of rare value. But the Bible is the only sacred book in the world that represents a righteous God working through long periods of history for the moral redemption of mankind.

. . . .

Our fathers interpreted the Bible in much the same manner which a lawyer uses in interpreting the statutes. . . . It was all an exact statement of fact and truth, and was to be so understood. The King James version was printed as prose, and it was not until a hundred years later that it was discovered that the psalms were poetry both in form and spirit. It has also been ascertained that the Hebrews, like all ancient people, conceived and stated truths in forms of the imagination. Therefore we have in their literature fable, parable, legend, the traditions which mothers told to their children at eventide, the proverbs of their wise men, the songs of warriors, the allegories, the idylls, the stories by which literary men enforced important truths. The discovery that the Bible is a library of many volumes, of many different types of literature, has led scholars to interpret the different books by their appropriate canon. Consequently we know much more accurately than did the men of a few generations ago precisely how God dealt with this people.

. . . .

[One] method by which science has influenced religious thought is through the introduction of the scientific spirit and the scientific method into theology. Let us bear in mind that theology is ever to be distinguished from religion, as botany is distinct from flowers. Theology is our theory of religion, as botany is the science of flowers.

The theologies of the past have been discarded one by one, not through lack of logical articulation, but because these mighty structures were reared upon shaky premises. Discredit the major premise and the superstructure collapses. Grown wise by the experience of the past, and thoroughly imbued with the scientific spirit, our leading thinkers in the religious world do not assume some broad generalization, such as the fall of man, or the sovereign decrees of the Almighty, upon which to build imposing systems of thought. On the contrary, they are keeping very close to facts of human experience; they deal almost exclusively with the near end of truth. And while undoubtedly their interpretations of the facts and truths may change with advancing knowledge, the foundations are secure. Their appeal is not to dogma, but to life.

.   .   .   .

In former days when religion dwelt in a gloomy tenement of uncharitable dogmatism, and science lived in a new and somewhat shaky house across the way, they did shout invectives at each other. But that time is passing. There are common premises upon which they can live together in peace, with science on the ground floor and religion supplying the motive and the home atmosphere.

The common house is the spirit of man. Man is the reconciliation of science and religion. Science shows him the laws of the world in which he lives and which he must obey. But above this order of time and sense there is another world of values and spiritual forces whch he knows as truly as he knows the temporal order. Here he finds an interpretation of the meaning of the life, a refuge in times of distress, lofty motives which hold him true to his ideals, and power pouring into his being from the reservoirs of the Unseen.

All scientific minds of the first rank are religious in their purpose of utter loyalty to the truth, and in their emotion of wonder, reverence, and humility; and many of them have possessed to the full the consolation and the strength which a spiritual vision of man and the universe gives.

.   .   .   .

There is only one attitude for a religious man to take in this age of science. Let him not stand with closed mind and closed fist in front of the venerable theories and systems of the fathers, determined to defend them to the last breath. Rather let him remember that the Holy Spirit is the spirit of truth, and that he works wondrously in every age. His glory shines not only from the pages of the Old and the New Testament, but also from the oldest testament written by the finger of frost and fire in the rocks, and from the newest testament as he discloses his nature and purposes through the minds of saints and seers who have lived since the canon of the scriptures closed. If we believe in the Holy Ghost, we must believe that more of his light will ever break from every testament. All light comes from one source and harmonizes with itself; let us receive it with gladness.

No one believes more profoundly than I do in the faith once delivered to the saints. It has been handed down from generation to generation by a glorious succession of redeemed men and women. The essentials of that faith can be realized in experience and cannot be overthrown. But these unchanging truths are interpreted in every age according to the language and point of view of that period. Therefore the forms of religious philosophy are constantly being modified, yet the substance changes not.

Science will greatly modify our theories and speculations; she can never disturb the deeper interests of the soul. Man is incurably religious. He is a little creature living in a universe terrible in its vastness and in its power. He asks great questions. He cannot be persuaded that they will remain unanswered. He will never believe that he has light to find his way amid the things that are temporal, only to lose it amid the things eternal. Confidently he will ever hold that the light within him, and in the spiritual geniuses of history, is the true light, given for safe guidance.

The tragedy of history has been that the church has so often mistaken the temporary form of her faith for the eternal substance. She has neglected her gospel of love in her fierce zeal for dogma.

.   .   .   .

What I wish to claim is this: Science does not have knowledge and religion simple faith. The lover, the artist, the musician know, so does the saint. Religion has always used the word "knowledge" freely and always will, because no lesser term expresses her experiences. Both science and religion begin with an act of faith. Both reach results. Those of science are sufficiently verified for a man to base his actions and his civilization upon them. Those of religion are so tested that one can build his whole life upon them with ever increasing satisfaction both to his mind and to his soul.

There is this difference to be noted between scientific and religious knowledge. A scientific experiment may be performed in an hour and its results demonstated, but moral and spiritual truths require centuries for their vindication. We believe in liberty so implicitly that we consider no sacrifice too great to conserve it, yet to establish beyond cavil that freedom of thought and speech is better than intellectual servitude would require the whole range of human history. In a very short time you can prove that two atoms of hydrogen will unite with one of oxygen to form water; but to validate the statement that righteousness exalteth a nation demands the experience of many generations. Yet am I more positive of the one than of the other? Shall I affirm of the former, "I know," and of the latter, "I believe?" Any such distinction would do violence to our convictions and to our habitual use of language.

Moreover, scientific knowledge is independent of the personal equation. A murderer can perform a chemical experiment as well as a saint. Religion, on the other hand, is more personal. Its knowledge is conditional on character. Only the pure in heart can see God; only the unselfish and obedient can realize his love.

.   .   .   .

Science can neither affirm nor deny immortality, but she has opened great spaces for this faith to live in. A man trained to our modern world-vision, gazing back over the long, toilsome, costly process from the fire mist up to man, and from primitive man to our present highly organized society, cannot readily believe that he is contemplating the haphazard whirl of unintelligent forces, a riot of chance! Rather he detects an increasing purpose running through the ages, working towards man and the development of the race. Surely the unfolding purpose is prophetic of an outcome worthy of the process. If materialism is right, and humanity returns to the dust from whence it came, and the earth is at last only a burned-out cinder; if the struggle of the ages, the prayers of the holy, the sacrifices of the martyrs, the devotion of the brave, ultimate in dust and ashes, then we are put to "permanent intellectual confusion." The ages have toiled and brought forth nothing. The Eternal has blown a soap bubble, and painted it with wondrous colors at awful cost of agony to the iridescent figures, then allowed it to burst! The wisdom, the power, the sacrificial love revealed in the long and orderly upward movement create the expectation that the culmination will be worthy of the cost.

The evolutionary hypothesis gives to this argument another turn. There was a time when the highest form of life upon the planet was a jellylike mass, floating about in the water. It was without power of locomotion, sightless, senseless, capable only of absorbing such food particles and the primeval ocean drifted against it. But the push of nature was in it. As the centuries and millenniums passed, life acquired the power of locomotion; it developed the faculty of vision; it accumulated experiences, becoming conscious and then self-conscious; it attained the noble faculty of reason; it distinguished sensations, and choosing between them, became aware of freedom; it formed glorious ideals of a nobler self; it began to crave to be fashioned in the likeness of the Perfect Righteousness, to commune with the Infinite Goodness, and to crown all these achievements it dreamed of immortality! In this steady acquisition of riches there is a foreshadowing of the future. If life in its long upward journey has acquired locomotion, sense-perception, reason, consciousness, self-determination, a feeling of moral responsibility, it is not incredible that when it thirsts for immortality the craving is a prophecy that the desire will be satisfied.

.   .   .   .

Let me sum up the argument of this lecture. The contrast between science and religion is not a contrast between knowledge and belief, but between two different kinds of knowledge. Religion can use the word "know" as legitimately as science. When we become aware of ourselves we are aware of a power not ourselves. By co-operating with this power we can develop characters of moral strength and spiritual beauty. Virtue and its transforming energies we know as well as we know any scientific fact, even better for we have the sure test of daily experience. Experience warrants us in affirming that God is the "Power, not ourselves, which makes for righteousness." We take a step further. Power is an anthropomorphic term, and so is personal spirit; but the latter is more significant, it represents higher worth. God cannot be inferior to the highest symbol we use in interpreting him. God cannot be less than personal; he may be infinitely more. By faith, therefore, we think of him as a living spirit operating through the electric framework of the world. When we seek him as the Father of our spirit in whom dwells all that we desire, we put this belief to the searching test of life. Thus trusting and obeying we meet with those responses which change faith into an assurance which often finds even the word "know" too feeble to express the experience.

We may know the redemptive energies summed up under the name of Jesus Christ, and our deepening knowledge of him will lead to a high faith in the significance of his nature.

Science can neither affirm nor deny a life hereafter, but if man

in his long journey has made such marvelous progress, and now aspires
to something further on, it is a rational faith to believe that when

> The white sail of the soul
> Rounds the mystic cape,
> The promontory death,

it will move in brave adventure over the deep until it comes to a blessed
country where a glorious company look upon the very face of God.

From Charles A. Dinsmore, *Religious Certitude in an Age of Science* (Chapel
Hill: University of North Carolina Press, 1924), pp. 20–24, 28–29, 31–35,
89–91, 100–102.

Fundamentalism is the most sinister force that has yet attacked the freedom of teaching.

JOSEPH V. DENNEY, 1923

We must have an intelligence established on faith, built in prayer, and nourished by good will.

HENRY N. SHERWOOD, 1925

Without God, is it education?

BENJAMIN S. WINCHESTER, 1927

4. Embattled Academe

THE decade following World War I was a critical era in the history of American education. The war itself had varied and profound effects upon the nation's schools and colleges. It dramatized the educational needs of a people living in a technological age and prompted many educators to question whether the existing schools could equip men to meet the problems of modern society. Their search for a more effective educational orientation, which was apparent in the numerous innovations in pedagogical theory, curriculum, and teacher training, coincided with rapidly rising enrollments at all levels, from the elementary school through the university. But not only were more people attending schools in the 1920s, they were receiving instruction from a new generation of teachers more familiar with the methods and results of modern scholarship and conscious of the importance of academic freedom to their profession. Their formal training, as well as the general disillusionment bred by the war, served to lessen their faith in the sufficiency of traditional educational formulas. The younger teachers in the 1920s were primarily interested "in creating critical-minded students and in giving educational processes effectiveness in our complex modern life."[1] Walter Lippmann summarized the differences between the old and new concepts of edu-

[1] Howard K. Beale, *A History of Freedom of Teaching in American Schools* (New York: Charles Scribner's Sons, 1941), p. 236.

cation when he remarked: "The child is not taught to believe. He is taught to doubt and to inquire, to guess, to experiment, and to verify. The teacher no longer pretends to transmit wisdom. Instead he strives to develop wise habits."[2]

This new concept of education not only disturbed those wedded to educational tradition but also ran afoul of the widespread fear of criticism nurtured by the war. It was often viewed as the equivalent of modernism in religion. And those who warned clergymen to "stick to the fundamentals" and avoid substituting social service for the gospel were likely to make similar demands upon teachers. Americans anxious about the moral standards of their children were inclined to be as forceful in their exhortations to teachers as to ministers. Their assumption that the values of the future generation were largely determined by the state-supported school was itself perhaps a tacit admission of the waning influence of the church. At any rate, the various defenders of orthodoxy—whether they represented patriotic societies, chambers of commerce, or fundamentalist religious groups—simultaneously sought to insure the perpetuation of their ideals by forcing schools to conform to them.

Although each of these groups concentrated on achieving a specific aim, their tactics and over-all goal were remarkably similar. They tended to identify virtually any departure from traditional methods and concepts with an ideology alien to the American Way and attempted to eliminate such heresies by statute. Legislation might be enacted to guarantee the patriotism of students and loyalty oaths created to require teachers to confirm their belief in capitalism and private property; but for many Americans these legal devices, though important, failed to touch upon something more basic to the preservation of "safe and sane" values among the future generation. In their view, such a task necessitated safeguards for the theological precepts which determined these moral values. Regardless of the difficulties raised by the principle of separation of church and state, the classrooms of publicly supported educational institutions, no less than those of the denominational schools, were to serve as the chief agencies for perpetuating a morality undergirded by orthodox theology. The school became a prime target for

---

[2] Walter Lippmann, *American Inquisitors: A Commentary on Dayton and Chicago* (New York: Macmillan, 1928), p. 84.

various elements dedicated to leading America "back to the Bible, Christ, and the Constitution."[3]

Throughout the 1920s religious fundamentalists were as active in combating what they considered "intellectual flapperism" in the schools as in waging warfare against modernism in the church. Their principal fire was directed at the teaching of evolution, which to them symbolized an amalgam of undesirable trends and phenomena in education responsible for the "moral bankruptcy" of modern society. The Bible Crusaders of America credited the religious infidelity of modern education to a vast conspiracy of agnostics, modernists, and evolutionists bent upon controlling schools as well as churches. "Now, it is no secret," remarked J. E. Conant, an active figure in the fundamentalist crusade, "that the Church and the Schools, broadly speaking, are in serious conflict with each other today."[4] In discussing the dangers inherent in modern education, Mayor John F. Hylan of New York warned against the practice "of inculcating in the plastic minds of the young such ideas, theories and hypotheses, not facts, which . . . may create a spirit of irreverence and sow the seeds of doubt where only those of faith should be planted."[5] In a similar vein Governor Cameron Morrison of North Carolina maintained that something was radically wrong with an educational system which "unsettled the religious faith our children."[6] The atmosphere of suspicion created by such anxiety meant that even teachers who displayed "prudence" toward the convictions of their students and patrons sometimes became victims of zealous "inquisitors." Yet, as one informed observer noted, "very frequently the difficulty arose because the teacher had failed to teach, and had insisted . . . on announcing strange and unpalatable doctrines which he held to be the truth."[7]

Although by 1920 secular education in state schools had largely replaced religious instruction in denominational institutions, many

[3] During the 1920s the Bible Crusaders of America waged its campaign under this slogan.

[4] J. E. Conant, *The Church, The Schools and Evolution* (Chicago: Moody Bible Institute Colportage Association, 1922), p. 9.

[5] John F. Hylan to William Jennings Bryan, June 21, 1923, William Jennings Bryan Papers (Manuscript Division, Library of Congress).

[6] "Warning from a Former Governor," *Crusaders' Champion*, I (January 15, 1926), 23.

[7] Lippmann, *American Inquisitors*, p. 94.

Americans questioned whether secular education could discharge the moral tasks previously performed by church schools. The experience of World War I and the "moral shabbiness" of the postwar era in general tended to increase their doubts. A more specific cause of their alarm was the findings published in James H. Leuba's study of religious beliefs prevalent on college campuses and statements by students who testified to the anti-Christian orientation of modern education. "The faith I had in my Bible is about all gone," one recent college graduate explained in 1921, "because in the classroom the Bible has been torn to pieces and Nothing Has Been Given Me To Take Its Place."[8] The fundamentalists determined to rectify this situation by requiring greater emphasis upon religious instruction in public institutions of learning and by ridding both denominational and public schools of all "teachings," teachers, and textbooks likely to weaken faith in the "old-time religion" which was essential to their conception of morality. Among the "teachings" none appeared more pervasively dangerous to the orthodox faith and its moral precepts than evolution. Despite all their efforts to demonstrate that evolution was "a mere guess" which teachers had no right to teach as a scientific fact, fundamentalists were less interested in whether evolution was right or wrong than in its effect upon religious faith. Whether true or false, evolution was "harmful to those who accept it" and should be banned because of its devastating effect upon man's spiritual life.[9]

Fundamentalists operated on the assumption that evolution was not a scientific question at all. Rather it was a religious question which invalidated the Christian concept of man. Precisely because of the religious connotations of evolution, they argued, the teaching of Darwin's theory in tax-supported schools was an unholy union of church and state. When fundamentalists themselves were charged with violating the principle of church-state separation, as they often were, they usually responded with one of two lines of argument: on some occasions, they claimed that if the state had no authority to teach Christianity, it likewise had no right to teach anti-Christianity under the guise of biological evolution; on other occasions, they turned the charge against their

[8] Quoted in Charles M. Sheldon to William Jennings Bryan, June 20, 1921, Bryan Papers.

[9] Lawrence Levine, *Defender of the Faith: William Jennings Bryan, The Last Decade, 1915–1925* (New York: Oxford University Press, 1965), p. 281.

critics by asserting that because "the teaching of organic evolution is teaching religion,"[10] evolutionists rather than antievolutionists were the real violators of historic principle. Fundamentalists defended their efforts to eliminate evolution from public schools supported by Christian taxpayers as a modern version of Thomas Jefferson's fight to free dissenting sects from being taxed to support an established church whose doctrines were repugnant to them. They insisted that their aim was not to infringe upon the rights of a minority of evolutionists, atheists, and agnostics, but to gain equal protection for the rights of the majority of American taxpayers who, by their calculations, were overwhelmingly orthodox Christians opposed to the teaching of evolution as detrimental to the religious faith of their children. In all sincerity, therefore, the fundamentalists could view the antievolution crusade as a democratic effort, a mightly struggle for "religious liberty," which expressed the "highest form of patriotism."

An impressive array of spokesmen both inside and outside the academic field challenged the fundamentalists' position as wholly incompatible with the principles of individual liberty and democracy. More specifically, they described the campaign to ban the teaching of evolution as inimical to the basic premises of American education because it struck at the heart of intellectual freedom and indeed threatened the essentials of liberal education itself. It marked an ominous step toward "educational serfdom." Although antievolutionists contended that they were primarily interested in preventing the teaching of a theory as a fact, their opponents hastened to classify such arguments as fallacious. They argued that any restriction on the teaching of evolution, however mild, would have the practical effect of prohibiting all discussion of the subject. In their view fundamentalists proposed to insure morality by resorting to "un-American means" and by forcing teachers to compromise their obligations "to present the truth as his training has led him to see" it.[11] Such a compromise by the teacher was itself immoral.

Educators active in the opposition to the antievolution movement

[10] *North Carolina Lutheran,* V (January 1927), 4.

[11] See *The Bulletin of the American Association of University Professors,* XI (January 1925), 93–94; Harry Chase, "Address to the Student Body," February 1925, University of North Carolina Papers (Southern Historical Collection, University of North Carolina at Chapel Hill).

employed several tactics in attempting to refute the charge that modern education was an enemy of orthodox Christianity. One approach was to maintain that the teaching of evolution, as well as other scientific theories, provided "powerful aids to religious faith" by clarifying "the power and Glory of God as manifested in His Works in the Universe." Another approach focused upon the unity of truth. "It is all God's truth," President Harry W. Chase of the University of North Carolina explained. "And I cannot believe that God is afraid of the sincere effort on the part of man to find out how He made the World."[12] As tangible evidence of their interest in the spiritual welfare of students, officials of state-supported colleges publicized the campus activities of denominational groups and the Young Men's Christian Association. President Frank L. McVey of the University of Kentucky assured the people of his state that "the morals, ideals and spiritual attitudes" of his student body could "not be excelled anywhere."[13] The proliferation of such statements by college executives during the 1920s revealed their growing anxiety about the mounting criticism by fundamentalists.

Such assurances by no means satisfied those convinced that the modern educational system was breeding religious infidelity. As a result both legislative and nonlegislative pressures were exerted upon schools in an attempt to effect a remedy. The most obvious of these corrective efforts were laws which required Bible reading and prohibited the teaching of evolution in public schools. No less significant and far more numerous were regulations by school boards, educational administrators, and college trustees, designed to eliminate from the classroom teachers and textbooks considered dangerous to the precepts of the orthodox Christian faith. In many areas community opinion or the mere threat of such legislative or regulatory actions was sufficient to achieve conformity. For public school teachers, dismissal was often the price of nonconformity. The National Education Association, long dominated by school administrators, refused to adopt a stand which encouraged teachers to take the risk, even if they had been so inclined. In contrast, the American Association of University Professors, an organization founded in 1914 and dedicated to the preservation of academic freedom, was far more active in asserting and defending the

12 Chase, "Address to the Student Body."

13 See Frank L. McVey, *The Gates Open Slowly: A History of Evolution in Kentucky* (Lexington: University of Kentucky Press, 1949), Appendix C, pp. 292–295.

rights and privileges of college teachers. Even so, numerous college professors, classified as evolutionists, modernists, agnostics, or some other form of "infidel," became the focus of controversies which frequently resulted either in their silence or dismissal. The retention of professorial positions by those who refused either to be silenced or to conform was generally hailed by the champions of academic freedom as a great triumph.

At issue obviously were two widely different views regarding the aims and content of education. Those professional spokesmen for modern education, interested in the establishment of a better social order, envisioned the school as an agency to develop a "capacity for life in a changing, growing world," by sharpening the individual's facility for independent, critical judgment.[14] Exposure to a variety of viewpoints, including those contrary to local mores and opinion, was necessary to accustom students to form their own judgments out of the conflicting forces present in American culture. If children were to escape the "inherited burden of ignorance," teachers trained in their respective fields, rather than nonprofessional laymen, should furnish the educational concepts and determine the curriculum of the schools. Religious fundamentalists, on the contrary, were concerned with the moral, rather than the social, aims of education. Hence the school curriculum, declared Clarence E. MacCartney, a spokesman of the orthodox wing of the Northern Presbyterian church, should include "definite instruction as to the existence of God, . . . morality, and . . . the moral nature of man."[15] Fundamentalists believed that the emphasis upon social goals in education was as misplaced as the emphasis upon the Social Gospel in religion. Sociology, they liked to proclaim, was no substitute for the gospel; morality must rest squarely upon the sanctions of orthodox Christianity rather than any secular foundation. Anything which cast doubt upon the tenets of the orthodox faith necessarily threatened moral standards and should be eliminated from the schools. And since the heart, not the mind, was the more important to this faith, the layman—the Christian taxpayer and parent—was as capable of judging what should be

[14] See R. Freeman Butts and Lawrence A. Cremin, *A History of Evolution in American Culture* (New York: Holt, Rinehart and Winston, 1953), Chapter 15; Beale, *A History of Freedom of Teaching in American Schools*, pp. 235–236.

[15] Quoted in "Shall We Force Religion Into the Public Schools," *The Forum*, LXXVII (June 1927), 816.

taught to insure the high moral standards as were intellectuals or professionally trained teachers. Fundamentalists vehemently denied that restrictions upon the teaching of evolution constituted an infringement upon the teacher's freedom. Bryan stated their position when he asserted that as individuals teachers were at liberty "to think as they please and to say what they like," but they had "no right to demand pay for teaching that which the parents and taxpayers do not want taught."[16] To compel children to attend schools where evolution was taught infringed, not upon the freedom of teachers, but upon the liberty of parents to direct the education, especially the religious instruction, of their children. Fundamentalists such as Bryan insisted that their position was legally sustained by the decision in the case of Pierce *v.* Society of Sisters in 1925. The decision, Bryan asserted, affirmed "the right of the parent to guard the religious welfare of the child and this . . . is decisive in our case."[17]

Although the fundamentalists were able to secure the passage of antievolution laws in only five states, it would be erroneous to assume that their effort to make the school a guardian of traditional morality and piety was largely a failure. What they failed to achieve by statewide statute was often accomplished by local regulations and administrative actions. Equally impressive was their success in using legislation to insure religious instruction or at least Bible reading in public schools. It is interesting to note that many states which refused to pass antievolution laws enacted measures to make Bible reading compulsory. Perhaps Bible reading was an acceptable alternative for the less combative fundamentalists who, though disturbed by the nonreligious orientation of education, considered movements to outlaw the teaching of biological evolution as likely to create more problems than they solved. The spectacle of the Scopes trial in 1925 strengthened popular skepticism regarding "monkey laws." Interestingly enough, in 1926, the year after the trial, eleven states made Bible reading compulsory while only one state enacted an antievolution law. Nor were the repercussions of the fundamentalist campaign confined to elementary and secondary education. The curricula of colleges and universities occasionally underwent adjustments as a result of the fundamentalist thrust.

Whatever the significance of their specific achievements, fundamen-

16 Levine, *Defender of the Faith,* p. 278.
17 William Jennings Bryan to Governor Austin Peay, June 27, 1925, Bryan Papers.

talists did focus attention upon the moral task of education. Their particular formula for its fulfillment well may have been unacceptable, but it forced educators to confront the issue and to search for bases upon which schools could legitimately perform the task in a pluralistic society.

Education Without Morality
William Jennings Bryan

In 1921 William Jennings Bryan delivered the Sprunt Lectures at Union Theological Seminary in Richmond, Virginia. Published under the title *In His Image,* these lectures constituted the most comprehensive statement of the theological position of the most famous lay spokesman of fundamentalism during the 1920s. In the following excerpts from this work Bryan makes clear his conception of education and his concern for the lack of moral content in the modern educational curriculum. Like most fundamentalist crusaders, he cited Professor James H. Leuba's study (1916) to support his contention that unbelief was spreading rapidly among the educated. The purpose of education, Bryan maintained, was not only to train the mind but also to produce "a good heart." The latter—conscience and morality—necessarily involved religion, because religion was the "only basis of morality." Therefore, anything in education which eroded the religious faith of the students jeopardized the future of American civilization. In his view, the propagation of the doctrine of evolution in schools and colleges was the most important single threat to Christianity and its moral standards. Learned professors devoted to the evolution theory destroyed the very basis of morality by replacing the biblical faith of students reared in Christian homes with a "clammy materialism." Bryan called upon taxpayers "to prevent the teaching in public schools of atheism, agnosticism, Darwinism, or any other hypothesis that links man in blood relationship with the brutes." He often reminded taxpayers of the financial lever by which they could force education to conform to their wishes.

———•◦•———

A boy is born in a Christian family; as soon as he is able to join words together into sentences his mother teaches him to lisp the child's prayer: "Now I lay me down to sleep; I pray the Lord my soul to keep; if I should die before I wake, I pray the Lord my soul to take." A little later the boy is taught the Lord's Prayer and each day he lays his petition before the Heavenly Father: "Give us this day our daily bread"; "Lead us not into temptation"; "Deliver us from evil"; "Forgive our trespasses"; etc.

He talks with God. He goes to Sunday school and learns that the Heavenly Father is even more kind than earthly parents; he hears the preacher tell how precious our lives are in the sight of God—how even a sparrow cannot fall to the ground without his notice. All his faith is built upon the book that informs him that he is made in the image of God; that Christ came to reveal God to man and to be man's Savior.

Then he goes to college and a learned professor leads him through a book 600 pages thick, largely devoted to resemblances between man and the beasts about him. His attention is called to a point in the ear that is like a point in the ear of the orang, to canine teeth, to muscles like those by which a horse moves his ears.

He is then told that everything found in a human brain is found in miniature in a brute brain.

And how about morals? He is assured that the development of the moral sense can be explained on a brute basis without any act of, or aid from, God.

No mention of religion, the only basis for morality; not a suggestion of a sense of responsibility to God—nothing but cold, clammy materialism! Darwinism transforms the Bible into a story book and reduces Christ to man's level. It gives him an ape for an ancestor on his mother's side at least and, as many evolutionists believe, on his Father's side also.

The instructor gives the student a new family tree millions of years long, with its roots in the water (marine animals) and then sets him adrift, with infinite capacity for good or evil but with no light to guide him, no compass to direct him, and no chart of the sea of life!

. . . .

James H. Leuba, a professor of psychology in Bryn Mawr College, Pennsylvania, wrote a book five years ago, entitled "Belief in God and Immortality." It was published by Sherman French & Co., of Boston, and republished by the Open Court Publishing Company of Chicago. Every Christian preacher should procure a copy of this book, and it should be in the hands of every Christian layman who is anxious to aid in the defense of the Bible against its enemies. Leuba has discarded belief in a personal God and in personal immortality. He asserts that belief in a personal God and personal immortality is declining in the United States, and he furnishes proof, which, as long as it is unchallenged, seems conclusive. He takes a book containing the names of fifty-five hundred scientists—the names of practically all American scientists of prominence, he affirms—and sends them questions. Upon the answers received he asserts that more than one half of the prominent scientists of the United States, those teaching biology, psychology, geology, and history especially, have discarded belief in a personal God and in personal immortality.

This is what the doctrine of evolution is doing for those who teach our children. They first discard the Mosaic account of man's creation, and they do it on the ground that there are no miracles. This in itself constitutes a practical repudiation of the Bible; the miracles of the Old and New Testament cannot be cut out without a mutilation that is equivalent to rejection. They reject the supernatural along with the miracle, and with the supernatural, the inspiration of the Bible and the authority that rests upon inspiration. If these believers in evolution are consistent and have the courage to carry their doctrine to its logical conclusion, they reject the virgin birth of Christ and the resurrection. They may still regard Christ as an unusual man, but they will not make much headway in converting people to Christianity, if they declare Jesus to be nothing more than a man and either a deliberate impostor or a deluded enthusiast.

The evil influence of these materialistic, atheistic, or agnostic professors is disclosed by further investigation made by Leuba. He questioned the students of nine representative colleges, and upon their answers declared that, while only fifteen percent of the freshmen have discarded the Christian religion, thirty percent of the juniors and forty to forty-five percent of the men graduates have abandoned the cardinal principles of the Christian faith. Can Christians be indifferent to such statistics? Is it an immaterial thing that so large a percentage of the young men who go from Christian homes into institutions of learning should go out from these institutions with the spiritual element eliminated from their lives? What shall it profit a man if he shall gain all the learning of the schools and lose his faith in God?

To show how these evolutionists undermine the faith of students, let me give you an illustration that recently came to my attention: A student in one of the largest state universities of the nation recently gave me a printed speech delivered by the president of the university, a year ago this month, to 3,500 students, and printed and circulated by the Student Christian Association of the institution. The student who gave me the speech marked the following paragraph:

And, again, religion must not be thought of as something that is inconsistent with reasonable, scientific thinking in regard to the nature of the universe.

I go so far as to say that, if you cannot reconcile religion with the things taught in biology, in psychology, or in the other fields of study in this university, then you should throw your religion away. Scientific truth is here to stay.

What about the Bible, is it not here to stay? If he had stopped with the first sentence, his language might not have been construed to the injury of religion, because religion is not "inconsistent with reasonable, scientific thinking in regard to the nature of the universe." There is nothing unreasonable about Christianity, and there is nothing unscientific about Christianity. No scientific fact—no fact of any other kind can disturb religion, because facts are not in conflict with each other. It is guessing by scientists and so-called scientists that is doing the harm. And it is guessing that is endorsed by this distinguished college president (a D.D., too, as well as an LL.D. and a Ph.D.) when he says, "I go so far as to say that, if you cannot reconcile religion with the things taught in biology, in psychology, or in the other fields of study in this university, then you should throw your religion away." What does this mean, except that the books on biology and on other scientific subjects used in that university are to be preferred to the Bible in case of conflict? The student is told, "throw your religion away," if he cannot reconcile it (the Bible, of course,) with the things taught in biology, psychology, etc. Books on biology change constantly, likewise books on psychology, and yet they are held before the students as better authority than the unchanging Word of God.

. . . .

The taxpayers should prevent the teaching in the public schools of atheism, agnosticism, Darwinism, or any other hypothesis that links man in blood relationship with the brutes. Christians build their own colleges in which to teach Christianity; let atheists and agnostics build their own schools in which to teach their doctrines—whether they call it atheism, agnosticism, or a scientific interpretation of the Bible.

If it is contended that an instructor has a right to teach anything he likes, I reply that the taxpayers must decide what shall be taught. The hand that writes the pay check rules the school. . . . A person can expose himself to the smallpox if he desires to do so, but he has no right to communicate it to others. So a man can believe anything he pleases, but he has no right to teach it against the protest of his employers.

Acceptance of Darwin's doctrine tends to destroy one's belief in immortality as taught by the Bible. If there has been no break in the line between man and the beasts—no time when by the act of the Heavenly Father man became "a living Soul," at what period in man's development was he endowed with the hope of a future life? And, if the brute theory leads to the abandonment of belief in a future life with its rewards and punishments, what stimulus to righteous living is offered in its place?

.   .   .   .

The purpose of education is not merely to develop the mind; it is to prepare men and women for society's work and for citizenship. The ideals of the teacher, therefore, are of the first importance. The pupil is apt to be as much influenced by what his teacher is as by what the teacher says or does. The measure of a school cannot be gathered from an inspection of the examination papers; the conception of life which the graduate carries away must be counted in estimating the benefits conferred. The pecuniary rewards of the teacher are usually small when compared with the rewards of business. This may be due in part to our failure to properly appreciate the work which the teacher does, but it may be partially accounted for by the fact that the teacher derives from his work a satisfaction greater than that obtained from most other employments.

The teacher comes into contact with the life of the student and, as our greatest joy is derived from the consciousness of having benefited others, the teacher rightly counts as a part of his compensation the continuing pleasure to be found in the knowledge that he is projecting his influence through future generations. The heart plays as large a part as the head in the teacher's work, because the heart is an important factor in every life and in the shaping of the destiny of the race. I fear the plutocracy of wealth; I respect the aristocracy of learning; but I thank God for the democracy of the heart. It is upon the heart level that we meet; it is by the characteristics of the heart that we best know and best remember each other. Astronomers tell us the distance of each star from the earth, but no mathematician can calculate the influence which a noble teacher may exert upon posterity. And yet, even the teacher may fall from his high estate, and, forgetting his immeasurable responsibility, yield to the temptation to estimate his work by its pecuni-

ary reward. Just now some of the teachers are—let us hope, uncon-
sciously—undermining the religious faith of students by substituting the
guesses of Darwin for the Word of God.

.   .   .   .

I am interested in education; if I had my way every child in all
the world would be educated. God forbid that I should draw a line
through society and say that the children on one side shall be educated
and the children on the other side condemned to the night of ignorance.
I shall assume no such responsibility. I am anxious that my children
and grandchildren shall be educated, and I do not desire for a child
or grandchild of mine anything that I would not like to see every other
child enjoy. Children come into the world without their own volition—
they are here as part of the Almighty's plan—and there is not a child
born on God's footstool that has not as much right to all that life can
give as your child or my child. Education increases one's capacity for
service and thus enlarges the reward that one can rightfully draw from
society; therefore, everyone is entitled to the advantages of education.

There is no reason why every human being should not have both
a good heart and a trained mind; but, if I were compelled to choose
between the two, I would rather that one should have a good heart
than a trained mind. A good heart can make a dull brain useful
to society, but a bad heart cannot make a good use of any brain, however trained or brilliant.

When we deal with the heart we must deal with religion, for
religion controls the heart; when we consider religion we find that
the religious environment that surrounds our young people is as favorable as their intellectual environment. As in the case of education,
lack of appreciation may be due in part to lack of opportunity to make
comparison. If we visit Asia, where the philosophy of Confucius controls,
or where they worship Buddha, or follow Mahomet, or observe the
forms of the Hindu religion, we find that except where they have borrowed from Christian nations, they have made no progress in fifteen
hundred years. Here, all have the advantage of Christian ideals, and
yet, according to statistics, something more than half the adult males
of the United States are not connected with any religious organization.
Some scoff at religion, and a few are outspoken enemies of the church.
Can they be blind to the benefits conferred by our churches? Security

of life and property is not entirely due to criminal laws, to a sheriff in each county, and to an occasional policeman. The conscience comes first; the law comes afterward.

Law is but the crystallization of conscience; moral sentiment must be created before it can express itself in the form of a statute.

From William Jennings Bryan, *In His Image* (New York: Fleming H. Revell Company, 1922), pp. 111–112, 116–120, 122–123, 186–187, 201–203.

Students Beware of False Teachers
Henry Clay Morrison

The chapel of the denominational college often served as a convenient platform for the protagonists in the modernist-fundamentalist struggle. Here the speaker could test his powers of persuasion upon a captive audience composed of those "impressionable minds" which figured so prominently in the verbal battle between the theological adversaries. Asbury College, a Methodist institution in Kentucky, was similar in many respects to numerous other small, church-related schools throughout the United States. Its president, Henry Clay Morrison, was a Methodist minister whose vigorous defense of the "old-time religion" placed him among the most conservative elements in Southern Methodism. During his administration the college brooked no "deviation from the saving Truths of the Holy Scriptures" as he interpreted them. In the following selection from one of his "chapel talks" President Morrison utilized many of the standard arguments advanced by fundamentalists in their war against "false teachers" and destructive critics of the Bible.

———◆◆◆———

. . . It will be found that those teachers who would discount the writings of Moses will also discount the words of Jesus. These false teachers do not hesitate to deny the Mosaic account of the flood, although Jesus places his endorsement upon that account. The same is true with reference to the Bible account of Jonah's peculiar experience. Jesus fully endorses this Bible record, but the false teachers deny with ridicule the Bible story of Jonah, notwithstanding Christ's statement with reference to the same.

The contradiction of these false teachers of the writings of Moses, the prophets, the teachings of Christ, and the writings of the Apostles are so frequent, emphatic, extensive, and irreverent that it is impossible to retain our faith in the inspiration of the Bible, in the virgin birth and atonement made by our Lord Jesus and at the same time accept the contradiction of these teachers and preachers who claim to be sent of God and to have a reliable message of helpfulness to mankind. Without doubt these men in high places and low who are making constant assaults upon the inspiration of the Bible are the false teachers spoken of by the Apostle Peter in our text. He speaks of them in the plainest terms. He says, "They will bring in damnable heresies." His words are positive. His meaning is plain. Their heresies can but lead to the loss of saving faith in our Lord Jesus, the casting away of the truth, the destruction of all spiritual life in the church, the undermining of all the high moral sentiment that arises out of Christian faith, and the ultimate destruction of countless human souls.

The destructive criticism of the Holy Scriptures which has been rampant in Germany for the past half century has wrought spiritual and moral ruin in that country. It has had time to produce its legitimate fruit, and the fearful conditions existing in that country and among those great and capable people at the present time reveal what must inevitably occur when the Word of God is discarded, the Son of God is rejected, and the Holy Spirit is grieved away. There are no greater people physically, mentally, and industrially than the German people. They are one of the most aggressive and productive peoples in the world; but for the false teachers in their universities and pulpits, they would be one of the most devout and spiritual people in the world today. The conditions which brought on the World War could not have existed, the savagery and ruin wrought by these otherwise great people, that has brought distress and confusion to the nations of the earth and laid a staggering burden upon the shoulders of the present generation and that which is to come, could never have come into our world but for the false teachers in universities and pulpits who brought in the "damnable heresies" that have turned loose fire and sword and plague, confusion, and death in the earth.

This same blight of heretical teaching is quenching the spiritual fires in England, has swept over Canada, and is becoming a widespread plague and curse in these United States.

It is a notable fact that these false teachers who deny the inspiration of much of the Bible have been at no pains to point out those portions of the scriptures that they believe to be inspired. They boldly declare in direct contradiction to the Word of God that there has been no fall of the race, but there is no such thing as inherited depravity—hence, no need of a new birth or cleansing away of sin and as a natural consequence no need of an atonement—therefore, no necessity for the tragedy of the cross, which they insist might have been avoided. Thus, they would rob us of the entire meaning of all the ancient sacrifices of the Israelitish people. They would strip the prophecies of all their deep and

wonderful significance, tear out from the Bible all account of the miracles performed by our Lord, with ruthless hands chop down the cross
and cut the heart out of the gospel, fling aside the teachings of the
apostles, tear up the hymn books, raze the foundations of the church,
and plunge the world into midnight darkness and blasphemous unbelief.

We must not pass without notice this word "privily." It is a most
significant and interesting fact that these false teachers bring in their
heresies in the very way indicated by St. Peter. How different the methods
of the disciples of doubt, the apostles of unbelief, in their propaganda
from the methods of John Wesley, General Booth, Charles Finney, and
Dwight L. Moody. These great evangelical teachers in their proclamation of the Gospel always sought the greatest possible publicity. They
strove to get to the multitudes of the people with the glad, good news of
a Redeemer mighty to save to the uttermost.

The destructive critics and this whole brood of false teachers use
shrewd and deceptive methods. They do not come bravely into the open
with their declarations; they dare not call a public convention of their
cult, openly declare to the public that the Bible is a forgery, that Jesus
Christ is not divine, that the Christian church is founded upon falsehood. They are not set on fire with a holy enthusiasm that leads them
to give up their salaries, surrender their chairs in Christian schools,
go out into the streets and highways like the true disciples of a newfound
truth, build their own churches and schools, support themselves, suffer
privation, and set on foot an active propaganda for the rescue of the
perishing, the salvation of souls, and the uplift of the race. Such procedure is entirely foreign to them, but they are careful to slip their
poison into the literature of the church and into the classrooms of the
schools. It is their delight to get before a summer school of young
preachers and dilute the pure faith of the ministry with their false
philosophies. They undertake and largely succeed in "privily" drawing
away young men, in theological schools and other institutions, from the
faith of the fathers and sending them out to preach—what! If the
Ten Commandments were written by ancient pagans who knew nothing
of God, they are not inspired and ought not to be preached as a divine
revelation. If the prophets of old knew nothing of the coming Messiah,
what they have written certainly has no place in the pulpit. If Jesus was
not of virgin birth—therefore not a divine being—and made no atone-

ment for sin on the cross, then of course he ought not to be offered to the people as a Savior. All of this heresy is the stock in trade of quite an army of false teachers in our country today who are eating the bread of the church while they "privily" pour their false teachings through the channels of the church and lead the people away from the faith in Christ that alone can save the souls of men. Like thieves in the night they are stealing away the beautiful and priceless jewels of the Gospel which is the power of God unto salvation to everyone that believeth.

From Henry Clay Morrison, *Crossing the Deadline or the Recrucifixion of the Lord Jesus Christ* (Louisville, Kentucky: Pentecostal Publishing Company, 1924), pp. 8–15.

Cast Out the Academic Philistines
T. T. Martin

Thomas Theodore Martin, one of the most vigorous opponents of evolution, claimed a varied career in teaching before becoming a full-time evangelist. At one point he apparently served as a professor of natural sciences in a Baptist college in Texas. In 1919 he was appointed Dean of the School of Evangelism at Union University, a small Baptist institution in Tennessee. During the next decade most of his energy was concentrated upon the activities of several nationwide organizations whose primary aim was to cleanse all schools and colleges of the "dirty theory" of evolution. He served as Director General of Campaigns in the Bible Crusaders of America and as Field Secretary of the Anti-Evolution League of America. Probably his most notable victory was in his native Mississippi where the legislators, after hearing his impassioned appeal, enacted an antievolution law in 1926. The following excerpts from his most famous tract reveal the nature of the attack that he delivered at numerous gatherings throughout the Southeast.

———•◦•———

But, if evolution, which is being taught in our high schools, is true, the Savior was not Deity, but only the bastard, illegitimate son of a fallen woman, and the world is left without a real Savior, a real Redeemer, and only hell is left for responsible human beings. The teaching of evolution leaves no room for Jesus Christ's being Deity, but forces the teaching that he must have had a human father as well as mother. Not only so, but evolution teaches not simply development within species,—every farmer, every stockman, every poultryman believes that; that is the reason we line-breed; that is the reason we send our children to school; evolution teaches that everything evolved from protoplasm, from the first amoeba, from the first living cell not as big as the point of a needle; that the different species, man included, were evolved from the first living thing just above the nonliving; that by very slight changes from generation to generation for millions of years, new species were evolved, up to and including man.

Now Genesis says positively ten times in the first chapter that everything brought forth "after its kind"; evolution says that there are ten lies in the first chapter of Genesis; that everything did not bring forth "after his kind"; Genesis says that God created man in his own image; evolution says that there is another lie in the book of Genesis—that the first man was midway between the anthropoid ape and modern man; Genesis says that the first man spoke plainly; evolution says that there is another lie in Genesis; that the first men chattered like animals in trees, having only exclamations of pain or pleasure.

The Savior endorsed Genesis as the word of God; Deity would not endorse these lies as the word of God; if evolution is true, and it is being taught as true in the high schools throughout the land, then the Savior, whom we trust for redemption and whom we worship, was not Deity, but only the bastard, illegitimate son of a fallen woman; therefore the world is left without a real Redeemer; therefore hell is the home of all responsible human beings.

John McDowell Leavitt: "Take Jesus from the world and you turn it into gloom." Take his deity and real redemption away and you turn the world into hell.

It will be shown . . . that the teaching of evolution is being drilled into our boys and girls in our high schools during the most susceptible, dangerous age of their lives. It is true that it is being taught in the lower grades of our public schools, even down to the primary department, as will be shown . . . ; and it is being taught in our state universities and state normals. But attention is especially directed here to evolution in the high schools, for three reasons: First, because it is the most susceptible, dangerous age of our young people; second, comparatively few of the high school students go through the state universities; vastly more, therefore, are being poisoned and eternally damned in the high schools than in the universities; third, the great state universities and state normals are barricaded behind strong political influences and millions of dollars, and they are hard to reach. From this barricaded position they can, in their high-browed arrogance, snap their fingers in our faces, until we can arouse the people to elect legislators who will cut off all appropriations wherever evolution is taught, and—mark my words—it will be done. Are we under the heel of a worse dictator than the Czar of Russia, to take our taxes from us and then ram down the throats of our children whatever they please? Ramming poison down the throats of our children is nothing compared with damning their souls with the teaching of evolution, that robs them of a revelation from God and a real Redeemer. Have we, while asleep, been dragged back under "taxation without representation?" The men are angels who will take my child from me and, under the plea of science, pour poison down its throat, compared to men to take my child away from home into the public schools, and, under the plea of science—when it is neither truth nor science—pour evolution into its mind and damn its soul.

The plea will be made that many pass through the high schools, and even the state universities and state normals, without being poisoned, without giving up the Bible as revelation from God and the Savior as Redeemer. That is true: in many cases the training in the home, under the pastors and priests and in the Sunday schools, has been so effective that they are able to escape; even so, many, because of the physical training, the strength, the health given to their bodies, are able to pass through our epidemics of smallpox and yellow fever, and many, many, as will be shown . . . , are being damned eternally by the teaching of evolution in our schools.

The third reason why this book is sent forth to warn against evolution in the high schools is that the scourge can be soonest reached and stopped there.

The boards of trustees of the public schools are absolute sovereigns; they can put in or put out whatever teacher they will; no power on earth can force teachers on them; in practically every school community in the land, Baptist, Catholic, Congregationalist, Disciple, Episcopalian, Lutheran, Presbyterian, and other professed Christian fathers and mothers are vastly in the majority; they can put on the boards of trustees only men and women who will not employ any teacher who believes in evolution; who will not employ any teacher who will not pledge to post himself or herself on the facts against evolution and expose it every time it comes up in any text book. And then carry the fight to the people and educate them until we can elect legislatures that will cut off all appropriation wherever evolution is taught. They have us by the throat—it is the only way to break their strangle hold.

.   .   .   .

It will be claimed that there are men who believe in evolution who are devout Christians. Let the reader consider:

First. There are men who are great along some lines of learning who are not clear in their reasoning; they are not logical in their thinking; they would not know logic if they met it in the road. Any man who will only think clearly and honestly knows that it is absolutely impossible to reconcile evolution and the ten-times-repeated statement in Genesis that everything brought forth "after its kind," and the Savior endorsing Genesis as the word of God, with the deity of the Savior; and if he was not Deity he was not a real Redeemer. If these things can be reconciled, WHY DON'T SOME OF THE EVOLUTIONISTS SHOW THE RECONCILIATION? This has been put up to them over and over, and they remain as dumb as oysters—and they will continue to pass it by in silence.

Second. Some men say they believe in evolution, when they mean by it development within the species, as the stalk of corn from the grain, the oak from the acorn, the chicken from the egg,—that is not evolution, and they know it,—they say they believe in evolution so as to appear learned.

Third. Men claim to be Christians and believe in evolution, when they do not, down in their souls, believe that Christ really redeemed us—actually died for our sins.

Fourth. Men claim to be Christians and believe that human beings are divine, that God is the Father of human beings, and so we are all divine; but down in their souls they believe that the Savior had a human father as well as mother—they have not the manhood to come out and say so—they do not believe he had pre-existence.

Fifth. I have never known a prominent evolutionist who claimed to be a Christian, who ever in public emphasized the fact of redemption through the blood of Christ, of redemption through Christ dying for our sins, until driven by exposure or by public sentiment to make such a statement.

.   .   .   .

Sixth. Some learned professors, by mental contortions or theological sleight-of-hand, may be able to believe in evolution and at the same time to believe the Bible to be really the word of God and the Savior to be real Deity and our real Redeemer; but your honest high school boy and girl who think cannot, and with many of them it will mean at last—hell; hence, the subject of this book, "Hell and the High School."

And the blame for their doom I lay at the feet of the fathers and mothers of America who, cowering before the sneers of a lot of high-brows supported by your taxes, will not arise and, through your local boards of trustees, drive every evolutionist from our high schools, and through your legislatures cut off all public funds where the Bible-denying, soul-destroying error is taught.

I know their pleas, I know their dodgings; they will be met fairly and squarely in this book.

. . . .

We gave our sons to save the world from being crushed by the Germans, and we did well; but they had already stealthily crept in and captured our citadels of learning, and now they and their dupes are damning our children. The soul of one high school boy or girl sent to hell by your German evolution is worth more than the bodies of all our brave boys killed in the great war in Europe. But they are being sent to hell by the thousands, as I shall show.

"But you are persecuting us professors!" Ah! Sissie! You have played the highbrow long enough. Now stand up and take your medicine.

But instead of standing up like men and meeting the issue, and meeting men in discussion and showing that their evolution is right, is the truth, and ought to be taught, they are, in their arrogance and pride, putting themselves above discussion and branding all who dare call their Bible-destroying, soul-damning teaching in question as a set of ignoramuses, sneering that their opposers are not "scientists." Well, a man does not have to be a hen to be a judge of an egg, and this is a nest full of bad eggs. Or, in their self-assumed superiority, they maintain a dignified, sublime silence,—on the principle that a fool may be considered by some as wise if he will but keep his mouth shut; or, as they are now beginning to do, they are playing the baby act, and whining for what they call "Academic Freedom," "Academic Liberty." One of them has recently put it thus: "The teacher should be allowed to teach as he sincerely believes. Not otherwise can he retain his self-respect, the confidence of his pupils, or the respect of the public." I deny it! Shall teachers be allowed to teach that there is no such thing as disease and keep smallpox pupils in the schools? But the teacher who would thus teach and spread smallpox through the school would do far less harm than the one who teaches evolution and spreads it among the pupils; for smallpox would only damn their bodies, while evolution would damn their souls. Should teachers be allowed "academic freedom" to teach the anarchistic-communistic proletariat, "Down with the Church! Down with the State! Down with private property!" That teaching could only damn the body; the teaching of evolution damns the soul. Shall the teacher be allowed "academic freedom" to teach a plurality of wives? Are we slaves? Are there no limitations? Where will you draw the line? In the nature of the case, the limitations must be drawn by those who pay for the teaching: where else can the line be drawn? A man, dead drunk, staggered out of a saloon to the street, waving his arms wildly, and hit a passer-by on the nose. The passer-by quickly hit the drunkard under the jaw and knocked him into the gutter. The drunken man staggered to his feet and stammered, "Don-don-don't you believe in personal liberty?" "Yes!" replied the gentleman, "but your liberty ends where my nose begins." Who is to be the judge? The ones who pay for the teaching. Let the teacher who wishes to teach otherwise have liberty to teach, yes, at his own expense, or at the expense of those who wish to pay for that kind of teaching.

From T. T. Martin, *Hell and the High Schools: Christ or Evolution, Which?* (Kansas City: Western Baptist Publishing Company, 1923), pp. 8–15.

The Great Conspiracy
Bible Crusaders of America

The Bible Crusaders of America was one of several national organizations created after the death of William Jennings Bryan in 1925 to continue his crusade in behalf of fundamentalism. It was largely the handiwork of George F. Washburn, a Boston capitalist and Florida real estate tycoon, who committed his religious zeal and financial resources to the fundamentalist cause. The following statement of the principles and strategy of the Bible Crusaders presents an indictment of the modernist-evolutionist invasion of schools and churches and a plan for insuring the restoration of the "Faith of Our Fathers." Although the conspiratorial theme appeared frequently in fundamentalist literature, it seldom received the detailed treatment furnished in this document.

———◦•◦———

First: Our objective is to persuade every state to safeguard its tax-supported schools, and to prevent the teaching of German philosophy which will discredit and destroy the Holy Bible, and ultimately endanger the perpetuity of the republic. Therefore, we urge every state to enact legislation in harmony with that of the National Congress, which requires by law that, "No partisan politics; no disrespect to the Holy Bible; nor that ours is an inferior form of government should be taught in any public school in the District of Columbia."

Thirty years ago, five men met in Boston and formed a conspiracy which we believe to be of German origin, to secretly and persistently work to overthrow the fundamentals of the Christian religion in this country. These men masqueraded as higher critics under the guise of superior literary attainments acquired in German universities. This betrayal of the Christian religion, now known as the "great adventure," was more serious than Benedict Arnold's betrayal of his country.

This invasion of German philosophy was more cunning, adroit, and ambitious in plan, and more disastrous, overwhelming, and successful in result than the German military plan to invade, overwhelm, and rule the world.

Second: That because "eternal vigilance, which is the price of liberty" has not been exercised by the American people over their educational and religious institutions, the original character and purpose of this Christian nation has been changed to an alarming degree.

Third: We believe that when the mothers and fathers of America learn and realize what is being taught their children in the public schools, there will be a righteous uprising in every state that will shake the nation.

Fourth: We claim that while 90 percent of the laity of the evangelical Protestant and Catholic churches of the country are fundamentalists at heart, they have allowed the other 10 percent, who preach and teach this German philosophy, to poison the minds and hearts of the children in our tax-supported schools, by the use of textbooks that ought never to have been allowed, and as a result, thousands of children from Christian homes are graduating each year from these schools as agnostics, modernists, evolutionists, and atheists.

Fifth: We charge that these evolutionists, as part of this conspiracy, control the textbooks used in the tax-supported schools of this country and teach doctrines to our youth that discredit and insult the Holy Bible. If the Bible cannot be allowed in the public schools, why should other books, that seek to discredit and destroy it, be permitted?

Sixth: We charge that these conspirators control our higher schools of learning—colleges and universities—that are largely supported by fundamentalists, without whose knowledge or consent they have used this money to assassinate the "Faith of Our Fathers" in the very institutions that were founded by them. We assert that this is not common honesty and is selling goods under false pretenses.

Seventh: We charge further that these teachers of German rationalism and their associates occupy the pulpits of Methodist, Baptist, Presbyterian, Protestant Episcopal, and other evangelical churches under the guise of "ministers of the gospel." This is "selling goods under false colors," and is a betrayal of Christ and the Bible for a paltry thirty pieces of silver.

We sound the warning that a deep, devilish, premeditated plan of propaganda exists to discard the Bible, discredit Christ, and destroy the church. The most pathetic picture of all is the paganist preacher who preaches away his pulpit, and himself out of a job, by substituting German philosophy for Christ and the Bible. By doing so he destroys the vital, dynamic force and energy of the gospel message, again buries truth, extinguishes the beacon light, and plunges the world into another period of sin, crime, and the dark ages.

Eighth: We further charge that the religious press of the country, with some exceptions, has shown a pitiable and pathetic surrender of Christ and the Bible to this German cabal, and this charge includes the Sunday school publications and publishing houses of some of the larger Protestant denominations.

Ninth: Not content with this invasion of America, these worldwide conspirators and their colleagues have included in their destructive plans the missionaries of the foreign fields. Posing as fundamentalists, they have secured funds, through the churches, by deliberate misrepresentation, not for the purpose of preaching the fundamental Bible doctrines, such as the virgin birth, the atonement, the redemption of mankind, and the resurrection, but rather substituting this false German philosophy for Christ, the Bible, and God.

Tenth: As two results of this destructive philosophy we suffered the world war and now endure a moral breakdown. The nation now is inundated by a great tidal wave of crime, embracing law violations of all kinds. Sunday desecration, an alarming increase in divorces, and a tremendous drop in moral standards and ideals.

Since this terrible indictment is true, is there not need of this crusade? Should the great American people longer be dominated by this German conspiracy? A thousands times, no! The fundamentalists in every state should rally to the flag of the Bible Crusaders and stand like Spartans at Thermopylae, with the courage of a St. Paul, to resist the invasion of the enemy. There are millions of fundamentalists in America. If they use their numerical strength, they will overwhelm the enemy.

The following are the ten remedies we offer:

First: Demand that your legislators shall enact laws in line with that of Congress, viz., that nothing that is disrespectful to the Holy Bible shall be taught in the public schools of our state, and vote to displace any legislator who refuses to do this.

Our crusade is not against true science, but is against the substitution of unscientific, evolutionary chaos for the Bible.

Second: Notify the modernist missionaries in foreign fields that your dollars will be withheld until they line up with Christ and the Bible, and discontinue teaching manmade philosophies.

Third: Immediately notify your Sunday school and church publications which teach this philosophy to cancel your subscription, and then substitute for them publications that are true to the teaching of Christ and the Bible and a miraculous change will result.

Fourth: Form a group of fundamentalists in your church and notify your rationalistic preacher that he is a misfit in an evangelical pulpit and that a change must be made.

The unfrocking of Bishop William Montgomery Brown for heresy places the Protestant Episcopal church in the forefront of fundamentalism.

Fifth: Withhold your fundamentalist gifts from, and your legacies to, rationalistic colleges and universities, and before long they will go out of business or become fundamentalist schools of learning.

Sixth: Likewise, do not send your boys and girls to these colleges and universities as students, and thus at the source cut off these streams of poison from the classrooms of the colleges that are making agnostics and atheists of your children.

Seventh: Organize laymen's leagues within the different denominations and elect only such delegates from your churches to church conferences, conventions, and presbyteries as are known to be "the old guard," and sound in the orthodox faith.

Eighth: Organize a battalion of Crusaders of all denominations in your community and help extend this movement to other communities, and then notify headquarters at Clearwater, Florida, and we will soon have an army of Crusaders throughout the country that will quickly restore Christ and the Bible to their rightful places.

Ninth: Likewise, organize the boys and girls of your community as junior crusaders, that they may be early taught to reverence and protect the Bible and thereby become the hope of the future, the defenders of the faith.

Tenth: Meet the modernists at every point and occupy their strategic positions, and we will soon restore this country to the "Faith of Our Fathers."

Under this flag fundamentalists will no longer be afraid or on the defensive, but will meet all comers without fear or favor, neither seeking nor giving quarters.

This is the greatest uprising of this country, and will overthrow the blighting influence of German philosophy, just as German militarism and imperialism were overthrown in the World War.

To further advance this cause, we invite chambers of commerce, other civic organizations, and groups of churches to arrange mass meetings in different states. We will supply scientists and lecturers of national reputation to address such meetings, or to meet in debate any and all advocates of this German philosophy who have like national standing.

If interested parties will send us copies of books on geography, biology, physiology, or other textbooks bearing on this question and used in the public schools of any state, our scientists will examine those books free of charge, and inform such parties as to what extent the teachings therein contained are false, misleading, and damaging.

From "The Bible Crusaders' Challenge," *The Crusaders' Champion,* I (February 5, 1926), 12–13.

California Textbook Investigation
Report of the Textbook Investigation Committee

The efforts of fundamentalists to rid public schools of "evolution textbooks" was almost as disturbing to the champions of academic freedom as their crusades to enact antievolution laws. Several states eliminated such works from the lists of approved textbooks and removed them from public school libraries. Under pressure from fundamentalists, the California State Board of Education ruled that evolution could be taught "as a theory but not as an established fact" and created a committee of distinguished educators to investigate twelve widely used textbooks in science. Cited below is the committee's report of 1924, which critics quickly denounced as further evidence that evolutionists actually controlled education. Their hostility was in part responsible for the passage of a measure in 1926 by the California legislature which empowered the State Board of Education to eliminate from public school textbooks any matter that it deemed objectionable.

———•◦•———

In response to the opportunity afforded by the [California] Board of Education to all parties present at the hearing conducted by the board on August 4, 1924, and to all others interested, briefs on the subject of evolution, with special reference to the teaching of that subject in state-supported schools, were presented by

> Rev. T. Hector Dodd, San Rafael.
> Rev. Harry Gill, Sacramento.
> Rev. Clarence Reed, Oakland.
> Rev. George L. Thorpe, Corona.
> Rev. E. E. Wall, Sacramento.

The members of the Committee of Nine have examined and considered those pages and sections of the twelve textbooks to which their attention has been specifically directed, and likewise the five briefs. The committee respectfully submits the following report:

The theory of evolution, in one or another of its phases, is referred to in these books—it could scarcely be omitted from any textbook on biology, or astronomy, or geology—and in a few of the books some of the evidence in support of the theory of evolution is presented. In our opinion, these books have treated the subject with moderation and circumspection. There appear to be no statements derogatory to the Bible, and in the few instances in which the possible bearing of evolution upon religion is discussed at all, the writers have taken special pains to assure the readers that there is no conflict between science and religion. Evolution is presented as a theory, and not as an established fact, although it is stated here and there that the theory of evolution is commonly accepted by scientific men, and that is true. On this phase of the subject the following quotations have bearing:

A. Moon's *Biology for Beginners,* pp. 329–331: "Some Things that Evolution does Not Teach. . . . 'That man is descended from a monkey.' That God can be left out of the scheme of Creation. . . . While we can not go into the argument here, rest assured that in the minds of the greatest scientists and philosophers there is no conflict between the conclusions of Science and Religion. To quote Davenport, 'The Creator is still at work, and not only the forces of Nature, but man himself, works with God in still further improving the earth and the living things which it supports.' "

B. Gager's *Fundamentals of Botany,* pp. 516 and 517. "The publication of Darwin's *Origin of Species* aroused at once a storm of opposition. Theologians opposed the theory because they thought it eliminated God. . . . The unthinking and the careless thinkers accused Darwin of teaching that man is descended from monkeys. Neither of these accusations, however, was true. Darwinism neither eliminates God, nor does it teach that monkeys are the ancestors of men.

"By slow degrees, however, men began to give more careful and unprejudiced attention to the new theory, and not to pass adverse judgment upon it until they were sure they understood it. 'A celebrated author and divine has written to me,' says Darwin, 'that he has gradually learnt to see that it is just as noble a conception of the Deity to believe that He created a few original forms capable of self-development into other and needful forms, as to believe that He required a fresh act of creation to supply the voids caused by the action of His laws.' "

The textbooks before us are concerned with presenting scientific facts and theories of which every person with any pretense to an education in the subject or subjects treated should be informed. All departures of the authors from this simple policy may be said to show due respect and consideration for the fundamental principles of religion, as presented in the Bible.

(Signed)   W. W. Campbell (Chairman)
              President of the University of California
            Ray Lyman Wilbur
              President of Stanford University
            Aurelia Henry Reinhardt
              President of Mills College
            Karl T. Waugh (acting for President R. R. von KleinSmid)
              University of Southern California
            Remsen D. Bird
              President of Occidental College
            James A. Blaisdell
              President of Pomona College
            V. L. Duke
              President of University of Redlands
            Tully C. Knoles
              President of College of the Pacific
            Catherine O'Donnell
              President of Dominican College

From W. W. Campbell, "Evolution in Education in California," *Science,*
LXI (April 3, 1925), 367–368.

Honest Teaching and Fundamentalism
Walter Lippmann

In 1928 the distinguished young journalist Walter Lippmann presented the Barbour-Page Lectures at the University of Virginia. Collectively entitled "American Inquisitors," his lectures inquired into the "predicament of the modern teacher under popular government during the conflict over religious fundamentalism and over patriotic tradition." In the following excerpt from those lectures, Lippmann indicates that a primary duty of the teacher is to appreciate the nature of his position in the context of prevailing conditions. The teacher of the 1920s had not only to recognize that American education was in the throes of a major transition as a result of the impact of science and the scientific method; he had also to understand the attributes of the fundamentalists' faith and abandon the notion that he, as a teacher, was a neutral. Because of the transitional state of education, the teacher had to concern himself with the minds and characters of his pupils as well as with the correct science of the day. Merely to teach modernism was to shirk the tedious task of "building a bridge from the ignorance of his pupils to the knowledge which he is trying to give them." Honest teaching, as opposed to sheer demagoguery, necessitated teaching in such a way as to make possible "the transition from fundamentalism to modernism." Obviously Lippmann did not prescribe any absolute rule of conduct for teachers, but his reference to newspaper editors offered a clue: "some prudence" in respect to the prejudices of subscribers was a prerequisite to their success.

———◆◆◆———

Until fairly recent times the role of the teacher was clearly defined. There existed a body of knowledge and certain well-established methods of thought which it was his task to transmit to the new generation. Essentially the ideal of education was that the child should acquire the wisdom of the elders. There were, no doubt, fierce disputes among the sects as to what was knowledge and what was error. But it was an accepted fact that in Catholic communities the child should learn Catholic dogma, that in Lutheran communities he should learn Lutheranism, that in Calvinistic communities he should learn Calvinism.

The growth of science has radically altered all this. For the ancient notion that there exists a completed body of knowledge, there has been substituted the notion of a growing and changing body of knowledge which is forever tentative and forever incomplete. Consequently, wherever science is the accepted mode of thought, the ideal of education must be, not that the child shall acquire the wisdom of his elders, but that he shall revise and surpass it. The child is not taught to believe. He is taught to doubt and to inquire, to guess, to experiment, and to verify. The teacher no longer pretends to transmit wisdom. Instead he strives to develop wise habits.

The scientific spirit now dominates the intellectual classes of the western world. They do not always obey it faithfully or successfully, especially where their material interests are involved. But they acknowledge that the scientific spirit ought to prevail in all fields of human knowledge, and the teacher, insofar as he is intellectually responsible, must consider himself bound by the code of science. In the scientific method he must find the only true and final allegiance of his mind.

But as a man and as a citizen the teacher is under contract to the state. He is in fact a subordinate official of the state, and in the state the sovereign power resides, not in the community of scholars, but in a majority of the voters. Now in this phase of history it is by no means certain that a majority of the voters understand the scientific ideal of the scholar or will tolerate it when they see the consequences of its application. The older method of thought still survives in great sections of the people, and they are by no means prepared to abandon their beliefs, or to adopt the newer method of holding beliefs and of arriving at them. The teacher therefore finds himself living at a time of transition from one kind of thinking to another. He is the servant of a community which is in part fundamentalist in its mode of thought and in part modernist. His intellectual duty is to modernism, this is to say, to the belief that the human reason has the last word. But politically, economically, legally, he is subject to the orders of those who may believe that the preservation of the ancient fundamentalism either in religion or in nationalism is the first duty of man.

Those who wish to evade this issue are fond of saying that reason and free inquiry are neutral and tolerant of all opinions. That, as we have seen, cannot be the case. Reason and free inquiry can be neutral and tolerant only of those opinions which submit to the test of reason and free inquiry. But towards any opinion for which the claim is made that it rests on some other method of verification than reason's own, reason is of necessity either partisan and intolerant, or indifferent. What cannot be tested by the method of science, reason will either ignore or reject. Carry reason and free inquiry to the utmost limits of their tolerance: what can they say to fundamentalism except that they are prepared to inquire whether there is reasonable evidence for believing that the tests of reason are not reliable?

The disagreement goes to the very premises of thought, to the character of thinking itself. It revolves upon the question of whether human reason is or is not the ultimate test of truth for men. The fundamentalist cannot admit that it is. He would cease to be a fundamentalist if he were no longer convinced that above human reason and the available evidence there is a gospel which contains a statement of facts that are the fundamental premises of all reasoning. His belief that there exists such a gospel certifies his opinions absolutely for him. He must conclude that where our reason contradicts these opinions, it is a sign not that the opinions are wrong, but that our senses have deceived us or that we have reasoned wrongly.

To ask the fundamentalist, therefore, to submit his belief to scientific inquiry is to ask him at the outset to surrender the most important attribute of his faith. It is evasive to tell him that science may after investigation confirm his opinion, or that it is possible to invent a formula which will reconcile his belief with the conclusions of science. The conclusions of science are radically different from the conclusions of the fundamentalist even when there is a nominal or superficial agreement between them. They are certified by different systems of thought. The effect, therefore, of asking the fundamentalist to approach the tribunal of reason is to ask him to accept the jurisdiction of a court which is not his own. It is asking him to say that while that which has been revealed may be true, it is not true because it is revealed.

Since the conflict between fundamentalism and modernism is essentially irreconcilable, the teacher who wishes to understand his position in the modern state must abandon the notion that he is a neutral. It is impossible for him or for anyone else to be neutral. Insofar as he makes any impression whatsoever on his pupils, he must tend either to confirm or to weaken the ancient modes of thinking; he must lead the child either toward the modern spirit or away from it.

Had he taught two hundred years ago he would hardly have been conscious of this dilemma anywhere in the western world. There are still vast communities where the ancient ways are still so strong that the teacher need make no choice. There are some communities on the other hand, not many as yet, I think, where the new ways are already firmly established. There the teacher is not faced with this problem. But in most communities in America today the old ways survive powerfully, either in religion or in nationalism, and yet the new ways are already powerful and insistent. The teacher in such communities is in genuine difficulties. And the more spirited and sensitive he is, the more profound those difficulties are likely to be for him.

I would not attempt to give teachers so situated advice as to how to conduct themselves even if I knew what advice to give them. For it is evident that any teacher who is capable of realizing his position in the modern state is also capable of deciding how he will conduct himself in the light of the exact circumstances in his particular case. The choice of a line of conduct is his personal affair, and I shall have failed altogether in these lectures if I have not at least suggested the complexity and risks of the transition in which the teacher occupies so responsible a place. For the introduction of modern habits of thought into the schools means a widening of the breach between the older generation and the younger. It means that parents and children may come to think so differently that neither can sympathize with or even comprehend the other. It means a dissolution of codes and rules which rest upon the ancient foundations. It means dangerous and bewildering experiment, not only in thought, but in action, and there is no certainty that any experiment will work out happily.

But while I do not know how far any particular teacher ought to go in evoking the doubts, the inquiries, and the experiments of modernism, of this at least I am certain: that the more clearly the teacher realizes the nature of this transition and its profound implications, the more successfully he will find his way through its perplexities. If he knows what he is doing, he will know better what to do. His predecessors were the custodians of a temple. But he belongs to a generation which amidst great hesitation, wild hope, and deep fear, is engaged in taking down the stones of the temple and in erecting something new, of which the plan is not quite clear, in its place. If he imagines that the ancient temple is still intact, he is hugging an illusion. If he acts on the assumption that the new structure is wholly erected, he will soon discover his error. Only by understanding that he is in the midst of a revolutionary change, and that he is a responsible agent of that change, can he hope to find out what his duty is.

The statement that the teacher today is a responsible agent of the change from the fundamentalist to the scientific method of thought leads, I think, to certain inferences which may clarify his position somewhat more. He is, let us remember, a teacher. He is not, let us remember, engaged in research to extend the boundaries of human knowledge. As a teacher he stands somewhere between the unlearned and immature on the one hand and the learned and the mature on the other. He has, therefore, to take into account not merely the correct science of his time but the minds and characters of his pupils.

Were he a scholar he could disregard entirely the ignorance of his pupils. He would address himself only to the problem under investigation, caring nothing who understood him or what impression he created. But being a teacher he is concerned primarily not with the discovery of truth but with its reception. He cannot merely announce the truth. He must communicate it. Because he must communicate it, he must take into account not merely what it is desirable to communicate but what it is possible to communicate.

If all the pupils in America could be present at meetings of learned societies where new discoveries are announced, the mere fact that they heard the words would not constitute education. For when the pupils heard these announcements, few of them would hear more than so many vocables. These vocables have significance only for those who can attribute significance to them. In the scientific announcement a whole chain of meanings and of previous agreements is taken for granted. It is assumed, for example, that the audience knows the vocabulary and the grammar which the scientist employs, that it knows the logical processes on which he relies, that it is aware of the history and meaning of the problem with which the new discovery deals. I am, for example, unable to appreciate Einstein's work. I do not know the meaning of the words and the symbols he employs. I cannot follow his mathematical processes. Above all I am too ignorant of physics to realize what it was that was inadequate in the Newtonian physics which raised the problems Einstein set himself to solve. If I, therefore, were to take up the study of Einstein's work, I should need to start far behind where Einstein began. I should need someone who not only understands Einstein, but also understands my ignorance, who knows not only what Einstein has discovered, but what I have not yet discovered, someone who can begin where my pitiably inadequate training ends and will with patience and ingenuity build a bridge for me. I need a teacher.

An adequate science would, of course, include not only Einstein's physics, but a knowledge of the ignorance, the stupidity, the preoccupations, and the indifference which prevent me from understanding Einstein's physics. The study of human ignorance is a science, a branch of psychology, on which all those who teach, in schools, in pulpits, in print, are compelled to draw. They are good teachers insofar as they are adept in human ignorance and skillful in dealing with it. I say skillful, because the manipulation of human ignorance cannot be reduced to cut and dried methods. The particular quality of the ignorance of each individual is a unique combination which can be dealt with successfully only by those whose general understanding is quickened by intuitive sympathy. The great journalist has this flair. The great orator has it. It is a sense of the audience, an awareness of the dim attitudes of those who are listening. And the only difference between what we call demagoguery and honest teaching is that the demagogue exploits the ignorance of his audience by solidifying it behind purposes that cannot be rationally defended; whereas the teacher is always trying to dissolve the ignorance of his audience by leading them to discover for themselves purposes that will stand the test of reason.

The true teacher is not concerned with persuading his hearers to accept his conclusion rather than their own. He is concerned with the rationalization of the process by which conclusions are reached. For that reason the teacher in a time of transition like the one amidst which we live, must make the transition itself the subject matter of his teaching. He does not do his work if he teaches fundamentalism. He does not do his work if he teaches modernism. He is a teacher only if he teaches the transition from fundamentalism to modernism.

I am persuaded that the failure to realize this situation accounts for many of the quarrels which come to public attention under the rubric of quarrels about the freedom of teaching. It does not account for all of the quarrels. There are, I am sure, many cases where scholars have been subjected to interference by the authorities who, out of prejudice or self-interest, object to their following out certain lines of inquiry. But I am not speaking here of scholars. I am speaking of teachers, and my own impression is that very frequently the difficulty arose because the teacher had failed to teach, and had insisted, sometimes rather provocatively, on announcing strange and unpalatable doctrines which he held to be the truth. The teacher who was in trouble had forgotten, or he had shirked, the tedious and difficult business of building a bridge from the ignorance of his pupils to the knowledge which he was trying to give them.

If the teacher had only to consider his pupils, these comments might be roughly sufficient. But of course the teacher is compelled to consider not only the state of mind of his pupils but the wishes of their parents. If he is an employee of the state, he is under orders from officials, who in their turn derive their authority from the voters. The teacher cannot teach these voters. He cannot build bridges for them. They constitute a force to which he must somehow accommodate himself. They hold the purse strings. They are the sovereign power. The final question then is: what shall be the philosophy of a modern teacher towards his employers and his sovereign, the reigning majority of the voters?

When I speak of philosophy I mean: what ought he to think of the majority? Of what he should do in the light of what he thinks, each man must again be his own judge in the light of the particular circumstances. Nobody can lay down a general rule as to what another John T. Scopes ought to do,—whether he ought to resign, or to fight, or to evade the issue. At least I cannot say it, because I do not think it is very good taste to advise other men whether or not they ought to be martyrs.

It would surely be very bad taste in a newspaperman, for no newspaper of large circulation can possibly represent the full, candid, unhesitating mind of its editors. They are compelled almost every day to weigh the advantages and disadvantages of candor, and to strike a prudent balance on which they act. I am telling no secrets. There are editors who do not have to be prudent because they have no imprudent opinions. There are editors who do not have to be prudent, because they have no readers whom they have to conciliate. There are editors who have to be prudent not to offend the majority, and there are editors who have to be prudent not to offend the minority. But prudence is an element in the judgment of every editor who has a following, the most liberal and the most conservative. Though timidity often makes it excessive, wherever men are bent upon persuading and influencing other men, some prudence in respect to their prejudices is necessary to success.

The question then is not how prudently the teacher ought to act in the presence of the will of the majority, but what weight he should inwardly give to it. When he is clear as to that, he is in no danger of confusing his timidity, his convenience, and his ambitions with a just prudence.

From Walter Lippmann, *American Inquisitors: A Commentary on Dayton and Chicago* (New York: Macmillan, 1928), pp. 83–96.

Protecting Education from the Mass Meeting
William H. P. Faunce

Surprised by the renewal of a controversy which had raged late in the nineteenth century, the aging president of Brown University, William Herbert Perry Faunce, manfully defended the theory of evolution and vigorously protested the surrender of education to demands of the "mass meeting." Convinced that evolution could not "explain the ultimate cause of anything," Faunce nonetheless insisted that it brought "the divine into the daily and hourly changes in the physical world" and provided "a new vision of the spiritual element in human life." As the head of a Baptist-related institution, he was only too well aware of the activities of the fundamentalist wing of the Northern Baptist Convention. At a Baptist gathering in 1923 John Roach Straton, a fundamentalist activist in New York, protested Faunce's right to speak on the grounds that he had "expressed views subversive to our faith." The views expressed in the magazine article below were largely responsible for Straton's protest. In the article the university president not only defended evolution but also maintained that the control of teaching must not be lodged in "an annual mass meeting," because it was "precisely the mass which needs to be educated and so is disqualified to direct education." Although Faunce's institution managed to escape the repercussions of the fundamentalists' assaults, other Baptist schools, especially those within the jurisdiction of the Southern Baptist Convention, felt the full impact of such efforts.

------◆◆◆------

We thought that forty years ago in America religion had been adjusted to the evolutionary theory, as it was adjusted in the sixteenth century to the far more startling Copernican theory. We thought that science had definitely yielded a large place to the unseen and intangible, and had agreed to Goethe's saying that "the universe divided by reason leaves a remainder." We thought that forty years ago it was established that the Bible was not a textbook of science—any more than is *Pilgrim's Progress* or *John Wesley's Journal*. Now, to the amazement of the whole world a large number of sincere enthusiasts are proclaiming that human progress is a delusion, that the ultimate catastrophe is close at hand, that all human institutions—home, school, state, and church—are soon to disappear, that the worse the world gets, the more reason we have to hope and are basing their pessimistic and nonco-operative attitude on the baldly literal interpretation of a few of the obscurest texts in the Bible.

What this recrudescence of medieval despair may do to the denominational colleges in some sections of our country is becoming clear. In one college a new professor happened in his first lecture casually to use the terrifying word "evolution." Whereupon the whole class hissed him and later explained apologetically that they had been taught that evolution and atheism are synonymous. In some colleges the control of teaching has been taken out of the hands of the trustees and faculty and lodged in an annual mass meeting. But it is precisely the mass which needs to be educated and so is disqualified to direct education. In other colleges the teachers are cowed and silent because of attacks of local publications which demand that all teachers repeat the shibboleths of a former generation or retire. The failure of the Kentucky legislature by a single vote to pass a law banishing modern science from the schools of the state, and the presentation of a similar bill in the legislature of Minnesota, show how fast and how far has gone the propaganda in favor of the world-view held in the sixteenth century. Political freedom has been achieved by whole nations and races since 1914. But freedom of teaching, liberty to declare the facts of history and biology and anthropology, as they are known to the foremost scholars in each department, is now threatened in the name of the religion which declares: "The truth shall make you free."

The college which surrenders to the control of the mass meeting not only is unworthy of the confidence of the public but utterly fails to prepare its students to face the realities of life. Sooner or later those students must meet the facts. . . . A college which should still teach the science of ancient Israel might fittingly call to its chair of astronomy "Uncle Jasper."

The colleges, however, will not permanently yield to obscurantism and reaction. Their roots are deep in the American principle, and all of them are striving to be true to the ideal embodied in 1764 in the charter of Brown University: "Into this liberal and catholic institution shall never be admitted any religious tests, but on the contrary all the members thereof shall forever enjoy full, free, absolute, and uninterrupted liberty of conscience."

The American Association for the Advancement of Science, representing over a thousand of the leading scholars of America, has just declared its undeviating belief in evolution as the method by which the world as we know it acquired its present form. Probably every teacher of physical science in every college or high school in the northern states agrees with this declaration of the American Association for the Advancement of Science. Every boy or girl attending a high school north of the Mason-Dixon's line is now being taught some form of the doctrine of evolution. The competent teachers of America and Europe are practically agreed that the physical world as we see it is a growth from simpler forms into more complex, and that so far as man is physical—of course he is vastly more!—he, too, is the result of the brain of an Aristotle and the heart of a Florence Nightingale.

These scholars do not affirm Darwinism or any other "ism." They are quite ready to acknowledge that Darwin overemphasized the struggle for existence in the organic world and that exaggerations and perversions of "natural selection" have given an excuse to imperialists, to exploiters of the weak, and to a pagan ethic which is all too prevalent. But perverse inferences do not disturb the fact. The fact is that the power of evolution—a doctrine as old as . . . the New Testament declaration of "first the blade, then ear, then the full corn in the ear"— is now as firmly established among scholars as the law of gravitation. Both of these laws are merely statements of how matter moves and how it has assumed its present form. Neither law sheds any light on ultimate causes or affects the conviction of the church: "In the beginning God." Neither law can be proved. Each is an hypothesis—a "guess," if one prefers to call it so, only remembering that it was by guess that Columbus discovered America and that all the advances in human knowledge have been made. Both gravitation and evolution are hypotheses—modes of thinking, ways of explaining the facts—and will be cast aside the moment some better explanation can be found. (Einstein is today questioning the adequacy of the theory of gravitation.) Both are consistent with Christianity or Buddhism or atheism; neither has anything to do with the truth or falsity of any religion. Whether gravitation attracts inversely as the square of the distance or not; whether species were created instantly as coins are stamped in the mint, or were created by process, as a gardner grows roses—that has nothing to do with the great fundamentals of religion: "Thou shalt love the Lord thy God with all thy heart and thy neighbor as thyself."

Indeed the doctrine of evolution, rightly understood and interpreted, is today one of the most powerful aids to religious faith. It has delivered thousands from perplexity amounting to despair. It has supplanted the old paralyzing conception of a "world-machine," a world mechanical and lifeless, grinding out human destiny without end. In place of that soulless mechanism we now have a growing organism. In the words of John Fiske, "The simile of the watch has been replaced by the simile of the flower." A developing world, still in process, ceaselessly unfolding, still to be shaped by human purpose and effort—that is the inspiring conception now placed in the hands of the church by modern science, a conception which formed the basis of the first Christian parable of "The Sower." Science is not yet able to discern a world-soul or a creator; it leaves that to religion. It has nothing to say about the purpose and goal of life or the spiritual presence in all things, which is the vital breath of religion. It has shown us a universe alive, progressing, climbing with many backward steps toward "one far off divine event." The doctrine of development has cleared away most of the difficulties in Old Testament ethics and enabled us to reconcile teachings which, given in different centuries, are yet united in one book. It has furnished the church with a powerful apologetic, which many of our leaders are now using.

From William H. P. Faunce, "Freedom in School and Church," *World's Work*, XLV (March 1923), 509–511.

Evolution and the Public Schools
Maynard Shipley

On the evenings of June 14 and 15, 1925, two widely publicized debates on evolution were held in San Francisco. In both sessions evolution was defended by Maynard Shipley, a vigorous opponent of fundamentalism who organized the Science League of America for the specific purpose of protecting the freedom of teachers and scientists. His opponents in the debates were Francis D. Nichol and Alonzo L. Baker, editors of the militantly fundamentalist weekly *Signs of the Times*. Both were former students of George McCready Price, "the leading fundamentalist scientist." On the first evening Shipley and Nichol debated the question: "Resolved, that the earth and all life upon it are the result of evolution." In the second debate Shipley was pitted against Baker on the question of whether "the teaching of evolution should be barred from tax-supported schools." The following selection is a portion of Shipley's argument in the negative on the second proposition.

———•◦•———

On the question, "Should evolution as a fact or evolution as a theory be taught in our schools?" we are bound to answer in accordance with the same principles that we would apply to the question, "Should physical geography be taught in the public schools?" or, "Should ancient history be taught in the public schools?"—including, of course, tax-supported colleges and universities.

Broadly speaking, anything that is true of nature or of man and society might well be taught in any school. But we live in an intensely practical world, a very busy world, and there are more subjects worthy of study than there is school time to devote to them. Hence, some purely arbitrary limiting choice must be made as to what should constitute the curricula of our schools.

To this end, we have state-supported educational institutions in which men and women receive special training in pedagogy, in the history of educational methods, in educational psychology, in science, and in such other studies as specially prepare them for their future work as educators.

Just as a physician must first devote years of study to physiology, anatomy, pathology, and allied subjects before he is given a certificate authorizing him to enter professional life as a medical practitioner, just so the educator must devote years of study to various fundamental branches of history, natural science, psychology, etc., before obtaining a certificate to teach in our tax-supported educational institutions.

It is these specially trained men and women to whom the lay public must intrust the task of working out the practical details of school curricula and administration; just as we intrust to structural engineers the building of our bridges, or to physiologists and pathologists solutions of the problems of health and disease, and the direction of medical schools and hospitals.

We also wisely delegate to these specialists selection of the subjects or theories of medicine which should be taught in medical schools. We apply the same principles and methods to our tax-supported schools of law, of art, of philosophy, or of theology.

The fathers and mothers of students of engineering, law, or medicine are never permitted, in their capacity of taxpayers, to prescribe the courses to be given in these schools and colleges. All such questions are decided by men and women who have been specially trained in one or the other of these branches of science, art, or law. The layman, as a taxpayer, is not consulted, nor does he presume to interfere in the administration of any of these institutions. Lawyers manage the law schools, doctors manage the medical schools, theologians manage the divinity schools, and so on.

On the same principles, scientists prescribe the studies in the science departments of our educational institutions, select the subjects for the required courses, determine what textbooks shall be used in the classrooms, what materials and instruments shall be employed in the laboratories; and the fathers and mothers of the pupils—the vast majority of whom know nothing whatever concerning the sciences in question —have ever been permitted—nor have they desired—to interfere with the administration of these schools.

A person might be a very good taxpayer and a very poor scientist.

The principle that science and science-teaching, art and art-teaching, law and the teaching of law, theology and the teaching of theology, must all be left in the hands of experts in these various departments of human knowledge, is universally recognized throughout the civilized world—excepting by a compartively small group of men and women who call themselves "Fundamentalists."

These sincere but—as I think—misguided citizens have challenged the right of educators to teach the theory of evolution in tax-supported schools. Our educational institutions should be placed under mob control, they tell us.

Here in the United States, for the first time in history, it is proposed by certain sectarian organizations that long-established educational principles—principles that have resulted in placing these states in an enviable position economically and culturally in the forefront of the most advanced nations—be now summarily overthrown.

The strange—not to say anti-American—doctrine is being advanced that control of our schools should be taken from men and women specially trained in pedagogy or in the aims and methods of science, and turned over to the control of laymen—to men and women who know nothing whatever either about science or about the teaching of science.

We are told that the taxpayer, as such, without regard to his educational status, even though he be illiterate, should decide the question of whether or not the facts and theories of evolution shall be taught in our schools and colleges. That is to say, in effect at least, the taxpayers are to be given the right and power to decide whether or not a scientific theory is true or false, or that, even if true, it may not be taught if found to be at variance with Babylonian and Hebraic mythology.

Never having devoted any time to the study of natural science, it should not take the average taxpayer long to decide what is true and what are "mere guesses" of men who have devoted a lifetime to patient and unprejudiced investigation of natural phenomena and natural laws.

If the taxpayers, as such, are to dictate to geologists and biologists what shall be taught in their classrooms, why not also allow the voters of the state to run the law schools, the medical colleges, and the theological seminaries? Why not enact laws making it a crime to teach any theology at variance with fundamentalist theology? But the antievolutionists are by no means so direct in their methods.

The fundamentalists tell us that the theory of evolution and the facts in support of that greatest and most useful generalization ever reached by the mind of man, should not be taught in our state-supported schools and colleges, because they have decided the theory of evolution is not supported by a single fact of astronomy, geology, paleontology, zoology, botany, or anthropology.

This assertion verges so closely on the ridiculous that it deserves no consideration, as a question of science. There is no living biologist or paleontologist of any repute who agrees with such an absurd and misleading assertion. That this declaration is untrue may be verified by anyone who should take the trouble to send out a questionnaire to the experts in geology, biology, anthropology, botany, zoology, comparative anatomy, morphology, or embryology, in any of our more important colleges or universities.

Ask any or all of these scientists if, in their judgment, the theory of evolution is supported by the results of their painstaking investigations. It is safe to predict that virtually all of them would reply in the affirmative. It is quite certain that at least 95 percent of them would so answer.

We may go farther, and say that even though we asked this question of professors of science in denominational colleges—sectarian institutions, Protestant or Catholic—we should find that at least 90 percent of them would endorse the theory of evolution as a valuable—if not necessary—working hypothesis.

In the nonsectarian colleges, evolution as a natural process of nature is practically accepted as a demonstrated fact; though it would be conceded by many of these experts that it is better, for the present, to account for the origin and development of plants and animals on this planet on the theory of evolution, without asserting that evolution is a demonstrated fact.

It is sufficient for educational purposes if it be shown that the phenomena of nature can be explained rationally and logically only on the theory of evolution—the theory that the higher organisms have been derived from the lower. And this is the position taken by nearly all teachers of science in our tax-supported schools, even though personally they may regard evolution as a demonstrated fact. To say "evolution" today is to say "nature," and vice versa.

If we disregard the few teachers of science who are not able to throw off the orthodox biblical teachings of their days of adolescence, we may say that the world of science accepts and utilizes the formula of evolution as a working method, and as truthfully representing the laws of the universe. This being true, it goes without saying that this theory and the facts upon which it is based should be taught in our publicly supported educational institutions. Moreover, I shall go so far as to say that not to teach this theory in our schools would be a virtual suppression of a large part of humanity's fund of painfully acquired knowledge, and would constitute nothing short of a social crime.

In passing judgment upon the validity of the theory of evolution, and in considering the value of the evidences offered by scientists in support of the explanation afforded by a process of evolution, the student should keep constantly in mind that if he rejects the general theory of evolution he must be prepared to offer some better explanation to take its place. For part of the evidence offered as giving validity to the evolutionist's explanation of how things came to be what they are found to be, is the absurdity of any other explanation which could be— or at least ever has been offered in opposition to evolution.

I insist that we must choose between the unsupported guesses of poets who wrote their views in a prescientific age, influenced by a belief in magic, which was universal in their day and age, and the modern theory of evolution, which recognizes in nature a process of gradual development with reference to the history of the earth in its entire career—a process of evolution of plants and animals from the relatively simple forms of the primordial world to the highly complex organisms of later geological ages.

In short, we must choose between belief in what are known by all scholars to be Babylonian, Persian, and Chaldean myths, and acceptance of the results of modern science, that is, natural processes under the uniform and immutable laws of nature—one of which, we now add, is a recognizable law of evolution.

To the unscientific mind, ancient or modern, there could not arise such a question as, for example, "How did the sun come into existence?" Either it would be asked "Who made it?" or, in former ages especially, its existence would be taken for granted. This for the simple reason that our solar orb was worshiped as a supreme god, hence as having always existed. The same is true with reference to the planets, one of which, like the moon, was worshiped by some peoples as a goddess, by others as a god. The earth itself was also worshiped by various races, at various epochs in history, as a goddess; hence as having always existed. There could, in such cases, arise no such question as, "Where did the earth come from, or how did it originate?"

It is true, however, that among various peoples, certain gods and goddesses were worshiped who are believed to be the offspring of older gods and goddesses. In some cases this was recorded in their tribal or national bible, their "Word of God," hence must be accepted without question as true.

This conception of deities as parents, as begetters of children, presented no difficulties for early peoples, or for that matter, for some supposedly modern minds.

. . . .

Yet the progressive element in our modern age of natural science is being told that it should be made unlawful to impart to the rising generation of this country a knowledge of the natural processes of evolution, or to present for their consideration a theory of evolution which accounts for the origin and development of living beings in terms of civilized thought and procedure. We are asked, meanwhile, to place the Book of Genesis on their desks, setting forth the barbaric notions of creation held by the ancient Oriental poets, with the implication that these stories are true because included among the books arbitrarily selected by the ancients as sacred writings. They are, we are told, to be "read without comment"—just where comment is most necessary, if our respect for truth and adherence to scientific methods are not to be overthrown and displaced by the dreams of pagan philosopher-poets, steeped in the superstitions and magical arts which abounded twenty-six hundred years ago in the valley of the Euphrates and the Tigris— thence transplanted to the soil of ancient Palestine.

It is an inherent and ineradicable tendency of the well-developed human mind not only to seek new knowledge, not only to search for new facts, but to try to set these facts in order, to classify them, and then to interpret them in terms of law. Man desires always not only to make new discoveries, but also to find new relationships and heretofore unknown laws in connection with the phenomena studied. We do this not only for the intellectual or "esthetic" satisfaction which such achievement brings in its wake, but also because we know that knowledge brings power, and power usually brings in its train increased health, comfort, and joy to humankind.

If scientists are forbidden by the nonscientific taxpayers to teach evolution in the schools, what are they expected to say when asked by pupils, as they inevitably will be, the meaning of the structural and functional resemblances between all mammalia, and especially the essential similarity between the structure of the higher apes and man?

Should the teacher be asked to suppress the information desired by the thoughtful pupil, because, forsooth, the nonscientific taxpayers regard the theory of evolution as being contrary to the teachings of the ancient Babylonians and Persians, as transmitted to us in the sacred writings of the ancient Hebrews?

Since no living paleontologist, morphologist, or anthropologist of international—or even national—eminence doubts that the higher plants and animals have been evolved from the lower, I contend that this expert conclusion represents the present state of our knowledge on this subject, and that the theory of evolution and the facts concerning evolution should be taught in our publicly supported educational institutions.

Every new discovery in paleontology—the science of fossil remains—in comparative anatomy, in anthropology, in biology and systematic zoology, in morphology, in physics, in chemistry and astronomy, adds new evidences in support of the theory of evolution. We may go farther, and say with Professor Henry Fairfield Osborn, dean of American vertebrate paleontologists, and eminent as zoologist and anthropologist, that evolution is a universal law of living nature and that evolution "has outgrown the rank of a theory, for it has won a place in natural law beside Newton's law of gravitation, and in one sense holds a still higher rank, because evolution is the universal master, while gravitation is one among its many agents."

From Maynard Shipley, *The San Francisco Debates on Evolution* (Mountain View, California: Pacific Press Publishing Association, 1925), pp. 145–158.

Fundamentalism and the Freedom of Teaching
Joseph V. Denney

The following excerpt from the presidential address delivered by Joseph
V. Denney to the American Association of University Professors in 1923
describes the fundamentalist movement as a serious menace to the freedom
of teaching. Fundamentalism was, in his opinion, all the more sinister because it was used by various nonreligious interests "to cover their own
purposes." Convinced that success of the movement would be disastrous both
for education and morality, he called upon the five thousand members of
the association to resist fundamentalist attempts to compromise the integrity
of the teaching profession.

———◆•◆———

The committee on Freedom of Teaching in Science has received
numerous complaints, during the last eighteen months. Efforts at coercion of college and university teachers have been open, direct, and, in
some parts of the country, successful. They have not usually originated
in the colleges themselves. Strong feeling has been first aroused by
agitation in outside bodies directly or indirectly controlling boards of
trustees and college administrators. In several of the state legislatures
attempts have been made to restrict or eliminate certain teachings by
proviso in appropriation bills. An un-American spirit of intolerance
and fanaticism has been engendered. The movement repeats with variations the conflict which raged in England and America after the
publication of Darwin's *Origins of Species.* The knowledge that this
conflict came to an end without injury either to religion or to science
has created an unwarranted feeling of security in the colleges of the
older parts of the country, where those not as yet affected are indifferent
to the danger.

As a matter of fact fundamentalism is the most sinister force that
has yet attacked freedom of teaching. Attempted coercion by commercial
and political interests has never shown a tenth of the vitality and earnestness of this menace. In the Southwest it has won sympathy and support
in two other widespread movements. As is to be expected in an effort
that is undoubtedly religious in original impulse but that inevitably be-

270

comes political in method and affiliation, it is used by other interests to cover their own purposes. While a dozen or more dismissals have occurred (two of them in state institutions) this fact does not begin to measure the evil effect of the movement upon the teaching profession, and in general upon the forces that ought to be co-operating for good in the nation.

This association distinctly acknowledges all of the legal, corporate, and legislative rights involved but regards the relentless invasion of freedom of teaching and research as ruinous to morality and education.

Resolutions, though without penalties, passed by state legislatures, denouncing "atheists, infidels, and agnostics," may appear harmless to the legislators who pass them in the hope of quieting clamor, but they increase intolerance. The only weapon of our organization is moral suasion. We cannot deny the legality of most of these intolerant acts, and we can understand the state of mind that prompts them.

This association is not primarily interested in defending evolution. We include professors of all subjects from all types of institutions and I doubt not we have members of all the Christian faiths. Our chief concern is to preserve to the teaching and research of the country, whatever the subject may be, the unhampered opportunity to find so much of the truth as it can and to make that known to minds ready to receive it. There are perils in such freedom, not the least of which in the last generation has been the so-called pride of science; but these perils are small compared with the only alternatives yet discovered—coercion, suppression of inquiry, intellectual stagnation.

No greater error was ever conceived in the popular mind than the belief, often concealing a fear, that a professor "may teach what he pleases." The present truth of any subject is determined by the co-operative labors of all who have ever devoted their lives and talents to the investigation of that subject. The truth is not determined by human fears, preferences, or hopes. The search for the truth implies the highest honor in its prosecution and the most scrupulous honesty of statement. This of itself is so impressive an obligation that no other can be conceived as of equal importance. It is a solemn responsibility not to be lightly assailed. The degradation of teaching means irreparable spiritual loss to the nation.

Any college or university, whatever its foundation, that openly or secretly imposes unusual restrictions upon the dissemination of verified knowledge in any subject that it professes to teach at all, or that discourages free discussion and the research for the truth among its professors and students will surely find itself shunned by professors who are competent and by students who are serious. It will lose the best of its own rightful constituency and will cease to fulfill its high ministry. The same results, disastrous to true education, will follow whether the restrictions are adopted voluntarily by the college itself, or are forced upon its administrative officers by a state legislature, an ecclesiastical body, or by powerful influence operating through trustees. The question of legality, and of good motive, is also irrelevant so far as moral and educational results are concerned.

The five thousand members of the American Association of University Professors in active service in some two hundred colleges and universities of the United States are of one mind on the fundamental necessity of preserving the integrity of the teaching profession. They realize that their work is a sacred trust that can be fulfilled only in freedom of conscience, loyalty to the truth, and a profound sense of duty and of personal responsibility. They claim the support of all good Americans whatever their creed in resisting measures that will prove ruinous to our institutions of higher learning.

From *The Bulletin of the American Association of University Professors* X (February 1924), 26–28.

The Protest of a University President
Harry W. Chase

Harry W. Chase, a native of Massachusetts and a psychologist trained by G. Stanley Hall, was inaugurated president of the University of North Carolina in 1920. Under his direction the university achieved new heights of excellence and acquired a national reputation for its fierce defense of academic freedom. Early in the 1920s fundamentalists in the state launched an attack upon the university as a prime example of an institution supported by Christian taxpayers which had allowed "foreigners" such as Chase and his "imported" faculty to substitute paganism for Christian piety as the dominant tenor of campus life. At one point their steady fire of criticism almost caused Chase to accept the presidency of the University of Oregon. Persuaded to remain at Chapel Hill, he assumed active command of a counter-effort to protect intellectual freedom from the fundamentalist onslaught. In 1925 he appeared in person before the state legislature to oppose the passage of the Poole Antievolution Resolution. The following selection is a letter written by Chase to Edgar W. Pharr, speaker of the North Carolina House of Representatives, while the measure was pending before the legislature. In this letter, as in public addresses and correspondence with other key political figures, the university president described what he considered the dangers inherent in such a bill. Although Poole's measure contained no penalty clause, Chase pointed out that the actual penalty was "the putting of genuine and honest men devoted to truth in the position of criminals in the eyes of the state."

———————•◦•———————

February 16, 1925

The Honorable Edgar W. Pharr
House of Representatives
Raleigh, North Carolina

Dear sir:

I hope you won't take it amiss if I take just a few moments of your time in this way to tell you just what the passage of the Poole [Antievolution] Resolution would mean to the University [of North Carolina] and to the other institutions in the state. If you take the University for example, I know you will agree with me [that] fundamentally the thing that gives it its distinction among Southern institutions and that makes it stand out as a real University is the quality of men that it is able to get and keep in its faculty. The quality of the faculty is the fundamental life-blood of an institution. Now, if any one thing is clear it is that you cannot get or keep men of the first quality under conditions that are contrary to their self-respect. The fact that the state should put on its statute books a resolution which would certainly be so construed as to harass, embarrass, and humiliate men of sincere convictions and of intellectual honesty is a blow made at the heart of the University. The question is not whether people are teaching evolution as a fact. It is the easiest thing in the world to read into utterances what was never intended. It is simply to accuse a man of things which he cannot disprove in this controversial region. The passage of the Poole Resolution would virtually set up a tribunal before which every teacher of science and related subjects would be badgered, worried, and disgraced. Good men simply will not teach in an environment of that sort. While the bill itself provides no penalty, the actual penalty is clear. It is the putting of genuine and honest men devoted to truth in the position of criminals in the eyes of the state any time that an utterance by one of these men may appear questionable . . . to any hearer. That is an intolerable position for men to find themselves in. It is an abridgment of the freedom of discussion and thought which will go a long way toward ruining the University, because it deals with the vital educational process itself, of which the appropriations and buildings are simply the means to create.

I think that you know me well enough to know that I have absolutely no sympathy with offensive and sensational statements which wound people's feelings and are destructive in character, but a net spread to catch the feet of one such man, let us say, would just as easily catch a hundred good and general servants of truth, and is a wound of the self-respect of every teacher.

So far as the situation at Chapel Hill is concerned, it is very serious, not only is the faculty discouraged by the holding up of the building programs necessitated if the Budget Commission's report prevails but right now the Dean of the graduate school . . . has an offer of a professorship of English in Johns Hopkins and the head of our extension work . . . is being approached by Wisconsin in the field of extension. One or two other men are also receiving offers from other institutions.

The passage of such a bill would not only mean instantly that such men would make up their minds to go, but other men would leave just as rapidly as offers developed, and the University would be set back twenty-five years in its development.

Please do not think that I am exaggerating the danger. . . . In a field of this sort misquotation is easier than anywhere else. For instance within the last week I have been accused editorially in the Charlotte *News* of having said that "the teaching of atheism was a matter of conscience," which is an absolute misquotation; and in the headlines of the Charlotte *Observer,* which furnished part of the material for Dr. Luther Little's sermon yesterday, I have been accused of talking about "Christian expediency," which is a phrase that I never used and that to my mind has no meaning, and has been distorted by Dr. Little to represent an idea which I never had remotely. . . . Suppose the Poole Bill were enacted, do you not see the possibilities of humiliation which any reputable citizen who believes in freedom of discussion is going to be subjected? These two personal experiences are simply in point which would be multiplied by a hundred under such a restrictive measure. . . .

> Yours truly,
> HARRY W. CHASE
> President

From Harry W. Chase to Edgar W. Pharr, February 16, 1925, University of North Carolina Papers, Southern Historical Collection, University of North Carolina, Chapel Hill, North Carolina.

A University in Jeopardy
Frank L. McVey

Among the presidents of state-supported colleges who jeopardized the financial status of their institutions by their bold opposition to antievolution bills was Frank L. McVey of the University of Kentucky. The fundamentalist crusade which began early in Kentucky unleashed one of the bitterest controversies in the history of the state. Although fundamentalists achieved considerable success in eliminating "heretical" professors from denominational colleges, their heaviest artillery was aimed at the state university. In 1922, when their antievolution bill appeared to be headed for victory in the legislature, President McVey publicly appealed to the people of Kentucky to preserve the academic integrity and freedom of the University. McVey's appeal, quoted below, contributed to the ultimate defeat of the legislation.

———•••———

TO THE PEOPLE OF KENTUCKY:

In view of the many statements, the confusion, and misunderstandings that have arisen relative to the bills introduced in the Legislature providing for the prohibiting of the teaching of evolution in the public schools and institutions of higher learning supported by taxation, it seems desirable that some direct comment should be made.

I have an abiding faith in the good sense and fairness of the people of this state. When they understand what the situation means and when they come to comprehend the motives underlying this attack upon the public schools of the state, they will hold the University and the school system in greater respect than ever before. While it is true that the proposed legislation prohibits the teaching of evolution in the public schools and educational institutions maintained by the state, the attack is narrowing itself more and more to one upon the University.

As President of the University, I desire to say as emphatically as possible that the charge that there is teaching in the University of atheism, agnosticism, and Darwinism (in the sense that a man is descended from baboons and gorillas) is absolutely false. No such teaching is carried on in the University. Moreover no member of the staff of the

University attempts, directly or indirectly, to modify, alter, or shape the religious beliefs of students.

The University, however, does teach evolution. It is, in fact, bound to do so since all the natural sciences are based upon it and failure to teach evolution would mean elimination of courses and textbooks relating to astronomy, botany, bacteriology, biology, geology, and zoology. The students in the University, as well as in the normal schools and high schools, would have to go elsewhere to get instruction in modern sciences. It does not seem to be generally appreciated what this means, but it means that the state would be shutting itself off from all contact with the modern world as a consequence of such an attitude on the part of the commonwealth.

Most of this discussion is due to lack of understanding and lack of knowledge of what has happened in the world of science.

What is evolution? Evolution is development; it is change; and every man knows that development and change are going on all the time. Evolution is a great general principle of growth. It is that idea that development goes on during long ages under varying influences of climate, surroundings, food supply, and changing conditions. It is the belief that the earth was formed ages ago and has evolved gradually and slowly. It is known today that man has lived on the earth a long time; that he has evolved from lower conditions to the one he occupies now. Science has brought to our knowledge some conception of the greatness of the universe. It has made clearer than ever before that God works through law and that men are to use their God-given minds in order that they may learn more of the power and glory of God as manifested in his works in the universe.

It is necessary to know that there are many theories of evolution; and the man who attempts to put in one phrase all the views regarding the development of the universe and state that evolution is comprehended in the phrase "man is descended from a monkey" is simply betraying his ignorance and his lack of an analytic mind.

There is a scientific theory of evolution; there is the theistic theory; there is the materialistic theory, and there is the so-called Darwinian theory.

The scientific theory of evolution seeks to determine the historical succession of various species of plants and animals on earth. It tries to arrange them according to natural series of descent. "This theory is in perfect agreement with the Christian conception of the universe, for the Scriptures do not tell us in what form the present species of plants and of animals were originally created by God."

The theistic theory of evolution regards the entire history of the world as a harmonious development, brought about by natural law. This conception is in agreement with the Christian theory of the universe. God is the Creator of Heaven and earth and if God produced the universe by a single creative act of his will, then its natural development by law implanted in it by the Creator is to the greater glory of his divine power and wisdom.

The atheistic theory of evolution maintains that the cause of the world's development was material and that through the process of law the development of the universe has proceeded to its present form, but such a theory accepts neither Creator nor Law Giver.

The theory of Darwin placed special emphasis upon the survival of the fittest, of sex selection, of hereditary influences in forms of life that appear today. The men of science have found that Darwin's theory does not explain the new facts that are being discovered from time to time, but the important thing is that Darwinism frequently stands in popular usage for all these theories of evolution. This use of the word rests upon a confusion of ideas.

The foremost thinkers everywhere, religious and scientific, have accepted the idea of evolution. The testimony of many men throughout the world is given again and again that there is no conflict between the theory of evolution and the Christian view.

If this be true, it follows that legislation of this character is unnecessary, particularly when the principle of it is already safeguarded in the public school laws, found in Section 4368 of the Kentucky Statutes. But more than this, such legislation is exceedingly dangerous in that it places limitations on the right of thought and freedom of belief, freedom of speech, and tolerance in religious matters. The Constitution of the State of Kentucky found in Section 5 of the Bill of Rights reads as follows:

No preference shall ever be given by law to any religious sect, society or denomination; nor shall any person be compelled to attend any place of worship, to contribute to the erection or maintenance of any such place, or to the salary or support of any minister of religion; nor shall any man be compelled to send his child to any school to which he may be conscientiously opposed; and the civil rights, privileges and capacities of no person shall be taken away, or in any wise diminished or enlarged, on account of his belief or disbelief of any religious tenet, dogma or teaching. No human authority shall, in any case whatever, control or interfere with the rights of conscience.

Adherence to the Bill of Rights means that such legislation as is proposed at the present time is unwise and unconstitutional.

The weakness of the position of those who are backing these bills is shown in the fact that the first bill provided for prohibition of the teaching of atheism, agnosticism, Darwinism, and evolution and attached fines of from $50 to $5,000, a prison sentence of from 10 days to one year, and revocation of charter of the institution. The second bill eliminated [the] prison sentence and [provided for a] reduction of fines from $10 to $1,000. The third bill is merely a declaration against the teaching of anything that will weaken or undermine religious faith of pupils in any school or college or institution of learning maintained in whole or in part in this State by funds produced by taxation. It provided no penalty but that of dismissal of teachers giving such instruction. Such provisions already exist on the statute books of Kentucky as indicated above and are entirely unnecessary.

In closing, I may say that the University has an unusually fine body of students. The morals, ideals, and spiritual attitudes of the students cannot be excelled anywhere. Last year two hundred men, during the winter, studied the life of Christ in classes that met in various fraternity and boarding houses near the University. These classes were conducted by members of the faculty. This year the same thing is being done, and the membership is now three hundred. The Y.M.C.A, the Y.W.C.A., and other religious organizations are active and well supported. There is absolutely no reason for this attack upon the University, and when analyzed it will be seen that it is really an attack on the public education that is maintained and carried on by the state.

From Frank L. McVey, *The Gates Open Slowly: A History of Education in Kentucky* (Lexington: University of Kentucky Press, 1949), Appendix C, pp. 292–295.

In the Name of Academic Freedom
American Association of
University Professors

The American Association of University Professors persistently opposed what it considered efforts by fundamentalists to restrict academic freedom. The association investigated numerous professorial dismissals allegedly occasioned by fundamentalist pressures and vigorously protested legislative attempts to prohibit the teaching of evolution. For example, its activities in Washington were largely responsible for the defeat of such a statute in that state. The following report released in 1924 by the Association's Committee on Freedom of Teaching in Science expressed the position of the organization in the fundamentalist-modernist conflict.

———◆•◆———

REPORT OF COMMITTEE M, Freedom of Teaching in Science.—The last few years have witnessed a revival of the spirit of intolerance which has asserted itself, especially in the opposition to the teaching of evolution. Attempts have been made to secure the passage of laws forbidding such teaching in state-supported institutions of learning, and teachers of biology in a number of colleges have been dismissed on account of their promulgation of evolutionary doctrines. These occurrences have aroused in the teaching profession, and also in the general public, considerable concern over the maintenance of that freedom of thought and speech which Americans have regarded as one of their most valued possessions. Recent events have demonstrated that public opinion in several parts of the United States is considerably less enlightened than had commonly been supposed, and manifestations of intolerance which we had generally come to believe were no longer possible have been of not infrequent occurrence. There are, in the opinion of the Committee on Freedom of Teaching in Science, certain general principles by which we should be guided in regard not only to the teaching of evolutionary theory, but in all other fields of inquiry. Notwithstanding the fact that the doctrine of evolution in some form is accepted by practically all competent investigators in every branch of biological science, it is not so much for this reason that the attempts to suppress the teaching of evolution should be condemned as because such attempts strike a blow at the fundamental principle of freedom in teaching and research. Opposition to the teaching of evolutionary theory is based mainly on ignorance and groundless fears. But the worst feature of the opposition is not that it is unscientific, but that it is un-American.

It is, we believe, a principle to be rigidly adhered to that the decision as to what is taught as true, or what should be presented as theory in science, or in any other field of learning, should be determined, not by a popular vote nor by the activities of minorities who are persuaded that certain doctrines are inconsistent with their beliefs, but by the teachers and investigators in their respective fields. It would be absurd for the laity to attempt to dictate to the teachers of medical science what should and what should not be taught as facts in colleges of medicine. Teachers and investigators may teach doctrines in one decade which are discarded in the next; nevertheless there is no body of individuals more competent than they to decide what doctrines are right, and if mistakes have been made, as they are bound to be, with the best of intentions, the teachers and investigators have proven themselves to be the first to discover and to rectify the errors without the assistance of uninformed outsiders. We are never absolutely certain as to what constitutes truth, but if there is any method of insuring that what is taught is true better than that of giving investigators and teachers the utmost freedom to discover and proclaim the truth as they see it, that method has bever been discovered. If those who know most about a subject sometimes decide wrongly, matters are not likely to be mended by putting the decision into the hands of those who know less.

Some of the proposed laws in regard to the teaching of evolution would forbid this doctrine to be taught as fact, while permitting it to be presented as theory. If such laws are justified at all, they should apply to all theoretical questions instead of singling out the theory of evolution for special attack. A teacher in any field is under a moral obligation not to teach as a fact a doctrine which is not yet established. But who is to decide what can reasonably be held as settled fact, and what is still in the realm of uncertainty? Most well-established generalizations begin as theories before they are finally accepted as truisms. This was true of the theory of the rotundity of the earth, although a minority might protest even now against teaching dogmatically that this theory is proven. The line between fact and theory would be drawn differently by different teachers. The attempt to settle such questions by law instead of allowing them to settle themselves in the light of advancing knowledge would create only endless mischief and confusion. The theory of evolution is one of those generalizations which are so far along on the high road to general acceptance as an established truth that teachers of biology differ as to whether, for practical purposes, it should be classed as fact or theory. So long as students as well as teachers are aware that there is a small measure of uncertainty attaching to most things regarded as facts, the distinction between what is called fact and what is an extremely probable theory is not one which urgently needs to be recognized by legislative enactment, especially since there is no way in which such questions can really be settled except through the advancement of knowledge.

The attempts which have been made to suppress all teaching of evolutionary theory, even as theory, are a menace not only to freedom, but to liberal education. Whatever one may think of the doctrine of evolution, he cannot fail to recognize the fact that it has profoundly influenced thought not only in the biological sciences, but in psychology, sociology, education, ethics, political science, philosophy, and many other fields of human knowledge. It is a doctrine, therefore, with which every person with any pretense to a liberal education should be familiar. Efforts to keep students from knowing about it are not only futile, but they constitute a violation of the rights of students to know what is the consensus of the best opinion on a great problem. Students have a right to know the pros and cons of controverted subjects and to express their own position in regard to them. It is only the things that are not true which have anything to fear from freedom of discussion, and it is only by the maintenance of this freedom that we create conditions under which the truth will most rapidly prevail.

From *The Bulletin of the American Association of University Professors*, XI (January 1925), 93–95.

Religion and politics are mightily mixed these days. Preachers will take a larger part in the campaign than usual this season, and politicians will misquote more of the Bible than ever before.

ARCHIBALD JOHNSON, 1926

5. *Piety and Politics*

O NE manifestation of the anxiety and insecurity so prevalent in the
United States in the period after World War I was the determined
effort to replace the "unsettlement" of the present with the comfortable
certainties of the past. To a remarkable degree, legislation became the
chief vehicle for the achievement of this end. Civic, patriotic, and religious groups demanded the legal exclusion of virtually all phenomena
which they considered causes or manifestations of the turbulent "new
era." Their support of numerous restrictive measures concerning alcohol,
movies, sexual immorality, immigrants, and Communists testified to the
popular faith in the efficacy of legislation to recapture their lost world
of stability and certitude. For many, the legal regulation of minds and
morals was essential to the obliteration of those dark, satanic ideas and
forces which jeopardized the safety of their eternal verities. When the
theory of evolution came to be considered the most pervasively dangerous
of these ideas, it too became the subject of restrictive legislation.

Some politicians, either out of sympathy with the aims of the
fundamentalist crusade or for the lack of other issues, gained considerable mileage from the antievolution agitation. One critical observer described the political spokesman of "the theology of the plain people"
as "artful masseurs of self-esteem" who capitalized on the ignorance and

prejudice of their constituents.[1] Obviously, Senator Cole Blease of South Carolina, no less than legislators in various states, used the controversy over evolution as an occasion to place himself "on the side of Jesus Christ."[2] Unquestionably the use of "ape laws as political medicine" helped spread the notion that "the professors are lined up against the folks."[3] Legislative defenders of the "folks" and their theology frequently cited as proof of such an alignment the statement by President Nicholas Murray Butler of Columbia University that decisions about educational curricula had been delivered into the hands of the intellectually unfit.[4]

Many, if not most, politicians, however, would have been happier if the teaching of evolution had remained outside the legislative arena, not because they were evolutionists or theological modernists, but because they recognized the perils of legislating in such sensitive areas. For some who opposed "monkey laws" the fear of political repercussions in the next election seemed to leave no alternative but acquiescence. Others searched, and sometimes found, less offensive substitutes for "monkey laws." But the introduction of antievolution bills clearly placed many politicians in a dilemma: to deny such measures any consideration whatever and thereby avoid outbursts of emotionalism within the legislative halls was to risk being charged with the same spirit of intolerance credited to antievolutionists. This fear of being accused of intolerant, undemocratic procedures was reflected in their responses to antievolution legislation. For example, the Maine legislature at first refused even to refer an evolution bill to a committee, but misgivings about such summary treatment of the measure prompted it to rescind its earlier action. Ultimately the bill was referred to a committee and granted a public hearing, then defeated by the committee. In North Carolina the opponents of a similar measure attempted in vain to appease the antievolutionists by what they considered a less obnoxious substitute bill which merely called for "a renewal of religious liberty" in the state. Throughout the 1920s statutes requiring Bible reading or religious instruction in public schools, which appeared to deal with many of the

[1] Duncan Aikman, "Ape Laws as Political Medicine," *The Independent*, CXVI (May 8, 1926), 543–544.

[2] U. S., *Congressional Record*, 69 Congress, 1 Session, LXVII, 12615.

[3] Aikman, "Ape Laws as Political Medicine," *The Independent*, CXVI (May 8, 1926), 543–544.

[4] See Woodbridge Riley, "The Fight Against Evolution," *Bookman*, LXV (May 1927), 282–289.

issues raised by antievolutionists, provided useful alternatives to "monkey laws." This was particularly the case after the Scopes trial of 1925 had tarnished the reputation of antievolution legislation. For legislators concerned about the image of their states and cognizant of the popular anxiety regarding the moral content of education, laws requiring some form of religious instruction in the public schools seemed to avoid the risk of ridicule and to satisfy the desires of their anxious constituents.

The antievolution measures which attracted the attention of legislators from Maine to California during the 1920s appeared in diverse forms and achieved varying degrees of success. In some states, full-fledged acts and joint resolutions either prohibited the teaching of evolution in publicly supported educational institutions or merely registered the opposition of the legislature to such teaching; in others, amendments to educational appropriations bills and textbook laws were designed to accomplish the same purpose. Generally, the restrictions were against teaching "as a fact" Darwinism or any theory which linked man in blood relationship with lower animals. Despite the diversity of opinion among antievolutionists regarding penalty clauses, some measures stipulated that any teacher convicted of violations was to be fined and/or denied the right to teach in the state for a specified period. In view of the magnitude of the furor over evolution, relatively few states passed any type of antievolution legislation. Some bills died in committee without fanfare; others, though the subject of noisy hearings, were either killed by adverse committee reports or defeated on the floor of the legislature. The fate of an antievolution measure often hinged on the role played by the state's educational leadership. Both in North Carolina and Kentucky the vigorous opposition of college and university spokesmen, who dared to jeopardize their institutional appropriations, was probably decisive in defeating antievolution bills, whereas the timid performances of educators in Mississippi, Florida, and Tennessee contributed to the success of similar measures in those states. But whether or not a state passed an antievolution bill was scarcely an index of its enlightenment or its embrace of modernist theology. Certainly the failure of antievolution measures in New Hampshire and Georgia was little reason to assume that either was a citadel of religious modernism and advanced culture. Timing as well as the presence of various political, intellectual, and socio-psychological factors often determined the success or failure of such legislation. In many areas the agitation over evolution was sufficient to cleanse the schools of "the Darwinian heresy" without the existence of a specific statute.

Regardless of the state or region in which legislative struggles occurred, the defenders and opponents of "monkey laws" employed practically the same arguments. Most antievolutionist legislators not only described themselves as friends of religion but also proclaimed their support of public education and "true science." Evolution, they argued, was an anti-Christian, unscientific doctrine that had no place in an educational curriculum. Most legislative advocates of antievolution statutes invoked, in one form or another, William Jennings Bryan's dictum that the final authority over public schools rested with the taxpayers.[5] They began with the assumption that most taxpayers were Christians opposed to the teaching of evolution, then proceeded to characterize restrictive legislation as an expression of popular democracy. They also maintained that if the state were forbidden to teach Christianity, it likewise possessed no right to propagate anti-Christianity under the guise of science and evolution. In their view biological evolution was basically a religious question that could only be introduced into the public school at the risk of violating the principle of separation of church and state. Furthermore, the theory was "a mere guess" and could not be taught as science without defying all accepted definitions of scientific knowledge.

In their turn, legislators opposed to antievolution laws were careful to avoid any argument that might raise questions about their own theological orthodoxy. Some argued that evolution was wholly unrelated to the essentials of Christianity; others insisted that evolution could be construed as a powerful ally of the historic faith; and still others, reversing the argument of the fundamentalists, maintained that antievolution legislation clearly violated constitutional guarantees regarding freedom of thought, speech, and religion. Whatever their approach, these legislators demonstrated that they, no less than fundamentalists, were adept at rhetorical juggling. Their particular problem was to make sure that a defense of academic freedom and science did not obscure their adherence to the "old-time religion." Opponents of antievolution legislation generally appeared to feel more at home in discussing the practical implications of such measures. They argued that if the legislature

5 Lawrence Levine, *Defender of the Faith: William Jennings Bryan, The Last Decade, 1915–1925* (New York: Oxford University Press, 1965), p. 278.

outlawed the teaching of evolution, it would open the gates to all kinds of restrictive legislation. In the future the legislature would be called upon to prohibit other ideas and theories which the populace, for the moment, found objectionable. It was not so much a question of the legislators' authority to enact such laws as it was the propriety of doing so. The discovery of truth, whether in science or religion, was achieved through the free competition of ideas rather than the majority vote of the legislature. The unfavorable publicity focused on Tennessee as a result of the Scopes trial in 1925 provided legislators with additional arguments against "monkey laws." After the trial, fewer were willing to jeopardize the "good name" of their states by passing such legislation. Certainly many legislators, including theological conservatives who personally objected to the evolutionary theory, refused to support legal restrictions which seemed likely to create more problems than they solved. Theirs was a pragmatic opposition to politico-religious legislation in general. But their votes against antievolution bills, whether in Minnesota or Tennessee, could scarcely be interpreted as license for flying in the face of orthodoxy.

Tennessee Senators Debate
Nashville *Banner*

The history of antievolution legislation in Tennessee reveals that even the most famous "monkey bill" in the United States succeeded only after a strenuous battle. In 1923 an antievolution measure failed in both houses of the Tennessee legislature. But the activities of numerous revivalists, several antievolution organizations, and William Jennings Bryan during the next two years helped created a climate far more favorable to the passage of such legislation. On January 20, 1925, Senator John A. Shelton introduced a bill to "prohibit the teaching of evolution in the public schools," and on the following day John Washington Butler dropped a similar measure in the legislative hopper of the lower house. Within six days Butler's bill, which, unlike Shelton's, included a penalty clause, passed the House of Representatives by a vote of seventy-one to five. Despite the swift action of the House, the fate of antievolution legislation in the Senate was uncertain. The Senate judiciary committee, having adversely reported the Shelton bill, proceeded to deliver a similar report on Butler's House Bill 185. At this juncture Senate Speaker Lew D. Hill rescued the measure from oblivion by leaving the speaker's chair to plead for its enactment. Following Hill's performance, the judiciary committee requested more time to study the bill which it ultimately recommended for passage. The following selection is a newspaper record of the Senate proceedings during the final three-hour debate on the "monkey bill." The most notable feature of the debate was the lengthy address by Senator Giles H. Evans in opposition to its enactment. Despite Evans's efforts, the Senate passed the Butler bill by a vote of twenty-four to six.

——◦•◦——

The Senate convened at 10:20 A.M. and was called to order by Mr. Speaker [L. D.] Hill. The Rev. R. J. Craig, chaplain, offered the invocation.

House Bill No. 185, by Mr. [John Washington] Butler, the "evolution bill," came up at once on third and final reading as a special order of business. The bill prohibits the teaching of "any theory that denies the story of the divine creation of man as taught in the Bible, and . . . that man has descended from a lower order of animals" in any of the "universities, normals, and all other public schools which are supported in whole or in part by the public school funds of the state."

The bill was the one reported by the judiciary committee for rejection, but was re-referred to the committee before the recess. Upon its latest consideration, the bill was reported for passage.

Mr. [John A.] Shelton declared he was one of those who believed very earnestly that this bill should be passed. He said he did not believe the right of any person to worship God as he sees fit should be interfered with, but contended that this measure would not interfere with the worship of any man. . . .

He said he considered the doctrine that man has a blood relationship with animals of a lower order is the most dangerous that could be taught the school children. "Whenever the belief in the existence of a human soul is destroyed, you will have destroyed the happiness and hope of mankind," Mr. Shelton declared, and contended that this faith is shaken by the teaching of the evolution theory. He declared that he did not believe men who believe in the divine creation of man should be compelled to help support schools in which the theory of evolution is taught.

Mr. [Hugh T.] Bennett offered an amendment to prohibit the teaching of the theory that the earth is round and affirmed the belief that the earth is "as flat as a fritter." Speaker Hill ruled that amendment was not germane to the matter under discussion.

Mr. [C. P.] Simonton offered an amendment to provide that the bill shall be construed to prohibit the teaching of any theory that man was not made in the image of God. . . .

Mr. [Sheldon] Maiden moved that the amendment go to the table. He declared that he regretted that this bill had been introduced, but since the issue had been raised, he believed he could justify himself in voting for the bill on the ground that an overwhelming majority of the people of the state disbelieve in the evolution theory and do not want it taught to their children.

"I know I lay myself open to the charge that I am narrow in voting for this bill, but I believe literally the story of creation as told in the Bible. I am not going to enter into any technical discussion of the matter, being quite satisfied with my own belief.

"This bill does not attempt to interfere with religious freedom or dictate the belief of any man, for [it] simply endeavors to carry out the wishes of the great majority of the people."

Mr. Maiden declared that the original bill was very clear and simple.

He urged that it not be encumbered with any amendments, either serious or jocular.

Mr. Simonton stated that his amendment had been offered with utmost sincerity for the purpose of clarifying the situation resulting from the presence of the word "evolution" in the caption of the bill and its absence from the body of the bill.

The amendment was tabled by a vote of 20 to 11.

Mr. [Giles N.] Evans was recognized and delivered an extended address in opposition to the bill. He said he regretted to take issue with Mr. Speaker Hill, who had vigorously urged the passage of the bill in an address before the recess.

He declared that he doubted the constitutionality of the bill and quoted the sections of the federal and state constitutions on the question of religious legislation.

. . . .

Continuing, Mr. Evans said in part:

"But Mr. Speaker, aside from the constitutional questions involved, I cannot support the passage and must favor the rejection of this measure by this body. Irresistibly forcing me to this determination . . . are several reasons to my mind potent and forcible.

"Mr. Speaker, I believe that the house and the gentlemen of the Senate supporting this measure do not oppose evolution being taught, as it has been demonstrated to mathematical certainty in the several sciences of geology, botany, biology of the lower animals, chemistry, and zoology. I think it is only the theory of man's originating from a monkey that the gentlemen would prohibit, a mere straw theory set up by the greatest of all disturbers in political and public life for the last twenty-eight or thirty years, I mean William Jennings Bryan—and never literally asserted nor advanced as I understand it by any scientist or scholar who believes in the chronological development of man—which is the true theory of evolution—not the development from a monkey to his present status—nor a mere spontaneous creation in his present form, with his present attainments, attributes, and inclinations, from mere dust, but man as he is today developed through the processes of evolution or changes from the prehistoric man of the prebiblical days, the existence of whom God's tablets of stone have revealed to us through geology.

"But, aside from these reasons, I contend that the true theory of

evolution, not alone the phase thereof that man and other animals may
have evolved or originated from a common origin—probably dust with
the breath of life—but the full scope of evolution that teaches the development of man from the prehistoric savage of giant stature . . . the
existence of whom God's great Book, the earth in which are revealed
his secrets, has proved to us the development of the plant life from the
primitive wild flower to the highly bred, long-stemmed rose or the cut
flower produced by the botanist of today, the development of the long-
nosed razor-backed swine to the thing of beauty, the Duroc Jersey
of the best farms, the development from a stunted wild fruit found to
have a pleasing taste to the seedless orange . . . all of which, Mr.
Speaker, as I understand it, is a part of evolution—I say that the theory
of evolution does no violence to the biblical story of the origin of man;
that it does no violence to the biblical theory that upon his tablets
of stone God revealed his laws to Moses. Mr. Speaker, I believe the
trouble between real evolutionists and the orthodox antievolutionists
lies in the fact that the true evolutionist has a conception of our God
as greater and bigger and broader than that of the literal text of orthodoxy and dogmatism. It is said, 'In the beginning God created the
heavens and the earth.' Mr. Speaker, no man with one ray of intelligence
. . . can deny or gainsay the fact that our Creator in the beginning
created the heavens and the earth. But what is the beginning? Is it an
instant of time, a day of the length of our present day . . . ? Or is it
that long period of time in which the Creator was bringing together the
organisms of life, the molecules of matter to shape them after his own
kind and in his own image?

"It is again said that the earth was without form and void; darkness was upon the face of the deep and 'the spirit of God moved upon
the face of the waters.' . . . I submit, Mr. Speaker, that this beautiful
language and this wonderful history so concisely written cannot possibly
be accepted in its present-day literal sense. It begins by saying that on
the first day God created the heavens and the earth, that the earth was
without form. It later says that on the third day God made land appear
and therefore created and named it earth.

"It is useless to review the story of his first seven days; but on the
first day he made light, and under the literal interpretation it was on
the fourth day that he made the two great lights, the sun . . . and the
moon. . . . Mr. Speaker, is this story not the figurative, concise history

of that greatest of all developments, occupying millions of our years, but as mere days to our Creator, the formation of our universe . . . ? Mr. Speaker, such a construction of Genesis, Leviticus, and Numbers, concurs with, and is but a symbolical, short, concise expression of, the origin of the universe as taught by true evolution.

"But again it is said that upon Mount Sinai God revealed his laws, his works to Moses. . . . Can anything be more concurrent with, yet a more concise, symbolical expression of, the teaching of evolution? And is it not true, Mr. Speaker, that throughout the last few centuries there have been many Moses who have gone on and into many Mt. Sinais and there found written in the tablets of stone by the fossils and remains of the ages . . . [a grander conception of God]? If we would ban the teaching of evolution, Mr. Speaker, we would ban this broader, grander theory of God, more omnipotent and more omnipresent, for the strict literal teachings, if construed for the narrow confines of today's literality, of the theory of the early origin and conduct of man.

"Mr. Speaker, I do not understand that evolution has questioned the immaculate birth of Jesus Christ, but that that quarrel lies not between the evolutionists and the orthodox, but between the modernists and the fundamentalists of the orthodox faith. I do know that the grand scope of the theory of evolution as applied to all the sciences does no violence whatever to the teachings of the lowly Nazarene, whose philosophy has stood the test of the ages . . . and will continue to do so.

"Why, my colleagues, if the broad field of evolution be truth, why attempt to crush it to the earth? If it be error will it not die of its own follies and will we not by trying to legislate against it thus advertise it and promulgate it? For, Mr. Speaker,

> Truth crushed to the earth will rise again;
> The eternal years of God are hers.
> Error wounded writes in pain,
> And dies among his worshipers.

Mr. Speaker Hill declared that he had the most profound respect for the judgment and ability of the senator from Lincoln [Evans] and that he was surprised that in this case he had made "such a poor analysis" of the pending bill. He declared that the measure only prohibits the teaching of theories at variance with the Bible's story of divine creation of man.

"We say that this is a Christian nation," declared Judge Hill. "The foundation of Christianity is the divinely inspired origin of the Bible. There never was a time when the teaching of pure Christianity was more needed than now. Christ Himself did not come to impose His beliefs upon others, but to teach.

"The beliefs of men and women is [sic] formed by their instruction as children. That is what causes men and women in Oriental countries to be Confucians and Buddhists. I say it is unfair that the children of Tennessee who believe in the Bible literally should be taught things contrary to that belief, in public schools maintained by these parents.

"Here is the reason for this bill: you can't teach children things when their minds are plastic and expect them to believe otherwise when they grow older. If you take these young, tender children from their parents by the compulsory school law and teach them this stuff about man originating from some protoplasm or one-cell matter . . . , they will never believe the Bible story of divine creation—that God created man after his own image and blew into his nostrils the breath of life."

Mr. [T. Benton] King declared that the Bible seemed to be "as well entrenched here today as the public utilities act was yesterday."

He said that he was opposed to this bill and he was an earnest Christian. He declared that he was not afraid that his faith could be shaken by any scientific theories and regarded this measure as a child of religious intolerance. "It is not the teaching of evolution as a reasonable, interesting theory that is ruining the children of this country, but the lack of care and attention shown them in the homes," he said.

Mr. [Frank D.] Fuller declared that he didn't believe that he was descended nor ascended from a monkey, but he thought that the surest way to spread a doctrine is to legislate against it. For that reason he was going to vote against it, he said.

Mr. [J. P.] Owen asserted that 95 percent of the people of Tennessee wanted this bill passed so that the "damnable doctrine" of evolution may be taken out of the public schools.

Mr. [Cecil] Sims said that he believed in a Supreme Being and the immortality of the soul, but he also believed that he should not vote in violation of the letter and spirit of the constitutions of the United States and Tennessee.

"We forget that our nation was founded because of religious oppression," said Mr. Sims. He asserted that this bill was the first step toward an effort to teach religion in the public schools. "It isn't a question of whether you believe in the Book of Genesis, but whether you think the church and the state should be kept separate," he asserted.

"The trouble is that we have here a subject that is not a proper one for legislation. No man could teach in the schools an interpretation of any book of the Bible that would meet with the belief of all parents.

"There are people who confuse science and religion, but science breathes a purpose into religion. Without science there would be untold hardship and suffering in the world. Science is a help given us by the same Being that created us. I urge that we should not be jealous or hateful or fearful of where the study of science may lead us.

"It is a mistake for us to try to make a statute in the state of Tennessee to unravel the mysteries of creation. We are quibbling over words. I hope the day will never come when we must choose between science and religion, but if it ever comes it will be caused by such radical legislation as this."

Mr. [Hervey] Whitfield said that he thought "the trouble with the gentlemen" who are opposing this bill is that they do not distinguish between religion and Christianity. "We are a Christian nation. We do not ask that Christianity be taught in the schools, but we do ask that nothing contrary to that belief be taught," he said.

"There are children in Davidson county who are being taught in the public schools to be infidels, that there is no immortality of the soul, that there is no heaven or hell. We have had circular letters from a group of men who were discharged from the state university because they taught evolution." He asserted that a small percentage of the "modernists" believe in God or the immortality of the soul.

Mr. Whitfield assailed the Rev. Mr. [Richard L.] Owensby of Columbia for his sermons in which he criticized the pending legislation and asserted that his actions had been inspired by a desire for advertisement. He attributed the unrest in the nation today to the "teaching that there is no hereafter."

Mr. [J. H.] Trice said that he had agreed with Speaker Hill on almost all subjects, but that he disagreed with him over his statement that he was glad this bill had been introduced. Personally, he was very sorry that the issue had ever been raised.

"No law can shackle human thought. No law can impede human progress," Mr. Trice declared. He asserted that nothing could shake his faith in God and in the immortality of the soul.

"I could have written two essays on this subject, one appealing to prejudice and the other appealing to imagination," he declared. "I am an orthodox member of the Baptist church, but I want to say that Jesus Christ himself was in a certain sense an evolutionist. He taught his disciples to hate the hypocrisy of the Pharisees. He taught them to evolve from their plane to a higher order. If evolution taught there was no God and that the Bible was not inspired of God, I would say 'Down with evolution.' " But he declared that he knew plenty of evolutionists who believe in and practice the doctrines of the Nazarene.

Mr. Trice condemned efforts to stir up prejudices and asserted that the subjects taught in the schools could be safely left to the educational department.

Mr. Simonton declared that he would take pleasure in casting his vote in accordance with the Bryan belief in the Bible.

Mr. [W. A. S.] Furlow said that he was almost inclined to believe that "we did come from monkeys after listening to this three hours' argument on a subject that we don't know a thing about. I wish I had sent down to Palm Beach for a bunch of coconuts to spread around in this chamber."

Mr. Furlow declared that the senators knew they were not descended from monkeys, but they wanted to enact a law merely to tell the world that they did not believe it. He earnestly affirmed his own belief in the scriptures, but assailed the pending bill as one leading to an era of religious legislation and stirring up of strife.

The previous question was called for, and the vote resulted in the passage of the bill 24 to 6.

From the Nashville *Banner*, March 13, 1925.

North Carolina Refuses to Legislate
Raleigh *News and Observer*

Antievolution leaders generally considered North Carolina a "pivotal" state in their drive for restrictive legislation. They contended that the enactment of an antievolution bill in North Carolina would ensure success elsewhere in the South and enhance the prospects of federal legislation. It was not surprising, then, that the state became an important battleground in the struggle over evolution. Encouraged by Governor Cameron Morrison's elimination of several state-adopted textbooks in 1924 on the grounds that they included references to evolution, the fundamentalists made an unsuccessful attempt to secure the passage of a "monkey bill" the following year. Their efforts in 1927 again proved to be futile. At the opening of the legislative session of 1925, D. Scott Poole, a small-town newspaper editor and a prominent Presbyterian lay leader, fulfilled his campaign promise of the previous year by introducing an antievolution bill. His House Resolution Number Ten stated:

> it is the sense of the General Assembly . . . that it is injurious to the welfare of the people of the state . . . for any official or teacher in the state, paid wholly or in part by taxation, to teach or permit to be taught as a fact either Darwinism or any other evolutionary hypothesis that links man in blood relationship with any lower form of life.

The bill was the subject of a noisy hearing before the House education committee in which the University of North Carolina became the principal target of scathing criticism for its teaching of the "infidel" theory. Once on the floor of the House, the measure prompted a series of complicated parliamentary manuevers by those legislators anxious both to satisfy their religiously orthodox constituents and to prevent the state from being "embarrassed" by its enactment. The following selection is a journalistic account of the final phase of the "evolution debate" in the House.

———•◦•———

[Zebulon Vance] Turlington opened the debate with a denial that the Poole [antievolution] resolution was an attempt to curb free speech. "If it meant that, I would be against it," he declared. He made the point that the resolution does not prevent the teaching of the truth nor prohibit the mention of evolution, but only that a theory shall not be taught as the truth.

He had been taught to love, cherish, and reverence the University of North Carolina, he explained, but he had been shocked beyond expression when he had heard President [Harry] Chase of that institution reply, when asked what he would do about the teaching of atheism, that it was a matter of conscience.

"I parted company with the present management of that institution when I heard him say that," Turlington declared with earnestness.

He read sections from both the state and federal constitutions relative to freedom of speech and of worship and submitted that they did not have reference to atheism but were bottomed upon religion.

"Who is backing the opposition to this resolution?" he asked and, answering his question, declared that while he could not prove it, he believed that the representatives of textbook publishers were.

"The smoothest article I have ever seen is the textbook lobbyist," he declared. "There are men who are whispering in the ears of legislators that they dare not adopt this resolution. These men do not care a snap of their finger about North Carolina."

Granting that they were not doing that which he charged, he declared that the people of North Carolina believe they are doing it and that they are attacking the sacred book of their faith in an underhanded way and argued that it is just as important that the people believe that it isn't being done as it is that the book of their faith be not attacked. He argued by analogy that people must not only get justice in their courts but must believe they are getting justice and that both go together and cannot be separated.

He warned the General Assembly that if the resolution did not pass, the representatives of the people would be in Raleigh two or four years hence with a demand that appropriations for state educational institutions be reduced.

"Let us demand now that they respect our sacred book," he exclaimed. The churches are the bulwarks of safety in North Carolina, he declared.

"Suppose somebody in our state institutions was teaching that Bolshevism had been tried and proved a success in Russia," he continued. "What would people say? Would they say that we must respect freedom of speech? No, they would rise up in their wrath and drive out such teachers."

"It is come to the point where the professors of our great educa-

tional institutions are lined up against the great masses of the people,"
he urged. "It is the hardest blow that I have ever received. Don't say that
it is religious bigotry. The great masses of our people are hoping that
the state institutions will not be hurt and that their sacred book will not
be hurt."

Concurring with what Mr. Turlington had said, Prof. R. L. Madison
declared that the resolution was simply a warning, an admonition. He
did not think liberty should be confused with license. All freedom that
society knows is freedom under the law, he explained, and submitted
that as society grows more complex, freedom of its members will be
more circumscribed.

"I can walk on the grass in the country but not in your city parks,"
he illustrated.

He described the two great books, the book of nature that reveals
the glory of God and all his works and the Bible that reveals him as
spirit. He read the nineteenth Psalm as illustrating this twofold revelation of God.

He submitted that there is not a single fact that can be given to
prove that man is descended from the lower animals. Darwin dealt only
with similarities and was forced to admit that man at maturity is quite
different from any animal. He said that the evolutionary theories are
for the most part a tissue of guesses and false inferences, and that highbrow professors and so-called scientists substitute hypotheses for fact.

The evolutionary theory cannot account for the moral nature of
man nor for his soul, he continued. Evolutionists undertake to explain
this by suggesting that there might have been a great cataclysm.

"Truth crushed to earth will rise again," he concluded.

"Such a resolution as we now have before us serves no good purpose
except to absolve monkeys from all responsibility for the human race,"
declared S. J. Ervin, of Burke, who declared that the only purpose that
the resolution could possibly serve would be as an attempt to curb free
speech.

"You can attempt it, but you can't do it by law, thank God," he
explained as he pleaded with great earnestness for the legislature not to
do a foolish thing.

"Anything can be proven by the Bible, if one wants to prove it,"
he argued, and cited as an instance the reading of a defense of human
slavery based on the Bible which he found last Sunday in a book pub-

lished in 1830. There is nothing in the Bible to justify woman suffrage, he declared.

He submitted that it would be an insult to the Bible, an insult to Christianity, to adopt such a resolution, he explained.

"I think the Christian religion can stand against anything, and a religion that can't stand against anything can't save a man's soul," he declared. "I have more respect for the Christian religion than to think it will not stand unless we pass some weak-kneed resolution. Every minister at my home has asked me to vote against this resolution for the reasons I have named."

R. O. Everett, of Durham, . . . read from a court decision rendered by the late Chief Justice [Walter] Clark in which he declared that it is outside the province of any legislature or court to regulate the religious views of men. He paid a tribute to the jurist as a champion of religious and economic freedom.

Out of the turmoil and strife of the years have come principles and utterances that men should not willingly lay aside. He had no fear for the truth, believing that it would prevail if it were the truth and that if it were error it would perish.

Because he believed the resolution to be outside of legislative authority, he moved to have it tabled.

[Everett's motion to table the Poole Anti-Evolution Resolution failed by a vote of 49 to 53. The measure itself was defeated by a vote of 67 to 46.]

From the *News and Observer* (Raleigh, North Carolina), February 19, 1925.

Antievolution Victory in Mississippi
Journal of the House of Representatives of the State of Mississippi, 1926

On March 11, 1926, the legislature of Mississippi approved House Bill Number 77 which prohibited the teaching of evolution in all state-supported schools and colleges. Any teacher convicted of violating this law was subject to dismissal and a maximum fine of $500. The measure was passed only after a strenuous fight in the legislature in which opponents employed practically every parliamentary obstuction at their disposal. That the bill finally became law was due in no small measure to the activities of T. T. Martin and the Bible Crusaders of America who descended upon the state while the antievolution bill was pending before the legislature. The Crusaders staged mass meetings and organized teams of ministers throughout the state who persuaded their congregations to bombard the legislature with resolutions in support of the bill. Martin, a native of Mississippi, addressed the House of Representatives regarding the evils that resulted from the teaching of evolution. Only when the governor received the bill for his signature did the Chancellor of the University of Mississippi, Alfred Hume, voice his objections, and only after the governor had signed it did a few major newspapers offer any editorial protests. The absence of opposition outside the legislature gives additional significance to the efforts of those legislators who forthrightly opposed the passage of a "monkey law." The following documents indicate the line of argument pursued by the legislative protagonists.

———◦——

REPORT OF COMMITTEE ON EDUCATION

Mr. Speaker:

The Committee on Education has had under consideration the following Bills referred to them, and have instructed me to report them back with the following recommendations:

H.B. No. 77: An Act prohibiting the teaching that man descended from a lower order of animals, in all the Universities, Colleges, Normals, and all other public schools of Mississippi which are supported in whole or in part by the public funds of the state, and providing penalty for the violation thereof.

Title sufficient. Do not pass.

A Minority report is herewith filed advocating the passage of the Bill.

A. C. ANDERSON, Chairman.

MINORITY REPORT ON H.B. NO. 77

Mr. Speaker:

We the minority of the Committee on Education do not agree with the majority report on House Bill No. 77 and recommend that the Committee Substitute Bill be considered.

Title sufficient. Do pass.

We assign for our reasons the following stated facts:

1st.—Evolution of any variety has no educational value and it enables men of small intellectual powers to pose as wise men—Men who cannot teach elementary mathematics are imposing on the children as science teachers and teaching evolution.

2nd.—There are no facts to sustain the theory of evolution. The fundamental teachings of Darwin and his followers have been exploded by Agassiz, Cuvier, and others whose names are the greatest in the field of science.

3rd.—Infidels, agnostics, modernists, and all the mongrel forces that tend to destroy virtue, truth, and the institutions that have held together and promoted the welfare of the human race are using our educational institutions as propaganda bureaus to bring into their ranks the children of America.

4th.—It is a principle of American education to exclude questions of religious differences from our schools.

5th.—This being true it is a brutal injustice for the state to take the Christian parent's tax money and use it to propagate agnosticism, infidelity, and modernism.

L. WALTER EVANS, of Leake,
H. F. SANDERSON, of Chickasaw,
O. N. ROBINSON, of Itawamba.

EXPLANATION OF VOTE ON H.B. NO. 77 (ANTI-EVOLUTION)

We voted against H.B. No. 77 for the following reasons:

First, this is a direct challenge to the freedom of speech, which conflicts with the foundation upon which this Government is based.

Second, it opens up the great question of entangling church and state in that it sets a precedent on recognizing certain religious beliefs and prohibits the exercising of certain other religious beliefs, a precedent that will in the near future bring before the law-making bodies favorable or unfavorable legislation for enactment in behalf of, or in opposition to, certain other modes of religious convictions.

Third, it is a very forward step against freedom of speech about which millions of people have paid the death penalty on battlefields. We predict that if the passage of this Bill prevails that very soon, efforts will be made to abridge free press and speech.

Fourth, we think the enactment of such Laws will do more to spread the teaching of evolution than if the matter were left alone. It will carry it to every boy and girl in the state who otherwise would never have thought of it. The papers will now publish evolution and antievolution articles, which did not exist before the agitation accompanying this legislation.

Fifth, we believe it will result in great harm to the schools, both public and private. It will cause strife and confusion in schools resulting in tearing down which will be very detrimental to public good. It will result in continual strife and division in the religious organizations, thus extending into every home, dividing members of the same church, school, and neighborhood.

We would have supported a Bill eliminating the adoption of free school books teaching the theory of evolution, as is shown in the Journal, but we are certain that the present Bill will do more harm than good from every view point, and will develop the practice of studying this unfortunate theory to a greater extent within a period of two or three years than has been exercised in the last century.

For the above reasons we cannot support the bill.

S. S. GORE,
J. A. ADAMS,
W. C. GRAY.

From *Journal of the House of Representatives of the State of Mississippi, 1926* (Jackson: Herderman Brothers, 1926), pp. 330–331, 1235–1236.

The "Fight for Righteousness" in Minnesota
Saint Paul *Pioneer Press*

In few states was the agitation over the teaching of evolution more protracted or more shrill than in Minnesota. The movement to outlaw this "soul-destroying doctrine" focused in the diverse activities of William Bell Riley, the minister of the First Baptist Church in Minneapolis, who vigorously attacked the University of Minnesota and Baptist-related Carleton College for allowing the propagation of Darwin's theory. Riley described his anti-evolution campaign as a "fight for righteousness." His efforts to place legal restrictions on the teaching of evolution in state-supported schools began in 1922 when William Jennings Bryan addressed the legislature on the subject. But the hostile reaction of legislators, coupled with Riley's serious illness at the time, precluded a test of the question. During the next five years Riley continued his antievolution crusade, and in 1927 he was ready for a legislative showdown. The following newspaper accounts of the climactic episodes indicate that his stringent antievolution bill, which made even the teaching of evolution "as a theory" a misdemeanor, had substantial support in the lower house of the legislature. Only grudgingly, however, did the Senate even allow a public hearing on the measure. At the hearing Lotus D. Coffman, the president of the state university, directly confronted Riley, whose bill he described as a serious infringement on both civil liberty and academic freedom. When the Senate finally killed the bill, Riley's friends in the House attempted to secure the enactment of "a compromise measure" which merely prohibited the teaching of evolution "as a fact." Introduced by Representative F. O. Frederickson of Caledonia, the compromise measure had twenty-nine co-authors. The certainty of defeat in the Senate prompted the House Committee on Education to shelve Frederickson's bill permanently. Whatever the validity of Riley's claim that a vast majority of the voters desired an antievolution statute, many apparently agreed with the editor who asserted that such a law would make Minnesota "the laughing-stock of the nation."

———— •••• ————

Members of Minnesota's Senate Committee on Education have their minds made up with regard to the theory of evolution.

Also they have already decided, they said Wednesday [March 2, 1927], as to how they will vote when it becomes necessary for them to recommend for passage or indefinite postponement the bill which would make it a criminal offense to teach evolution in the schools of the state.

But despite this fixity of their opinions, they were compelled by public demand Wednesday to agree that an open hearing should be held on the measure by a joint committee of the Senate and the House before any definite action is taken on the bill.

The evolution bill was declared by Senator K. K. Solberg of Clarkfield, its author, to be "one of the most important measures now before the Legislature," when he appeared before the education committee Wednesday to explain his bill.

Senator Frank A. Day, a member of the committee, told his colleagues that since the session began he had received more than 1,000 letters from constituents regarding the measure. And Senator W. B. Anderson of Minneapolis echoed the thought that the evolution bill was of too much interest to the people generally throughout the state to be acted on without a hearing.

In view of these statements, members of the committee, who a few minutes before had voted informally, 9 to 2, to dispose of the measure without a public hearing, reversed their stand and by a vote of 5 to 4 agreed they would hold an evening meeting at which opponents and proponents of the bill might speak.

While this action was taking place in the Senate committee, a companion bill to the Solberg measure was introduced in the House carrying the name of 15 authors.

In granting Senator Solberg's request for a public hearing, the Senate committee specified that it would allow but an hour and a half for Dr. W. B. Riley, Minneapolis fundamentalist leader, and his associates to present their arguments, and the same amount of time for the opponents of the measure. Moreover, the committee indicated that the discussion must be limited to the question of whether or not the proposed measure is a fit subject for legislation by the state.

Adoption of the plan for a public hearing was made contingent upon the House Committee on Education taking similar action. The antievolution bill was introduced in the House Wednesday afternoon and the House committee took no action on it. The Senate committee decided that if the House committee desires to hold a hearing on the bill, members of the Senate committee will join with it for a joint session.

Strong opposition to any kind of hearing on the bill was expressed in the Senate committee when it took the measure up for the first time Wednesday afternoon.

"The question has been advertised over and over again," Senator J. E. Madigan of Maple Lake, said. "What will be said in any hearing here will not change one vote in the committee, and I don't think we owe the public any duty to give any more advertising to these men who want to get this bill passed. They have had headlines in the papers for months. Why should we waste our time in a hearing of this nature when there are so many other measures demanding attention?"

Senator Henry Steen of Winona and Senator Lloyd E. Lilygren of St. Paul also said that all members of the committee had made up their minds on how they would vote on the proposed law and that a public hearing would not change a single vote.

Senator Victor Christgau of Austin asked if senatorial courtesy required that they grant a hearing to authors of the bill or its proponents outside the legislature. Senator Madigan replied that senatorial courtesy was all right but he didn't think that it would be stretched to cover this extremity.

From the Saint Paul *Pioneer Press*, March 3, 1927.

Before a capacity house that hissed and applauded, speakers for and against the antievolution bill filled a strenuous three hours of debate in the Minnesota House chamber Wednesday night [March 9, 1927].

Men seeking the passage of the bill, which would prohibit the teaching of evolution in the schools of the state, told the joint committee on education that the teaching of this theory is undermining the Christian faith of students, that it is not science, and asked the legislators to make such instruction illegal. Opponents of the bill declared it was an attempt to force on the schools the creed of a particular group.

Every aisle and every inch of standing space was packed with men and women anxious to hear the argument. Some brought their lunch and at 6 P.M. were eating sandwiches in the House gallery. About 300 were seated half an hour later, and at 7 P.M. it was nearly impossible to get in or out of the room.

Speakers were interrupted by hisses, comments, and applause.

"We had to take the Bible out of the schools," Rev. W. B. Riley, fundamentalist leader of Minneapolis, and the chief proponent of the bill, shouted. "When we do this, we say that you dare not put this atheistic philosophy in its place."

President Lotus D. Coffman, of the University of Minnesota, declared the bill represented an attempt by law to enforce on the schools of the state the creed of a particular group, an act inconsistent with the whole American spirit of tolerance and freedom.

"The spirit of America will wither and decay when the correctness of scientific theories is decided by legislation or by the counting of heads," President Coffman said.

"If that method had been followed in the past, as is proposed today, we should be meeting tonight clothed in the skins of beasts we had killed with bows and arrows.

"Squatted around a campfire in a cave, we should be trying to decide whether to burn or behead some member of the tribe who said the god of the harvest was greater than the god of the hunt."

Ministers of a large number of churches joined in asking that the bill be defeated, while others added their forces to the plea of Dr. Riley that it be passed.

Meanwhile, crowds packed the chamber and the galleries of the House, hissed and applauded, or laughed and cheered over the verbal battle.

Senator A. L. Thwing, Chairman of the Senate Education Committee, warned the audience at the outset that demonstrations would not be permitted. Hardly had the first speaker finished, however, before the audience began in vigorous fashion to express its sentiments. Hisses and "boos" followed most of the talks of Dr. Riley and his associates, while addresses made in opposition to the bill generally met with hearty applause. The audience was plainly on the side of opponents of the bill, judging from the demonstrations.

Senator Thwing several times had to pound the gavel to prevent interruption or curb the demonstrations of protest and approval that followed some of the talks. At one point Dr. Riley sought to interrupt Howard Haycraft, a university student, who was making a statement to the committee.

Shouts of "put him out, put him out" filled the chamber, and it was only with difficulty that order was restored.

Dr. Riley declared that he and his associates had talked in 200 Minnesota towns and that nine tenths of the people in these towns were in favor of the passage of the antievolution. The University of Minnesota is making a strenuous campaign to defeat the bill, he said, but the people want it to pass.

He declared the evolutionary hypothesis taught in the schools is an unproved theory, but it is not science.

University professors who spoke against the bill asked who should decide what is science, scientists or those who are not scientists. This brought a retort from Dr. Riley in his concluding speech.

"Every time I hear the argument that this is a controversy between experts on the one hand and, as someone has said, 'organized ignorance,' on the other, I smile," Dr. Riley said. "This is not a debate between the educated and uneducated."

"Five times in recent weeks men and women have come to me and said the teaching which we are trying to prohibit had destroyed the Christian faith of their children. Three of these children were recent graduates of the university. Everywhere there is a growing protest to this teaching.

"I can show from these books that I hold here in my hands that every fundamental of our Christian faith is being taught against in the University.

"Now I don't like to have my boy of 13 come home and ask, 'Am I descended from a monkey?' Maybe some of my ancestors were hung, but they never hung from a tree by the tail.

"Deism destroyed France. This doctrine has wrecked Germany already. Now it threatens the faith of our children."

Dr. Coffman made one of the principal talks against the bill.

"Long ago I learned the simple truth that men cannot be made or kept religious by law," Dr. Coffman said.

"And how can I refrain, both as a university administrator and as a citizen, from decrying the use of the police power of the state to fine and terrorize the teachers in the schools because one group of citizens does not see eye to eye with other citizens?"

Freedom is necessary for the building of a great university, just as it is necessary to obtain progress in science, Dr. Coffman said. Passage of the bill would not only bring ridicule on Minnesota, he declared, but would hamper the work of the university in many fields.

"This bill mentions only man," he said, "but it should apply, it would seem equally well, to all animal and plant life. If that is so, the doctrine ought to yield a whole flock of bills that would close our stock- and fruit- and plant-breeding experiments for fear that they might discover something unpleasant to the advocates of the measure."

President Coffman reminded the audience that the attempt to enact legislation about science is very old.

"Scripture was used by the Greek church to keep many of the Russian peasantry from raising and eating potatoes," he said. "The Scotch once opposed the use of fanning mills for winnowing grain, and thought it reason for excommunication because contrary to the Biblical text 'the wind bloweth where it listeth.' "

Others who urged passage of the antievolution bill included: A. V. Reike, Minneapolis attorney; Rev. L. A. Vigness, former president of St. Olaf College and editor of "The Lutheran"; and Mrs. Sue M. Dickey Hough of Minneapolis, former legislator.

Opponents included Dr. Arvid Reutherdahl of St. Paul; Rev. Roy Smith, pastor of Simpson Methodist Church; Rev. Phillips E. Osgood, pastor of St. Mark's Church; Rev. Frank S. Hickman, pastor of the Wesley Foundation; and Rev. J. A. O. Stub of Central Lutheran Church, all of Minneapolis.

From the Saint Paul *Pioneer Press,* March 10, 1927.

A Monkey Bill Has A Hearing in Maine
Daily Kennebec Journal

The agitation for an antievolution law in Maine was concentrated in the sparsely populated districts of the extreme north. The spokesman for the antievolutionists in the state was Benjamin C. Buber, a minister of the United Baptist Church in Blaine. Failing to win the Republican nomination for a seat in the legislature in the primary of 1926, he ran unsuccessfully as an independent candidate in the general election of that year. Undaunted by these political setbacks, Buber was still determined to protect the school children of Maine from the evil influence of the evolution theory. He drafted a bill which prohibited both the teaching of evolution and the use of textbooks subscribing to any theory that made man a descendant of lower animals. Violations by teachers and public school administrators were punishable by suspension and maximum fines of $500. Much to the bafflement of legislative officials, he sent to the state House early in 1927 his proposed bill addressed to the "Leading Active Anti-Evolutionist in the Legislature." Since no legislator was anxious to assume such a label, it appeared as if the bill would go without a sponsor. Finally, Representative Henry E. Roy, a Democrat from Lewiston, introduced it merely as a "matter of courtesy towards the citizens with whom it originated." Immediately, Representative Blin W. Page of Skowhegan had the bill tabled. When it was taken from the table on February 17, 1927, Robert Hale of Portland, the majority leader of the Republican-dominated House, moved that consideration of the measure be postponed indefinitely. Like Hale, other legislators were opposed to any consideration of the bill on the grounds that it would result in "unintelligent action" and would tarnish Maine's reputation as a "sound and conservative state." But after Hale discovered that some of his colleagues wanted the bill to have a proper hearing, he managed to have it referred to the education committee. Despite the efforts of Buber and his followers during the hearings, the committee killed his antievolution measure. The following stenographic report of the House action regarding Hale's motions reveals much about the attitude of the Maine legislators toward "monkey bills."

[February 17, 1927]

On motion by Mr. Page of Skowhegan, it was voted to take from the table House Paper 834, an act to prohibit the teaching of evolution, tabled by that gentleman earlier in the session.

MR. [Blin W.] PAGE OF SKOWHEGAN: Mr. Speaker, I yield to the gentleman from Portland, Mr. Hale.

MR. [Robert] HALE OF PORTLAND: Mr. Speaker, I move the indefinite postponement of this bill.

MR. [Ellsworth] PIPER OF JACKSON: Mr. Speaker, I move that we adjourn.

A viva voce vote being doubted, a division of the House was had.

Forty-nine voting in the affirmative and 43 in the negative, the motion to adjourn prevailed, and the House adjourned until ten o'clock tomorrow morning.

.   .   .   .

[February 18, 1927]

THE SPEAKER: The Chair lays before the House the unfinished business of yesterday, an act to prohibit the teaching of evolution, H.P. 834, tabled yesterday on the motion of Mr. Hale of Portland for indefinite postponement.

MR. HALE OF PORTLAND: Mr. Speaker, on yesterday afternoon I moved indefinite postponement of this bill. In doing so I intended no injustice to any member, least of all to . . . the gentleman from Lewiston, Mr. Roy, who introduced this bill. I do know, as most of the members know, that this bill in question has been circulating in the State House for some period. I did feel that a large number of the members of the House were inclined to treat the bill jocosely. I did fear that it would be difficult to have the bill given serious consideration, and I did feel, and do now feel to some extent, that a committee hearing on the bill would be the occasion of a demonstration which might be not very seemly nor very profitable. On the other hand, I have become aware since last night of a considerable sentiment on the part of the members of the House that the bill should receive a hearing before a committee. I know that there are some members . . . who wish to have their say in court upon this measure, and I should be the last to wish to deprive any man of a fair hearing. Therefore, Mr. Speaker, I would like to make a motion which will take precedent over my motion of yesterday afternoon and move to commit the bill to the committee on education in accordance with the recommendation of the committee on reference of bills.

MR. [Frederick] ROBIE OF GORHAM: Mr. Speaker, I suppose this is a debatable question. Some of the members who voted to adjourn yesterday in order to save this bill from immediate defeat did so for the express purpose of sending it to the committee on inland fisheries and game or the committee on Maine publicity or to joint standing legislative committees. They plan to have it rival the famous porcupine bill. To the public at large, we are a serious, deliberative organization. We are elected and paid for that purpose. Maine has the reputation of being a sound and conservative state, and we should not go on record throughout the country as having entertained this bill even long enough to have wasted the State's money in having the thing printed. I trust the motion of yesterday to indefinitely postpone will be definitely settled now, and I trust that the motion of . . . Mr. Hale will not prevail.

MR. [Henry E.] ROY OF LEWISTON: Mr. Speaker, I would like to give some explanation of this measure. This originated in the northern part of Maine—Aroostook County—and many have ridiculed the proposition. Now, we members of this House are representatives of the people. The people have a right to bring a proposition before this legislature and we should respect that right. Now this bill isn't any different from any other bill. There are some far more ridiculous than this is, and I don't see why we should not allow it to go before a committee and allow the people, the citizens, to come here and express their opinions, and after it goes to the committee, then it is up to us either to put it through, or kill it. I, myself, am not in favor of this proposition, but as a member I merely introduce it as a matter of courtesy towards the citizens with whom it originated. A member is not merely bound to support a measure that he presents in this House, but everybody should have a right to bring their propositions before this House: but now we say it may be ridiculed by other people. What about that? The first man who started this bill was ridiculed. Fulton when he built the first steamboat . . . was considered ridiculous. . . . We should not stop at that. We should let this bill go before a committee, and that is the only place where the citizens have a right to express themselves.

This question of evolution is not sufficiently proven to be permitted to be taught in our schools. If it is true, it will gradually come up no matter what we do. There is no power on earth that can keep the truth down. Now, I see by some of the papers that I am the father of the "monkey bill." (Laughter) Now, this evolution originates with a man who does not believe that we are descended from lower animals. . . . I say in justice to our citizens we should allow this bill to go before a committee. We are not afraid of the question. If you are afraid to see the other fellow's side, it proves that your side is very weak.

Mr. [Arthur W.] Patterson of Castine: Mr. Speaker, perhaps it is unfortunate that this matter of evolution comes up on Friday to those who are in any degree superstitious. I am going to direct my remarks to the statement made by . . . Mr. Robie, that this bill should not be considered at all, not even be printed, because it will subject the State to ridicule. Now, I personally . . . am a believer in the theory of evolution. If this question was to vote upon the bill itself, I should vote no, but certainly I believe it would be very discourteous to the people of Maine who believe that evolution should not be taught in the schools. I believe it would be very discourteous not to allow them a hearing . . . I am absolutely opposed to anything that would prevent the teaching of the theory of evolution or the theory of special creation in the schools of Maine; but certainly the people who presented this bill are entitled to a hearing . . . and it will not in any way subject the Legislature to ridicule. I think the Legislature would be in a much more unfortunate position if they denied the bill its proper hearing before a committee.

Mr. [E. D.] Merrill of Dover-Foxcroft: Mr. Speaker, I think there is a great danger of unintelligent action on this bill. As I understand the whole question of evolution, it has nothing whatsoever to do with a belief or disbelief in God. It is simply a question of the orderly progress of nature from the simple form to the complex, which has been so abundantly demonstrated that it has ceased to be a question in the minds of scientific men. It has absolutely nothing to do . . . with the question of an overruling Providence or a God to whom you must look beyond any question of evolution to the giver of life which permitted evolution; and for that reason I would not like to see this Legislature take unintelligent action and believe it is much in the position of the alderman who was elected to . . . the board of alderman from a ward in which he had done valiant service in politics but who was a very illiterate man. On the first session of his attendance, a gentleman, also a member of the board, who had recently returned from Europe, said: "Gentlemen, I have a suggestion to make, and my mind has turned to the question because of my experience in Venice. I was so impressed by the beauty and gracefulness of the gondolas floating over the waters in Venice that it seemed to me it would be a wonderful thing if we could have some of them in the waters of a lake in our beautiful park, and I would like to see a dozen of these gondolas floating over our beautiful lake." The illiterate politician then said: "I have no objection to spending the city's money but I see no reason for squandering our money on twelve of them birds. I would move that we buy a pair of them and let nature take its course." (Laughter) Now, it is to avoid such unintelligent action as that, and for the reason aforesaid, when the question is studied it will be found that I am absolutely correct in stating that a belief or disbelief in the teaching of evolution has nothing whatsoever to do with a belief in God; and for these reasons I am heartily in support of the motion of ... Mr. Hale.

THE SPEAKER: Is the House ready for the question?

MR. [John R.] SLINT OF MONSON: Mr. Speaker, I found out by experience that it was not well to indefinitely postpone a bill before it went to a committee. This bill is no more absurd or ridiculous than the hedgehog bill to me. (Laughter) I hope the motion of the gentlemen from Portland [will pass].

THE SPEAKER: Is the House ready for the question? The question is on the motion of . . . Mr. Hale, that this bill be referred to . . . the committee on education. Those in favor of this motion will say aye; those opposed no.

A viva voce vote being taken, the motion prevailed.

MR. [John M.] STURGIS OF AUBURN: Mr. Speaker, I would ask for a division of the House.

A division of the House was had.

Ninety-two voting in the affirmative and seven in the negative, the motion to refer to the committee on education prevailed.

From *Daily Kennebec Journal* (Augusta, Maine), February 18, 19, 1927.

Darwin and the Dakota Legislature
Grand Forks *Herald*

The fundamentalist agitation in North Dakota reached a climax in 1927 when Representative L. O. Richardson introduced an antievolution bill in the state legislature. The measure made the teaching of evolution a misdemeanor and imposed a penalty of $25 to $100 for each offense. The chairman of the House committee on education, in presenting an adverse report, argued that the passage of such a bill would mean that the legislature would ultimately be called upon "to express itself concerning the authenticity of the origin of the Bible, Mendel's law, or Einstein's theory." The obvious approval with which the House greeted his comments persuaded the author of the bill and its vocal advocates to forego a showdown on the floor of the legislature. Before its death at the hands of the committee, however, the Richardson bill was a topic of lively discussion throughout the state. The following selection is a journalist's account of a committee hearing on the proposed measure in which three Protestant clergymen engaged in a heated exchange before a sizable audience. In the aftermath of the much publicized Scopes trial, it was relatively easy for the North Dakota legislature to defeat a "monkey bill"; yet the same body enacted a law requiring school officials "to display a placard containing the Ten Commandments of the Christian religion in a conspicuous place in every school room."

Three churchmen, one of them the most militant, debated the theory of evolution with special reference to the Richardson bill which bars the teaching of the theory in North Dakota schools, before the committee on education of the house of representatives.

Rev. S. F. Halfyard, Methodist, and Rev. F. H. Davenport, Episcopal clergyman, opposed the bill, while its passage was vehemently demanded by Rev. C. J. Fylling, Lutheran. All three of the pastors are from Mandan.

Mr. Halfyard, who was the first speaker before the committee, declared himself to be a believer in the evolution theory and he gave a brief resume of the evidence in its favor. . . .

"How do we know man came from the lower animals?" he asked. I go to the rocks and read the story," and he then described the formation of fossils and told how the history of the earth can be traced from these forms. He laid particular emphasis on the evolution of the horse as revealed in the fossil. "That story is written as plainly as anything you can read in books," he declared.

Passing to the immediate question of the enactment of the proposed law, Mr. Halfyard asked how it could be enforced without making the state ridiculous in the event it should be passed.

"If a law like this passes, we should have to throw most of our present history textbooks and practically all of our textbooks in geology, biology, etc., out of the schools," he said. "If such laws become general throughout the country, we should have to close our museums, and our whole system of education would be so torn up that we should never find our way out."

"Worst of all, we would have lost our intelligent freedom which was won by our fathers."

In closing, Mr. Halfyard pointed out, there is nothing degrading in the evolutionary theory and that it in no way denies the divine origin of man. The evolutionist believes that God created man, but he believes He did it through the methods which are shown in the records, he declared.

Mr. Fylling, who spoke immediately at the close of Mr. Halfyard's address, opened his remarks by attacking the previous speaker for the views he had voiced.

"I would be ashamed to be a pastor and say to you what the pastor has said to you tonight," he declared, and continued with the claim that he is voicing the sentiment of 62 percent of the Protestant people of North Dakota when he said that he wanted very much to see the bill passed.

Mr. Fylling did not discuss the geological evidences regarding evolution in any way but based his argument entirely on the Bible.

"Either the Bible is the Word of God, or it isn't," he said and asked how Mr. Halfyard, a pastor who claims to believe in the Bible, can take a position which he said was entirely contrary to the book of Genesis.

"It is not right to take our money for public schools and teach things against our religion in those schools," he said. "A law ought to be enacted to prevent the teaching of such things. We have no right to speak against the Holy Bible as it has been spoken against here tonight."

"I believe that God created Adam and Eve not as babys [sic]

but as full-grown people and when he created the world he created the world full grown.

"We are living in a land of religious liberty, but we can have no right to say anything against religion in the public schools."

Mr. Davenport, who was the last speaker, expressed his regrets that personalities had been brought into the argument. "After listening to the argument here tonight I think you can readily see what a mess you would get the state into if you passed the bill," he said. "I would certainly be opposed to having any such law put on the statute books."

The issue, he said, was whether or not the state was to be put in the position of having to defend the literal truth of the book of Genesis and expressed the view that it was no part of the business of the state to do this since religion is specifically barred from the public schools.

His address ended the formal discussion. The committee took no action on the bill at its conclusion but will probably act within the next few days.

The hearing was held in the Burleigh county court room which was crowded with legislators and others.

From Grand Forks *Herald* (Grand Forks, North Dakota), February 16, 1927.

The People Act in Arkansas
Initiative Petition

Arkansas was the last state to restrict by law the teaching of evolution in its state-supported institutions of learning. The Arkansas law was unique in that it was placed on the statute books by popular referendum in 1928. When the state legislature refused to enact such a measure the previous year, various local and national antievolution organizations utilized the initiative to force a referendum on the issue. The people outlawed the teaching of Darwinism by a vote of 108,000 to 63,000. In 1928, the same electorate which prohibited the teaching of evolution also cast its vote for Alfred E. Smith of New York for president. The following selection is the Initiative Petition which was signed by enough voters to require the holding of a referendum.

———•••———

INITIATIVE PETITION, STATE OF ARKANSAS.

To the Honorable Jim B. Higgins,
    Secretary of State of Arkansas:

We the undersigned legal voters of the State of Arkansas, respectfully propose the following law, to-wit:

Act No. _____. . _____

FOR AN ACT TO BE ENTITLED "AN ACT TO PROHIBIT IN ANY UNIVERSITY, NORMAL PUBLIC SCHOOL, COLLEGE OR OTHER EDUCATIONAL INSTITUTION IN THE STATE OF ARKANSAS THAT IS SUPPORTED IN WHOLE OR IN PART, FROM PUBLIC FUNDS, THE TEACHING THAT MAN DESCENDED OR ASCENDED FROM A LOWER ORDER OF ANIMALS AND PROVIDING A PENALTY FOR THE VIOLATION THEREOF."

Be it enacted by the people of the State of Arkansas.

Section 1. That it shall be unlawful for any teacher or other instructor in any University, College, Normal, Public School, or other institution of the State, which is supported in whole or in part from public funds derived by State or local taxation to teach the theory or doctrine that mankind ascended or descended from a lower order of animals and also it shall be unlawful for any teacher, textbook commission, or other authority exercising the power to select textbooks for the above mentioned educational institutions to adopt or use in any such institution a textbook that teaches the doctrine or theory that mankind descended or ascended from a lower order of animals.

Section 2. Be it further enacted, that any teacher or other instructor or textbook commissioner who is found guilty of violation of this Act by teaching the theory or doctrine mentioned in Section 1 hereof, or by using or adopting any such textbooks in any such educational institution shall be guilty of a misdemeanor and upon conviction shall be fined not exceeding five hundred dollars ($500.00); and upon conviction shall vacate the position thus held in any educational institutions of the character mentioned above or any commission of which he may be a member.

Section 3. This Act shall be in force and effect from and after its adoption by vote of the people of Arkansas.

Section 4. That all laws and parts of laws in conflict herewith be, and the same are, hereby repealed.

And by this, our petition, order that the same be submitted to the people of the said state, to the end that the same may be adopted, or rejected by the vote of the legal voters of the said State at the regular general election to be held in said State on the 6th day of November, 1928, and each of us for himself says:

"I have personally signed this petition; I am a legal voter of the State of Arkansas, and my residence, postoffice address, and voting precinct are correctly written after my name."

From *Evolution* (July 1928), p. 9.

Skirmishes in Congress
Congressional Record

The forensics of the evolution controversy first echoed within Congress on May 3, 1924, when Representative John William Summers, a Republican from Washington, introduced an amendment to a District of Columbia appropriation bill. His amendment was designed to exclude from District schools all teaching "of partisan politics, disrespect to the Holy Bible, or that ours is an inferior form of government." Only Representative Tom Connally of Texas among the few congressmen present at the session directed any questions to Summers. Following their brief discussion, the amendment passed the House and was later approved by the Senate without debate.

MR. SUMMERS of Washington: Mr. Chairman, I offer an amendment which I sent to the Clerk's desk.

THE CHAIRMAN: The gentleman from Washington offers an amendment, which the Clerk will report.

The Clerk read as follows:

Amendment offered by Mr. Summers of Washington . . . insert: Provided, that no part of this sum shall be available for the payment of salaries of any superintendent, assistant superintendent, director of intermediate instruction, or supervising principal, who permits the teaching of partisan politics, disrespect to the Holy Bible, or that ours is an inferior form of government.

MR. BLANTON. Mr. Chairman, I shall not make a point of order to that.

MR. SUMMERS of Washington. Mr. Chairman, this is a limitation, and of course it is in order.

I think everyone will agree with me that no teaching of this kind should be permitted in the District or in the public schools of any city or town in any State in the Union.

I have spoken to a number of members, and it is an exception to find one who does not say that his children have come to him with complaints in regard to one or the other of the points mentioned in the amendment.

In the interest of the highest possible standard of education in this city, and because I believe that the schools here should be as nearly as possible a model for those throughout the country, I think this thing ought to be stopped, and this amendment will have that effect.

If it should be contended that no one is guilty of permitting this, then the amendment will do no harm. If they are guilty of permitting it knowingly, then it should apply.

MR. CONNALLY of Texas. Mr. Chairman, will the gentleman yield?

MR. SUMMERS of Washington. Yes; I yield.

MR. CONNALLY of Texas. Has the gentleman information that such things are going on in the schools which his amendment is intended to reach?

MR. SUMMERS of Washington. I have.

MR. CONNALLY of Texas. Who will pass upon the question as to whether this is happening or not? Who will be the arbiter?

MR. SUMMERS of Washington. The school board.

MR. CONNALLY of Texas. Will not the man who issues or pays these warrants be the one? This being a limitation on this appropriation, will they not pass the question up to the accounting officers of the Government?

MR. SUMMERS of Washington. All right.

MR. CONNALLY of Texas. In a practical way, I would like to know how that is going to work.

MR. SUMMERS of Washington. It might be up to the accounting officers. Anyhow, there would be a way then by which one might file a complaint and stop the payment of salaries to anyone who has been permitting this pernicious teaching. It has unquestionably been going on for years, and is going on in this present year.

MR. CONNALLY of Texas. Does not the gentleman think that the Board of Education can control this matter? Does the gentleman think it wise to put a limitation upon the appropriation?

MR. SUMMERS of Washington. Yes, I do; because I know of no other way to reach it. This will stop it.

MR. CONNALLY of Texas. An Act of Congress would reach it in the regular way.

MR. SUMMERS of Washington. There is no other way that I know of whereby we can reach it in a practical manner. In the interest of our children and of the government itself this teaching must stop.

ported.again

MR. CHAIRMAN. The question is on agreeing to the amendment offered by the gentleman from Washington.

MR. LOWERY. Mr. Chairman, may we have it again reported?

MR. CHAIRMAN. Without objection, the amendment will again be reported.

The amendment was again read.

MR. CHAIRMAN. The question is on agreeing to the amendment.

The question was taken and the amendment was agreed to.

From *Congressional Record,* 68 Congress, 1 Session, LXV, 7796.

The Summers Amendment, passed in 1924, elicited little interest until Loren H. Wittner, an employee in the Treasury Department long known as a champion of the complete separation of church and state, used it as the basis of a test case against the District of Columbia school officials in the following year. His petition requested the court to enjoin the fiscal agents from paying salaries to any instructors who taught evolution. Although Wittner's case failed on technical grounds, it served to attract attention to the Summers Amendment. In March 1926, when a District appropriation bill was again before the House, Representative Bill G. Lowrey of Mississippi (an old acquaintance of T. T. Martin, Secretary of the Anti-Evolution League of America) attempted to attach to it an amendment whose purpose was identical to that of Summers's measure two years earlier. When Lowrey's amendment was ruled out of order, Representative Thomas L. Blanton of Texas tried in vain to keep it alive by appealing the decision of the chair. Failing in this effort, Blanton gained the floor by offering a *pro forma* amendment to another section of the bill. He discoursed on the dangers of "turning teachers loose upon unsuspecting pupils and letting them teach any kind of doctrine they want." Smarting from the newspapers' derision of fundamentalists, he advised his colleagues that "they had better pay some attention to what is going on" in the schools and colleges of America. Unlike the dispirited exchange over the Summers Amendment in 1924, Blanton's remarks prompted comments from James T. Begg of Ohio, John C. Ketcham of Michigan, Martin B. Madden of Illinois, and Fiorello La Guardia of New York. Blanton's most effective adversary was La Guardia, who alluded to the "ridiculous" Lusk Laws passed in his own state and counseled the House to avoid emulating the foolish conduct of some state legislatures.

MR. BLANTON. Mr. Chairman, I offer the following amendment.

The Clerk read as follows:

Amendment by Mr. Blanton: Page 38, line 1, strike out the word "text-books," and in line 8 strike out the words "in their discretion."

MR. BLANTON. Mr. Chairman, this is a *pro forma* amendment to enable me to use a few minutes. I think what is known as the Summers amendment was good legislation. It is the law now and will be the law of the land until July 1, 1926. It provides that teachers here shall not teach partisan politics, or disrespect for the Holy Bible, or that this is an inferior form of government. I do not believe in turning teachers loose upon unsuspecting pupils and letting them teach any kind of doctrine they want. My colleagues, of course, sustained the chair in holding that that was not a limitation.

MR. BEGG. Where are the supervisors that they do not keep them from doing that?

MR. BLANTON. The gentleman will remember that during the war there was a teacher suspended for doing that very thing.

MR. BEGG. That might happen.

MR. BLANTON. For teaching disloyalty. The teacher was suspended. She belonged to an organization and that organization demanded that the teacher be reinstated and her back salary paid for all the time she was out. She was reinstated and the back salary was paid, and she continued to do what she pleased.

But I want you to know that in the colleges and universities of the United States you had better pay some attention to what is going on before you send your boys there. You had better pay some attention to what is being taught in all schools before you send your children there. I know the newspapers make fun of us and call us "fundamentalists" whenever we want to inquire into what the children are being taught.

MR. MADDEN. It is a good thing. I think they ought to find out.

MR. BLANTON. I think it would be a good thing to have the Summers amendment in every State in the land. Why should they not be taught to have respect for the Holy Bible? The Government has enough respect to place on the dollar the words "In God We Trust." Why should we not require the teachers of the District of Columbia to show proper respect? Why should we not prevent them for teaching partisan politics in the schools here? Let them learn partisan politics on the floor of the House. There is plenty of it here, and this is a good place to learn partisan politics.

I wanted to say this, that some members do not like to be in the minority vote. When I believe that I am right I would vote to support my convictions, if I were the only man voting that way. It is not a question of voting with the majority; it is a question of voting one's sincere convictions. . . .

MR. KETCHAM. Will the gentleman yield?

MR. BLANTON. Yes.

MR. KETCHAM. Granting the gentleman's argument, what does the gentleman think about putting this provision in a great appropriation bill that has to do with the schools of the United States capital, practically admitting that these things are done?

MR. BLANTON. It was placed in this bill last year, and it is now law but it will expire July 1, 1926.

THE CHAIRMAN. The time of the gentleman from Texas has expired.

MR. BLANTON. I withdraw the *pro forma* amendment.

MR. LA GUARDIA. Mr. Chairman, I rise in opposition to the withdrawal of the amendment. I sympathize with the gentleman from Texas when he states that he votes very often in the minority. I also vote very often in the minority. I always follow my own convictions and vote accordingly.

MR. MADDEN. I think every man should follow his own convictions.

MR. LA GUARDIA. Exactly so; and I have voted so often in the minority that I am accustomed to it. I do not agree in this instance with what the gentleman from Texas has said.

MR. BLANTON. Will the gentleman yield?

MR. LA GUARDIA. Let me get started first.

MR. BLANTON. Right on that point.

MR. LA GUARDIA. I have not made any point yet; let me get started. I do not believe there is the slightest danger in what is being taught in our public schools and colleges in this country. Our children are in the care of the finest group of men and women in the country, and as a class there are none more loyal and more devoted to the country than our school and college teachers. But when it comes to saying that any teacher might create a notion in the mind of a student that this is an inferior form of government, and that this sort of thing should be stopped, it is a bit hysterical and getting excited over something which does not exist. Of course, we are to have criticism of government in the study of civics and political history. If anyone who criticizes our form of government is guilty of a serious offense, then Abraham Lincoln was guilty of such a charge. He repeatedly stated at one period of our national life that a country that permitted slavery was an inferior form of government, and that it should be changed, and the Constitution was amended. That amendment made a fundamental change in our form of government.

We cannot stand still in the science of government. We cannot stand still and accept as permanent what was good and what was proper and what was fair and just 140 years ago when the Constitution was adopted under different conditions. Every amendment to our Constitution shows the need of constant changes in governmental fundamentals to meet changed conditions.

As times change, so must your government change. When the Constitution of the United States was adopted we had no railroads, we had no congested districts, we had no farm problems. . . .

We went through a period of hysteria in New York, and a stupid sort of law purporting to test the loyalty of our school teachers was passed. It turned out to be so ridiculous that it was repealed and wiped off the statute books in three years. At this time there seems to be a wave of intolerance in thought and everything else. He who does not accept as permanent and perfect an existing order of things and ancient fundamentals in all things is immediately suspected and charged with every crime under the sun. Intolerance has never stopped thinking. In fact, it stimulates it. . . . We should at least give a good example to State legislatures by what we do here and not try to follow the mistakes and foolish conduct of any State legislature. Our children are safe in the schools; they are learning to think; and as they grow up they will be able to look after their Government and to make laws to meet changed conditions and to bring about a more equal distribution of happiness and the good things of life.

MR. FUNK. Mr. Chairman, I move that the committee do rise.

The motion was agreed to.

From *Congressional Record,* 69 Congress, 1 Session, LXVII, 5748–5749.

The most direct reference to the evolution controversy within Congress appeared in the form of an amendment to the Dill Radio Control Bill, offered on July 2, 1926, by Senator Cole Blease of South Carolina. The amendment prohibited radio broadcasts dealing with "the subject of evolution." Although Blease obviously was not optimistic about the passage of his amendment, it at least allowed him an opportunity to voice his objections to the evolution theory and to let the world know that he was "on the side of Jesus Christ." Senator Thomas Heflin of Alabama, who agreed with Blease regarding evolution, nonetheless opposed the amendment on the grounds that it interfered with free speech. Heflin devoted most of his semijocular discussion to a reiteration of hackneyed antievolution jokes. The author of the radio control bill, Senator C. C. Dill of Washington, confined his remarks to correcting Blease's extravagant claims about the censorship powers of the proposed radio commission. Closing the brief debate was Senator Royal Copeland of New York, who urged the defeat of Blease's amendment. He publicly confessed that he was at the same time a religious man and a believer in evolution. The defeat of the Blease amendment marked the end of congressional skirmishes related to the evolution controversy. Despite their grandiose claims, the fundamentalists never came near achieving a full scale federal antievolution act, much less a constitutional amendment.

MR. BLEASE. Mr. President, I offer the amendment which I send to the desk.

THE VICE PRESIDENT. The amendment will be stated.

The Chief Clerk. On page 59, after line 15, it is proposed to insert the following as a new section.

Sec. 25. The commission is further empowered to make and enforce regulations to censor and prohibit all discourses broadcast from stations under its control regarding the subject of evolution.

MR. DILL. Mr. President, that is an amendment, as the Senate can readily see, which gives the commission the power to censor. I am willing to let the Senate vote on it, and if the Senate cares to accept it, it can go to conference.

MR. BLEASE. Mr. President, I am willing to have the amendment voted on. I should like to have an expression of the Senate of the United States on the subject as to whether or not we are going to create a commission and let them censor almost everything in the world except the question of religion without anyone having a say as to what subjects along that line shall or shall not be discussed.

Personally I want to go on record on it. It does not make any difference to me whether the Senate adopts the amendment or not, but I am willing for the world to know that on this proposition I am on the side of Jesus Christ.

MR. DILL. I want to correct a statement which the Senator has made. The Senator from South Carolina, I know, does not want to make a misstatement. The bill does not give to the commission the power to censor programs, but instead it specifically prohibits the commission from censoring programs in any way. I wish that statement to go in the record, to clear up any misapprehension that might arise.

MR. BLEASE. That does not change my position, Mr. President.

MR. HEFLIN. Mr. President, I took the position yesterday and the day before that people ought to be at liberty to discuss anything they want to over the radio, and that the special interests ought not to be able to suppress free speech. The Senator from South Carolina [Blease] and I occupy the same position with regard to the Bible theory of creation—that God made man just as the Bible tells us He did.

Last year, when I was delivering a few addresses about the country, a gentleman asked me on one occasion if I was going to discuss evolution. I said, "No; not particularly." "Well," he said, "most of our people here believe that God made man, but there are a few who hold to the Darwinian or evolution theory regarding the origin of man." "Well," I said, "I have no desire to hurt the feelings of anybody. So far as I am concerned, I find a great deal of comfort and satisfaction in the belief that God Almighty made my ancestors, but I am willing for those who hold to a contrary view regarding theirs to think as they choose upon the subject. If they insist that they sprung from monkeys, I shall not quarrel with them, because they know more about their ancestors than I do, and they may be right about it." [Laughter]

I told him what occurred in my home county in Alabama. I said "That question has been settled. The Negroes had an immense mass meeting out at the Greenwood Church in Chambers, Alabama. They assembled at 10 o'clock one Sunday morning and held forth until 5 in the afternoon. They read various passages of the Bible pertaining to the creation of man, and at 5 o'clock old Uncle Rufus got up and offered a resolution which was unanimously adopted. The resolution said: *Resolved*, God Almighty made all the niggers and most of the white folks, but all them white folks what thinks they sprung from monkeys is right about it." [Laughter in the Senate and galleries]

THE VICE PRESIDENT. The question is on the amendment offered by the Senator from South Carolina.

MR. COPELAND. Mr. President, I could not bear to have this amendment go without one word. I can not see why the Senate of the United States should be disturbed over the subject of evolution. You may be surprised, Mr. President, to know it, but I believe in religion and try to be religious; even so, I believe in evolution, and am glad to give public testimony to both these facts. I hope the amendment will be defeated.

SEVERAL SENATORS. Vote!

MR. VICE PRESIDENT. The question is on the amendment offered by the Senator from South Carolina.

The amendment was rejected.

From *Congressional Record*, 69 Congress, 1 Session, LXVII, 12615.

The contest between evolution and Christianity is a duel to the death.

WILLIAM JENNINGS BRYAN, 1925

6. Modernists and Fundamentalists at Armageddon: The Scopes Case

I N mid-July 1925, the drowsy little town of Dayton, Tennessee, became the focus of international attention. The cause of its sudden emergence from obscurity was the trial of a local high school coach and science teacher, John Thomas Scopes, who was accused of violating the state's antievolution law. Failing to enact a "monkey law" in 1923, the fundamentalists were able to achieve their goal two years later largely because of crusades by numerous itinerant evangelists, rallies by William Jennings Bryan, and lively discussions of the evolution controversy in the press. Upon signing the bill into law in 1925, Governor Austin Peay publicly characterized it as merely "a protest against a tendency to exalt science, and deny the Bible." "Nobody believes," he declared, "that it is going to be an active statute."[1] Despite the fact that the state made no effort to enforce the measure, the mere existence of a legislative enactment designed to ban the teaching of evolution attracted much attention and aroused considerable alarm among those who considered it a serious blow to academic freedom or "a leap backward into the Dark Ages."

That Dayton was the scene of a legal case to test the constitutionality of the antievolution law was no accident. Rather it was the result of well-laid strategy by a group of prominent Daytonians, including F. E. Robinson, chairman of the local school board, and George W.

[1] Nashville *Banner*, March 24, 1925.

Rappelyea, manager of the Cumberland Coal and Iron Company. The motives for instituting the legal contest were complex; but apparently they were prompted in part by a genuine hostility to the law and in part by a desire to "put Dayton on the map" by taking advantage of an offer by the American Civil Liberties Union to finance a test case. At any rate, they approached Scopes about the possibility of standing trial. Although his regular classes in chemistry and algebra provided few opportunities for violating the statute, Scopes had been the substitute teacher in the biology class for two weeks during the illness of the regular teacher and had made assignments in George Hunter's *Civic Biology*, the state-adopted textbook which embraced the Darwinian theory of the origin of the species. Scopes was uncertain whether he had explicitly violated the antievolution law, but he was nonetheless willing to become the defendant in a case to test the constitutionality of a legislative enactment contrary to his basic values. The announcement of Scopes's "arrest" was the signal for frenzied activity in preparation for what William Jennings Bryan extravagantly described as the "duel to the death" between Bible Christianity and infidelity.

The trial developed into a first-rate attraction starring two nationally known personalities: Clarence Darrow, a famous criminal lawyer who, for many, symbolized the secular, agnostic cast of urban America; and William Jennings Bryan, the folk-hero of rural America, who was convinced that the "fate of Christianity hangs on the outcome" of the case. Retained by the American Civil Liberties Union, Darrow headed a team of distinguished legal talents including Dudley Field Malone, Arthur Garfield Hays, and Bainbridge Colby. The World's Christian Fundamentals Association arranged for Bryan and his son to assist the prosecution. But the fierce forensics of the two star performers, Byran and Darrow, occupied the center of the courtroom stage. Yet neither of them was credited with the most eloquent oration of the trial, an honor that apparently belonged to Malone.

A bizarre conglomeration of people crowded into Dayton to witness the spectacle. The town, in fact, assumed the appearance of a carnival where hot dog vendors competed with booksellers hawking Bibles and evolution tracts. Journalists from all parts of the world vied for news stories, while personnel from Chicago's radio station WGN pioneered in remote-control broadcasting in order to keep Americans informed of "the strange happenings in the Tennessee hills." Famous scientists and theologians, on hand to testify for the defense, rubbed shoulders with T. T. Martin, the evangelistic secretary of the Anti-Evolution League of America, and with Deck Carter, who claimed to be the only person with whom God had communicated directly since Joan of Arc. The high priest of irreverence, Henry L. Mencken of the *American Mercury,* facetiously pronounced the trial "the greatest since that held before Pilate"[2] and delighted in describing the Tennessee hill people as "gaping primates" and "yokels." Darrow's cohort, the urbane Arthur Garfield Hays, listened with utter disbelief as a group of gyrating Holy Rollers screamed: "Thank God I got no education. Glory be to God."[3] Michael Williams, a journalist for more than a quarter of a century who covered the trial, described Dayton as an "agreeable little country town among charming, wooded hills, forty miles from the nearest city, and a million miles away from anything urban, sophisticated, and exciting."[4] Despite his confession of being wholly unprepared for his Dayton assignment, he recognized that behind the farce and comedy of the Scopes trial lay issues deeply disturbing to the generation of the 1920s.

In the course of the trial (July 10–21, 1925), Judge John T. Raulston, a lay preacher, never attempted to hide his fundamentalist sympathies. When he ruled out the scientific testimony of fifteen experts, many thought that Darrow's whole defense had been destroyed. But Darrow regained the advantage when Bryan was induced to take the stand as an expert on the Bible and allowed himself to be maneuvered into admitting that he did not accept all scripture literally. Such an admission was a serious blunder, causing much disaffection within fundamentalist ranks. As Bryan's biographer points out, however, the Commoner had not entered the fundamentalist movement primarily to defend biblical literalism, and "his literal acceptance of the Bible did not lead to his rejection of evolution so much as his rejection of evolution led to his willingness to accept literally portions of the Bible."[5]

After less than ten minutes of deliberation, the jury returned its expected verdict of guilty. Neither the defense nor the prosecution

---

2 H. L. Mencken to Howard W. Odum, June 28, 1925, Howard W. Odum Papers, (Southern Historical Collection, University of North Carolina at Chapel Hill).

3 See Arthur Garfield Hays, *Let Freedom Ring* (New York: Boni and Liveright, 1928), p. 40.

4 Michael Williams, "At Dayton, Tennessee," *Commonweal,* IV (July 22, 1925), 262.

5 Lawrence Levine, *Defender of the Faith: William Jennings Bryan, The Last Decade, 1915–1925* (New York: Oxford University Press, 1965), pp. 349–350.

was disappointed. Although Bryan probably sensed that the trial had harmed his cause, he could take comfort in the fact that it had sustained the antievolution law. As for Darrow and his colleagues, they were delighted that the verdict afforded an opportunity to appeal the case. The argument on the appeal took place in June 1926, before the Tennessee Supreme Court, which found a way both to prevent appeal to the federal Supreme Court and to avoid offense to public sensibilities: its decision in January 1927 upheld the antievolution law but reversed the decision of the Dayton court on the grounds that Judge Raulston had improperly imposed the $100 fine upon Scopes. By directing the attorney general to nol-pros all proceedings in what it termed this "bizarre" case, the court appeared to endorse Governor Peay's view that the antievolution law was not a statute to be enforced.

Scopes himself was not present when the appeal was argued before the Tennessee Supreme Court. Once the fine had been paid, he was a free man. A scholarship fund arranged by a group of distinguished scientists had enabled him to begin graduate study in geology at the University of Chicago in the fall following the trial. By 1927 the fund was depleted, and Scopes applied for a regular university fellowship. Unfortunately for him, his notoriety as "the Monkey Trial defendant" prevented him from receiving the fellowship. In fact, the university president suggested that he take his "atheistic marbles and play elsewhere."[6] Stunned and disappointed by such an attitude, Scopes abandoned his doctoral program and took a job with an oil company in South America. Even so, he was never able to escape completely the effects of his experience in Dayton.

But the significance of the trial was by no means limited to its effect upon Scopes's personal career. Of major importance was its impact upon the fate of the evolution controversy. The trial had a sobering effect upon many Americans who, disturbed by the moral and intellectual drift of the era, were repelled by the ludicrous spectacle. Rather than bringing solace, it had raised serious questions about attempting legislative and legal solutions to religious and moral problems. Whether justifiable or not, the impression that fundamentalism was allied with bigotry, ignorance, and intolerance was enhanced by the millions of words of newsprint and radio broadcasts emanating from Dayton. Un-

[6] John T. Scopes and James Presley, *Center of the Storm: Memoirs of John T. Scopes* (New York: Holt, Rinehart and Winston, 1967), p. 240.

questionably the press coverage of the trial also "dramatized the conservative religious temper of the South and popularized the Bible Belt stereotypes."[7] Tennessee, in particular, was depicted as the home of benighted yokels bent upon thwarting enlightenment by statute. To be sure, the widespread nonsouthern criticism of Tennessee and the South in general "activated defensive psychological mechanisms" in the region and prompted *Manufacturers' Record* to characterize the trial as "one of the South's supremest advertisements" in publicizing its "pure and undefiled" religion.[8]

For entirely different reasons, the Dayton affair elicited a defense from the famous literary group at Vanderbilt University known as the Fugitives. The Scopes trial and the journalistic attacks on the South prompted by it played a decisive role in the metamorphosis of this group which spawned the Agrarians. Before the trial "none of the future Agrarians had in any way distinguished themselves as champions of their region." By 1927, however, Donald Davidson, Allen Tate, John Crowe Ransom, and other Fugitives had made a "striking reversal" by becoming champions of "the principles of the Old South" including its religious orthodoxy. While they distinguished between "bad" and "good" fundamentalists—between those who displayed a "belligerent ignorance" and those who clung to "poetic supernaturalism against the encroachments of cold logic"—they were inclined to believe that even the "bad" ones did "no great harm."[9] In their view fundamentalism at least stood for "moral seriousness" and offered a "sincere, though a narrow, solution to a major problem of our age: namely, how far science, which is determining our physical ways of life, shall be permitted also to determine our philosophy of life."[10] An "unorthodox defense of religious orthodoxy" originating with the Vanderbilt group was John Crowe Ransom's *God Without Thunder* (1930).

At the same time the Fugitives were initiating their defense of the South and its historic, orthodox faith, Edwin Mims, also of Vanderbilt, was lamenting the recrudescence of religious obscurantism in the re-

[7] Kenneth K. Bailey, *Southern White Protestantism in the South in the Twentieth Century* (New York: Harper and Row, 1964), p. 90.

[8] *Manufacturers' Record*, LXXXVIII (August 20, 1925), 70.

[9] See Alexander Karanikas, *Tillers of A Myth: Southern Agrarians as Social and Literary Critics* (Madison: University of Wisconsin Press, 1966), pp. 9, 12, 26–27, 145.

[10] Donald Davidson, "First Fruits of Dayton: The Intellectual Evolution in Dixie," *Forum*, LXXIX (June 1928), 898.

gion.[11] Many shared Mim's concern that the cultural advancement of the South had failed to keep pace with its material progress. Although southerners were obviously divided in their reaction to the Dayton affair, there was little evidence of popular support for a similar trial elsewhere. Undoubtedly few teachers in the region were willing to take the risk that Scopes had taken, but many fundamentalists, especially those of the passive variety who well might have encouraged a "monkey trial" in their own states prior to Dayton, were quick to abandon such notions after the midsummer of 1925. Many had become weary of the "whole monkey business"; even civic boosters were sufficiently concerned about the reputations of their communities and states to avoid the odium heaped on Tennessee and Dayton. Tennessee was for many southerners what the South was for the nation: by focusing on the "shame" of Tennessee it was possible for Americans generally to gloss over their own faults and shortcomings.

This is not to say that the Scopes trial marked the end of the fundamentalist movement. Actually, the noisiest phase of the crusade occurred in the two years following the trial. But the furor was the work of a relatively few zealots. The shrillness of the clamor seemed to increase in direct ratio to the decline of their cause in popularity. A partial explanation for this development lay in the effect of Bryan's death shortly after the trial, an event which bestowed an ambiguous legacy upon the antievolution crusade. On the one hand, it furnished the movement with a martyr around whom the remnant of dedicated zealots such as the Bible Crusaders of America, an organization formed to continue the battle begun by the "fallen Elijah," rallied. On the other hand, the removal of Bryan from the scene created a vacancy in the leadership of the cause, and though there was no dearth of aspirants for his mantle, no one was ever able to co-ordinate the antievolution effort as he had. The direction of the movement was diffused among rival organizations and individuals whose free-wheeling activities and preposterous claims scarcely elicited broad support even from those segments of the population classified as fundamentalist. In a sense, then, both Bryan and his cause were casualties of the Scopes trial.

Technically the question before the court at Dayton was whether

11 See Edwin Mims, *The Advancing South: Stories of Progress and Reaction* (Garden City: Doubleday, 1926).

Scopes had violated the state's antievolution law, but the American people viewed the trial as involving far more significant issues. Both the defense and prosecution attorneys were well aware of this popular conception. Bryan, the self-styled defender of Christianity, came to Dayton "to protect the Word of God against the greatest atheist or agnostic in the United States!"[12] Convinced that nothing less than intellectual freedom itself was on trial, Darrow conceived of himself as the champion of intelligence and enlightenment. Contemporary observers, no less than historians later, displayed a wide diversity of opinion regarding the significance of the Scopes case. It has been described as a decisive event in the historic struggle between science and biblical faith, "a grand colic in the bowel of American folk-religion," and merely an entertaining "teapot tempest."[13] In one respect at least there was little disagreement: the personalities, the social setting, and the popular conception of the issues involved in the trial were the stuff of which headlines were made in the 1920s. Those who viewed the trial as a "duel" in which the outcome would determine the future of science, religion, or intellectual freedom in America were extravagant in their expectations. In such matters Dayton was scarcely decisive. In 1965 a Baptist clergyman provided a perceptive assessment of the Tennessee antievolution law and the Scopes trial when he wrote:

The old Tennessee law was never law and never mattered. It was a flag, but that is all. Dayton settled nothing. The forces of change were other than courts can deal with and were already, slowly, in ferment.[14]

12 T. T. Martin, "The Flag of Fundamentalism Borne Aloft?" *Crusaders' Champion*, I, (December 25, 1925), 20.

13 See *D-Day at Dayton: Reflections on the Scopes Trial*, edited by Jerry Tompkins (Baton Rouge: Louisiana State University Press, 1965), p. 130; Joseph Wood Krutch, *More Lives Than One* (New York: William Sloane Associates, 1962), pp. 143ff.

14 Quoted in Tompkins, *D-Day at Dayton*, p. 136.

Origins of the Scopes Trial
John Thomas Scopes

Late in the summer of 1924, John Thomas Scopes accepted a "coaching- and-teaching job" in Dayton, Tennessee. The unexpected resignation of the football coach left Central High School there "without a coach or anyone to teach algebra, physics, and chemistry." The son of an English-born father proud of his reputation as an independent thinker, Scopes was taught "always to stand up for what I thought was right." An easy-going, personable young man, he quickly became a popular figure in Dayton. Although he was aware of the Butler Antievolution Act passed by the Tennessee legislature in 1925, he showed little interest in it until a group of prominent Daytonians persuaded him to become the defendant in a legal case to test the constitutionality of the law. The following selection is his recollection of how the "monkey trial" originated and how he became involved in it. Significantly, Scopes recalls that although he agreed to stand trial, he was not at all sure he had taught evolution.

In the middle of our game, a little boy walked up and watched us smack the ball back and forth. He was waiting for me and when we had finished a point, he called, "Mr. Scopes?"

I nodded and trotted over to him.

"Mr. Robinson says, if it's convenient, for you to come down to the drug store," he said. The boy didn't work at the drug store. He had been summoned off the street to fetch me.

There was no urgency in the message. Fred E. Robinson, the owner of Robinson's Drug Store—"Doc," as we called him because of his profession as a pharmacist—also was chairman of the Rhea County school board, and I assumed he wanted to talk to me about school business. We finished the game. I was wearing a shirt and trousers, and the shirt was stained with sweat. It was about three quarters of a mile downtown to the drug store, and I walked there dressed as I was.

Robinson's Drug Store was a social center for Dayton, where people would get together for a soda and stay to discuss any local issues or just to pass the time of day. Toward the back of the drug store, near the fountain, there were wire-backed chairs arranged around wooden-topped tables. It was always a pleasant refuge from the outside heat.

That afternoon there was plenty of heat inside. Past the screened double doors at the front was the fountain, and at a nearby table were half a dozen men in the midst of a warm discussion. In addition to Doc Robinson, there was Mr. Brady, who ran the town's other drug store; Sue Hicks, the town's leading lawyer, who had been arguing for the Butler law; Wallace Haggard, another attorney, whose father owned the leading bank and was "Mr. Dayton"; a fellow who worked at the post office; and George Rappelyea.

Robinson offered me a chair and the boy who worked as a soda jerk brought me a fountain drink.

"John, we've been arguing," said Rappelyea, "and I said that nobody could teach biology without reaching evolution."

"That's right," I said, not sure what he was leading up to.

A copy of George William Hunter's *Civic Biology* lay on a nearby shelf. Robinson's Drug Store supplied Rhea County's textbooks. Hunter's was the text used in Tennessee for biology. It had been used since 1909. The state textbook commission had adopted it in 1919 and although the contract had expired in 1924, no other book had been adopted in the meantime. I got a copy of it and showed it to the men at the table.

"You have been teaching 'em this book?" Rappelyea said.

"Yes," I said. I explained that I had got the book out of stock and had used it for review purposes while filling in for the principal during his illness. He was the regular biology teacher. I opened the book and showed them the evolutionary chart and the explanation of evolution. "Rappelyea's right, that you can't teach biology without teaching evolution. This is the text and it explains evolution."

"Then you've been violating the law," Robinson said.

I didn't know, technically, whether I had violated the law or not. I knew of the Butler Act; I'd never worried about it. At the end of the term I had substituted in the classes of the principal while he was ill; I assumed that if anyone had broken the law it was more likely to have been Mr. Ferguson.

"So has every other teacher then," I said. "There's our text, provided by the state. I don't see how a teacher can teach biology without teaching evolution."

Robinson handed me a newspaper. It was the Chattanooga *News,* the afternoon paper, and he pointed to an advertisement, placed by the American Civil Liberties Union, which offered to pay the expenses of anyone willing to test the constitutionality of the Butler law forbidding the teaching of evolution in any public school.

"John, would you be willing to stand for a test case?" Robinson said. "Would you be willing to let your name be used?"

I realized that the best time to scotch the snake is when it starts to wiggle. The snake already had been wiggling a good long time.

I said, "If you can prove that I've taught evolution, and I can qualify as a defendant, then I'll be willing to stand trial."

"You filled in as a biology teacher, didn't you?" Robinson said.

"Yes." I nodded. "When Mr. Ferguson was sick."

"Well, you taught biology then. Didn't you cover evolution?"

"We reviewed for final exams, as best I remember." To tell the truth, I wasn't sure I had taught evolution.

Robinson and the others apparently weren't concerned about this technicality. I had expressed willingness to stand trial. That was enough.

Robinson didn't indicate that my acquiescence would lead to an ordeal, and I didn't suspect it. Nor did he suggest that trouble might come out of the trial in any way. Instead, he walked over to the telephone and called the city desk of the Chattanooga *News*.

"This is F. E. Robinson in Dayton," he said. "I'm chairman of the school board here. We've just arrested a man for teaching evolution."

I drank the fountain drink that had been handed me and I went back to the high school to finish playing tennis with the kids. I assume everyone else in the drug store went about his normal business too.

Afterward, Rappelyea wired the American Civil Liberties Union and got a promise to assist in my defense.

Rappelyea had argued with the townspeople over the Butler law before that afternoon. He would sit in Robinson's Drug Store and expound his views on evolution and the law. He said he had first got the idea of holding a test case in Dayton as he read the Chattanooga *Times* before dinner on Monday, May 4—the day before our encounter. An article stated that Superintendent of Schools Ziegler in Chattanooga had refused to sponsor a test case there. If Chattanooga backed down, then why not have the trial in Dayton? So Rappelyea had reasoned. The following afternoon, he precipitated the incident in the drug store.

Rappelyea already knew me as an independent thinker, and he knew that I had subbed as biology teacher during that spring. He reasoned that, if Doc Robinson asked me, I would agree to become a defendant in a test case. Relying upon this analysis of my character, he convinced the businessmen of the town that the publicity of such a case would put Dayton on the map and benefit business. His was a convincing argument and the businessmen went along with it.

I don't know what Rappelyea's personal motives were. But I am convinced that he must have had a special reason for getting the case started. Possibly he hoped to open up the Tennessee coal business or win some new industry as a result. I didn't see how he could gain by the trial; at the same time I knew him well enough to realize he wouldn't have done the things he did if he hadn't had an angle.

As things turned out, I had been tapped and trapped by the rush of events. That was all right with me. It appeared that Rappelyea and the businessmen of Dayton and I were entering the test case with different motives, and that was all right too, as long as we shared the goal of testing the constitutionality of the Butler law. I would lend my name, and possibly my reputation, to the case; they would handle the technicalities of my "arrest" and bond. I had no idea the un- dramatic drug store scene would trigger the big news story that followed. I knew there would be a certain amount of publicity and that a great portion of our society would believe I had some kind of horns. At the same time, I knew that sooner or later someone would have to take a stand against the stifling of freedom that the Butler Act represented. It seemed still early enough to keep emotions from getting out of hand. Flareups are always probable in issues concerning religion, sex, and other intimate topics. Evolution held great potential as a roiler of emotions. If the trend toward prohibiting the teaching of evolution could be stopped before the people's emotions flared up unreasonably, then we would be able to apply reason; therein lay my hope.

Logically, the principal should have stood trial instead of me. He was the regular biology teacher. He also was a married man with children and, when he had been asked, he wouldn't consent to partici- pate in a test case. Who could blame him? He had something tangible to lose, and he felt first responsibility to his family, as he should have. After him, I was the next logical defendant. I was a bachelor.

From John T. Scopes and James Presley, *Center of the Storm: Memoirs of John T. Scopes* (New York: Holt, Rinehart and Winston, 1967), pp. 57–62.

Billy Sunday Advises Bryan
William A. Sunday

Before assuming his role as a prosecutor in the Scopes trial, William Jennings Bryan requested leading fundamentalists throughout the nation to suggest "a line of thought" appropriate for use in the courtroom. Among those who responded to his request was Billy Sunday, the famous evangelist and ardent foe of evolutionists and modernists. Convinced that Americans were "groping through a fog of infidelism" which paraded under the name of science and philosophy, Sunday had long been active in the campaign to lead them "back to the old-time religion." A former baseball player whose picturesque language often seemed more appropriate in the outfield than in the pulpit, he described evolutionists as "loud-mouthed, foreign-lingo-slinging, quack-theory-preaching bolsheviki." His letter to Bryan, cited below, included random thoughts about the relationship of evolution to education, science, and religion. Clearly, Sunday equated "the old-time religion" with Americanism.

———◆◆———

Dear Mr. Bryan:

I have been away. Just returned. Thank God for W.J.B. Sorry I cannot be there [Dayton].

I hasten to send you some ideas that may suggest a line of thought.

Daniel Webster said "any attempt to educate the people without giving them at the same time religion and moral sentiment is low, vulgar deism and infidelity."

The compact in the cabin of the Mayflower was for the Glory of God and the advancement of the Christian religion.

Atheism is a public enemy. Evolution is atheism.

I do not believe a man can be an Evolutionist and a Christian at the same time. Natural evolution is always downward and not up. If man evolved from a monkey, why are there any monkeys left? Why didn't they all evolve into humans? If we should take . . . specimens of a monkey and breed and train them for thousands of years we would have nothing but monkeys now.

Evolutionists seem set on ejecting God from the universe and destroying the authority of the Bible.

Wendell Phillips said:

The answer to the Shasta is India.
  „   „   „   „   Koran „ Turkey.
  „   „   „ Confusianism „ China.
  „   „   „ the Bible   „ America.

Evolutionists say 100,000 species came from 4 species. The law of the universe tells us that starting in one species it keeps on in that species. If there were only 4 to start with there would be only 4 now. There has never been a case of progression upwards. If cells did not maintain their ancestral characteristics, they would have perished ages ago.

Prof. Agassiz said he found in a reef in Florida the remains of insects thousands of years old. They were the same as the insects found there now.

I hope you may find a thought in the enclosed. All the believing world is back of you in your defense of God and the Bible.

Your friend
As ever
W. A. Sunday

Hood River, Oregon
July 4, 1925

From William A. Sunday to William Jennings Bryan, July 4, 1925, William Jennings Bryan Papers, Manuscript Division, Library of Congress, Washington, D.C.

The Meaning of the Scopes Trial
Russell D. Owen

The presence of so many journalists and reporters at Dayton indicated that they saw in the Scopes Trial the ingredients of "good copy." For several weeks in the summer of 1925 their observations of the event dominated the columns of the newspaper and periodical press in the United States. Among the reporters at Dayton was the veteran correspondent of the New York *Times,* Russell D. Owen. A magazine article which he wrote shortly after the close of the trial at once constituted one of the most perceptive analyses of the issues and personalities involved in the affair and a vivid description of the socio-intellectual atmosphere in which it occurred. Owen maintained that the real issue at stake in this episode in "the age-old struggle between rationalism and faith" became evident in an extra-legal exchange between the dominant personalities in the case, William Jennings Bryan and Clarence Darrow, when each in a moment of anger stated his reason for being at the trial. Bryan claimed that he was there "to protect the Word of God from the greatest atheist and agnostic in the United States"; Darrow insisted that his purpose was "to show up Fundamentalism" and "to prevent bigots and ignoramuses from controlling the educational system of the United States." In Owen's view Bryan, who "had not been an altogether unmixed blessing to the young Tennessee prosecutor," was the most obvious casualty in this "meeting of the great forces of skepticism and faith."

When two vitally opposed schools of thought meet in conflict, there is much smoke and dust of battle, many grievous wounds, but seldom any advance toward a reconciliation of their views. So it was at Dayton, the little town in the smiling Tennessee Valley, which for two weeks was the center of the world's news while John Thomas Scopes was being tried for teaching evolution in a public school.

Each side withdrew at the end of the struggle satisfied that it had unmasked the absurd pretensions of the other, but all they did was to collide in what, because of the limitations of present-day civilization, was a bitter verbal combat instead of a massacre. It is not likely that the faith of a single fundamentalist was shaken, or that a believer in evolution was won over to the acceptance of the literal interpretation of the Bible. What may happen in the years to come, with every Ten-

nessee library swamped by demands for the works of Darwin and Huxley, Kellogg and Osborn, is another story. The "Chinese wall" of the
literalists may crumble under the impulse of a human curiosity.

The trial was not merely to determine if a schoolteacher should
or should not teach evolution. The fundamentalists were striving with
all their might to protect their children from the blight of modern
thought, from agnosticism, to protect their literal Bible from the attacks
of unbelievers; while the forces which rallied about Scopes were there
for the purpose of saving Tennessee from the intellectual disaster, and
to use the trial as a means of awakening the country to a new sense of
spiritual and intellectual freedom. The court was a forum, a debating
ground for these opposing groups. But although the trial was in one
sense a symptom of the age-old struggle between rationalism and faith,
occurring, as it did, in this twentieth century, with airplanes flying
overhead, with its picturesque setting, its vivid moments, and sudden
and dramatic end, it was perhaps the most exciting of all such meetings
since they were settled by the sword.

.   .   .   .

Dayton is a small town, the center of a fruit-growing section. It
has become prosperous with a reviving South. Its people are pleasantly
hospitable and do not think too deeply on abstract subjects. Its public
meeting place is Robinson's Drug Store, where about the fire in winter
and the soda fountain in summer the social life of the place centers.
The antievolution bill caused quite an uproar there last May, just
at the end of the school term, and John Thomas Scopes, teacher of
biology, wearing his twenty-four years lightly, denounced it bitterly
as an unconstitutional restriction upon freedom of thought and teaching.
Asked if he would be a martyr for science, he consented, and was
arrested. That is how Dayton came to be the center of the world's
news for three weeks.

The real issue involved in the bill became apparent with Scopes's
arrest, and it was seen that here was provided an opportunity to thrash
out those questions of fundamentalism and modernism which have been
plaguing the churches in recent years. Interest in the case began to
spread, as it was discussed from one end of the United States to the
other, and papers abroad began to tune their ears to this strange
rumble out of the New World. It was the first definite test of strength,
and when William Jennings Bryan, the great apostle of the inerrancy

of the Gospels, girded up his loins and rushed to the aid of Tennessee, those on the other side rose to defend science. The American Civil Liberties Union became interested, and through their efforts and those of lawyers to whom they appealed, Clarence Darrow, whose agnostic views were the antithesis of Bryan's, was brought into the case. Darrow was wanted because of his brilliant legal mind, his skill in examination and his relentless fighting ability in a courtroom. As his two chief aids he had Dudley Field Malone, whose fiery oratory won even Dayton, and Arthur Garfield Hays, who has gone to jail for defending what he believed to be right.

It was the first to arrive on the field. He walked the streets of Dayton in his shirt sleeves, wearing a pith helmet; and the people gathered and worshiped him as the champion of their faith. Never in his greatest political days did he receive such complete adulation as from the people of the Tennessee Valley, and he basked in it, radiating good fellowship and happiness. Far different was his demeanor toward the end of the trial, when he had been racked by the pitiless words of Darrow, and retired, heartbroken, to the cottage where he died a few days later.

It was a simple town into which Bryan walked, but a town excited and transformed by the great happening which had come to it. Dayton was half a street fair and half a religious revival meeting. Hawkers of religious books had their booths along the street opposite the Court House; on the lawn where Bryan later underwent his terrible ordeal itinerant singers of sad hymns sat under the trees; speakers drew crowds at night under the flare of lanterns to listen to exhortations against the temptations of this world and the reward to come, while signs everywhere warned people to read their Bible lest they perish. In the daytime worn women in calico dresses gathered their children about them, after a long drive in from hill farms, and waited for a sight of Bryan.

It had an effect almost of exaltation upon the Commoner. Here was unaffected and wholehearted support of his views. He expanded under it, and when, in his first speech at the little hotel the night of his arrival, he stretched out his arms as if to gather them to him and spoke to them in the persuasive tone which he knew so well how to adopt, they were moved so that they spoke of him the next day in hushed voices. It was in that speech that Bryan announced what many took to be his plan to make a national campaign upon a religious issue, for he said that if defeated in the courts he would appeal to the people, and that constitutions were made by the people and could be amended by them. If he had not died, there is no doubt that he would have done his best to carry out his expressed intention.

From the very first session of the trial it became evident that the fate of John Thomas Scopes was the most unimportant issue involved. Even the question as to the constitutionality of the law became relatively insignificant. What each side was there to argue was the momentous topic: "Is the Bible true?" And so deeply did this inquiry touch the hearts and minds of those on both sides that the necessity for Bryan's fervent words and Darrow's scorching logic became obvious. In all the nine days of the trial, which began on July 10, there were only three hours of testimony, all of it for the prosecution. The court room, packed to suffocation with men in their shirt sleeves, women in their thinnest dresses, even young girls and boys who were drawn by the greatest show ever offered for their entertainment, was turned into a debating hall, where hour after hour men thundered scornful and bitter words. Nothing happened according to schedule, and nobody could guess what the next day might bring forth.

The prosecution had three things it wished to prove: That the Bible was the inspired word of God; that it was to be accepted literally; and that the account of creation as given in the first and second chapters of Genesis was the only account which should be believed by Christians. The defense wished to show: That the Bible account of creation was allegorical and could be reconciled with the evolutionary theory of creation; that the Bible was not to be taken literally and was not so accepted by many good Christians, some of them theologians; and that a belief in science did not necessarily imply that one must be an agnostic.

Technically, of course, the prosecution was compelled to prove only that Scopes taught a theory of creation contrary to the Bible, and that "man descended from a lower order of animals." But all Bryan's eloquence was to be called upon to hammer home the truth of the inspired Word, and it was gall and wormwood to him when Darrow called him as an expert on the Bible and out of his own mouth drew an admission that the Bible need not be taken literally as to the "six days" of creation.

The defense had a much more difficult problem. They were compelled to rely altogether upon expert testimony to show what evolution is, and to attempt to prove that the Bible is not the revealed word of God but was written by men who knew nothing of science and were therefore extremely liable to error. That it was a great book, a book which had brought consolation and happiness to millions, a book in which many of their own scientific witnesses believed, they were willing to grant, but not that it was or could be a textbook of science. It was this problem of the defense which governed the whole course of the trial, for as soon as Darrow saw that Bryan and Attorney General Tom Stewart would fight the admission of scientific testimony, he tried to force an argument on this question and adopted the policy of fighting desperately for every possible point. It was because of this that he made his great speech on the motion to quash the indictment.

Darrow rose to new heights in his defense of Scopes. Always a brilliant criminal lawyer, perhaps the most famous in the country, the antievolution law brought out every resource of his versatile nature. He proudly admitted he was an agnostic when that was hurled in his face as an epithet by Attorney General Stewart, and with his long arms folded about him, his gaunt shoulders hunched up about his ears, his eyes flashing indignation, he damned Tennessee's antievolution law as "the most brazen and bold attempt to destroy liberty as was ever seen since the Middle Ages." He saw early in the trial that there would be no opportunity to outline the case for evolution and against the Bible that he had hoped for, and although he never ceased to press for a possible decision favorable to his cause, he and his associates directed most of their efforts to getting before the country by methods never seen before in a court the arguments they had hoped to produce from witnesses.

Up to a certain point their challenge was accepted by Attorney General Stewart, a brilliant young lawyer with an eloquence which he whipped to a startlingly effective use in replying to Darrow. "I want to know," Stewart cried, his arms raised and his voice shaken, "that beyond this world there is happiness for me and for others. Would they have me believe that I was a worm and writhed in the dust, and that I will go no further when the breath has left my body?" Against this faith all the legal resources of Darrow, Malone, and Hays were blunted.

Judge John Raulston, himself a raw-boned mountaineer with the sing-song voice of an evangelist, whose talks were more often like prayers than court opinions, ruled consistently with the State. He is a typical product of the primitive hill life of Tennessee, and religion is as much a part of his nature as the law. He was born in a little place known as the Fiery Gizzard, a cove in the mountains near Winchester, and his mother led him on mule back over the hills to school and back every day, and read the Bible to him at night when he was a boy. His forgiveness of Darrow after Darrow had defied him to cite him in contempt and later apologized, was the forgiveness of a minister in the pulpit to an erring brother. He was perhaps the most amazing figure of this extraordinary case, part priest and part judge, who was seen in the street with a Bible under his arm as often as a book of law.

All that Darrow and Hays could do with their heated arguments for the admission of scientific testimony was to obtain permission to have statements of what they would have proved placed in the record for purposes of appeal, but they got around this obstacle to some extent by having the statements prepared over the weekend and gave them to the newspapers in time for publication the day they were presented the Court. And then Darrow caused the great sensation of the trial.

The court had moved out to a little platform on the lawn because of a crowd so dense in the court room that the Judge feared the floor would give way. On this platform Bryan had preached a sermon and the Rev. Charles Francis Potter had preached for the modernists. Every night some one discoursed there on religion. The two groups of lawyers now gathered on opposite sides of the rough pine structure; Judge Raulston sat in the middle; Mrs. Bryan was wheeled out in her chair and took a position where she could watch her husband with eyes so quick in comparison to her bodily stillness. Reporters gathered around as best they could, and out in front a great throng of men and women clustered on the benches under the trees and stood in a great circle reaching nearly to the fence, their faces turned eagerly upward.

For days Darrow and Malone and Hays had debated whether or not Bryan would take the stand if they should call him as an expert witness on the Bible, ostensibly to show Judge Raulston that the Bible was not a scientific book. Hays completed his reading of the scientific testimony and made a few perfunctory motions, and then Darrow in a quiet voice asked Judge Raulston if he might call Mr. Bryan. The Commoner, who had been fanning himself beside Stewart, turned with a start of surprise. He could not refuse, and said so quickly, but made the condition that he in turn should be permitted to question Darrow and his associates on their religious beliefs. There was no precedent for this and all court procedure was at once forgotten. As Darrow said with a sarcastic smile that he would be glad to be questioned by Bryan, the entire audience became tense with expectation. And then Bryan walked forward and took a seat in front, gazing up alertly into the gnarled, quizzical face of Darrow, who leaned against the edge of his table and tapped his spectacles speculatively against his arm as he began.

It was the meeting of the great forces of skepticism and faith, and there was only one possible result. Bryan, calmly contemptuous of this intellectual upstart as he answered the first questions, became restless under Darrow's relentless prodding, and finally lost all control of his temper. Darrow, seeking flaws in the Commoner's unshakable answer, "I believe," roused by Mr. Bryan's retorts and the applause of the crowd, gave way to anger and turning to the throng under the trees during one outburst, cried: "Why don't you cheer?"

Darrow had wrung from the shaken Bryan some damaging admissions, for after Bryan had stated with absolute conviction that he believed the whale swallowed Jonah, that Eve was made from Adam's rib, and that Joshua made the sun stand still, he admitted that the days of creation might not be litcrally days of twenty-four hours, but might each be millions of years. That God made man in his own image in one act of special creation he did not doubt at all, but he was stumped when it came to explaining how Cain got his wife. He admitted that he knew nothing of geology, of philology, of the comparative study of religions, of ancient civilizations, of any of the things which one might expect a man who had written for years on religion and evolution to be familiar with, and his one invariable answer was that he had not considered it necessary to study these matters very deeply, that the Bible was sufficient authority for him on any subject.

The scene as these two men, each representing such diametrically opposed principles, fought back at each other with all the resources of their years of rich experience on the platform was an unforgettable one. In the end Attorney General Stewart tried to come to Bryan's rescue by protesting that the examination was illegal, outside the bounds of court procedure. "What is the meaning of all this?" he asked, and both men sprang forward and hurled their answers at each other.

"To protect the Word of God from the greatest atheist and agnostic in the United States!" cried Bryan, shaking his fist at Darrow.

"To show up Fundamentalism!" roared Darrow. "To prevent bigots and ignoramuses from controlling the educational system of the United States."

In this burst of anger they gave what to each was the real issue involved in a trial which had continued for nine days of argument, without either side achieving its purpose. But in a moment they stripped off all pretense of legal procedure and in those brief, sharp words gave the real meaning of the Scopes trial.

When Bryan came to court the next day he was a weary, heartbroken man. He had realized the position in which his answers the day before had placed him, he knew that they had gone all over the world and that he would never be able to catch up with them. His ignorance of many things on which he had professed authority had been made a record for every one to read, and he knew that he would never be able to retaliate, for after he had left the stand there was a long and stormy conference between him and Attorney General Stewart. Bryan had not been altogether an unmixed blessing to the able young Tennessee prosecutor. There were undoubtedly times when he wished that he had been able to get rid of his famous, but embarrassing, colleague, who knew little law, and kept stirring up the lions on the other side. So much was admitted after the trial was over. And that night he told Bryan that there would be no more extralegal examinations, that Bryan would not be permitted to take the stand again, and that he would not be permitted to examine Darrow.

The only thing left for Bryan was his speech, the speech on which he had been working for three months and which he was scheduled to deliver in summing up as the final speaker for the State. It was to be a crushing reply to Darwin and Darrow, and this Darrow snatched from him. When the court opened Darrow asked that his client be found guilty, a suggestion which Stewart jumped at, and all debate was shut off. As it turned out, Bryan could not have delivered his speech anyway, for the defense had planned to refuse argument after the first speaker for the State had finished, which would have automatically prevented further argument.

So, although Scopes was found guilty of misdemeanor for teaching evolution and was fined $100, Bryan was beaten and beaten badly, and when he left court on the last day he was a bitter and disappointed man. All the fires of religious hate had been stirred in the long days of argument, and it had had a crushing effect upon him. A few days later he died in the cottage where he had written and issued an autobiographical sketch to show that he was not an ignorant and uneducated man.

From Russell D. Owen, "The Significance of the Scopes Trial: Issues and Personalities," *Current History*, XXII (September 1925), 875–883.

Dayton: Good Advertising for the South
The Manufacturers' Record

By the 1920s the *Manufacturers' Record,* a mouthpiece of industrialism published in Baltimore, had become "the patriarch of Southern boosters." During the decade its editorials seemed to indicate that the industrial progress of the region was dependent upon preventing the encroachment of various forms of "radicalism" from the North and West. In 1924 Gerald W. Johnson, a perceptive student of the South, suggested that southern manufacturers quietly supported fundamentalist religion among the masses as a means of providing an outlet for emotions which otherwise might be manifested in strikes. The following editorial from the *Record,* published shortly after the Scopes trial, tended to corroborate Johnson's view of an alliance between religious and economic conservatism. The editorial was in response to a sermon by the well-known New York Unitarian clergyman Charles Francis Potter in which he "sounded the call for a missionary campaign to introduce liberal religion in the South." Displaying a common psychological reaction to such critics of the fundamentalists' effort at Dayton, the *Record* described the trial as "one of the South's supremest advertisements" which would "do boundless good" in attracting "tens of thousands of people" from the North and West seeking to escape the "agnosticism and atheism" so prevalent in those sections. A kind of Promised Land, the South was one place in America where the absence of "the alien foreign element" and the presence of a "pure and undefiled" religion guaranteed that children could be reared in "an atmosphere of Christianity." Ironically, the *Manufacturers' Record* found itself allied in a religious cause with the same Bryan whose economic and political views it had so long opposed.

———◦•◦———

Dr. Potter's desire to improve the religious life of the South will not meet with enthusiasm of any intelligent people in the South. The people of this section do not need any of Dr. Potter's liberalizing religious propaganda, nor do they need to regard Darrow as a close approach to Abraham Lincoln. When Dr. Potter has regenerated New York, when he has cleansed that city of its unspeakable crimes, its debauchery, its gun-toters, its murderers, then perhaps it will be time enough for him to think of turning his thought to the betterment of the South, especially in religious lines.

The South rejoices in the fact that it still believes in the Bible, that it still upholds the teachings of Christ, and it neither asks nor needs any instruction from Dr. Potter or any of his associates in his line of thinking.

Despite all the tomfoolery of the monkey business in which Darrow and others demonstrated that the monkeys of Jungleville, if they had sense enough to express themselves, might have well rejoiced that they were not the progenitors of those who were seeking to discredit in every way possible the teachings of the Bible, the Dayton trial, instead of injuring the South in the minds of intelligent people, will benefit it. The very activities connected with that trial, and the demonstration of the firm religious views of the people of Tennessee and of other southern states, will ultimately prove to be an advertisement of immeasurable value to the South.

There are millions of people in other parts of the United States who do not want to raise their children in an atmosphere of agnosticism and atheism so prevalent throughout the North and West, where the alien foreign element is so dominant, and who, having learned as a result of this trial that there is a section in this country where religion pure and undefiled still holds sway, will turn their eyes longingly to that Land of Promise, hoping that in the South they may be able to have their children raised in an atmosphere of Christianity rather than an atmosphere of anti-Christianity. These people will not regard the Dayton trial as demonstrating any backwardness on the part of the people of the South, but they will hold that the influence which the trial demonstrated that religion still has upon the southern people will be of immense value to this section and will bring to the South thousands and tens of thousands of people who will seek to escape for themselves and their children from the agnosticism and atheism which curses much of the North and West. Despite all of its monkey business, therefore, the Dayton trial will be one of the South's supremest advertisements, and an advertisement which will do boundless good.

From "Why the Dayton Trial Will Resound to the South's Good," *Manufacturers' Record*, LXXXVIII (August 20, 1925), 70.

Dayton: A Fundamentalist View
John Roach Straton

Many Americans undoubtedly agreed with William Jennings Bryan's contention that the principal issue in the Scopes case was the "right of parents to guard the religion of their children against efforts made in the name of science to undermine faith in super-natural religion." Many also contended that the trial was a test of the principle of majority rule. The following excerpt from a piece written by John Roach Straton and published in his *The American Fundamentalist* provided a succinct statement of the fundamentalist view of the issues in the Dayton trial. Straton was convinced that the small minority of skeptical, agnostic intellectuals represented by the defense attorneys was engaged in an "anti-American defiance of majority rule." He resented the intrusion of Darrow and his "Evolutionist Bund" from Chicago and other urban centers debauched by "religious modernism and a Godless materialistic science" into a region whose orthodox faith and robust conservatism offered some hope of salvation for the nation. For Straton, the central issue in the Scopes trial was what Bryan said it was—whether taxpaying parents "shall be made to support the false and materialistic religion, namely evolution, in the schools, while Christianity is ruled out, and thereby denied their children."

———————◆◆———————

. . . the real issue at Dayton and everywhere today is: "Whether the religion of the Bible shall be ruled out of the schools and the religion of evolution, with its ruinous results—shall be ruled into the schools by law." The issue is whether the taxpayers—the mothers and fathers of the children—shall be made to support the false and materialistic religion, namely evolution, in the schools, while Christianity is ruled out, and thereby denied their children.

And with this goes the even deeper issue of whether the majority shall really have the right to rule in America, or whether we are to be ruled by an insignificant minority—an "aristocracy," . . . of skeptical schoolmen and agnostics.

That is the exact issue in this country today. And that it is a very real and urgent issue is proved by the recent invasion of the sovereign state of Tennessee by a group of outside agnostics, atheists, Unitarian preachers, skeptical scientists, and political revolutionists.

These uninvited men—including Clarence Darrow, the world's

greatest unbeliever, and Dudley Malone, the world's greatest religious What-Is-It,—these and the other samples of our proposed "aristocracy" of would-be rulers, swarmed down to Dayton during the Scopes trial and brazenly tried to nullify the laws and overthrow the political and religious faiths of a great, enlightened, prosperous, and peaceful people.

And the only redeeming feature in all that unlovely parade of human vanity, arrogant self-sufficiency, religious unbelief, and anti-American defiance of majority rule was the courtesy, hospitality (even to unwelcome guests), forbearance, patience, and Christlike fortitude displayed by the noble judge, and the Christian prosecuting attorneys and people of Tennessee!

There was an element of profound natural irony in the entire situation. Darrow, Malone, and the other members of the Evolutionist Bund vicariously left their own communities and bravely sallied forth, like Don Quixote, to defeat the windmills and save other communities from themselves.

They left New York and Chicago, where real religion is being most neglected, where law, consequently, is most defied, where vice and crime are most rampant, and where the follies and ruinous immoralities of the rising generation—debauched already by religious modernism and a Godless materialistic science—smell to high heaven, and they went to save from itself a community where women are still honored, where men are still chivalric, where laws are still respected, where home life is still sweet, where the marriage vow is still sacred, and where man is still regarded, not as a descendant of the slime and beasts of the jungle, but as a child of God, with the wisdom and love of a divine Revelation in his hands, to guide him on life's rugged road, to give him the knowledge of a Savior from his sins, and to plant in his heart the hope of heaven to cheer him on his upward way!

And that is the sort of community which Darrow, Malone, and company left Chicago and New York to save!

Think of the illogic of it! and the nerve of it! and the colossal vanity of it!

Little wonder it is recorded in Holy Writ that "He that sitteth in the Heavens shall laugh" at the follies of men! And surely the very battlements of Heaven must have rocked with laughter at the spectacle of Clarence Darrow, Dudley Malone, and their company of cocksure evolutionists going down to save the South from itself!

It is all the other way around! The religious faith and the robust conservatism of the chivalric South and the sturdy West will have to save America from the sins and shams and shames that are now menacing her splendid life!

A great religious revival is the most urgent need of America at the present hour, and it will come not through pride of scholarship and the vanity of man's mind, but through faith and love, and that beautiful modesty which enables sinful man to humble himself under the mighty hand of God that in due season he may be exalted!

From John Roach Straton, "The Most Sinister Movement in the United States," *The American Fundamentalist,* II (December 26, 1925), 8–9.

Dayton: Then and Now
Joseph Wood Krutch

Joseph Wood Krutch, the distinguished American critic and man of letters, devotes almost an entire chapter of his memoirs to the "Monkey Trial at Dayton" which he covered as a reporter for *The Nation*. Born and reared in Knoxville, less than fifty miles from the scene of the trial, Krutch returned home in 1925 to witness what he interpreted as a "sorry" spectacle produced largely by the cowardice of the state's educators and legislators in the face of a "militant and sincere" bigotry. Reflecting upon the Dayton affair thirty-five years later, Krutch admits that at the time he was "inclined to see the threat of rural fundamentalism as a more serious threat than it actually was." The following excerpts from his memoirs indicate that what he once saw as a "real and present" danger was later viewed more as a comic "teapot tempest."

———◆◆———

The Monkey Trial at Dayton was a teapot tempest which attracted international attention and is now enshrined in the intellectual history of twentieth-century America. More than thirty years after it took place, it was almost simultaneously the subject of a successful play and of a widely read, completely documented study. References to it still turn up not infrequently in the conversation of intellectuals, and I can still become the center of attention if I announce portentously, "All of it I saw and part of it I was."

Nevertheless, it is difficult to see the whole affair in any true perspective and it has almost always been oversimplified by those who have attempted to describe or to assess. If it was partly a witch hunt, it was also a jape elaborately staged for their own amusement by typical intellectual playboys of the exuberant Twenties, and the real villains were not either the benighted rustics nor the playboys but the responsible citizens and officials of Tennessee who should never have allowed it to happen.

When Marcelle and I arrived at Dayton, the little town was already in a state of excited bewilderment and almost of shock at the discovery that it had been selected as the site of an Armageddon. The great world had never noticed it before. Now it was swarming with reporters, a whole galaxy of famous warriors had descended upon it, all because astonishing attention had been called to a local political farce of a familiar sort and one which would probably have been soon forgotten had not several unexpected things happened.

It all started unsensationally enough. A back-country member of the Tennessee legislature had been distressed to hear that the daughter of one of his constituents had lost her fundamentalist faith when she heard at school something of the Darwinian heresy. Inspired by the same naive trust in the efficacy of moral legislation which had saddled prohibition on even the most sophisticated parts of the United States, the legislator introduced into the lower chamber a bill forbidding the teaching of the theory of evolution in any part of the state's educational system. No politician wanted to go on record as opposing God or religion, and the bill was passed in the lower house by legislators, some of whom later stated that they had confidently assumed it would be killed in the Senate. The Senate thereupon passed the buck to the Governor, certain, so they said, that he would veto it. But the Governor was not disposed to center all the ire of the fundamentalists on himself alone. Accordingly he signed the bill with the remark that he did not expect it to become an operative law.

Probably it would have been soon forgotten if John Scopes, athletic coach and professor of biology at the Dayton High School, had not called the attention of his principal to the fact that the textbook he was using seemed to violate the law. He was told to ignore the fact and would no doubt have done so had it not been for a local citizen (an outlander, by the way) named George Rappelyea who was manager of a local coal mine. He had been increasingly irritated by the antics of the fundamentalists and he asked Scopes if he would be willing to co-operate in a test case by submitting to an indictment brought against him. Scopes consented, and the Civil Liberties Union in New York agreed to subsidize the defense.

Originally the Civil Liberties Union had intended to employ only local counsel, but when William Jennings Bryan, whose star had been waning fast, announced that he would come to Dayton as the champion of Christianity against atheism, the Union revised its plan and enlisted the services of three oddly assorted national figures shrewdly selected for their diverse talents: Clarence Darrow, coat-sleeved wizard with all juries including those of such "plain men" as he himself pretended to be; Arthur Garfield Hays, veteran of many civil liberties suits who knew the ins and outs of the law as Darrow did not; and Dudley Field Malone, a silver-tongued orator whose talents had been most often employed in divorce cases but whose ornate rhetoric might be expected to fall persuasively on the ears of the simple. John R. Neal, an eccentric teacher of law in his own private school at Knoxville, tagged along.

Probably Dayton had been slow to believe that all America and much of Europe would take seriously what was happening there, but by the time we arrived excitement was running high and the little town was doing its best to acquit itself well in the role of host to guests of a very unfamiliar kind. The circus and the religious revival were the only festive occasions with which it was familiar and the atmosphere was strongly suggestive of both. Signs and banners—some welcoming the strangers, many of the where-will-you-spend-eternity? kind—adorned the principal street. Preachers, official and self-appointed, had come into the town to harangue from soapboxes whomever they could persuade to listen. Private citizens offered bed and board to the many who could not find accommodation in the one hotel and the overcrowded boarding houses. The Chamber of Commerce, which saw the whole thing as a chance to put Dayton on the map, gave separate dinners in honor of the two champions, Bryan and Darrow, while the more intellectual citizens, though firmly asserting their loyalty to Bible and church, expressed frank satisfaction in the anticipated opportunity to hear the great questions debated by the most famous defenders of religion and atheism.

As for the hangers-on like myself, we quickly converted the soda fountain in the drug store into a cafe where not only we but most of the leaders and many of the interested citizens discussed everything which was happening in full amiability, though one paradox was soon noted. Only the Great Commoner held himself aloof. Guest of a leading citizen, he fraternized with no one—not with his opponents, nor with the reporters, nor with the ordinary citizens. He was glimpsed only occasionally in a large black limousine, and on the one occasion when he entered the drug store he let it be known that he was not amused by the soda clerk who asked if he would have grape juice, of which he was a famous advocate.

Here, there, and everywhere was the broad, beaming face of H.

L. Mencken. A few days later he enjoyed in the courtroom what were perhaps the happiest moments of his life, contemplating, and in a sense presiding over, a spectacle which seemed arranged for his delight. He was in the middle of that Bible Belt he had done so much to make famous, and its inhabitants were behaving precisely as he had always described them. Had he invented the Monkey Trial no one would have believed in it, but he had been spared the necessity of invention. He fraternized exuberantly with everyone; and everyone, including even the street-corner preachers, was delighted with him—until the first of his dispatches got back to Dayton and many of those with whom he had genially conversed could hardly believe that he could be the author of the brutally contemptuous account he gave of them. One preacher, I remember, protested more in sorrow than in anger, that Mencken had seemed to listen with sympathy to his arguments; then had flung into his face the reply, "Oh well, I have always said I would be converted to any religion for a cigar and baptized in it for a box of them."

Much as I admired Mencken, this was one of several occasions when I found in him a brutal rudeness too strong for my taste, and at the time I could not help contrasting it with the courtesy of the fundamentalist proprietor of a little boarding house at one of the "Springs" which served Dayton as summer resorts. I had driven out for dinner with Darrow and several others, each of whom introduced himself and was cordially greeted. Darrow came last and when he murmured his name the host recoiled for a moment as though the gates of hell had just opened in his face. Then he remembered his manners, swallowed twice, and extending his hand he said: "I am glad to meet you, Mr. Darrow." A prince, even a Prince of Darkness, obviously deserved no less.

Though I am no lawyer and hence subject to correction, I assume that, from a strict legal standpoint, the defense did not have a leg to stand on. John Scopes had obviously violated a duly enacted statute and "guilty as charged" was the only possible verdict. Most of the strangely mixed crowd which moved from the drugstore and the streets into a courtroom crowded to the doors and windows must have been aware of this fact, and it must have been in part responsible for both the calm confidence of the inevitably prejudiced judge and that section of the audience which genuinely believed in its own essential rightness. The

Lord had delivered the enemy into their hands—and on home ground too.

But the defense had, of course, no interest in the inevitable verdict or even in the question of the constitutionality of the law which, if raised, could only have been settled at some distant day in some other court. Since it was interested in propaganda rather than in a verdict, the defense's strategy was to turn nominally legal proceedings into the meeting of a debating society, and the question to be discussed was not the legal guilt or innocence of John Scopes but fundamentalism versus modern thought as typified by the theory of evolution. Its thesis—and a very strange one to be defended by the Ingersolian atheist Clarence Darrow—was simply that the theory of evolution was in no way incompatible with either Christianity or the essential truth of the Book of Genesis.

Since this was not, after all, the question which the jury would be called upon to decide, the locally elected Judge Raulston, who presided, might, I presume, have ruled out as irrelevant almost everything which was said in the course of the trial. Probably he was not shrewd enough to do so, and it is even less likely that he wanted to do anything of the sort. He was known to all as a staunch supporter of those to whom the fantastic statute seemed sound common sense. He had probably never in his life heard anyone question in other than timidly apologetic terms the combination of ignorance, superstition, and (sometimes) hypocrisy for which he stood; and he was confident that, so far at least as his world was concerned, the debate as well as the legal verdict would be in his and his community's favor.

After perhaps fifteen minutes during which shutters clicked and flash-bulbs flashed while the judge basked in this recognition of his importance while protesting feebly against it, he gravely welcomed the visiting counsel. "Rest assured," he seemed to be saying, "we shall annihilate you as gently as possible." The first hint that the defense did not intend to be polite had come when Darrow astonished the court by objecting to an opening prayer on the ground that it was prejudicial. But after the objection had been overruled, the atmosphere was again relatively calm until the fourth day of the trial. Then Darrow, coatless and conspicuously suspendered as though to assure Dayton that he was as plain a man as any of its own citizens, rose to launch his impassioned if legally irrelevant attack.

He began, as all before him had begun, with trivial courtesies. He ironically thanked the judge for having bestowed upon him the title "Colonel" and the judge, with a twinkle of good fellowship in his eye, bade him "take it back to Chicago." The vicious circle of empty courtesies seemed to have been re-established when Darrow, after a transition too quick to be noticed, was suddenly in the midst of an impassioned oration, shaking his finger in the face of the astonished judge and denouncing in angry, insulting words what he called the ignorance, intolerance, arrogance, and bigotry of that community of which the judge was known to be a typical member. Upon the face of the latter was written shocked amazement, and the correspondents rubbed their ears to be sure they heard aright. "With flying banners and beating drums we are marching backward to the glorious age of the sixteenth century when bigots lighted fagots to burn the men who dared to bring any intelligence and enlightenment and culture to the human mind."

Much that followed was farce, though not without sinister overtones. When the prosecuting attorney made his principal harangue, he accepted the assumption that Darwinism rather than John Scopes was on trial, and he translated the question into East Tennessee terms. Long, drawling, lanky, and with an air of rustic simplicity which was, like Darrow's, partly synthetic, he reached the climax of his performance when, taking the jury into his confidence, he asked them to contrast Genesis with Darwinism. "The defense has told you that they mean the same thing. Let's look at the record. The Bible says that God made man" (here he stooped to the floor and then flung his hand into the air) "out of the dust of the earth. What does this theory of evolution say? It says that God set some sort of a scum floating on the water and then said, 'Give me a few million years and I'll try to make something out of you.' "

Darrow's reply was in the form of a brief cross-questioning of the obviously not very bright adolescent whom the prosecution had summoned to establish technically the fact that Scopes had indeed taught the forbidden doctrine. The cross-examination went something like this: "Now, son, I understand that you were taught the theory of evolution. Tell me exactly what you were taught." (Long pause and with hesitant embarrassment) "That all life comes from an egg." "Was that all you were taught?" "Yes, sir." "Well, son, I suppose that when you heard that all life comes from an egg you stopped going to church, didn't you?" "No sir." "Witness dismissed."

As tension mounted it was obvious that even many of the Dayton citizens who had come to see the infidel discomfited and then destroyed had begun to take a genuine interest in the drama. Plainly impressed by the vigor, the confidence, and the competence of the enemy, they tended to forget which side they were on and to take delight in the contest for its own sake; sometimes even bursting into applause which the judge not too sternly repressed when a good hit had been made or some rhetorical flight was executed by Darrow in a style not too different from that they had learned to appreciate at a fundamentalist camp meeting. But they were also reassuringly aware that their own champion was merely holding himself in reserve and that when the time came he would know how to deal with those who now threatened to mislead them.

Many a time during the days when the heathen raged or when Darrow, Hays, or Malone rose for a few seconds to voice some legal objection in terms which unmistakably implied their contempt for a court from which they expected no fair play, the eyes of the spectators turned toward the Peerless Leader from whom they awaited vindication and triumph. Though for several days Bryan continued unbroken the silence he had been maintaining, the reddening of his neck, the tightening of the lines about his mouth, and the increasing speed with which he waved his palm-leaf fan showed that some of the arrows were reaching home and that his heart was stung by the realization that here were men of undoubted if undeserved eminence who scornfully refused him the respect he had once been accustomed to enjoy. Finally he could stand it no longer. He rose to say merely that in due time he would answer. And the applause which greeted this statement showed clearly how satisfactorily his audience expected him to fulfill his promise.

At last his moment came and he began with a plea for the exclusion of all testimony from either scientists or theologians. Though he himself, he boasted, had been certified as learned by the many colleges which had bestowed honorary degrees upon him, there is no such thing as a Bible expert. Learning is useless. The opinion of a bushman just converted is as good as that of a scholar who has devoted a lifetime to the study of the text. Faith alone counts.

His case could hardly have been stated more ineffectually and the

audience which had long awaited some convincing retort to the heresies
it had been hearing, was aware of the fact. He used the word Faith
but it was no glowing or even positive thing. It was not something
which triumphed over difficulty and doubts but which fled from them.
Almost as in a parody, he equated it with ignorance and reduced it to
something of which no one could be proud. Any passionate revivalist
from the hills could have been ten times more effective. He would have
believed. Bryan merely refused to doubt. The Champion upon whom
Dayton depended had let it down and Dayton knew that he had. At
that moment not only confidence but hope went out of its heart and it
was prepared to applaud, as presently it did, the flamboyant oratory of
Dudley Field Malone—not primarily, perhaps, because it believed or
even understood what he was saying but because he at least had in his
liberal platitudes the faith which Bryan seemed to lack.

Malone was a spellbinder of much the same variety that Bryan had
once been, and his audience responded as similar audiences had once
responded to Bryan's spell. He pleaded for fair play, stated the simple
case for light against darkness, then taunted Bryan as a coward who
had first declared before the world that the trial at Dayton was a duel
to the death between religion and science and then refused to fight
the battle he himself had so loudly called for. When Malone, swelling
with pride over his triumph, stalked over to Mencken to receive the
praise he obviously expected, what he got was, "Dudley, that was
absolutely and without any possible exception the loudest speech I
ever heard." Coldly considered, this was perhaps a just assessment, but
the most effective debater is not necessarily the one who stands best
the test of cold consideration, and Malone was precisely right for the
occasion. The applause which broke out from a predmoinantly hostile
audience was twice as great and twice as long as that which had
greeted Bryan.

Under cross-examination the defeated champion provided an even
sorrier spectacle as he retreated further and further into boastful ignorance. Asked if he did not know that there were records of civilization
far older than biblical chronology could include, he replied that he
was not accustomed to seek evidence which might damage his faith.
Asked finally if he denied "that man was a mammal," he replied,
"I do," probably because he had only a very vague idea what the
word meant. And it was at this point that Mencken fell with a loud

crash from the table upon which he had climbed to get a good view of the show. Perhaps it was the accident he pretended it to be, but I have always suspected that it was to mark with an exclamation point an interchange which he wanted no one to forget.

One was almost sorry for the great leader who had fallen so low. Driven from politics and journalism because of obvious intellectual incompetence, become ballyhoo for boom-town real estate in his search for lucrative employment, and forced into religion as the only quasi-intellectual field in which mental backwardness and complete insensibility to ideas could be used as an advantage, he already knew that he was compelled to seek in the most remote rural regions for the applause so necessary to his contentment. Yet even in Dayton, as choice a stronghold of ignorance and bigotry as one could hope to find, he went down in defeat in the only contest where he had met his antagonists face to face. Dayton itself was ashamed for him.

It knew very well who had won the debate, though many may have still believed that it was Truth which had been defeated in what was, after all, no more than a debate. So far as the legal verdict was concerned it was no more in doubt than it had been before the trial opened. From a legal standpoint the judge was, I suppose, quite right to have kept the jury out of the courtroom during most of the technically irrelevant proceedings. It had, as a matter of fact, been present for not more than fifteen minutes during the entire trial. And it did not, of course, take long to agree that John Scopes was indeed guilty of having taught the theory of evolution in defiance of a law passed by both houses of the legislature and signed by the Governor.

A few days later William Jennings Bryan died suddenly while still in Dayton. It was commonly (and probably truly) said that gluttony had prepared the way for his death; but I suspect that a broken heart was the immediate cause. Mencken staged a grotesque dance over his grave in one of the best and most characteristic of his essays, "In Memoriam: W. J. B." A few days after we had left Dayton he wrote me a note: "God aimed at Darrow, missed him, and hit Bryan. But our loss is Heaven's gain." And it is interesting to imagine what Bryan himself would have said had it actually been Darrow rather than he who was struck down at the end of the debate.

·   ·   ·   ·   ·   ·   ·   ·   ·   ·   ·   ·   ·   ·   ·   ·   ·   ·   ·   ·

Those who wrote the recent book and recent play are too young to have known at first hand the atmosphere of the Twenties, and their interpretations seem to me for that reason to miss the tone of the proceedings as well as what time has made the most significant aspect of the whole affair. Almost inevitably they see it in terms of the grim ideological conflicts of our own day rather than as, in part at least, a typical jape to be gleefully reported in *The American Mercury*. They see a witch trial and miss the fact that it was also a circus; that the defense had deliberately baited their victims; that they had nothing to fear for themselves at least; and that they were enjoying themselves thoroughly.

What took place was more farcical than ominous for the simple reason that Bryanism was not, as it has been made to seem, roughly equivalent to McCarthyism but was, instead, as typical of its decade as McCarthyism was of the Fifties. Bryanism could not possibly have become that Wave of Future which communism or fascism may be, because it was only a backwashing ripple from the past. No one (except Bryan) got hurt and no one on the side which was unpopular only in Dayton and other fundamentalist communities could conceivably have been hurt very much. The wooden swords with which the antagonists fought provided a fine theatrical spectacle but it was a sham battle—not because Bryan was not in earnest but because he had nothing to fight with. Neither the principals, nor such camp followers as I, were Freedom Riders who would be beaten and jailed. Is it any wonder that those who were young then look upon the much maligned Twenties as in some respects a golden age?

From Joseph Wood Krutch, *More Lives Than One* (New York: William Sloane Associates, 1962), pp. 143–161.

The fiction of the last year in particular has mirrored an extraordinary interest in the problems of religion.

WALTER V. GAVIGAN, 1927

7. Reflections in the Literary Mirror

THE modernist-fundamentalist conflict of the 1920s coincided with a spectacular burst of creative energy in the cultural life of the United States. Broadly speaking, the struggle against orthodoxy by "modernists" in literature, art, architecture, and music bore some resemblance to the position of the theological modernists. Perhaps the similarity was greatest between the innovators in literature and "the advanced elements" in theology. If religious modernism was criticized for its "connivance with naturalism," so was modern fiction. Writing in the *Atlantic Monthly* in 1925, Eleanor Duvall maintained that a "new paganism" reigned supreme in contemporary literature. "That our modern fiction holds the mirror up to nature,—pagan nature,—whether of the individual or of social groups," she wrote, "is fairly true; yet it is a menacing truth of disintegration and decay."[1] Obviously the parallel between the new literature and the new theology can be easily exaggerated; in many respects their differences overshadowed their similarities.

A literary revolt against the genteel tradition under way for some years culminated in the 1920s in the efforts of such writers as Sinclair Lewis, F. Scott Fitzgerald, and Ernest Hemingway. Theirs was a rebellion against the values of what they considered the culturally sterile,

[1] See Ellen Duvall, "The New Paganism," *Atlantic Monthly*, CXXVI (November 1925), 633–637.

materialistic, and conformist middle class addicted to Puritanism and smug hypocrisy. Tendencies discernible in the intellectual life and literature of the "lost generation" included a robust skepticism, a hedonistic pursuit of pleasure, large doses of Freudianism, and a rejection of social reform for a concern with the individual, especially one's self. One of Fitzgerald's characters insisted that his generation found "all Gods dead, all wars fought, all faith in man shaken,"[2] while a character in Hemingway's *A Farewell to Arms* protested that he was "not made for thinking" and explained that rather he was made to "eat and drink and sleep with Catherine." George Jean Nathan, the drama critic, disclaimed any concern whatsoever in the "the great problems of the world," including theological problems, and H. L. Mencken proclaimed that "Doing good is in bad taste."[3] The church, like democracy, was identified with the reign of middle-class values; it was viewed as the instrument for forcing conformity to Puritan mores.

The attitude of the intellectual rebels toward religion was perhaps best revealed by the omission of any article on the topic in the critique of American culture *Civilization in the United States*, edited by Harold Stearns and published in 1922. Although Stearns recognized the immensity of the church's physical apparatus and conceded that Americans were a "church-going people," he had to forego an essay on religion and settle for whatever comments the authors of the articles on "Philosophy" and "Nerves" made on the subject. Stearns explained,

The bald truth is, it has been next to impossible to get anyone to write on the subject; most of the people I approached shied off. . . . Almost unanimously . . . they said that real religious feeling in America had disappeared, that the church had become a purely social and political institution, that the country is in the grip of what Anatole France has aptly called Protestant clericalism, and that, finally, they weren't interested.[4]

Although the religious theme, in the broadest sense of the term, was not altogether absent from the writings of the rebellious literati, they could scarcely be expected to produce major works with serious theological motifs. Of course, their critiques of middle-class institutions included

[2] The remark was by Amory Blaine in Fitzgerald's *This Side of Paradise*.
[3] Quoted in William E. Leuchtenburg, *The Perils of Prosperity, 1914–32*. (Chicago: University of Chicago Press, 1958) p. 150.
[4] Harold Stearns, *Civilization in the United States* (New York: Harcourt, Brace, 1922) pp. v–vi.

scathing indictments of organized religion and lurid caricatures of the clergy, most notably in Sinclair Lewis's *Elmer Gantry*.

Students of American literature have been impressed by the obvious decline in religious fiction during the era of the modernist-fundamentalist conflict and the Scopes trial. James D. Hart has pointed out that "during the entire decade there was no best-selling American novel that could be called religious in theme and attitude" and only a few that even had "a slight aroma of Christian faith."[5] Another scholar has asserted that "biblical influence on American fiction probably reached its nadir" in the 1920s.[6] In 1928 Edwin A. McAlpin, an adherent of orthodox theology and an enthusiastic defender of religious fiction, lamented the decline of Christian themes in the literature of "our nontheological age" and found inspiration in the "great" novels of the pre-1920 era.[7] An article in *The Bookman* by an anonymous author deplored the course of religious fiction "from *In His Steps* to *Elmer Gantry*" and clearly indicated that the writer preferred Charles M. Sheldon's book with its inquiry "what would Jesus do?" to contemporary literature which poked fun at the clergy and ridiculed organized religion.[8] The perennial popularity of *In His Steps* throughout the 1920s indicated that many Americans shared this preference. In explaining the apparent disparity between the popular interest in religious questions and the decrease in the number of best-selling religious novels, one historian has suggested that the debate over modernism and fundamentalism was of greater interest to the newspaper reading public than to "the somewhat more sophisticated readers of fiction."[9]

But it would be erroneous to assume that issues involved in the modernist-fundamentalist conflict were in no way reflected in the more sophisticated fiction of the 1920s. Throughout the decade, for example, science posed problems for the literary artists no less than the theologian. And the alternatives pursued by those writers who wrestled with the

---

[5] James D. Hart, "Platitudes of Piety: Religion and the Popular Modern Novel," *American Quarterly*, VI (Winter 1954), 315.

[6] See Carlos Baker, "The Bible in American Fiction," *Religious Perspectives in American Culture*, edited by James W. Smith and A. Leland Jamison (Princeton: Princeton University Press, 1961), pp. 243–272.

[7] See Edwin A. McAlpin, *Old and New Books as Life Teachers* (Garden City: Doubleday, Doran, 1928).

[8] "From *In His Steps* to *Elmer Gantry*," *Bookman*, LXV (May 1927), 380–381.

[9] Hart, *loc. cit.*

new scientific interpretations of man and the universe often paralleled the positions assumed by theologians. In assessing the struggles of the writers, Professor Frederick Hoffman wrote:

The dreadful suggestion that science, having long since reduced man's significance in the universe, was in the process of destroying God as well (or weakening Him and making Him all but morally useless) forced them to one of several strategies: they had to find the kind of "glory" that [Bertrand] Russell recommended in courageously accepting the universe as science revealed it; they had to take advantage of every loss of scientific confidence; they had to hold firmly to a fundamentalist position . . .; or they had to distinguish between scientific and aesthetic orders of perception either to destroy the confidence in the scientific or to restore the aesthetic to the level of useful knowledge.[10]

Perhaps the change so evident in the short story of the 1920s was indicative of sophisticated fiction in general. Unlike those of the pre-World War I period, the short stories of the postwar era demonstrated a moral, rather than an intellectual, doubt of God's nature. "The conflict between doctrine and feeling," according to Professor Austin M. Wright, "is significant because it shows that formal religious faith does not have a clear priority as a source of values. The typical religious problem of the twenties is the difficulty of finding out what one really believes."[11]

Whatever may have been the status of sophisticated religious fiction, there is ample evidence that the issues raised in the modernist-fundamentalist conflict received substantial treatment in the popular literature, both fiction and nonfiction, of the 1920s. A survey by the National Association of Book Publishers in 1927 revealed that "there is today an unprecedented demand for religious books." In explaining the causes for this demand, John Farrar wrote:

there has been a widespread recrudescence of interest in religion, partly induced by the war and partly by the challenge which natural science has urged upon religious formulae. It cannot be said that we are in a great spiritual awakening; it can be said that we are on the verge of an intellectual awakening as regards religion.[12]

10 Frederick Hoffman, *The Twenties: American Writing in the Postwar Decade* (New York: Viking Press, 1955), pp. 290–291.

11 Austin M. Wright, *The American Short Story in the Twenties* (Chicago: University of Chicago Press, 1961), p. 144.

12 "Readable Religion," *Bookman*, LXV (April 1927), 115–116.

Charles W. Ferguson, writing in *The Bookman* in 1928, suggested that not only had "clerics learned to write" but also that the term "religious literature" had acquired a "new meaning" since World War I. The new religious literature included far more than collections of tedious sermons or "lessons" of the Sunday school variety. It embraced a "hodgepodge of works," both fiction and nonfiction, dealing with topics ranging from the salvation of souls to the traits of Bantu worship. "Obviously," Ferguson concluded, "the sharp line of demarcation between religious and general books is fading away."[13] The fact that the Religious Book-of-the-Month Club, organized in 1928, made a work by Gamaliel Bradford its first selection seemed to corroborate his interpretation.

Certain best sellers of the 1920s suggest a correlation between popular reading and the public interest in theological issues. For example, the national concern with science, which was undoubtedly quickened by the modernist-fundamentalist debate, was reflected in the popularity of such works as Albert Wiggam's *The New Decalogue of Science* and J. Arthur Thomson's *Outline of Science*. At the same time works involving various aspects of the Christian faith attracted a wide audience. One of these was Harold Bell Wright's novel *God and the Groceryman* which, though popular, failed to elicit the enthusiasm accorded similar works published before 1920. In a critical evaluation of "religion in fiction" at the end of 1927, Walter V. Gavigan concluded that such novels as Reginald W. Kauffman's *A Man of Little Faith*, Edith Wharton's *Twilight Sleep*, and Marie Conway Oemler's *The Holy Lover* were superior to Wright's "sentimental and saccharine" work.[14] Among the nonfiction best sellers were two bizarre studies of the life of Christ, Giovanni Papini's *Life of Christ* and the less reverent *The Man Nobody Knows* by Bruce Barton.

More relevant to the themes implicit in the modernist-fundamentalist conflict were various novels by Willa Cather and T. S. Stribling. The sense of disenchantment with the scientific and industrial orientation of America which became increasingly evident in Miss Cather's literary efforts reached a climax in her symbolic novel *The Professor's*

[13] Charles W. Ferguson, "The Clerics Learn To Write," *Bookman*, LXVII (April 1928), 129–133.

[14] See Walter V. Gavigan, "Religion in Recent Fiction," *Catholic World*, CXXVIII (December 1927), 360–369.

House, published in 1925. The principal character in this essentially religious novel is Godfrey St. Peter, a professor in a midwestern university, whose familiar, orderly world is shattered by a scientific invention. The commercial exploitation of the invention not only corrupts the university and his own family but also forces him from his old house. The novel chronicles the defeat and spiritual withdrawal of St. Peter, who is saved from committing suicide by an ignorant, devout seamstress and her "little religious book." Professor St. Peter's response to a question posed by a student named Miller reveals his disenchantment with a science which gave man "a lot of ingenious toys" while destroying something far more valuable—man's feeling of personal involvement "in a gorgeous drama with God." In the words of Maxwell Geismar, *The Professor's House* was "a novel of death and rebirth—of a spiritual purging and regeneration, and of that second coming which, formalized in the central rituals of religions, is actually part of the deepest experience of man."[15]

Numerous novels of little literary merit, as well as hundreds of poems whose quality destined them to obscurity, probably mirrored more accurately than sophisticated fiction the popular interest in scientific and religious questions. In 1928, for example, *The Bible Champion,* the organ of the Bible League of North America whose editorial board was a virtual roster of fundamentalist leaders, serialized Glenn Gates Cole's *Jungle Poison: A Novel Reflecting Present Tendencies.* Cole's novel described in gory detail the ruinous effect of evolution and modernist teachings upon America's Christian civilization. The evolution controversy and the Scopes Trial in particular spawned a plethora of verse and short stories and at least one play. Early in 1927 the well-known Hungarian playwright Ferenz Herczeg became the first dramatist to use the Dayton trial as the theme of a play, which he entitled "Monkey Business"[16] and described as a fantastic comedy. Herczeg's work was superseded a quarter of a century later by the highly acclaimed Broadway production of Jerome Lawrence and Robert E. Lee's *Inherit the Wind,* a play based on the Scopes trial.

15 Maxwell Geismar, *The Last of the Provincials: The American Novel, 1915–1925* (Boston: Houghton Mifflin, 1947), pp. 187–188.
16 See New York *Times,* January 2, 1927.

Abner Teeftallow in Court
T. S. Stribling

Among the novelists of the 1920s whose works included references to the resurgence of fundamentalism was **T. S. Stribling**, a native of Tennessee and the author of several popular books. Published the year after the Scopes trial in 1925, his *Teeftallow* was a fictional account of life in the Tennessee hill country which revolved around the career of an untutored orphan, Abner Teeftallow. The following excerpt from the novel is a scene witnessed by Abner during a session of the county court when the local justices of the peace convened to perform their legislative and judicial duties. Before the court decided whether Abner should be required to attend school, it heard a plea from "Professor" Lem Overall, the local pedagogue and man of culture, in behalf of a petition requesting the legislature to prohibit the teaching of evolution in all state-supported educational insitutions. The court approved the petition after an impassioned oration by a well-known traveling evangelist by the name of Blackman who shared the "Professor's" views regarding the evil influences of evolution. Apparently convinced of "the weakening influence of literacy on the mentality," the justices also relieved Abner of any requirement to attend school. Those who interpreted Tennessee's antievolution law and the spectacular trial which it inspired as the work of a rural, culturally deprived people undoubtedly found support for their view in Stribling's novel. Although "Professor" Overall and "Brother" Blackman might well appear as stereotyped fundamentalists to sophisticated critics, it is interesting to note the remark of the court's presiding officer following the endorsement of Overall's petition: "Now, gentlemen of the court," he said, "le's git to work on somethin' we know somethin' about."

***

Laughter filled the courtroom as the clerk drawled out, "Professor Lem Overall and Brother Blackman want to put a proposition before the court."

As he spoke the two men mentioned arose from the crowd and entered the chancel. A trickle of dismay went over Abner on seeing the stranger with Professor Overall. His black coat and a certain unsmiling quality about his long sallow face stamped him for a preacher. Abner's spirits sank and sank at these elaborate preparations to force him to go to school and thereby weaken his mind. He began to doubt even if Railroad Jones could rescue him from such a situation.

375

Professor Overall took the floor and stood rolling his prominent eyes about the room for several seconds, after the approved fashion of Lane County orators, then began with the utmost solemnity:

"Honourable Judge and justices of the court, Brother Blackman an' me has come before you today to address you on what I an' all the scholarly world considers to be the most important base on which our civilization rests, an' that is the edjercation of the young. Ain't that right, Brother Blackman?"

"Amen, Brother Overall," rumbled the minister in a basso profundo.

"Brother Blackman, as a great many of you all know, is an evangelist now holdin' a meetin' at Shady Grove Church on Big Cyprus, an' from all reports, God shore has been blessin' him in a wonderful manner with a great outpourin' of the spirit." He turned for corroboration to the minister.

"That's right, Brother Overall," assented the divine in his sepulchral tone, "we shore have got the devil on the run on Big Cyprus."

"But in his work of savin' souls," continued the pedagogue, "Brother Blackman goes jest a grain furder than savin' the ol' sheep from destruction; he's after the innocent lam's, the little children of this county an' them that's to come in the fewcher."

A pause here as the room became intensely quiet except for a whisper somewhere, "edjercated fool, but he shore han' les a speech. . . ."

"Brother Blackman ast me as a man of science an' as a representative of the edjercational intrusts of this county to git up an' tell you-all what I thought of his plan. I want ter say I'm with him heart an' soul. I want you justices to hear what he is goin' to ast you to do an' you do it. It'll be a blessin' to you an' yore children the longest day you'll live. Honourable Judge an' justices of the court, lemme interduce Brother Blackman."

The evangelist stepped forward as the pedagogue retired.

"Gentlemen of the court," began the minister in his profound voice, "Brother Overall says it will be a blessin' to you as long as you live. I say it will be a blessin' to you through eternity. I tell you the angels are leanin' this minute over the battlements of Heaven, waitin' with hushed breaths an' beatin' hearts to see what the justices of Lane County air goin' to do here at this hour an' this minute!"

The minister paused with a certain effect of embodying the supernatural world, of solidifying it in the air somewhere above their heads. He proceeded in his ponderous voice, and inquired slowly and solemnly, "My frien's, do you b'lieve yore great gran'daddy was a monkey?"

He paused, then with the revivalist's trick, shouted the same question with a different stress at the top of his lungs, "Do you b'lieve yore great gran'daddy was a monkey?"

This jarred the nerves of his audience. The preacher brought down his fist on the chancel rail with a sounding blow, "Is there a man in the sound of my voice that b'lieves his great gran'daddy was a monkey?

"Oh, brethren, don't you know the Bible says man was made in the image of God! Then how can he be made in the image of a monkey?

"Brothers, judges," gasped the divine, pausing to mop his dripping face, "you know that our school books air full of this damnable doctrine. What air ye goin' to do about it? Air ye goin' to let the deceivin',' agnostic, hell-bound college perfessers send our children to hell? Air they goin' to cry fer bread an' you give 'em a stone! It's a sin unto God an' a cryin' out of unrighteousness from the earth! What air ye goin' to do—what you goin' to do? I'm talkin' to you justices now, what you goin' to do?"

Reverend Blackman shook a long forefinger at the justices.

"You know what you can do," he replied to his own question, "tear this infidel doctrine out of the school books! Tear it out! Give the old devil a thrust in the heart with the sword of truth! Strike a match to his sulfurious fires an' roast him out of the school books our blessed little children's got to read. Roast him out! Ain't I right, Brother Overall?" he bellowed, beet-coloured.

"You're right, Brother Blackman!"

"Then, let's all be right!" chanted the preacher. "Now, brothers an' justices of Lane County, when the clerk passes aroun' the petition I have drew up, I want ever' man who believes in God and wants to meet his children in Heaven—I want him to sign it. I want you to tell our legislatur' that we don't want no more infidel doctrines of the Godless Yankees sent down here in our school books, an' we won't have it! Let 'em know ol' Lane stan's fer God, an' God stan's fer ol' Lane! An' we do this hopin' our county escapes the destruction that God is shore to send on our Sodom an' Gomorrah Nation! Brethren, let us pray!"

The parson lifted his hands and the whole courtroom bowed its head. His prayer was as vehement as his address and covered the same points. When he made an end, he retired, dripping with perspiration, while the blond clerk, rather hastily, passed around a petition which the minister had drawn up asking the Tennessee state legislature to remove all traces of the science of evolution from the school books of the state.

The justices looked at it rather blankly and signed one after another. One of the court hesitated a moment. "Professor Overall," he asked, "does our present school books teach there ain't no God an' our gran'fathers were monkeys?"

Professor Overall rolled his prominent eyes on the questioner reprovingly. "They certainly do, Brother Boggus. You can take my word as a teacher and a scholar."

"I jest wanted to know," said the justice in a chastened tone, and signed his name hurriedly.

There was some slight cheering among the audience when the petition went back to the table. The judge of the court rapped for silence.

"Quiet! Quiet! Now, gentlemen of the court, le's git to work on somethin' we know somethin' about. Mr. Clerk, what's nex' on docket?"

From T. S. Stribling, *Teeftallow* (New York: Doubleday, 1926), pp. 23–27.

A Manse-Dweller Encounters Modernism
Luther Little

Among the works of fiction which might qualify as a "fundamentalist novel" is *Manse-Dwellers* by Luther Little, a clergyman in North Carolina who actively participated in the fundamentalist crusade of the 1920s. Described as a "thrilling romance," Little's work may well have been autobiographical. More temperate than Glenn Cole's *Jungle Poison*, it nonetheless shared Cole's penchant for nostalgia and sentimentality. The central theme of Little's romance focused upon the "joys and sorrows" of the Reverend James West, the minister of a prosperous church in Tarrytown whose congregation subscribed to a theology no less orthodox than his own. One of the most disconcerting experiences in West's career, described in the following selection, was an encounter with a young theological heretic in the person of his assistant, David B. Stamps, who was ultimately forced to vacate his post in the Tarrytown church.

———◆◆———

Dr. West had been out of the city nearly two weeks touring the state in the interest of the "Veterans' Reward." He returned to his study on Friday morning of the second week in high, happy mood. His trip had been successful, for pastors and congregations, where he had spoken, were in full accord with his campaign. More than two hundred thousand of the million dollars had been secured since the meeting of the convention in which his commission had been created. It was now clear that before the next convention he would see half of the amount fully raised. Two years had been the time limit set for finishing the task. On that Friday morning the pastor was happy and hopeful. He greeted all the office force and they were glad to see him back. He was the fine, moving spirit among all, and everyone of them was loyal to him. He even sought out Black Jerry and greeted him by saying, "Hello, Jerry, did you run everything well while I was gone?" Jerry grunted and said, "Doctor, I done de best I could, but it seems de Lawd done hid away hisself when you goes off." Dr. West laughed but did not catch the significance of Jerry's remark "the Lord hides away when you go off."

On the previous Sunday the pastor had left his pulpit to be

379

filled by his assistant, Dr. David B. Stamps, who usually took the duties of the pastor in his absence. Dr. Stamps was not a regular preacher in the accepted meaning of the term. He had taken his degree at the state denominational college, but it was the degree of Doctor of Philosophy. He was a man of religious feeling and turned toward the life of a lay-preacher. He was highly educated and a person of charm and culture. He was finely fitted to do the kind of work that was needed in the Tarrytown church. He was popular and influential, always knowing his place and filling it. He was devoted to Dr. West and did his best to help forward every movement of the church. This young assistant seemed to have been just the man for the place, and Dr. West considered himself fortunate. He had held the place of assistant for several years and was clearly conversant with all the program of Dr. West and the church, and both had his sympathy, so far as he knew how to give it.

When the morning greeting was over, Dr. West settled himself in his study and soon was getting his sermons for the following Sunday. After lunch he was ready to dictate some important letters, so he asked Mrs. Black to come in. When the dictation was finished, he asked her just how the affairs of the church had gone during his absence. Mrs. Black, who had been with the church since he came, was easily the best person from whom he could get real facts. She was one of those quiet, loyal souls who could see from the heart. In addition to being an incomparable secretary, she was a "buffer" who preferred to take the blows intended for another and bear them herself. She was also a great discerner, and knew what things should be reported, but never in the spirit of tattling. So that Friday afternoon she gave a report of the sermon preached by Dr. Stamps the preceding Sunday. Though unintended, the sermon was clearly radical and dangerous. Dr. Stamps disclosed the fact that he believed there were parts of the Bible not inspired, and he took the position of the naturalist. Of course, all of this was a grief to the pastor, for he loved Stamps; besides he at once could see the danger of exposing the minds of the young people to such serious errors spoken by one so popular as the young assistant. Here was a new and surprising problem. His first thought was to interview Stamps, and, if he found the report to be correct, to see to it that he leave the position promptly. But two facts deterred him. If possible he wanted to save Stamps, and besides he knew it would cause friction to discharge so popular a man. So Dr. West decided to wait for further developments, and also to see what had been the impression made on the church. The words of Black Jerry now began to unfold to him. "The Lord hides when you go away." Had Stamps hidden the Lord in his naturalistic interpretation of the scriptures? Sunday came and a larger congregation greeted the returning pastor. His sermon, preached on the subject "The Rock of the Holy Scriptures," was timely and well received. Many of the devout members wept as they spoke to him of the words of Stamps on the previous Sunday. On the other hand, he heard a few echoes of how it pleased many of the younger people. This gave Pastor West an additional alarm. So the wise course was followed. The pastor first made an investigation as to what influence had worked to produce this effect upon his young assistant. He did not have to go far to find out that one or two of the favorite teachers in the denominational college in the state had planted the seed in the mind of the young student and now the flower and the fruit were in evidence. To Dr. West, here was one of the most serious things in the Christian and state education of the day.

The usual routine of the church went on for several weeks and Pastor West was hearing so much of this new doctrine that he saw some move must be made or all would be lost. Finally he asked Stamps to spend the morning in his study. The conversation was opened by Pastor West who assured Stamps of his love and esteem. He also told him how he wanted to help save him from these errors. Stamps was frank and open. He told the pastor how these thoughts were given him in college and how the modern trend of education was to throw away the old traditions, so that in his sermon he was only reproducing what many young men were absorbing in their college life. After the whole morning spent together Dr. West asked Stamps if he would not write out his full belief and submit it to him within a week's time. To this request Stamps agreed and they were to meet in the study one week from that day for further discussion.

The week passed and now they were face to face with the written creed which is as follows:

Jesus was born of a human father and mother. He was divine only as are other men. He was the greatest of prophets and ethical teachers. He attained the highest degree of trust in God. We are to imitate his religious life. He is himself not the object of religious trust and worship. His recorded miracles are mainly myth and fiction, the imaginings of fond disciples. In some cases of healing he exerted a kind of magnetic power, such as we often observe today in so-called "divine healers." There was no real resurrection and ascension.

There was, doubtless, belief in the resurrection, but it was based on manifestations like those of modern spiritualism. They are simply psychic phenomena of the subjective kind. There was no objective ground of forgiveness in His death on the Cross. He taught that God forgives the penitent and desires fellowship with men, but other prophets taught the same. Christ's present influence is like that of many great men who have lived. It is mediated to us through the Gospels, especially the Sermon on the Mount and related ethical teachings. The New Testament records themselves are conglomerates of a little truth and a great deal of fiction drawn from the surrounding ethnic religions or the imagination of the writers themselves.

After this statement had been read and understood by West and Stamps, the Pastor said to his assistant: "Stamps, are you willing to let me read this to the church next Sunday morning, so that the members of our church may know and understand your position just as you and I know it?" Stamps, being a man of open and candid mind, gladly consented to the request. The conversation between these two church leaders was so fraternal and cordial, it was evident that whatever the outcome, these men would remain personal friends. They both knew that intellectual and theological verities would prosper best in an open and thoroughly understood statement.

Following the Sunday morning service, the statement was read to the church. Its reading produced a strange effect. Instead of division and hate, the evident feeling was that of regret, sympathy, and the spirit of prayer. One could easily see that the occasion was not one of contest between West and Stamps, it was conflict between Stamps and Revelation. As one of the members put it, "Not that we love Stamps less, but we love the Bible and God more."

The church was heartbroken and bewildered. So far as West was personally concerned, he saw that he was safe from the results that might follow, but he was not hunting for individual victory, rather he was seeking the triumph of truth and the saving of his young comrade from the withering touch of "Naturalistic Philosophy."

After the church had spent an hour in prayer and meditation, they all went home with tear-bathed faces and trusting hearts, having left the entire matter with Dr. West to settle, knowing his mastery in the hour of crisis and having seen his great leadership before, the church knew it could safely trust him in this one.

From Luther Little, *Manse-Dwellers* (Charlotte: Presbyterian Standard Publishing Company, 1927), pp. 143–149.

The Last Heretic
Carl Van Doren

The following story by Carl Van Doren, a distinguished man of letters, describes the conditions following the triumph of the fundamentalists' crusade for conformity. The chief character, Randolph Schuyler, who by 1970 was "the last heretic," had miraculously survived the Preliminary Census of 1929 and the Final Inquisition of 1940. Clearly, he dissented "from every sovereign tenet" of the theological and political fundamentalism foisted upon the nation by a combination of religious zealots, Ku Kluxers, and prohibitionists. In his opinion, civilization in the United States had capitulated to the demands of a minority of "barbarians who hated science and reason" no less than Catholics, Negroes, Jews, and aliens. Under the rule of an Anglo-Saxon oligarchy, the American people had been forced into a "drab Protestantism and a touchy nationalism."

It must have been about 1970 that I first met Randolph Schuyler. I had, it is true, noticed him before that time going in and out of his house in Charlton Street, but I had thought no more about him than that he obviously belonged to the old regime which even then seemed so dim. Our actual meeting came about, I remember, by accident. Having backed gradually up his stoop in order to see over the heads of a sidewalk full of people who had gathered to watch a Klan parade go by, I had the misfortune to tread upon the toes of the old gentleman who had just emerged from his doorway. He met my apologies, which I doubtless made profuse because of my feeling that he would hardly understand our honest modern manners, with a pardon at once so kindly and so ironic that I found my interest in him many times enlarged. A few days later I greeted him on the street, and not long after that took occasion to carry to his house in person a letter which the postman had carelessly left in my box. The details of our ripening acquaintance have now escaped my memory, but I am not likely soon to forget the memorable evening when, having been invited to dine with him, I stumbled upon his secret.

Here was a man who had been overlooked not only by the Preliminary Census of 1929, but also by the Final Inquisition of 1940, and who dissented, so far as I could learn, from every sovereign tenet of the Fundamentalists.

Why I did not immediately turn him over to the police is a mystery to me. I had been taught in as strict a school as any in Manhattan, and at Amherst had heard with conviction the prescribed lectures on Fundamentalism, Americanism, and Censorship. There was, however, something diabolical about the charm of this cheerful rebel, and I succumbed, as I venture to think most men would have done in the circumstances. My defection proves, it seems to me, that the Fathers of the Inquisition were right in their ruthlessness toward the heretics in those bitter days. A few such survivors as Schuyler would have imperiled the whole victory.

"You are clever to guess my secret," he said when my face had suddenly betrayed my horror. "I suppose I should be more worried than I am. The secret, as a matter of fact, has been something of a burden. It has condemned me to an extraordinary loneliness. If you report me to the police, I shall be first a nine-days' scandal and then a living example just long enough to die for my offenses. Little as I care for these aspects of fame, I cannot truly say that they are altogether painful prospects. After all, I have lived for thirty years among Fundamentalists of an unrelieved orthodoxy, and the most uncomfortable exit from the world has therefore its advantages."

I dare say it was some quirk of curiosity which got the better of me, for I thereupon solemnly promised, to my own astonishment, that I would keep his secret.

"In that case," he thanked me, "I can do no less than be quite frank with you. If, as I suspect, you are merciful because you consider me a sort of specimen too rare to be lightly thrown away, I must try to make your museum entertaining. What shall I tell you first?"

"But how—how—" I stammered.

"How did I avoid the inquisitors? I simply do not know. You are of course aware, though you are too young to remember, that New York was the last region to be subdued. Our own Fundamentalists had to summon aid from the Ku-Klux Klan in the South, the White Ribbon Legion in the Middle West, and the Watch and Ward Crusaders in Massachusetts. Even then the task was difficult. I do not like to think of the blood which flowed in Greenwich Village. At the time I was so desperate that I made no effort to save myself. This may explain my incredible good fortune, if I may call it that. The Final Inquisition through some error passed me by, I lived here quietly undisturbed, and in the end I came to breathe freely once again. Out of the millions of the unpersuaded possibly there were others whose fate was similar to mine, but I was too discreet to look for them, and no one of them ever found me out. I honestly believe that I am now the last heretic in the United States. You will forgive me if I take a certain pleasure in the distinction."

2

"Have you," I asked, perhaps too gently, "no sense of sin?"

"None whatever. And I have generally observed that those who have a strong sense of sin have very little of any other kind. After all, consider where that feeling comes from. To have it a man must be sure that he has done what is displeasing to the gods; and to be sure of that he must know what the gods require of men. Now, I have gone here and there over the earth a great many thousand miles without ever happening upon a god, talking to him, or learning the demands which he and his fellows make of me and mine. I have questioned numerous men who were sure they were in the counsels of the gods, yet I have never entirely trusted one of them. The best of such men disagree among themselves, doubtless for the reason that they all argue from what I, in my modest fashion, must call inadequate evidence. They tell me that the gods whispered their secrets to men who lived long ago, and who wrote their knowledge down in books. Reading these books, however, I find them full of manifest absurdities regarding history and science and full of manifest contradictions regarding morals. I can consequently do no better than choose among them the precepts and examples which confirm my own experiences. But this I do with other books which no one calls inspired. Nor do I find myself more thoroughly convinced when I examine the great traditions which, first based upon the holy books, are in some quarters held to have broadened down and gradually to have included the whole truth. Looking over the chronicles of these traditions, I discover that they have regularly resisted novel truths and persecuted the truth-seekers as long as it was possible, never learning anything from the fact that they have so often had eventually to confess themselves mistaken and honor persons whom formerly they dishonored. As neither the books nor the traditions bring me face to face with the gods whom they proclaim, I suspend my judgment and do not scourge myself for deeds which this or that authority calls unlawful."

"What appalling egotism!" I burst forth, partly to shield myself from his supple arguments. "You set yourself up against all the collective wisdom of mankind."

Schuyler smiled brightly.

"Why, so I must seem to you to do. It is so long since I have discoursed with a contemporary that I had quite forgotten how insolent an independent thought would look to him. But let me remind you that groups of men, large or small, have their egotisms, too, which often clash with din and fury. And my researches, to say nothing of my recollections, assure me that the smaller groups have not seldom overthrown the larger, and that mere individuals in their time have brought majorities round to their way of thinking."

Here I saw that I had the better of the argument and, though I was Schuyler's guest and junior, I did not hesitate to press it.

"Then you must admit the logical consequences of your position. You see truth emerging from the clashes of one party with another. Why can you not perceive that the truth has finally emerged, after centuries of wrangling, into the clear light of Fundamentalism? If truth has a history, as you maintain, it is naturally most powerful in its latest form."

"This is most refreshing," said the incorrigible old man. "I see I have denied myself a considerable amount of entertainment by getting out of touch with the younger generation. It may distress you, but I do not believe that truth, for all it has a history, is necessarily progressive. It moves, I note, in cycles, ebbs and flows, rises and falls, advances and slips back. I have always suspected it to be one of the whimsical devices of the gods, about whom I know so little, that the reason, after reaching a certain point, is once more engulfed by a wave of sentiment or ignorance and then has slowly to struggle into power again. It had struggled to that certain point at the beginning of this century, whereupon the uninstructed and the unimaginative, as if envying it its prosperity, rose and destroyed it. As I view the matter, this was merely another barbarian invasion. I so viewed it in 1940. If I had been shaped of the clay of martyrs I might have fought the Final Inquisition and lost my head for my pains. Instead, I bowed my head as the civilized Greeks no doubt did when they saw their reasonable opinions being overturned by the jangling Oriental sects which had invaded their world. My world was being invaded by barbarians who hated science and the reason. They were stronger than I. I smiled and settled down in my own dominions in Charlton Street. The barbarians have furnished me one unbroken comedy ever since."

I saw I could not endure this blasphemy any further, so I turned the conversation from theology to politics.

3

In this realm, it turned out, Randolph Schuyler was no less incorrigible than in the other. Though he was, as his name indicated, of strictly native stock, he made merry at the expense of true Americanism.

"How the trail of Amerigo Vespucci comes down through the ages! Amerigo probably never made the voyages he bragged about, but he wrote a book and thus fixed his name on the new hemisphere. In something of this same fashion the outspoken Anglo-Saxons, though they have had the help of many other races in building the United States, have fixed their language, or one a good deal like it, upon the nation, and so claim the whole credit for the undertaking. At the time of the Final Inquisition about one tenth of the Americans were colored, and about one sixth Catholic, and a large proportion so decidedly not Anglo-Saxon that they were not even Nordic; yet the White Protestant Nordics forced their will upon the rest and made the Government an unblushing oligarchy."

"Surely you realize the importance of having one country, one flag, one speech, one culture."

"I realize the importance of such a unity to the oligarchs, but I am afraid the importance to the country is not so great. Recalling the folk-songs of the Negroes, and their powerful emotional impulses, I think the land is a much less desirable place to live in, now these particular Americans have been condemned to the rank of songless, sullen helots. Recalling the secular light-heartedness of the Catholics, though I never liked their theology, and the international sympathies of the Jews, I take emphatically less pleasure in the American scene, now all these tribes have been obliged to settle down to a drab Protestantism and a touchy nationalism. It seems to me that the Fathers of the Inquisition were about as wasteful of precious human materials as their ancestors had been of the natural resources of the continent."

"Then why don't you go back—"

"To the land from which I came, whatever be its name? Forgive me if I cap verse with you out of an old song which was sung during the Preliminary Census. But I am refreshed to a pitch of frivolity by your question. I have lived, you see, so long to myself that I had forgotten that such witty repartee still exists. As to your question itself, I might be willing to go back if it were not for one thing, which is that I am, in my way, an American, and have nowhere else to go. I belong to an American minority. Come to think of it, I am the American minority. In the circumstances I feel almost what a Fundamentalist would call a duty to stay here. I believe the country ought to have a minority within its borders. Doubtless in the blithe economy of the gods I have been spared to play this necessary role. To be sure, I have not been conspicuous, but that is because the majority is at the moment so overwhelming. If another party of dissent arises, I shall declare myself and hand on to its members the torch which I have kept alight, however feebly, within my prudent bosom. When that fortunate day appears, the young minority, remembering me, will not have to blush at the thought that they inherit a past which, even for a second, once lacked any minority whatsoever."

I nearly suffocated as I listened to his words. Not only did he insist that the old days of varying opinions might come back, but he insisted that such a thing was philosophically desirable. So great was my sense of horror that I could not speak.

"That unborn minority," he went on, "will discover that if we have a Constitution, we have also a Bill of Rights. They will investigate our history and discover that we are a federation of States and also a federation of cultures. The dream of an absolute unity, they will understand, was a vain dream, because it was an unscientific dream. It assumed that the original Anglo-Saxon element could assimilate all sorts of foreign elements to itself and show no differences. What chemistry! And what anthropology to hold that the unchecked dominance of one racial group would produce a richer civilization than a natural mixture of all the component group!"

4

I saw it was hopeless to expect any sound views from such a creature. It took all my resolution not to recall my promise to keep his secret and not to rush out to the police. But I reflected, in the midst of my anger, that he really did no harm, and I did not like to run the risk of being suspected of complicity. If he should later become talkative, the Censors would know how to deal with him.

Meanwhile, however, Schuyler cherished in his library, which was stowed away in a vault beneath his house, books which would have driven the Censors to distraction. Not a book was expurgated. With an irresistible inquisitiveness I looked into several of them that evening, at the same time listening to a shameless series of comments from the heretic. He showed me volumes, printed in the United States before the establishment of the Censors, which moved nonchalantly among the most devilish theories. Some weighed the relative value of all the religions ever invented; some compared the political systems of the world and actually found others at some points preferable to the American; some expounded chimerical schemes for peace or utopian notions about what they called a just division of goods among mankind; some set forth without dissent the most fantastic proposals for innovations in the arts; some actually praised the ancient heretics. The pre-Fundamentalist poets and dramatists and novelists, in all their nakedness, here held up their heads quite unabashed. Though I read hastily, it was with a fearful fascination. I had not dreamed, having been nurtured in a purer age and taste, that such things could ever have been written. I felt my face flushing, my hands trembling with excitement. Yet Schuyler had lived so long among these evil books that he was unperturbed. He even laughed at me for my distress.

"You remind me," he said, "of the unimaginative moralists who used to set up an elderly twittering about 'free love' whenever a novelist looked for a moment behind the scenes and caught a glimpse of the strings which pulled the puppets in the dance of sex. It was they who brought the Censors into power, they and the unimaginative patriots who strangled political speculation by calling it sedition unless it flattered the ruling oligarchs. In my more vindictive moments I wish these moralists and patriots could suffer from the reign of dullness which they have ushered in. My reason, however, denies me the pleasure of vindictiveness. I realize that dullness is their natural food and that they do not know what they are missing."

"But what order, what stability, could you expect in a world habitually confused by unsound doctrines and unclean pictures of human life?"

"Unsound? How can we know what doctrines are unsound until they have been proposed, tested, and accepted or rejected? Unclean? Do you blame a mirror for accurately reflecting the faces which look into it? The earth is nothing if it is not a trying-ground for all the ideas that the poor creatures on it can invent. Most of them are sure to perish while they are still ideas, without ever taking root in the soil of conduct. That soil, however, always grows dry and sour unless it is constantly rejuvenated by these new seeds, fertile or not.—But I am afraid that I am becoming solemn, or I should never use so unscientific a metaphor. To answer your question most directly, I could not expect a Fundamentalist order and stability in a world kept stirred by new ideas, but then, neither should I desire it. Though my voluntary survival during thirty years of Fundamentalism may not indicate it, I genuinely prefer a noisy life to a peaceful death."

This abominable frivolity both saved Schuyler from my wrath and saved my soul from his contagion. I often wish I could have so far escaped from the sly influence as to denounce him and let him pay the penalty. Still more do I wish I could be sure that in my mercy there was no fear of him. And yet, remembering those days in which my conscience tormented me with the demand that I make his existence known, I confess that nothing dissuaded me as much as the certainty that if I gave him up he would laugh at me. He was not merely a faithful rebel; he was a cheerful rebel. If I had informed the Censors, they would have had to turn to me for evidence, and I should have had to face him in their presence. That hour, I am afraid, was what I felt that I could not endure. Much as I should have rejoiced to see him punished for his contumacy, I should not have been able to meet that amused smile of his as he listened to my version of his opinions, perhaps explaining it to the Censors in language more precise than mine. He would have ridiculed us in the lethal chamber, I am convinced. With right and virtue on our side, we should nevertheless have been made uncomfortable by the ironical confidence of his manner. This, perhaps, is by itself a reason why the land is better off since it is rid of him. Minds like his, free minds they call themselves, are such enemies of our upright and dignified society that there can be no truce between them and it.

From Carl Van Doren, "The Last Heretic," *The Century Magazine,* CVII (April 1924), 929–934.

Alice in Literal-Land
John F. Scott

The following "allegory of the war in the churches" by John F. Scott, modeled after *Alice in Wonderland,* describes the imaginary journey of a young girl also named Alice. After a flight astride her "preacher-bird's back" she entered the Cave of Controversy where she was forced to choose between two routes to salvation: one promised excitement and adventure but involved certain risks of confused directions; the other guaranteed safety and comfort so long as the traveler obeyed all prescribed rules. Choosing the latter, Alice arrived in Literal-Land in time to witness a major heresy trial. While in Literal-Land, she wandered into the Denominational Chamber of the Episcopalians where a kind gentleman attempted to force her to attend a school. Repelled by this idea, she first hid behind a curtain, then felt her way along a dark passageway until she reached a "much larger and brighter corridor" crowded with people coming from passageways similar to that through which she had just escaped. Soon the travelers stood before the Gates of Paradise, and regardless of the route that had brought them here, "nobody argued" as they glimpsed "the Holy City all bright and shining."

The sermon was very dull—to Alice. She had tried hard to listen, but the words were awfully long, and she didn't have the slightest idea of what it was all about. Now and again when the preacher raised his voice, she would look up and marvel at his excitement.

"How much like a big bird he looks when he waves his arms that way!" thought Alice. "I wonder if he could fly." The idea fascinated her, and the more she wondered about it, the more possible it seemed. It was well for her that she had given the matter some thought; otherwise she might have been very much surprised and startled to see him jump out of the pulpit and sail right down to her pew. As it was, it seemed the most natural thing in the world.

"Would you like to come with me on a flight of the imagination?" said he.

"I'd love to," Alice replied.

"Hop on my back and hang on tight," said the minister.

Alice did as he bade her, and off they flew together, right out of the window. On and on they went, up and up, over cities and forests and lakes and prairies and mountains and river systems.

"How strange everything looks from up here!" said Alice, talking to herself. I should think God would get very dizzy looking down from his throne, because his altitude is so much higher. But I suppose he has got used to it. Anyway, people must seem very funny to him, they are all so little, even smaller than the pygmies in 'Gulliver's Travels.' " So Alice talked on, sometimes not knowing what she was saying. After a while, however, she ran out of words, and as it seemed to her that they must be nearly at the journey's end, she thought it would be nice to know just where in the world they were. So, very carefully, she crawled up a little farther on the preacher-bird's back, and shouted as loud as she could right in his ear:

"Where are we now?"

"Up in the air," he called back to her.

Alice thought it a very uncivil answer, but she couldn't help wondering if that wasn't the reason she had talked so much. Before she had time to come to any decision in the matter they ran into a huge, black thundercloud. Alice was so frightened that she shut her eyes tight, and tried to hide her head under one of the flapping wings.

Suddenly, things grew strangely quiet; the rushing wind stopped; then came a series of violent jounces, thumpety, thump, thump, thump, and Alice, taken unawares, fell to the ground.

"Well, here we are at last," said the preacher-bird, turning around to look at her.

"Where are we?" snapped Alice, still a bit upset by her fall. He kindly disregarded the tone of her voice.

"We are now at the beginning of a theological adventure."

Alice was about to ask the same question again, but was afraid she might appear stupid, so, putting on her best company manners, she said:

"Oh, indeed. How interesting." But, really, she was very much excited.

After a short walk they arrived before two large iron doors set in the side of a hill. Two or three newsboys ran up to them, shouting:

"Wuxtra! wuxtra! all about the war of the churches! Everything split wide open!" But the preacher paid no attention to them, and walked straight up to the iron doors, where he knocked three times, and repeated some words that sounded like "Open Sesame." Of course that wasn't what he said, but it worked just the same. The great doors slowly opened, and the preacher turned to Alice and said:

"We are now going into the Cave of Controversy. Keep your head, and you will be all right."

Alice hesitated for a moment, but after assuring herself that her head was still with her, she followed her guide.

2

Hardly had the doors closed behind them when Alice was seized violently by two wild-eyed men, one on each side, pulling her in opposite directions. She was so startled that she couldn't say a word, and, besides, she didn't have a chance.

"This way to salvation!" shouted the one on her left. "Nice, quiet, and comfortable; all your thinking done for you by experts; no effort required."

"Come with me!" cried the other, pulling at her right arm. "I'll show you how to blaze a trail of your own. Don't listen to that other chap: he's all wrong. I can prove it."

"You see," said the first one again, "he has nothing to offer you. You would get lost with him. The way I know is perfectly plain; it has been the same for years. It's all—"

"It's all overgrown with grass and weeds," interrupted the other. "You can't believe him; he has a creedal complex."

"You're a cuckoo!" shouted the first one, growing apoplectic.

"You're a coward!" the other retorted.

"You're a traitor!"

"You're a liar!"

"My, it's getting quite warm!" thought Alice as names flew thick and fast. "I wish I knew what it was all about."

In their interest in their own arguments the men seemed to have forgotten her entirely, so she slipped out from between them and left them struggling together. But it was much the same everywhere in the cave, people wrangling and shouting and calling names as if their life depended on it. Alice was much confused. "It's just like the Tower of Babel," she said to herself, and looked up, half-expecting to see the ruins before her. She did see something, but not what she had expected.

There, away up high in the darkness, appeared the head of the Cheshire Cat.

"Hello!" said Alice, with a friendly wave of her hand. "What are you doing here?"

The cat only grinned and responded: "Remember what I told you in the wood on the way to the March Hare's? It's the same here."

"Oh, yes," said Alice, after a moment's thought, "I remember. 'We're all mad here.'" The cat nodded his head and grinned more broadly, as if well pleased with himself. "Thank you so much for telling me," Alice went on; "that explains a great deal." She was about to ask what it was that everybody was mad over, but the cat had vanished.

The noise and confusion were so great that she could scarcely distinguish her own thoughts. She could make no sense out of all the different sounds that filled her ears. It was very irritating to have everyone shouting and not to know what they were saying. Finally, Alice lost her patience.

"I can make a noise, too," she said, and started to recite the "Jabberwocky" in as loud a voice as she could. It seemed to fit the occasion nicely, as she didn't have the slightest idea what it meant.

She felt a great deal better after this, and found herself laughing at the two men who were still fighting where she had left them. They were so absurdly serious! And now that she had slipped away from them, it really did not matter which of them won. Just then someone tapped her on the shoulder, and she turned to find the preacher at her side.

"Have you decided which way you want to go?" he asked.

"What do you mean?" said Alice. "Is there some way out of this?"

"Why, yes, indeed," explained the preacher; "there are two ways out. One is up there, through the forest and over the mountains. It's quite dangerous in places, and sometimes people get lost. But the air on the mountains is clear and bracing, and there are some wonderful views. And most people find it worth all the risks. The other way is much easier and more comfortable; as long as you obey the rules you are safe."

"M-m-m-m," said Alice, thinking for a moment, "I guess I'll choose the second one. I'm pretty tired, and it will seem nice to be safe at least. What is it called?"

"It is Literal-Land," replied the preacher. "Right over this way," and he led Alice over to one side of the cave, where there were several openings in the wall. They were all of the general shape of the human body, some for fat people and some for thin people, some for the tall and some for the short. But in each case the space for the head was tilted almost at right angles with the neck.

"That's queer," said Alice. "What is that for?"

"That," the preacher explained, "is the peculiar bent people have to have for this sort of thing."

"But my head doesn't grow like that," protested Alice.

"Oh, that's very easily arranged," the preacher assured her. "All you have to do is to take one of these Doctrinal Pellets for Prospective Pilgrims." He handed her a little purple-and-gold pill dispensed by a very regal-looking elderly lady sitting on a throne before the openings in the wall.

"I don't believe it," said Alice.

"Really, it's very simple," the preacher continued. "All you have to do is swallow the pill, shut your eyes, take a deep breath, and say, 'I believe' three times. Let's try it together."

Alice did so. Very timidly she opened her eyes, and was rather surprised to find everything just as it was before.

"I don't feel any different," said Alice, "and it didn't hurt a bit."
"No," said the preacher; "that's the nice thing about it; it's quite painless, and you don't notice any change in yourself. But I think we can go in now."

3

The first thing that caught Alice's eye on the other side of the wall was a golden church-like building that stood near to where she had come in. It was very beautiful, and out from it there issued the sweetest song she had ever heard. It made her want to sing, too. On each of the four sides of the building were words engraved in large letters. They were strange words to her; she couldn't even pronounce them, and contented herself with spelling them out. On one side, C-O-N-C-I-L-I-A; on another, B-I-B-L-I-A; on the third, T-R-A-D-I-T-I-O; and on the front, E-C-C-L-E-S-I-A. While she was admiring the building, the song suddenly stopped, and out from the top there flew a pure white dove, which disappeared through one of the openings in the wall.

"Did you see that?" Alice exclaimed. "It got away!"

"Sh-sh," warned the preacher. "When the building was erected, they forgot to put on the roof; but nobody knows that in here."

"Oh, I see," said Alice, "and they think it's in there all the time."

"Yes," answered the preacher, "and it gives them a great deal of comfort."

Turning around, Alice discovered that they were in a great hall shaped something like a huge circus tent, only much larger, and with a high, vaulted roof.

"My! it is quiet in here after all that racket outside, isn't it?" she said, thinking out loud. "Everything is so neat and orderly! One does feel safe here, too," she added, as she watched a squad of soldiers drilling close by. "And here come some others. They don't keep together at all, and they have different banners. It's a funny army, isn't it?"

"Yes," answered the preacher. "You see, they can't agree on their officers, and so they all drill separately."

"How silly!" thought Alice, "and dangerous, too, if an enemy should suddenly—" She forgot to finish the sentence, for just then one of the squads disappeared through a doorway off from the main hall. Alice noticed then, for the first time, that there were similar doorways at intervals down both sides of the larger room, and up over each entrance was a sign such as shopkeepers have over their stores. "Where did they go, and what are all those doorways?" asked Alice.

"Those," answered the preacher, looking where Alice was pointing— "those are the Denominational Chambers. Would you like to look in some of them?"

"Do you think I could?" Alice inquired, hesitatingly.

"Well, I don't think any one would object if we just looked in from the doorway. At least we can try it," said the preacher. And they started over toward the one where the soldiers had disappeared.

They had gone only a short distance when they were met by a very grave-looking man who, in solemn tones, invited them to tea. Alice, though she hadn't realized it till that moment, was quite hungry, but she wasn't sure what was best to do. She looked inquiringly at the preacher, and as he nodded his head, she said in her politest manner, "Thank you so much. You are very kind." As their host was leading the way to the other end of the hall the preacher whispered to her behind his hand, "Every newcomer has to take tea here the first afternoon. You may not like it; it's theological tea, you know. But try not to offend any one."

4

Presently they were led into a stuffy little room, very poorly lighted with candles. The walls were lined with large and heavy books, all showing signs of great age. Around a table in the center of the room were five or six men in long black gowns, pondering over several large volumes. Now and again they would get into an argument over something they had read, and would take down other books to settle the question; and then when finally they came to an agreement, one of them would write down the answer on a large slip of paper. They kept this up for some time. Alice didn't know exactly how long, for the clock on the wall wasn't going,—in fact, it looked as if it had run down centuries ago,—but Alice was getting worried about the tea, and, besides, it was very close and uncomfortable.

"Don't you think we might have a window open?" she said by way of beginning conversation. Every one apparently was very much shocked, and most of all the grave men with the books. The one who had been writing stood up and addressed her in a very deep voice.

"Young lady, no one speaks his own mind here. There is nothing in the 'Fathers' about opening a window. It has never been done. Fresh air would spoil our theological atmosphere."

Alice didn't agree with him on the last point, but she kept her peace. Seeing that she was quiet, the man turned to his companions and announced, "Let the tea be prepared." Then holding up his paper, he began: "Five tablespoons of the councils." Five men went to a large cupboard at one end of the room and returned each with a spoonful of dry leaves, which they dropped into a large kettle of water boiling in the fireplace. "One teaspoon of Ignatius," he continued, "one of Irenaeus, two of Origen, two of Athanasius, three of Augustine."

"That's the strangest tea I ever heard of," thought Alice, and turned inquisitively to the preacher. He only made a wry face at her and said nothing.

"Bring up your cups," the chief steward announced. "Children allowed two lumps of sugar, scholars a grain of salt, those with special dispensation may dilute it with a little milk. Alice had begun to feel ill already, but she took her cup with the sugar, and held it up to be filled.

Fortunately for her, just at the moment, a herald opened the door and called out:

"Learned Doctors, the trial is about to begin; the judge requires your presence."

Immediately the doctors dropped everything, and forming in double file goose-stepped solemnly out of the door after the herald.

"What trial is it?" asked Alice of the preacher, and before he had time to answer, she added, "Can we go to it?"

"Yes," said he; "I think it is a heresy trial."

"That ought to be interesting," Alice responded. "I've never been to a hearsay trial. What do they do?"

"We shall see," the preacher answered.

5

The trial had already begun when they arrived. The prisoner, with a handkerchief tied over his mouth, was standing before the judge. The prosecuting attorney, whom Alice recognized as one of the men who had shouted at her as she entered the Cave of Controversy, was reading the charge.

"Item I," he began. "The prisoner is charged with asserting that there is no such place as hell."

"He'll soon find out that he is mistaken," said the judge, with a very undignified wink at the sheriff.

"Item II," continued the prosecutor. "The prisoner is charged with not meaning what he said."

"I object," interrupted the prisoner's attorney. "That isn't correct. The defendant did mean what he said, but in so doing, he didn't say quite what he meant."

"Objection overruled," shouted the judge. "In either case, he is guilty of dishonesty."

"Item III. The prisoner is accused of stating that a semicolon is missing from the Bible."

"This is very serious, indeed," observed the judge. "The jurors will please consider this carefully; our whole religion is at stake. If one can put in a semicolon at will, we may just as well place a question-mark at the end of the Bible. Furthermore, it is exceedingly presumptuous of this young man, or anybody else, to attempt to improve upon the punctuation which the Almighty Himself inserted. Next."

"Item IV. The prisoner is accused of claiming and practicing the right to think for himself."

"Enough! enough!" cried the judge, jumping up and tearing at his hair. "We need no more. Gentlemen of the jury," turning to the learned doctors, "consider your verdict."

"But I protest, your Honor," cried the defendant's lawyer. "The prisoner should be allowed to speak for himself, to answer the charges."

"They need no answer from him," said the judge. "That handkerchief must not be removed; there's no telling what he might say in our presence. Let it be thoroughly understood that a man in his position may feel for himself and hear for himself, he may eat and even die for himself, but it is forbidden him to think and speak for himself. I will therefore pronounce sentence."

"But, your Honor," objected the attorney, "the jury has not given the verdict."

"We'll have the sentence first, and the verdict afterward," ruled the judge. "He is guilty, anyway." And pulling a parchment scroll out of his pocket, he proceeded to read: "I sentence the prisoner to a public scourging at the whipping-post in the outer court until he shall consciously repeat the creed; I sentence the prisoner to ten months in the School of Discipline, where he shall give special study to theography, ancient mystery, and the higher ecclesiastics; I sentence the prisoner to drink two cups of clear tea (unsweetened) every afternoon. The court is dismissed."

There was a great applause as the judge finished, and the people all hurried out to the whipping-post to watch the beginning of the punishment. Alice didn't understand any of the sentence except that about the tea, and she thought that alone was sufficient for almost any crime. However, she followed the others to the outer court.

The prisoner was already tied to the post, and two white-hooded gentlemen were swinging sticks with long tongues of leather on the ends. The orchestra started to play a solemn dirge, and the ceremonies began. It was all done to music, the "executioners" and the prisoner singing alternate verses of a disciplinary hymn, and the crowd joining in on the chorus, while the time was marked by the whip-cords on the victim's back. This was the hymn:

Executioners:

> The Bible is infallible, which you must not deny.
> Adam named the animals, and Enoch did not die.
> Take care you do not change it, for that would surely breed
> Distrust of our authority! Now, won't you say the creed?
> Will you, won't you, will you, won't you, will you say the creed?
> Will you, won't you, will you, won't you, won't you say the creed?

Prisoner:

> I cannot see your argument; it has no sense at all.
> To sin by eating apples is not a serious fall.
> There is no hell hereafter for which I feel the need,
> But if there were, I tell you now, I would not say the creed!
> Would not, could not, would not, could not, would not say the creed.
> Would not, could not, would not, could not, could not say the creed.

Executioners:

> Arius was a heretic; Apollinaris too.
> They sought to think things for themselves, much the same as you.
> The Apostles at Nicea—please give this careful heed—
> Drew up our sacred document Oh, won't you say the creed?
> Will you, won't you, will you, won't you, will you say the creed?
> Will you, won't you, will you, won't you, won't you say the creed?

Every one was quite out of breath by this time, and the "executioners" decided that they would postpone further action till the next day.

Alice looked for the preacher, but couldn't find him anywhere. She was terribly disappointed, because she did want to visit the Denominational Chambers. "Anyway," she said to herself, "I should think it would be all right to go to my own church. I believe I'll try it." She saw the sign nearby, "Protestant Episcopal Church." Someone, apparently, had tried to rub out the word "Protestant," but it was still faintly visible, if you looked hard enough.

6

I seemed quite natural to Alice inside. The people were separated into different groups, engaged in different occupations: some were singing gospel hymns, some were taking care of a sick man, some were polishing the candlesticks. Alice was trying to decide which group she would join when a kindly gentleman came up to her, and led her off to another part of the chamber, where school was being held. She did not like this at all, and when no one was looking she slipped away, and hid behind a curtain hanging on the back wall.

Imagine her surprise when she found herself in a long dark passageway. She was a bit frightened at first, and started to go back, but the thought of school and lessons gave her courage. She waited a moment till her eyes grew accustomed to the darkness, and then began to feel her way along the passage. Soon it brought her into a much larger and brighter corridor. There were other people here, all walking toward a great light off in the distance. They were coming from passages similar to that through which Alice had just come.

"How do you do?" said Alice, overtaking two who were walking arm in arm.

"Very well, thank you, little girl," one of them answered with a sweet smile. "Isn't it glorious here? And I was so afraid!"

"What were you afraid of?" asked Alice.

"Death," was the reply. "But it isn't bad, after all."

Alice was considerably shocked, but her curiosity was aroused, and she asked: "How did you get here?"

"Through the Methodist way, back there," her new friend answered, pointing to one of the passages. "And my dear neighbor here came the Roman Catholic way."

"Do you mean that each chamber has a passage leading to this place? My, wouldn't they be surprised if they knew it!" said Alice.

"And here we are at the gates of paradise," her companion announced.

There was a crowd gathered here, and some of them carried torches and told breathless tales of adventure in the mountains and forests of the way they had come. But nobody argued, and there was no controversy. Alice finally got close enough to the gates to look through. And what a sight she saw! There was, in truth, the Holy City all bright and glistening, lying four-square, and the walls all set with precious stones. It was beautiful. Alice clapped her hands in delight. And suddenly a great and mighty sound of many voices filled the air: "Hallelujah, give praise to our God, all ye his servants, ye that fear him, the small and the great." Alice did as they said, and, opening her mouth, began to sing as loud as she could, "Hallelujah." But one of the angels that watched at the gates turned, and put his hand over her mouth, so that the sound was smothered.

"Child, you mustn't do that; it's only for the choir," said a voice in her ear. And Alice looked up into her mother's face.

"O Mother," she said, "I've had such a wonderful dream! I saw the Holy City and everything."

"Yes, yes, my dear; you can tell me all about it when we get home," said her mother. So Alice sat there in the church, thinking of all the strange and beautiful things she had seen and heard. Only one thing bothered her: she did not know the moral.

From John F. Scott, "Alice in Literal-Land," *The Century Magazine*, CVIII (May 1924), 52–59.

The Poetic Effort
Raymond Browning
Preston Slosson
Arthur I. Brown
Quartet Music Company

A wide assortment of verse devoted to the issues in the modernist-fundamentalist conflict appeared during the 1920s. The first three selections are rather typical examples of the content and quality of such poetic efforts. The fourth selection, which represents a more bizarre use of verse, appeared as an advertisement of a music company in a fundamentalist magazine.

———◆◆◆———

EVOLUTION

Back in the dark of intangible nothing,
Billions of years ere the earth gathered form,
Somehow the gloom changed to volume and substance;
Some way came motion, came light, and came storm.

Nebulous fire floated up out of nowhere;
By some strange movement suns rolled from the flame.
Then by the millions came stars, moons and comets,
Found their own courses and rolled in the same.

This tiny earth like a dark lonely dust-mote
Wandered about for some million years more,
Gathered some atmosphere, rivers and mountains,
Made the land stable, set tides on the shore.

Then came the cell, or the small protoplasm,
Perhaps an amoeba—just happened, you know—
Stirred from its shapelessness, took form and motion,
Learned by experience just how to grow.

Thus as the ages dragged by it ascended,
Through all diversified forms that we see,
Till by environment made ape or monkey,
Scratched, grinned and chattered—then climbed up a tree.

Now if some son of an ape will come forward
And kindly remove the mysterious veil,
Perhaps he can tell how his nimble ancestry
Succeeded in shedding the fur and the tail.

This is the weird fable he puts above Genesis,
This gruesome myth of man's climb from the clod;
Maniac's dream in exchange for our Bible;
Nightmare of science instead of our God!

RAYMOND BROWNING

From the *News and Observer* (Raleigh, North Carolina), October 18, 1922.

FUNDAMENTALISM

God of the star-swarm and the soul,
The conscious Will that made the world
From ether drift and cosmic dust,
Such is the God we know and trust.

Our partial pictures of the Whole,
Our demigods from heaven hurled,
Our idols in the chapel nooks,
Our gods of stone, or wood—or books—

Forgive them all! We are but men,
Our thoughts must go a homely road,
We build as children in their play
Our frail theologies of clay.

Children will grow. More wisely then
Our race will tread a steeper road,

Lifting our thoughts from earthly sod,
From Threshold to the Throne of God.

No sin it is for childhood's mind
To lift a candle as the sun
The great is imagined in the small
Better than never seen at all.

But *this* is sin: To choose to blind
The sight to light that men have won,
Deny the truth that has been taught,
Fetter the Godward searching thought.

Creation's magic is too great,
They fear to view it open-eyed,
They wish the world a smaller place
Eternity a shorter space.

Their fear is swiftly turned to hate,
Truth dreaded soon is truth denied,
They call on Caesar to resist
God's fearless saint, the scientist.

PRESTON SLOSSON

Preston Slosson, "Fundamentalism," *Scientific Monthly*, XXII (May 1926), 463.

"BUNK" AND THE "MONK"

1. The scientist wise, with wondering eyes
    Smiles sweet on his dear monkey friend.
   To incredible words, names of reptiles and birds,
    He bids us attention to lend.
   We listen intent,—on learning we're bent,
    We're glad to know all our relations.
   So with awe-stricken gaze, and our minds in a haze
    We watch the professor's gyrations.

2. He can twist and can turn as we very soon learn
      When he tries to explain protoplasm;
   "How much do you know sir?"—the question's a poser,
      But glibly he bridges the chasm
   'Twixt that speck of sea-slime of long-ago time,
      And man the crown of creation.
   With arguments weird says, to him it appeared
      And earthworm's a distant relation!

3. This sea-slimy speck,—it's a fact, friend, by heck!—
      Really longed to wiggle his toe.
   So he wondered and thought—as the vision he caught
      And planned how to make himself go.
   With unequalled hustle he sprouted a muscle,—
      You believe me, my friends, I trust,—
   "One mile I will race at a moderate pace,"
      And he swore that he'd do it or "bust"!

4. Making muscle and bone, day by day, all alone,
      His cold blood grew hot as he toiled;
   He invents lungs and liver—the thought makes me shiver—
      How awful had these things been spoiled!
   But the marvel of all as he stretched and grew tall,—
      He, the organ most needed forgot
   For two million years!—Oh! I'm quaking with fear,—
      For this wee, careless, sea-slimy dot.

5. He was brainless from birth, yet this creature of earth
      Planned and thought as he changed to a "monk."
   No brains, yet could think, this first "missing link,"
      We learn this in "Science of 'Bunk'."
   With strong foot and hand he now swam to land
      There never was known such a work,
   This thing without brain, with fierce might and main,
      Has invented a leg with a jerk!

6. So, we're cousins to moles, to fish and tadpoles,
      Don't smile friends, beware,—that's called "science" today,

We've a "common ancestor"—you've heard of the quest, sir,—
  His old bones they do hunt night and day.
But though hot on the trail of this mythical tail
  There's no trace, of poor lost chimpanzee.
And this "brain-stormy" theory can't answer my query,—
  Not one ape roosts in my family tree!

                                    ARTHUR I. BROWN

From *The Crusaders' Champion*, I (December 25, 1925), 18.

ADVERTISEMENT: QUARTET MUSIC COMPANY

Is your church tossed in the Tempest of the Evolution Storm?
Do you feel your faith a-slippin'
As the 'Monkey Men' preach on?
When a College Prof. states boldly
That a monkey was his Dad,
Do you feel the comfort leaving
That in childhood once you had?
On the final Day of Judgment
Would you 'up a tree' be found—No?
—Then use our Searchlight Songs No. 1,
A book fundamentally sound.

From *Searchlight*, February 8, 1924, p. 3.

It is superficial to conclude that Modernism and Fundamentalism are vitally concerned with matters like the gullet of whales and the famous voyage made by Jonah. Today's controversy, and yesterday's are primarily outward expressions of a deeper issue. . . . The real problem . . . concerns the very nature of the mind itself and of its task and authority in human life.

ALBERT G. A. BALZ, 1927

8. *An American Phenomenon: Contemporary Interpretations*

CONTEMPORARY commentators on American life, both foreign and native, found the modernist-fundamentalist conflict of the 1920s, and especially its most dramatic manifestation, the struggle over evolution, an intriguing subject. Some of their efforts to explain this "American phenomenon" resulted in provocative suggestions regarding the nature and place of Protestantism in the United States. Their analyses of the causes, origins, and effects of the modernist-fundamentalist conflict, which included incisive diagnoses of the respective protagonists, were often presented within a commendable historical or sociological perspective. Those inclined to interpret the disturbance in a broad context related it to the peculiar character of America's public education and economic systems, the conflict between urban and rural cultures, the Puritan tradition, and the cumulative impact of Deism, Unitarianism, higher criticism, and science upon the established systems of Protestant theology. Although modernists generally fared better at the hands of the more or less detached contemporary observers, fundamentalism was given a sympathetic hearing, especially by theological commentators, in the late 1920s as its drive slackened.

Perhaps, as one European has noted, the three episodes that "most damaged the image of America the Golden in European eyes in the roaring twenties" were the execution of Sacco and Vanzetti, Prohibition, and the Scopes trial.[1] Throughout the decade Europeans followed with increasing amazement the progress of the modernist-fundamentalist struggle being waged across the Atlantic. If the Scopes trial was "the biggest and best newspaper story since the war" in the United States, it was only slightly less so in Europe. Failure to comprehend its meaning led many in Europe to join some Americans in viewing the disturbance as nothing more than a comedy—a source of considerable hilarity and amusement. A rather typical attitude was expressed in 1926 by a French visitor, Professor Desiré Pasquet of the University of Paris, who told his American host:

I want to see one of the "Fundamentalists." I have heard much of these "Fundamentalists" and "Modernists." I hope I shall have the very exquisite pleasure of seeing one while I am here.[2]

Describing the fundamentalist crusade in the United States as a "nationalist orthodox movement," Heinrich Hermelink, a professor of church history at the University of Marburg, boasted that Germany had attained "a stage of popular enlightenment that makes such a sensational episode as the Tennessee Monkey Trial inconceivable in our country."[3] Views of the American theological debate as an exercise in absurdity and its protagonists as quaint oddities resulted largely from sensational accounts of the more bizarre aspects of the evolution controversy which Pasquet described as a "great joke."

Other foreigners were unwilling to dismiss the conflict so lightly. Several British observers sought to explain it within the context of the prevailing temper of American society. Americans, they argued, were intensely earnest about their religion because it was the source of their idealism; therefore Americans would reject whatever might appear to endanger it. Furthermore, a vehement defense of religious creeds to complement 100 percent Americanism was a means of combating the unrest which new doctrines had provoked elsewhere in the world.[4] Taking a longer view, the noted British journalist S. K. Ratcliffe explained:

[1] See the *Times Literary Supplement* (London), February 9, 1967.

[2] Quoted in the *News and Observer* (Raleigh, North Carolina), April 12, 1926.

[3] Heinrich Hermelink, "Darwin and the Bible Abroad," *Living Age,* CCCXXVI (August 1925), 393–395.

[4] George H. Knoles, *The Jazz Age Revisited: British Criticism of American Civilization During the 1920's* (Stanford: Stanford University Press, 1955), pp. 111–112.

for a century or more, a great pioneer population had been engaged in subduing the land and laying the foundations for a new civilization. The swiftly expanding forces of knowledge and inquiry reveal, at this relatively late hour, that for many millions of these people, who, with their immediate ancestors have accomplished the world's greatest miracle in nation-building, there is coming the shock of a profoundly revolutionary discovery. It falls to the generation now reaching maturity to realize that the material progress of America has been made without a corresponding advance in mental enlightenment and spiritual experience. The conclusion towards which we are led by this latest uprising of obscurantism is that America is on the eve of a final encounter between its vast inertia of "plain Bible religion" and the spirit of the modern world.[5]

John Strachey, another distinguished British journalist, who interpreted fundamentalism as an "anomaly produced in backward sections," was convinced that the "controversy between the angels and the monkeys is not going to destroy the American union."[6]

Several French students of American culture, far better informed and more perceptive than Professor Pasquet, provided thoughtful critiques of the modernist-fundamentalist conflict. Bernard Faÿ, writing in the French Catholic Le Correspondant in 1928, provocatively analyzed the state of "Protestant America." Up to World War I, he argued, orthodox Christianity was "tacitly recognized as the religion of the United States," but the "social and moral crises" produced by the war had seriously challenged its pre-eminence. "The dogmas, the beliefs, and the moral system of Christianity," he maintained, "are being attacked . . . as they have never been attacked before." While "the vast mass of the people" continued to thirst for "a concrete religion," intellectuals were busy formulating a new morality based on the premise "that religious law should defer to scientific methods and teachings." Fundamentalists attempted to satisfy the demands of the former by "an emotional, literal religion of the senses," and the modernists sought to make sufficient adjustments in theology to attract intellectuals. Because of the dualistic tradition of American Protestantism, both fundamentalists and modernists could claim to be heirs of the historic faith. The modernists, according to Faÿ, harbored "a Calvinistic instinct that religion should not merely be a private affair, but should fill one's life, model society, and adapt

---

5 S. K. Ratcliffe, "America and Fundamentalism," Contemporary Review, CXXVIII (September 1925), 295.

6 Knoles, The Jazz Age Revisited, p. 112.

itself to present circumstances." It was in the matter of adapting Christian-
tity to the secular environment that modernism threatened to become
a "neo-paganism."[7] Another Frenchman, André Siegfried, who analyzed
"the American religious problem" at greater length, drew conclusions
that often paralleled those of Faÿ. Both agreed that Americans were a
generous and idealistic people who were "so strongly attracted by religious fervor, yet so eager to enjoy the voluptuous pleasures of this
world." Among the more significant aspects of Siegfried's study were
those that dealt with the relationship of the various protagonists in the
modernist-fundamentalist controversy to the economic community.[8]

Less detached, perhaps, but nonetheless instructive were the ap-
praisals by Americans who seriously reflected upon the nature and
meaning of the contemporary theological disturbance. As the conflict
began to abate late in the 1920s, interpretations of its impact and
results ranged from the rosily optimistic to the darkly pessimistic. The
optimists were inclined to ignore the whole conflict as an unfortunate
interlude and to pretend that with the return of theological peace the
church, unchanged and triumphant, would resume its normal course
as if nothing ever happened. At the other pole was the pessimistic
view summarized in the titles of such articles as "The Disruption of
Protestantism" and "The Break-up of Protestantism" which held that
Protestantism as "an organized religious force is moribund and shows
signs of rapid disintegration."[9] A different interpretation that also emphasized the polarization of theology was particularly evident in the
writings of contemporaries who attempted to assess the fundamentalist
crusade. They seemed to subscribe to a cyclical theory of Protestant
history. One writer insisted that historically in the United States the
theological pendulum rhythmically swung from one extreme to another,
from Jonathan Edwards's "Sinners in the Hands of an Angry God" to
churches being "mere gas stations on the way to heaven."[10] The resurgence of fundamentalism presumably represented an effort to swing
the pendulum away from the "gas station" position. Another commenta-

[7] Bernard Faÿ, "Protestant America," *Living Age,* CCCXXXIV (August 1928),
1193–1201.

[8] See the selection from Siegfried's *America Comes of Age* that follows.

[9] Herbert Parrish, "The Break-up of Protestantism," *Atlantic Monthly,* CXXXIX
(March 1927), 295–305.

[10] See especially Curtis E. Reese, "The Outlook of Religion," *Open Court,* XLI
(November 1927), 677–683.

tor, writing in the *Virginia Quarterly Review* in 1927, suggested that the theological warfare of the 1920s was but another of the periodic outbursts resulting from the basic dichotomy between faith and reason inherent in American Protestantism.[11] Secular historians such as Charles and Mary Beard, who attempted to place the theological clash within the broad stream of American history, rarely failed to conceal their sympathy for modernism. Often more balanced were the efforts of church historians and theologians who viewed the struggle from a socio-theological perspective. Of these, few were more perceptive than an essay by William Adams Brown, a liberal theologian unwilling to dismiss fundamentalism as a mere revival of superstition. Rather he attempted a sympathetic analysis of the forces which produced the movement and sought to offer some tentative answers to the question "After Fundamentalism, What?"

[11] Albert G. A. Balz, "The Yea and Nay of It," *Virginia Quarterly Review*, III (April 1927), 212–223.

A British View
S. K. Ratcliffe

In the following selection an Englishman, S. K. Ratcliffe, uses the Scopes trial as the focal point of a discussion designed to explain the fundamentalist crusade to his countrymen. His aim was to probe beneath the comic aspects of the trial and "account for Fundamentalism as a social product." Ratcliffe agreed with those foreign observers who concluded that the evolution controversy was evidence of America's failure to achieve an intellectual sophistication commensurate with its material success. But he detected implications which others failed to emphasize. For example, he believed that although fundamentalists had made "a bogey out of Darwin," they "would have been much nearer the mark if they had directed their main assault upon Freud." More significant, however, was his view of the modernist-fundamentalist conflict primarily as a direct confrontation of two widely different mentalities—a collision between Main Street and the intellectual elite—hastened and dramatized by the rapid expansion in American higher education.

There is, I submit, no social phenomenon in the contemporary world more singular, and there are few more regrettable, than the gulf between Britain and the United States, as revealed particularly in our general indifference towards the national life of the American people. Roughly speaking, we are interested in American affairs only at those times when some startling movement is discernible, not in politics, but in business, in conduct, or in belief. Prohibition is pre-eminently such a movement, for in England it arouses passion no less than curiosity. And to Prohibition there has now been added fundamentalism. Large numbers of English people have been amused and startled by the recent affair in Tennessee. They have likewise been greatly puzzled by it; and perhaps no recent event in America stands more in need of explanation, in all its bearings, than the verdict of "Guilty" in the Dayton trial and the fine imposed upon the high school teacher John T. Scopes for violating the Anti-Evolution Law of the State of Tennessee.

In THE CONTEMPORARY of July 1922, I described what appeared to be at that time the more salient characteristics of the reaction that was affecting the American churches and colleges after the war. The movement against enlightenment had gathered great force. An organised attack was being made upon liberal professors and ministers. In colleges subject to denominational influences religious tests were being applied. Modernist preachers were having to fight for the retention of their pulpits. There was a violent recrudescence of millennial belief, and when the movement called fundamentalism adopted its aggressive policy, a "drive" was made to get the early and visible second advent accepted as an item of the orthodox creed, no less essential than the inerrancy of scripture, the virgin birth, or vicarious atonement.

It would be accurate to say, however, that so recently as four years ago the fear of evolution that is now so much in evidence was not a governing part of the fundamentalist consciousness. At all events, it had not then obtained possession of the old-fashioned religious public, as, under the leadership of W. J. Bryan, it was soon to do. The first indication of the coming struggle that received widespread notice in the press was the introduction into the Kentucky Legislature of a bill designed to forbid the teaching of evolutionary doctrine in public schools and colleges. The defeat of this measure by one vote was treated as a political joke or an isolated curiosity. But those who knew the educational conditions of the southern states were aware that the attempt in Kentucky was the first manoeuvre in a campaign that would probably develop into a grave spiritual civil war involving the entire country.

The late W. J. Bryan was, from the beginning, the unchallenged leader of the lay forces of fundamentalism. No man in America knew so well as he the formidable strength of the country's religious conservatism. His extraordinary experience as a politician-evangelist had made him aware of the field of conquest awaiting him in the South and West. His party was rapidly organised, and it had large financial reserves to draw upon. No small section of the American business world is fundamentalist in sympathy, for a reason not at all difficult to understand: namely, the instinctive realisation of the fact that if traditional religious beliefs are questioned, there can be no security for the economic assumptions of existing society. Mr. Bryan, good Democrat that he was, calculated that by making an attack, state by state, upon the modernists and evolutionists he might hope to achieve, as the crowning work of his life, a triumphant affirmation in the laws of the United States of the doctrines which were to him the fundamentals equally of Christianity and Americanism.

Thus, for the fundamentalists, the passage of the Tennessee Anti-Evolution Law, early in the present year, was an important initial victory. It was made a misdemeanour for any person employed in a public school of the state to teach any biological doctrine which implied the descent of man from lower forms of animal life or contradicted the biblical story of the divine creation of man. The bill appears to have gone through without causing alarm in the educated minority of Tennessee. It ought, of course, to have been seriously opposed at every stage, especially by the teachers. But they, it would seem, shared the opinion that was expressed by the Governor of the state when he signed the measure—namely, that, like some thousands of laws upon the books of the United States, it would prove to be inoperative. As a matter of fact, the public challenge could easily have been foreseen by anyone who had taken the trouble to follow the activities of the American Civil Liberties Union. This body, working vigilantly from New York, exists for the purpose of upholding the rights of the citizens as guaranteed in the Federal Constitution and especially of resisting the invasions upon civic freedom which have become in recent years a grave menace in the United States. The Civil Liberties Union was seeking the opportunity for a good test case. The opportunity was afforded by Tennessee; and when it had been agreed that a teacher should be indicted for transgressing the law by taking his class through a textbook of evolutionary biology, everybody could see that the trial would become a national event, with all the agencies of publicity combining to exploit it.

There is no need for me to dwell here at any length upon the scenes of the Dayton trial. For a fortnight of this last July it provided an unparalleled tragicomedy, which, while provoking the world to laughter, could not be other than a grief and humiliation for educated and thoughtful Americans. The farcical elements were, inevitably, overplayed by the American press, but there are several points in the affair that need to be clearly brought out.

Both sides were resolved to make of Dayton something much more than the trial of J. T. Scopes, who, as it happened, was almost forgotten during the proceedings. "This is the day I have waited for," said W. J. Bryan, who went to Dayton in the conviction that he was leading the hosts of the Lord in a final grapple with the forces of Hell. The defence naturally embraced the opportunity. With Bryan advising the prosecution, it was certain that Genesis would be the battleground, and no less

certain that the defence would so lay its plans that the fundamentalist
leader might be enticed into the exposure of his own ignorance and
remoteness from the elements of modern knowledge. It was for no other
reason than this that the leading counsel for the defence was a famous
criminal lawyer of Chicago. Mr. Clarence Darrow would have had no
interest in the Tennessee case if the intention had been to fight it upon a
constitutional principle alone. He went into it with the passion of a
Bradlaugh presented with an almost certain chance of turning to ridicule
a popular leader who was untroubled by any doubts as to the absolute
rightness of his opinions and his faith. Bryan had made preparations for
a great display on behalf of the Faith, but he was not able to make it.
Instead, with a childlikeness that is almost unimaginable, he handed
himself over to his opponent. Although present in court as advisory attorney to the prosecution, Bryan consented to take the witness-stand and
submit to examination by a skilled cross-examiner who is also a militant
agnostic. The ordeal lasted for two hours: Darrow questioning in cold
scorn; Bryan answering questions upon incidents and characters of the
Old Testament, the Eden story, his belief in the verbal inerrancy of
scripture, and what not. The purpose of this grotesque exhibition was
twofold: to expose the ignorance and self-contradiction of the ingenuous
fundamentalist leader, and to draw from him the confession that, despite his assertions as to verbal inspiration, he did not believe that
everything in the Bible must be taken literally. The judge, who had
given up even the pretence of directing the court, on the following day
ordered the report of Bryan's examination to be expunged from the
record as irrelevant. Irrelevant also was the evidence of the men of
science, who had been brought to Dayton at heavy cost. Onc only of
these, a prominent zoologist, was allowed to testify in person. The evidence of the others was admitted to the record in the form of affidavits.
And, as a crowning absurdity, the jurors were sent out of court whenever
an approach was made to the subject of evolution. The newspaper reports indicate that the greater part of the proceedings went forward in
the absence of the jury, one of whom was admittedly illiterate.

The judge himself was a fundamentalist; and as such, presumably,
he began with the intention of allowing full discussion of the question
of evolution versus Genesis. But this could not be without the admission
of scientific evidence, and that he was determined not to allow. He
made it clear that the sole issue before the court was the charge against

Scopes of teaching in violation of the state law; and in the end the defence asked for a conviction in order that the case might be carried to the higher courts. The educated public in America appear to believe that the Supreme Court must declare the Tennessee law to be unconstitutional and void; but that is by no means a foregone conclusion. The case, however, cannot reach Washington for many months, and in the meantime it is to be presumed that the campaign in favour of further antievolution laws will be suspended. Oklahoma has lately rescinded its statute, and Georgia, which ranks among the most backward of states, has refused to follow the lead of Tennessee. The educational effect of Dayton upon public opinion may not be nearly so great as many people suppose. But at least the Fundamentalists must now fight hard for obscurantist legislation, wherever they may introduce it.

Complaints have been made by several prominent Americans in England that the press, on both sides of the ocean, has been concerned almost entirely with the comedic or spectacular features of the Dayton trial and of Bryan's crusade, while almost no endeavour was made to account for fundamentalism as a social product: to describe the religious and educational conditions in the fundamentalist states, the feeling of their people, and the circumstances which made the emergence of fundamentalism as an aggressive force practically inevitable. These complaints, I think, are not unjustified. Dayton is not an isolated incident. It is a symptom. W. J. Bryan was not an accident or a freak. He was a representative westerner, and a portent. Behind him and the agitation to which he devoted his marvellous energy and eloquence during his last years there lies a complicated social condition, the phenomena of which are certainly deserving of study.

Three quarters of a century ago James Russell Lowell described the American public as the most common-schooled and the least educated in the world. The common school is, in the North and West, a ubiquitous institution. In the progressive states public money is devoted to education on an immense scale. In the course of another generation the schools and colleges of these states will bring about a transformation of the common mind. But there are wide areas of the United States, especially in the South and South-West, where no such fortunate conditions prevail. And in trying to indicate the differences between the contrasted regions, I cannot, perhaps, do better than quote from two especially qualified students of present-day America.

Professor S. E. Morison, whose retirement from the Harmsworth Professorship of American History is a great loss to Oxford and to the Anglo-American cause, has given an illuminating analysis of the social conditions of Tennessee and kindred areas near the borderline between North and South. Tennessee, he reminds us, is a state more than one third larger than Scotland, with less than half the population. About one person in five is coloured, and about one adult white in ten illiterate. The white Tennesseans are the purest "Nordic" Anglo-Saxons in America. Less than three percent are foreign-born or of foreign-born parentage. They belong to the Upland-Southern stock, one of the three main divisions of the British race in America. The Southern Uplander, Professor Morison says, was a magnificent pioneer. But he lost all contact with civilisation on the frontier, and brought very little with him.

Tennessee is a backwater, untouched by any of the main currents of American life since 1865. So it is not surprising that modern scientific and social thought, even in the most diluted form, has never penetrated to these cultural depths, or that the conflict between science and theology that rocked England sixty years ago has just reached Tennessee.

By the side of this vivid summary, from one of the best of the younger American historians, we may place a description of the typical small town of the border, suggested by the scenes of the Scopes trial.

Mr. Frank R. Kent, an able journalist on the staff of the Baltimore Sun, in an article written just after the trial, asks us to believe that the real drama in Dayton was not in the court. It was in the townsfolk, who are typical of a great multitude of American citizens:

Religion—real religion, basic Bible religion—is the big thing in this country; the religion of the camp meeting, the revivals, prayer meetings and Sunday Schools of the evangelical churches in the little towns; and of queer, violent, acrobatic sects, creeds and faiths, all based on literal Bible beliefs, in the more isolated districts. The whole region is saturated in religion. Nine-tenths of the people are steeped in it. It is their mode of recreation, as well as their means of redemption: their single emotional outlet, the one relief from the deadly drabness of a cut-off existence.

In the areas here described there are almost no Catholics, Episcopalians, or Jews. There are Methodists, Baptists, Presbyterians, and half-a-dozen other denominations; and Mr. Kent makes the surprising statement that of the 2,000 people in Dayton not more than fifty are without some touch with one or other of the nine evangelical churches, and that this

proportion prevails in the towns throughout Tennessee, the neighbour-
ing states, and kindred regions further west. Take religion away from
such places, and the desolation and distress would be pitiable to contemplate, while to think of convincing these people, even the relatively
educated section of church members, of the soundness of evolution as
opposed to their view of Bible truth, would be fantastic.

There remains to say a word as to the wider results that may be
expected from the dramatic death of W. J. Bryan, on the Sunday following the verdict of the Dayton trial. The first thought of the European
reader would naturally be that the removal of this extraordinary man
at that precise moment is a shattering blow to fundamentalism, since
an aggressive movement must be crippled by the loss of a leader who
cannot be replaced. We may think that not even to the simplest Day-
tonian could this sudden death after a distressing collapse on the witness-stand be anything but a merciful release for a man who had done
his life-work and for whom realities were too strong at the end. But
we may well ask whether, as a matter of fact, this common sense view has
any relation to the popular feeling at present prevailing throughout the
rural states in which for thirty years the name of Bryan has been as the
sound of consolation and triumph. Let us remember that all fundamentalist America was with Bryan in his view of Dayton as the arena of the
conflict between the only truth and the lies of Satan, and that he was
the leader of the winning side. Mr. Kent, who sat through the hearing
says:

If during the trial a bolt of lightning from the sky had singled out Mr.
Darrow for slaughter, few would have been surprised. Many actually expected it. On the other hand, to thousands . . . it would have come as no
surprise if Mr. Bryan, having gloriously defeated the forces of unrighteousness,
were to be visited by an angel of the Lord who would whisk the old gentleman
off to heaven in a chariot of fire.

Will they not, indeed, say that this is almost exactly what occurred,
since their champion was silently translated during a Sunday-afternoon
sleep? Here, indeed, is evidence in favour of the immediate creation of a
Bryan legend, growing spontaneously among the simple people of the
farms and small towns—a legend, we may anticipate, that may be far
more pervasive and actual than the Roosevelt legend which family pride
and an interested patriotism have been employed in creating during the
past six years.

So far I have been dealing almost entirely with that large portion of the American public which inhabits the backward regions and is by geographic and social conditions remote from modern influences. I turn now to another important aspect of the subject, equally peculiar to North America.

There has been in the United States, since the beginning of the century, vast expansion of colleges, state universities, and technical institutes. Immense endowments from private donors have shown the world an example of the social use of wealth going far beyond anything known in Europe. The number of college graduates is constantly and rapidly increasing. There has come to exist the general notion that a college course is the right thing to aim at for as large a percentage of the population as possible. Now, in this connection we must have in mind the important fact that, as they say in America, the people as a whole "live on Main Street." In other words, the great majority of the youths and girls who obtain the coveted advantage of a college education come from the small town or rural community where social life is centered in the churches. They step into the stimulating atmosphere of a large institution, where the students are allowed the most complete freedom, and where, in the absence of the classical humanities, the main interest is concentrated in the departments of history, economics, and science—including, emphatically, the many-sided subject of psychology, which is pursued in America in a fashion that would be unrealisable in the older universities of England. The resulting situation is not difficult to imagine. The student goes from his home in Iowa or Nebraska to the state university, or to one of the vast conglomerate universities of Chicago, or some other centre. He makes the immediate discovery that the small body of religious and patriotic doctrine which is the whole of orthodoxy in his hometown has no place in the new world he has entered. The professors of history introduce him to a body of knowledge that makes his boyish Fourth-of-July notions of American origins seem like an infantile fairy tale. His memories of Sunday school dissolve in the laboratory, while his elementary studies in psychology make havoc of the simple notions of conscience and the soul with which he started out in life. Bryan and the fundamentalists, calamitously behind the times, have made a bogey out of Darwin. They would have been much nearer the mark if they had directed their main assault upon Freud and his American interpreters, and upon the young and powerful school of behaviourists. This newer psychology has made an extraordinary conquest of the United States. Its theories are, to a large extent, treated as final discoveries. Its terms have passed into current speech. The departments of psychology furnish employment throughout America for an army of professors and instructors, many of whom, it is alleged, make no effort to teach their subject with a restraint, but, on the contrary, find a particular interest in giving emphasis to a radical materialism. A similar complaint is made in relation to the teaching of physical and biological science. If these things are so, as seems likely enough, we cannot wonder that many parents, who may have no sympathy whatever with the fundamentalists, should be resentful in the knowledge that their sons and daughters are studying in institutions which, necessarily secular by American law and custom, are open to the charge of permitting and encouraging a multiple assault upon traditional faiths. Bryan's miserable plaint that the boys and girls go from home and church to college and become unbelievers has a certain plausibility if the many complaints of the kind I have referred to have any considerable foundation in fact. They point, one may remark, to a state of affairs in the American universities strikingly different from that existing in the English academic world. No one imagines that college life can afford protection in matters of faith. The student, obviously, must face all the risks for himself. But it would greatly surprise the parents of English youth at the university to learn that the teaching of any scientific subject could be accurately described as part of a definite materialist propaganda.

However these things may be, we may perceive the gathering evidence of conflict that cannot fail to be painful, destructive, and in its results incalculable. Over the larger part of North America, for a century or more, a great pioneer population had been engaged in subduing the land and laying the foundations of a new civilisation. The swiftly expanding forces of knowledge and inquiry reveal, at this relatively late hour, that for many millions of these people, who, with their immediate ancestors have accomplished the world's greatest miracle in nation-building, there is coming the shock of a profoundly revolutionary discovery. It falls to the generation now reaching maturity to realise that the material progress of America has been made without a corresponding advance in mental enlightenment and spiritual experience. The conclusion towards which we are led by this latest uprising of obscurantism is that America is on the eve of a final encounter between its vast inertia of "plain Bible religion" and the spirit of the modern world. If the fundamentalists elect to pursue the course marked out for them by Bryan, the main result will be a mass of wreckage, amid which the inevitable church schisms will be relatively unimportant. And, in any event, the central question of intellectual and social freedom still remains to be decided by the American people.

From S. K. Ratcliffe, "America and Fundamentalism," *Contemporary Review,* CXXVIII (September 1925), 288–295.

A French Analysis
André Siegfried

Alexis de Tocqueville, the most famous French observer of American life in the nineteenth century, provided an incisive analysis of the place of religion in the society of the United States. A century later, another French observer, André Siegfried, though not the equal of Tocqueville, produced a kind of up-to-date revision of that analysis. Touring the United States at the height of the modernist-fundamentalist controversy, he attempted to interpret the disturbance in terms of America's social structure and cultural heritage. In the following selection from his famous account, Siegfried views the conflict as an aspect of the urban-rural clash of the 1920s and relates it to America's materialistic success and Puritan legacy. His comments about the relationship of economic interests to modernism and fundamentalism are worthy of note.

———————•••———————

Protestant thought in the United States is divided into two schools, fundamentalist and modernist, which correspond more or less to the orthodox and liberal divisions of the French Reformed Church. This controversy between the letter and spirit is not new, but dates back in both the New and Old World to the middle of the nineteenth century. On the American side of the Atlantic, however, the modernists have been so active since the war that the fundamentalists have had to defend themselves with an ardor that cannot be imputed altogether to religious motives. This in fact is the very heart of the American religious problem.

American modernism has freed itself to a remarkable degree from dogma, ritual, and the literal interpretation of the scriptures; in fact, from all formalities extraneous to purely religious thought. It is no exaggeration to say that those who come under its influence soon abandon the last shreds of belief in dogma or in direct revelations from God. This phenomenon is all the more surprising on the part of a people whose churches are so closely associated with their daily lives. Modernism is, however, strictly in line with Puritan traditions, for its chief preoccupation is moral sincerity and social welfare. It insists that Christianity should come first of all through life, and that it should adapt itself to the conditions of the time, in order to fill its appointed role as guiding factor of the community. They contend that if religion does not occupy itself with morals or even politics, it cannot justify itself to the conscientious, and surely this is more important than formal belief in hidebound doctrines! Personally I think that it is owing to this penetration of religious thought into everyday life that America feels she is superior to the Orient.

This supremacy of the conscience is the essence of religion in its purest form. Nevertheless modernism conceals certain dangers from which the Puritan Fathers were not exempt, in that it emphasizes the confusion of the spirituality and the worldliness. The American is entirely at ease only in practical matters, for he is completely out of his element when he is not active, and pragmatism expresses his possibilities and limitations to perfection. Simply to exist is not enough; he must always express himself in some tangible way. In the study of science he values laboratory equipment rather than research, and in religious matters he is more interested in the bricks with which he builds his church than in prayers and meditation within it. The inevitable association between religion and his other activities ends by Christianizing his daily life, but it also runs the risk of bringing materialism into the church. After two weeks in the United States one is already aware of this collaboration, which permits a certain type of modernism to dominate religion. One often hears it said that a good Christian makes the best citizen, as he is more efficient in the office and the factory. From this it is only a step to the thought that in order to produce more the country must become more Christian, and after all this is really the doctrine of "big business."

Whenever a conflict arises between conscience and practical necessities, American optimism sidesteps it, not by hypocrisy, but by admitting that it is normal and desirable that religion should be a factor in social progress and economic development. Such conflicts do arise, when tender consciences question the motives of powerful interests, but bitterness is generally avoided. When the spiritual elite take it upon themselves to face social or ethnic problems, to denounce scandal, or to insist that a solution must be in conformity to Christianity, obviously they cannot please everybody. The rich, for example, overwhelm the churches and the welfare organizations with their generosity; but later they claim the right to dictate their political activities. Social uplift naturally pleases

the Christian capitalists only as long as they control it. They do not
hesitate to reprove the religious leaders if they ever attempt to put into
practice the more revolutionary doctrines of the New Testament, for
they maintain that the church should not meddle with problems which
it does not understand and is not equipped to solve; and immediately
no more money is forthcoming! In America social reform cannot be
accomplished without funds; so we cannot logically conceive of a church
which obeyed the dictates of Christianity without coming up against the
ill will of Money. We can picture scrupulous souls in the near future
undergoing the equivalent of the temptations of Christ. The Devil, a
banker naturally, will conduct them to the top of a skyscraper where he
will spread out beneath their feet all the immense riches they can acquire
to construct churches, schools, clubs, and hospitals—"all that I will give to
you." Mephistopheles will say, "to use to the best of your ability for the
benefit of social uplift; but only on the condition that you bow down
and worship me." And if the good souls really wish to carry out their
programs, they will bow down. But if they prefer to keep their spiritual
liberty intact they will have to refuse, and then grapple with the fact
that they must carry on in poverty.

Active modernism finds its chief recruits in the eastern states among
the vigorous rich manufacturers. To this attempt to attach the churches
to the chariot of production, the South and West have replied by a revival of fundamentalism, which is of course a reaction against other
things as well. They are faithful to the literal interpretations of the
scriptures, which they venerate almost more than God himself; for, like
their fathers, they try to believe in everything the Bible contains. They
swallow without reserve the divinity of Christ, the immaculate conception, the perfect holiness of his life, his physical resurrection, his ascension into Heaven in a materialistic sense, his promise to return to earth
again in the flesh, and for good measure they also accept the impossible
miracles of the Old Testament. They question nothing, for if they once
began, where would they end? During the Dayton Trial William Jennings Bryan, whose authority as the popular leader of the fundamentalist movement was boundless, replied as follows to the ironical questions put to him by counsel:

Q. Do you claim that everything in the Bible should be literally interpreted?
A. I believe that everything in the Bible should be accepted as it is given
there.

Q. But when you read that Jonah swallowed the whale—or that the whale swallowed Jonah—excuse me, please, how do you literally interpret it? . . . You believe that God made such a fish, and that it was big enough to swallow Jonah?

A. Yes, sir. Let me add, one miracle is as easy to believe as another.

Q. Perfectly easy to believe that Jonah swallowed the whale?

A. If the Bible said so.

There were ten newspaper columns in this strain. The skeptical lawyer thought that he was holding Bryan up to ridicule, whereas he was only giving him a martyr's halo in the eyes of millions of admirers. They might laugh at the fundamentalists in the East, and caricature them, but in the South he was taken seriously.

These fundamentalists come exclusively from Protestant sects, in particular from the Baptists of the country districts and the little towns which have been peopled for generations by the older type of Americans. In the South, where they have been soured by fifty years' fear of the Negro, they are especially numerous, and also in the Puritan colonies of the West. This does not mean that the western states are backward from the economic point of view; on the contrary, life there is very energetic, for the days of the pioneers are only just over, and initiative and progress are sought after and admired there more than anywhere else. But unfortunately the pioneer has no leisure to think, although he manages to read his fifty-page newspaper! All his energies are concentrated on material accomplishments, but in spiritual matters he is conservative. Though superficially free, he is mentally bound; and hence the peculiar paradox that, though he sincerely believes that he is leading the world into the future, in reality he belongs to the past.

The actual form of the fundamentalist movement is interesting. From the religious point of view it is essentially a reaction against the growing influence of the new thought imported from abroad, such as the scientific skepticism of Europe. Popery, and also many philosophies which sow doubt among the younger generation, are looked upon as a danger to the integrity of Protestant traditions. Confronted with these abominations, they turn back to the Bible, the Holy Book of their ancestors, which is still the rallying-point of the nation. From the moral point of view fundamentalism preaches a similar reaction against the customs of the present century, which, dangerous in themselves, become doubly so if they are imported from abroad. In their struggle to preserve the old moral tone, the bigotry and zeal of the ministers, especially the Baptists and Methodists, know no bounds. They give vent to furious diatribes against the modern Babylons of New York and Paris, and with rage they lay their curse on wine, dancing, and cigarettes. In the last analysis their following comes from the rural middle class in the South and West, who are generally Baptists or Methodists, sometimes Presbyterians or Congregationalists. They are the people who are opposed to the cities and financial domination they stand for.

The fundamentalists are the spiritual descendants of Cromwell, and they have remained faithful to his inflexible religious bigotry, until morally they are more insular than the English themselves. European visitors rarely encounter them, for they stand aloof, obstinate, and suspicious. The Ku Klux Klan expresses both their prejudices and their fears. They are instinctively hostile to the broader conceptions of social welfare, for they are hypnotized by the literal preservation of dogma, by the defense of old-fashioned customs against those of today, and by vague fear of an intrusion into the Negro question of the conscientious scruples of the North. In their objection to the socialization of the church, the fundamentalists of the South and East are in sympathy. The latter, though less numerous, actually comprise two hundred of the most bigoted millionaires in New England, who prefer that religion should not meddle with business. Though for different reasons, they both desire that the Protestant church should not drift toward the engrossing preoccupation of social problems. There are always certain questions that they believe should not be tackled.

What with the ice-bound faith of the fundamentalists and the nebulous beliefs of the modernists, it is difficult to know where to look for the true spirit of American Protestantism. Can we even legitimately express it in the singular? In spite of all these contradictions, an essentially American viewpoint on religion does exist. The seventeenth-century English Puritans brought with them the pessimistic doctrine of original sin, and although the fundamentalist minister still preaches it, it obviously no longer harmonizes with the general atmosphere. A hundred years of achievement crowned by magnificent material victories have inclined the American people to believe in man, though less in his original virtue than in his power.

From André Siegfried, *America Comes of Age: A French Analysis*, translated from the French by H. H. Hemming and Doris Hemming (New York: Harcourt, Brace, and Company, 1927), pp. 39–45.

An Historical Interpretation
Charles and Mary Beard

In their classic study of American civilization, written at the height of the modernist-fundamentalist conflict, Charles and Mary Beard attempted to place the phenomenon in its historical perspective. They interpreted modernism as a commendable effort to adjust Christian theology to modern civilization and fundamentalism as an attempt to hold fast to a theological system made obsolete by modern science. Fundamentalism was, in their view, "a popular movement, showing its greatest strength in rural districts where the machine process had as yet made little impression." Touching upon an important aspect of the fundamentalist crusade which has not yet received adequate attention, the Beards noted that American fundamentalists "received hearty encouragement from theologians in England, Scotland, and Europe who were themselves put in similar jeopardy by the inroads which modern learning was making upon their own domain." However provocative their observations regarding fundamentalism may have been, their study clearly revealed a strong bias in favor of modernism which precluded a balanced assessment of the fundamentalist position.

———————◦•◦———————

Besides the drive of secular concerns competing for the attention of the masses more and more absorbed in the machine process, the clergy of every sect had to reckon with all kinds of intellectual currents running against orthodoxy in thought. Without interruption the skeptical Deism of the early republic, the growing Unitarianism of the middle period, and the higher criticism of the gilded age, though they resulted in no great congregations of the faithful, continued to make inroads upon established systems of theological opinion. All the while a great army of geologists, biologists, astronomers, physicists, and historians poured out into the streets through books, magazines, and newspapers sensational and disturbing ideas that did not square with the cosmogony and chronology of the Bible, raising a cloud of queries and doubts in the minds of laymen and suggesting to theologians that explanations, modifications, or counterblasts were in order.

Frankly accepting the stubborn facts of science and higher criticism, one school, calling themselves modernists, tried to meet the situation by

restating the substance of Christianity in terms compatible with modern
knowledge. The thinker of this type, to use the language of Harry
Emerson Fosdick, simply could not

take in earnest the man-sized representations of God on which, it may be,
he was brought up—a god walking in a garden in the cool of the day, making
woman from man's rib, confounding men's speech lest they build a tower
too high, decreeing a flood to drown humanity, trying to slay a man at a
wayside inn because his child was not circumcised, showing his back but not
his face to a man upon a mountain top, or ordering the massacre of his
chosen people's enemies, men, women, and children, without mercy. He is in
revolt against all that.

From such "old literalism" the modernist demanded "intellectual lib-
eration"—emancipation to expound "Christ's imperishable Gospel freed
from its entanglements, the Shekinah distinguished from the shrine, to
be preached with a liberty, a reasonableness, an immediate application
to our own age such as no generation of preachers in the church's history
ever had the privilege of knowing before."

Far from surrendering to the iconoclasm of modern science, theologians of an opposite tendency, known as "fundamentalists" clung
with unshaken loyalty to what they were pleased to call "the old faith"—
their own selected essentials of Biblical theology. In a strict sense, of
course, the Catholic church, though occasionally disturbed by the writings of modernists within its own fold, was prefundamentalist in doctrine, claiming, as it did, an unchanging and unchangeable creed of
invariables which embraced contentions quite as difficult for natural science as the virgin birth. But it was the conservatives of the Protestant
persuasion who started the new vogue in dogmatism. Picking out a few
tenets deemed necessary for salvation, they rejected the validity of scientific methods in theological criticism and declared war on free thinking of every type. In general they agreed on four or five points as tests
for separating the sheep and the goats; such, for example, as the verbal
inerrancy and inspiration of the Bible, a literal interpretation of its cru-
cial passages, the fall of man, virgin birth, the scheme of atonement and
salvation through the crucifixion, and the resurrection of Christ.

Lest there be uncertainty as to their position, fundamentalists proclaimed their views in unmistakable language. The Baptists, for instance,
at their northern convention in 1922, specifically resolved

that the Bible was written by men super-naturally inspired; that it has truth without any admixture of error for its matter; that as originally written it is both scientifically and historically true and correct; and therefore is and shall remain to the end of the ages the only complete and final revelation of the will of God to man; the true center of Christian union and the supreme standard by which all human conduct, creeds, and opinions should be tried.

This broad and emphatic profession was followed by eight additional declarations pertaining to the Trinity, the acceptance of the Genesis account of creation "literally not allegorically or figuratively," virgin birth, atonement for sin, grace in the new creation, the mission of the church, immersion, the resurrection and second coming of Christ, and the condemnation of evolutionary doctrines. Affirming its faith in dogmas similar in character, the Presbyterian church at its general assembly in 1923 prefaced its bill of particulars with the assertion that "it is an essential doctrine of the Word of God and our standards that the Holy Spirit did so inspire, guide, and move the writers of the Holy Scriptures as to keep them from error." Whatever criticisms could be leveled against the fundamentalists, it was admitted that they left no doubt as to the verbal forms of their beliefs.

By competent authorities the origins of the fundamentalist movement have been traced to Bible institutes founded in various parts of the country for the purpose of training religious workers whose preliminary education did not, as a rule, qualify them for the theological schools tinctured by scientific and historical methods. It was in essence a popular movement, showing its greatest strength in rural districts where the machine process had as yet made little impression. Unquestionably, it was highly organized, well-financed, and resolute.

Not content with making war on the modernists in theology, fundamentalist leaders strove to get possession of state legislatures and force the enactment of statutes forbidding the teaching of evolution in schools supported either in whole or in part by public funds. With comparative ease, they accomplished this object in Tennessee, precipitating in the summer of 1925 a spectacular battle in the trial and conviction of a young teacher accused of imparting to his pupils the doctrine of evolution in violation of the law.

Among the freethinkers of two continents, especially among those who looked neither around nor back, the Tennessee case aroused amusement at the expense of the American hinterland; but undisturbed by scorn from such quarters, the fundamentalists announced that they intended to carry on their campaign—preaching their gospel and forcing legislatures to pass bills against evolution until they had made their creed the faith of the American nation. And while the doubters scoffed, the straight sect of literalists, in their warfare on science, received hearty encouragement from theologians in England, Scotland, and Europe who were themselves put in similar jeopardy by the inroads which modern learning was making upon their own domain.

From Charles and Mary Beard, *The Rise of American Civilization,* II (New York: Macmillan, 1927), 750–753.

Assessment of an American Theologian
William Adams Brown

William Adams Brown, a Presbyterian educated at Yale and the University of Berlin, was a distinguished member of the faculty at Union Theological Seminary. For years he was a leading spokesman for liberal Protestantism in the United States. His *Christian Theology in Outline* (1906) was a classic statement of liberal theological thought which "interpreted the gospel in terms of its social thrust." In 1922 he published his *The Church In America*, a "study of the present condition and future prospects of American Protestantism," which displayed considerable hostility toward the recent resurgence of virile fundamentalism. In the following essay, written four years later, his attitude toward the fundamentalists was substantially more sympathetic, although Brown himself had by no means abandoned the liberal cause. In spite of the crass and unintelligent ways in which fundamentalists often stated their case, he maintained that the movement represented a protest against "a form of religion which would substitute reliance upon man for dependence upon God." Essentially then fundamentalism was "a reaffirmation of the central experience of all religion—the discovery of God." After surveying various forms through which contemporary religion expressed itself, Brown concluded that religion "will begin and end in the quest for God and will not be satisfied with any substitute."

———◆●◆———

Recent happenings in religious circles seem to show that the fundamentalist movement which has held so prominent a place in public attention during the last half dozen years has reached its crest and is on the ebb. Both in the Northern Presbyterian and in the Northern Baptist churches the efforts of the extremists to commit the church to a policy of exclusion have failed. The Presbyterian General Assembly, accepting the report of the Special Commission of Fifteen appointed a year ago, has recognized the existence of different parties in the church and refused to commit itself to the policy of strict construction which has been strongly urged upon it by the conservatives. The Northern Baptists, in their General Convention, have shown a similar tolerant spirit, and in spite of the protests of the fundamentalist minority have endorsed the conciliatory policy of their present leaders by substantial majorities.

The danger of a split, very real a year or two ago in these two great denominations, seems now to have been definitely averted.

This does not mean that the fundamentalist movement is over or that the conservatives in the churches may not still win notable victories. Whatever the decision in the Scopes case, we are likely for some time to come to see the aid of the state invoked to check the rising tide of modernism. But whatever temporary inconvenience these attempts may cause, they are not likely to have the serious consequences once anticipated. The effort of the fundamentalists to capture for their cause, or if not successful in this, at least to split, one or more of the major denominations, is not now likely to be realized.

It becomes timely, therefore, to ask what were the forces which account for this widespread reactionary movement. To dismiss fundamentalism by calling it a revival of superstition gets us nowhere. Some powerful motive must have been at work to arouse such deep conviction—a motive which will continue to operate until it is recognized for what it is and its legitimate demands are met. It will be worth our while to ask what that motive is and what is likely to be its influence on the future development of religion in America.

Many different influences have combined to produce the movement we call fundamentalism, but in its deepest meaning it is a protest, largely instinctive, but nonetheless deep seated and passionate, against a form of religion which would substitute reliance upon man for dependence upon God. In the past religion, however different its forms in detail, has meant to its devotees the worship of a God who has made his will known in definite and recognizable ways—One to whom one could speak, confident of being answered; on whom one could rest, knowing that one's trust was well founded. This simple, trustful attitude toward religion has become increasingly difficult for many cultivated people. They realize acutely the obstacles which the scientific temper puts in the way of faith, and while they are still interested in religion, their interest has become that of the critic who desires to understand rather than that of the missionary who desires to share. They have exchanged the position of the participant for that of the observer.

A recent number of *The Atlantic Monthly* contained two articles about prayer. One was by a Harvard professor who wrote with all the technique of the scholar; the other by an amateur who had no other qualification for writing than the fact that he had rediscovered the art of prayer and could not rest until he had shared with others the joy of his discovery.

Professor Kirsopp Lake begins by telling us what prayer has meant to praying people in the past, and then goes on to explain why it cannot mean the same thing to us who are living today. One by one he takes up the familiar forms of prayer: petition, intercession, and the like, and shows why they are no longer possible to modern men. He concludes with a forecast of what prayer will be like in the future when it has been stripped of all its superstitious elements and reduced to its simplest form as the reverent contemplation of our own highest ideals.

Glenn Clark writes in a very different spirit. He brushes all . . . theoretical difficulties aside in face of the one fact that matters for him, the fact that since he has rediscovered the art of prayer, his entire life has been transformed. What has happened to him he dares to hope may happen to others who are willing to repeat his experiment, and he proceeds to outline a series of simple rules which he has found helpful in the conduct of his own devotion.

The contrast between these two articles measures the distance between our own generation and the generation which preceded it. We live in an age in which large numbers of people have been exchanging the attitude of Glenn Clark for that of Kirsopp Lake. Where their fathers and mothers prayed, they philosophize about prayer. They have ceased to be participants and have become critics of religion, and in the process something has dropped out which has left a gap which for many has not yet been filled.

How far this process had gone in some modernist circles may be learned from a recent book of Professor Kirsopp Lake, included by *The New Republic* in its list of the best books of the year. He calls it *The Religion of Yesterday and of Tomorrow*. In this book he gives reasons why the older forms of religion, whether Catholic or Protestant, no longer satisfy many people. He describes the newer religion which he believes to be in process of formation—the religion of tomorrow. Its most notable feature, if he rightly interprets it, will be the substitution of the attitude of self-reliance for the dependence which has hitherto been characteristic of religious people. Whereas, according to Professor Lake, the fathers were drawn to religion by their consciousness of weakness, their sons approach God conscious of their strength. The former looked up to an all-powerful God for the help they needed and found their need met through a series of supernatural acts, which together make up what theology calls revelation and redemption. The latter are using the methods of modern science to discover the laws of life, and through this discovery are able progressively to emancipate themselves from the controls of the older religion. The religion of yesterday was one in which God revealed his will to man. The religion of tomorrow will be one in which man discovers the right life for himself. In the old religion God judges man. In the new religion man will judge God.

Not all modernists, to be sure, go as far as Professor Lake. Many avowed liberals have as vivid a God consciousness as any fundamentalist. Men like Dr. Fosdick and Dr. Merrill regard the discoveries of modern science as data which help them to understand more clearly how God reveals Himself. But of the fact of revelation they have no doubt. Nonetheless it is true that the temper in which they approach the religious life is different from that of their predecessors. For submission they substitute inquiry, for acceptance criticism. The line which once used to separate reason from revelation has been blurred. Doors once thought to be closed forever have been opened, and no one can set limits to the changes which may follow.

So long as this attitude was confined to a scholar here and there, its effects were negligible. There have always been men in the church who have thought of religion very much as Professor Lake does. But they have been in a minority, which had little influence on the church as a whole. When the critic became troublesome, the church found ways of dealing with him, each denomination in its own way. The case of Dr. [Charles S.] Briggs might stir the Presbyterians, or that of Dr. [Algernon S.] Crapsey the Episcopalians. But so long as the controversy remained within a single denomination, the members of other communions could shrug their shoulders and thank God they were not as other churches. But when the results of the new teaching began to extend from the seminaries to the universities and colleges, and from the colleges to the schools, a new situation was created. Newspapers and periodicals began to popularize the new religion, and it lost nothing of sensation in the process. In widespread circles the word went about that religion was in danger, and in various ways men organized for its defense. In addition to the steps taken by the conservatives within the different denominations, interdenominational organizations were formed. Large sums of money were raised for propaganda, and the battle was carried from the church to the school and from the school to the legislature. Mr. Bryan, silver-tongued orator though he was, could not have produced the effect he did if he had not made himself the voice of a widespread popular movement.

It is easy to depreciate the significance of the fundamentalist movement because of the crass form which it has often taken and the unintelligent way in which its case has been put by many of its defenders. But at its heart it is the reaffirmation of the central experience of all religion—the discovery of God. To one man the discovery comes in one way; to another in another. But however it comes, it has this common characteristic, that it carries within itself its own evidence. Vital religion is always supernatural religion. To the arguments of reason, telling us that this or that is impossible, it has one simple and convincing answer: "God has said . . . Let God be true though every man be a liar." This vivid consciousness of a reality carrying within itself its own evidence has been characteristic of religious revivals in every age: and when it is lost religion languishes. It is not only simple and uneducated people who feel the need of assurance and certainty which fundamentalist religion seeks to supply. In modernist circles too there is evidence that all is not well.

I have quoted *The Atlantic* for evidence of the decline of the unquestioning faith which was the characteristic of the older religion. Let me turn to it again for evidence of the growing longing for what that unquestioning faith alone can supply.

In a revealing article by one who styles himself a modernist, the writer tells us the story of his progressive disillusionment with contemporary religion. One by one he has followed the paths opened to him by the modern spirit, only to find them ending in a cul-de-sac. Biblical criticism, the new theology, the social gospel, he has tried them all and come back empty-handed.

He is not alone in this failure, he tells us. He finds himself one of a multitude of seekers looking for something which they have not found. He quotes the experience of one of them, a man whom he had long respected for his sincerity, devotion, and spiritual insight, who recently came to him to tell him of a dream. "I thought," he said, "that I saw you standing on a hilltop, and we, a great host of us, were crowded around waiting eagerly for what you might say. We could see your lips framing the word, but no sound came out of your mouth. We tried to help you by calling out the word your lips were shaping; but we also were dumb. And that word was God."

In the light of experiences such as this, it is not hard to appreciate the mood of wistfulness which is so characteristic of our time, or to understand why the thoughts of many persons all about us are turning longingly to religion in quest of some new light which shall illuminate the darkness from which otherwise they see no hope of deliverance.

What are the prospects that this longing will be satisfied—that those to whom the blind submission to authority which fundamentalism demands is no longer possible will find the present God of whom their hearts are in quest?

Three ways are being taken by contemporary religion, each of which has many advocates. Some find in the growing consciousness of social solidarity the door of access to the presence of God. Others, following the clue given by the mystics of all religions, seek to win through detachment from the world an inner assurance and peace not possible in any other way. Still others find God through the church and, in such movements as the Anglo-Catholic Revival and the more recent Eucharistic Congress of the Roman church, see God manifesting himself anew to each age through the historic institution which is the organ of his revelation and the mediator of his grace.

One of the characteristic features of the religious life of the last generation was its growing emphasis upon man's social relationships. The older individualistic Christianity in which men were thought of as separate units, each having his own direct relationship to God, was challenged . . . as one-sided and selfish. Men were to be saved one by one, to be sure, but not simply as men, but as fathers, teachers, husbands, employers, patriots, and the like. And it was easy to show that salvation of this kind was impossible without far-reaching changes in the social organization. It was religion's function to save not only individuals from the consequences of their sins, but society from the influences which were producing sinners. And this it appeared was a complex process which required for its success the co-operation of many different specialists. So Christians began to concern themselves with the relations of the church to industry and race and were found working for the eight-hour working day, better wages, the right of labor to organize for its own protection, the safeguarding of women and children, the abolition of lynching, and similar reforms. The social settlement was a product of this new social emphasis; but it was only one of a number of like kind, some of them directly connected with the church, others the result of influences which the church set in motion.

We are witnessing a reaction against this early enthusiasm. The high expectations entertained by many of the converts to the social gospel have not been realized in fact. There was a time within the memory of many who are still in the prime of life, when it seemed to many earnest spirits as if the Kingdom of God would immediately appear. The plans for the new social order were already drawn; the foundations were laid. All that seemed needed was enough willing hands to build the superstructure. Today our mood has changed. The war that was once for all to put an end to oppression and tyranny has left as its aftermath a host of ugly shapes that mock our hope of a better world. The old selfishnesses and prejudices of which we hoped that we were rid forever, are with us still, and with them a new brood even more hateful and baffling. The failure, at least the indefinite post-ponement, of the social hope has turned the thought of many from this world to another and made them more than usually sensitive to the fundamentalist appeal. As in the early church the trials and persecutions which fell to the lot of the Christian converts led many to despair of happiness here and made them hospitable to the millennial hope with its promise of a supernatural salvation, so in our day the disappoint-ments that have come to many through the failure of their hopes of social reform have made them willing to lend an ear to anyone who can promise an easier and more satisfying salvation.

But while this is true of many once socially minded Christians, it is by no means true of all. On the contrary, what has happened has made some of them not less but more alive to the need of radical social transformation. They differ from their predecessors not in their con-viction that it is the Christian's duty to work for the Christianization of society as a whole, but in their clearer perception of the greatness of the task and the obstacles which prevent its accomplishment. In a work so great, mightier resources are needed than these early reformers com-manded. It is not enough to substitute the love of man for the worship of God. We must win from our faith in God the active power that will nerve the will for the sacrifices that must be made. In the past Christianity has been a transforming and liberating influence, releasing new energies and bringing new things to pass. And this it must still be to us today if it is to meet our present need. All the more because the task is not simply individual but social, do we need the resources which religion alone can supply.

So we see men and women in all countries turning with new enthusiasm to Christianity, confident that they will find in it the social enfranchisement they need.

The most striking illustration of the effect of the new social spirit in after-war religion is the movement known as "Copec," which culminated in the great congress held in Birmingham in April 1925. "Copec" is short for Conference on Christian Politics, Economics, and Citizenship. The movement began in the attempt of a group of British Christians, sobered by the tragedy of the war, to think through for themselves the spiritual implications of the Christian gospel. Their enterprise aroused widespread interest and in due time received the official endorsement of many of the British churches. Commissions were formed for the study of various aspects of the problem. Associates were enlisted to push the movement and provide for its support. After five years of preparation the congress met at Birmingham, and after a week of frank discussion of the most pressing social problems of the day adopted certain resolutions defining the duty of Christians in the field of industry, race, education, morals, and politics. Those responsible for the movement have planned to carry it on through a continuation committee, and anticipate the time when the standards which they have defined for themselves will be accepted by the church as a whole.

No gathering of equal size and impressiveness has been held in this country, but similar influences have long been operative. The Federal Council's Commission on Social Service brings together the social service commissions of the different denominations, and in co-operation with the National Welfare Council of the Roman Catholic Church has repeatedly made studies of important social issues. The pronouncement on the eight-hour day in the steel industry was a notable example. The Committee on the War and the Religious Outlook, a committee formed by the Federal Council and the General War Time Commission of the Churches to consider after-war problems, has published a series of volumes dealing with various phases of the church's social responsibility. Similar studies have been made by another group of Christians who have created an informal organization for the study of the relation of religion and social problems under the name of "The Inquiry."

In these and similar ways the effort is being made to bring religion into all phases of human life and to prove anew the truth of the Master's word: "Inasmuch as ye have done it unto one of the least of these My brethren, ye have done it unto Me."

Not all Christians, however, find their way to God by way of the social gospel. Some there are, by no means fundamentalist in their sympathies, who regard it as a blind alley serving only to mislead and confuse. No one has been more unsparing in his criticism of "Copec" than the Dean of St. Paul's. . . .

To find God, according to Dean Inge, we must turn our thoughts in and not out. The Christian way as he conceives it is the mystic way, and in saying this he is voicing the experience of many beside himself. In widely different circles we find a revived interest in mysticism—an interest anticipated by William James when in his well-known Gifford lectures on the *Varieties of Religious Experience* he pointed out the central place which the mystical experience holds in the life of religion. The United States, always hospitable to new religions, has a score of cults which find in the immediate experience of God a way of deliverance from the sorrows and sins of life. Christian Science, New Thought, Theosophy—these are but a few examples of an interest which is growing. In Christian Science, as the title of Mrs. Eddy's book implies, the motive which draws most of its votaries to the new cult is the desire for physical healing. The intimate relation between mind and body, long a familiar fact to those who have had much to do with sickness, is here made the center of a religion which promises healing to diseases of the soul as well as of the body. But Christian Science is but the best known of a large number of cults which profess a similar faith and practice similar methods. A recent study, made by Miss Alice Paulsen for the Committee on Public Health of the New York Academy of Medicine, describes the methods of a number of these cults. All bid their devotees seek their remedy within; all inculcate relaxation and receptivity; all divert attention from that which is feared and fix it upon that which is desired; all appeal to faith as the key to a satisfying life as well for the body as for the spirit.

No one who has studied the facts will deny that many who follow such methods find what they seek. The use of the mystical discipline in Roman Catholicism and the cures reported at such shrines as that of Our Lady of Lourdes and Our Lady of Mount Carmel are well known to all students of religion. It is natural to conclude that what has been so beneficent to some will be equally adapted to all. So we find an ever increasing number of unlicensed practitioners extending the procedure of the older cults to cover phases and experiences that are not ordinarily included in the mystic way. There is nothing that the heart of man desires that is not promised by these new evangelists to those who have faith. "Success, money, efficiency, power over men, the love of women,—whatever you have tried to reach and failed in reaching—only have faith in me and in my method and it shall be given to you." This is the gospel which is being preached in many a hotel parlor today in the name of the new psychology.

For just as the social interest of our day has had a double influence upon religion, leading some men to despair of any large success from the methods of the social reformers, while for others it has filled these methods with a divine meaning, so psychology, turning men's thought in upon themselves, has made faith in God impossible for some, while for others it has rationalized the faith they had. As the laws of the social life may be interpreted either as a substitute for Divine Providence or as the method by which God evolves his social purpose, so the laws of the individual life may be regarded either as man's way of creating God or as God's way of revealing himself to man. Not a few in our day are choosing the latter alternative and finding in the inner life the shrine in which the human spirit meets God face to face.

Many of those who follow the mystic way are extreme individualists and have broken with historic Christianity. But this is by no means true of all. There are many—and I believe an increasing number—who find their most effective help to realizing the divine presence in the symbols of historic religion. God, who transcends all human definition, draws near to them in visible and tangible shape in the sacraments of the church, and in the miracle of the altar and of the font makes the familiar objects of everyday experience the vehicles of his supernatural revelation. The assurance which some find in social service and others in the silence of their own spirit, these seekers win through God's revelation in his church. This is the third of the three doors through which earnest spirits in our day are entering into the presence of God.

A notable example of this churchly approach was the recent Eucharistic Congress in Chicago. A faith which can assemble 200,000 persons in one place to participate in a single act of worship is evidently very much alive. Those modernists who write of Catholicism as an outworn form of religion may find food for thought in what happened in the great auditorium by the lake in those memorable days of June.

.   .   .   .

Such are some of the forms through which the spirit of contemporary religion is expressing itself. Which promises the shortest and the most direct way to the desired goal, he would be a bold man to say. It may well be that, as so often in the past, no one way will be found practicable for all travelers, and that in the future as in the past they will make their journey by different routes. But one thing we may confidently predict: that unless human nature shall radically change, the religion of the future will still be religion. It will begin and end in the quest for God and will not be satisfied with any substitute. May we not hope that the earnest effort that is going into this quest in our day will not fail, and that the generation upon which we are entering will find its God and will be able to speak his name so clearly that all who hear will understand and recognize in what they hear the answer to their deepest need?

From William Adams Brown, "After Fundamentalism—What?," *The North American Review,* CCXXIII (September–November 1926), 406–419.

A Note on Secondary Sources

The historical literature devoted to the modernist-fundamentalist conflict of the 1920s is diverse in scope, emphasis, and interpretation. Some historians have explored the subject in detail at the grass roots level; others have attempted broad, comprehensive analyses of the national conflict within the framework of American religious and intellectual history. Most numerous, perhaps, are those monographs that focus upon a single aspect of the boarder phenomenon, namely the popular agitation over biological evolution that erupted in the era after World War I. Such studies rarely explore the relationship between this phase of the dispute and the earlier debate over evolution in the late nineteenth century. And they devote little attention to fundamentalist activities during the Progressive Era. In fact, scholarly efforts have concentrated to an extraordinary degree upon the Scopes trial and its implications. But in spite of differences in approach and focus, scholars generally agree that the modernist-fundamentalist conflict was "a terribly confused and complex phenomenon" which involved more than a clash between divergent schools of theology or different reactions to a biological theory. Rather it was a socio-intellectual disturbance of considerable dimension which revealed much about the American mind in the post–World War I decade.

Lest the controversy between modernists and fundamentalists in the 1920s appear as merely an aberration in the American experience, it is necessary to place it in its proper cultural and religious context. To do so one needs to consult general works on the history of Protestantism in the United States. For the experienced scholar no less than the neophyte, the four volumes of the *Religion in American Life* (Princeton: Princeton University Press, 1961), edited by James W. Smith and A. Leland Jamison are indispensable, especially R. Nelson Burr's critical bibliography. Two concise works which provide intelligent introductions to the history and theology of Protestantism are Winthrop Hudson, *American Protestantism* (Chicago: University of Chicago Press, 1961) and William Hordern, *A Layman's Guide to Protestant Theology* (New York: Macmillan, 1957). Equally useful are the two volumes of narrative and documents by H. Shelton Smith, Robert T. Handy, and Lefferts A. Loetscher, *American Christianity: An Historical Interpretation With Representative Documents* (New York: Charles Scribner's Sons, 1963). Somewhat similar in format, though briefer and with more narrative than documentary material, is Edwin Scott Gaustad, *A Religious History of America* (New York: Harper and Row, 1966). An excellent historiographical essay on American Protestantism is Paul A. Carter, "Recent Historiography of the Protestant Churches in America," *Church History*, XXXVII (March 1968), 95–107. A useful bibliography is provided in Robert T. Handy's "Survey of Recent Literature: American Church History," *Church History*, XXVII (June 1958), 161–165.

Several significant works concentrate upon the religious history of the United States since the Civil War. Among these are two highly readable volumes, Winfred E. Garrison, *The March of Faith: The Story of Religion in America Since 1865* (New York: Harper, 1933) and William W. Sweet, *The Story of Religion in America* (New York: Harper, 1939), and Sidney Mead's provocative essays on the changing nature of American Protestantism which have been collected and published under the title of *The Lively Experiment* (New York: Harper and Row, 1963). Numerous denominational histories exist, but Lefferts A. Loetscher's *The Broadening Church: A Study of Theological Issues in the Presbyterian Church Since 1869* (Philadelphia: University of Pennsylvania Press, 1954) is a model case study of how one major denomination wrestled with theological problems in the post–Civil War era. The reaction of Protestant churches to the challenges of an industrialized, urban society has been explored in depth in such first-rate studies as C. Howard Hopkins, *The Rise of the Social Gospel in American Protestantism, 1865–1915* (New Haven: Yale University Press, 1940), Aaron I. Abell, *The Urban Impact on American Protestantism, 1865–1900* (Cambridge: Harvard University Press, 1943), and Henry F. May, *Protestant Churches and Industrial America* (New York: Harper, 1949). Two monographs of a similar nature which are directly related to the era of the 1920s are Robert Moats Miller, *American Protestantism and the Social Issues, 1919–1939* (Chapel Hill: University of North Carolina Press, 1958) and Paul A. Carter, *The Decline and Revival of the Social Gospel: Social and Political Liberalism in American Protestant Churches,*

1920–1940 (Ithaca: Cornell University Press, 1956). Chapter IV of Carter's work is an especially perceptive analysis of "the social meaning of fundamentalism." These five works just cited, used in conjunction with Herbert W. Schneider's *Religion in 20th Century America* (Cambridge: Harvard University Press, 1952) and a collection of writings edited by Arnold S. Nash and entitled *Protestant Thought in the Twentieth Century* (New York: Macmillan, 1951), help considerably in placing the modernist-fundamentalist conflict of the 1920s in historical perspective.

The history of fundamentalism and modernism in the United States before 1920 has by no means been exhausted as a field of research. Substantially more scholarly probing is needed on the theological, social, and cultural aspects of fundamentalism and modernism before any definitive history can be written. An admirable attempt to give some theological perspective to these two schools of Protestant thought is Robert T. Handy, "Fundamentalism and Modernism in Pespective," *Religion in Life*, XXIV (Summer 1955), 381–394. Probably the most comprehensive treatment of the fundamentalist movement prior to the 1920s is Carroll E. Harrington's "The Fundamentalist Movement in America, 1870–1921," (Unpublished Ph.D. dissertation, University of California, Berkeley, 1959), a work which strikes a neat balance between narrative and interpretative analysis. For a brief assessment see H. Richard Niebuhr, "Fundamentalism," *Encyclopaedia of the Social Sciences*, V, 527. The need for more research regarding the origins of fundamentalism is implied in Ernest R. Sandeen's provocative essay, "Toward a Historical Interpretation of the Origins of Fundamentalism," *Church History*, XXXVI (March 1967), 66–83. Among the commonly accepted notions which Sandeen challenges is the idea that fundamentalism was "an agrarian protest movement centered in the South." A thoughtful critique of Sandeen's essay is provided by LeRoy Moore, Jr. in his "Another Look at Fundamentalism: A Response to Ernest R. Sandeen," *Church History*, XXXVIII (June 1968), 195–202. The fact that modernism was a less coherent, definable theology than fundamentalism undoubtedly helps explain why it has been neglected. The deficiency is only partially compensated by F. H. Foster, *The Modern Movement in Theology* (New York: Fleming H. Revell, 1939), various general histories of American Protestantism, and such brief mention as appears in Chapter 24 of Stow Persons, *American Minds: A History of Ideas* (New York: Holt, Rinehart, and Winston, 1958). Useful in determining the relationship of fundamentalism and modernism to science both before and after World War I are John Dillenberger, *Protestant Thought and Natural Science* (New York: Doubleday, 1960), Edward A. White, *Science and Religion in American Thought: The Impact of Naturalism* (Palo Alto: Stanford University Press, 1952), John C. Greene, *Darwin and the Modern World View* (Baton Rouge: Louisiana State University Press, 1961), Stow Persons, *Evolutionary Thought in America* (New Haven: Yale University Press, 1950), and several illuminating articles by Bert James Loewenberg on the reception of Darwin's theories in the United States in the late nineteenth century. Of course, there exists a vast literature on the relationship of science and religion. As scientists ponder religion and theologians ponder science, the literature continues to expand at an accelerated rate.

That the modernist-fundamentalist conflict of the 1920s has been a topic of perennial interest to scholars is evident in the number of books, essays, and graduate theses dealing with various aspects of the subject. Two early works, Stewart G. Cole, *The History of Fundamentalism* (New York: Harper, 1931) and Gaius G. Atkins, *Religion in Our Time* (New York: Round Table Press, 1932), are still valuable but should be used with discretion. The most comprehensive treatment of the modernist-fundamentalist conflict to appear in a general history of the 1920s, of which there are several, is that in William E. Leuchtenberg, *The Perils of Prosperity, 1914–1932* (Chicago: University of Chicago Press, 1958). But Paul A. Carter's free-wheeling little volume, *The Twenties in America* (New York: Thomas Y. Crowell, 1968), raises some interesting questions about the nature of the conflict. Though deficient in some respects, the volume which more than any other has shaped the interpretation of the modernist-fundamentalist disturbance is Norman F. Furniss, *The Fundamentalist Controversy, 1918–1931* (New Haven: Yale University Press, 1954). Two excellent unpublished theses, Kenneth K. Bailey, "The Anti-Evolution Crusade of the Nineteen-Twenties," (Ph.D. dissertation, Vanderbilt University, 1953) and LeRoy Johnson, "The Evolution Controversy During the 1920's," (Ph.D. dissertation, New York University, 1953) are often more perceptive in critical areas than Furniss. Another thesis which offers some insight into the complex issues involved in the struggle is William N. Crow, "Religion and the Recent Evolution Controversy With Special Reference to the Issues in the Scopes Trial," (Unpublished Bachelor of Divinity thesis, Duke University,

1936). For the state of religion in general in the later 1920s see an incisive essay by Robert T. Handy entitled "The American Religious Depression, 1925–1935," *Church History*, XXIX (March 1960), 3–16. And Louis Gasper's *The Fundamentalist Movement* (The Hague: Mouton, 1963) is an enlightening treatment of the course of fundamentalism after 1931.

Specialized studies of one phase of the larger conflict between fundamentalism and modernism, namely the controversy over evolution, exist in abundance. The works of Furniss, Bailey, Johnson, and others cited above explore this phase of the struggle in some depth. The meaning of the evolution fight in the South has been described in two early works, Virginius Dabney, *Liberalism in the South* (Chapel Hill: University of North Carolina Press, 1932) and Wilbur J. Cash, *The Mind of the South* (New York: Alfred A. Knopf, 1941). Cash offers some astute observations about the fracas over evolution, which he saw from the vantage point of a student at Wake Forest College in the 1920s when the institution and its president were under fire because of the teaching of Darwin's theory there. The treatments by Cash and Dabney have been superseded by Kenneth K. Bailey, *Southern White Protestantism in the Twentieth Century*, (New York: Harper and Row, 1964), a masterful synthesis which devotes a chapter to the battle over evolution. Since the fundamentalists achieved their most notable legal victories against evolution in the South, it is not surprising that the controversy in the region has been explored in detail at the grass roots level. Willard B. Gatewood, Jr., *Preachers, Pedagogues and Politicians: The Evolution Controversy in North Carolina, 1920–1927* (Chapel Hill: University of North Carolina Press, 1966) is a monographic study of the struggle in a state which national fundamentalist leaders considered "pivotal" to the outcome of their crusade. The controversy in four other Southern states has been described in Kenneth K. Bailey, "The Enactment of Tennessee's Anti-Evolution Law," *The Journal of Southern History*, XVI (July 1950), 472–490; Elbert L. Watson, "Oklahoma and the Anti-Evolution Movement of the 1920's," *The Chronicles of Oklahoma*, XLII (Winter 1964-1965), 396–407; R. Haliburton, Jr., "The Nation's First Anti-Darwin Law: Passage and Repeal [Oklahoma]," *The Southwestern Social Science Quarterly*, XLI (September 1960), 123–135; R. Haliburton, Jr., "The Adoption of the Arkansas Anti-Evolution Law," *The Arkansas Historical Quarterly*, XXIII (Autumn 1964),

271–283; and R. Haliburton, Jr., "Kentucky's Anti-Evolution Controversy," *The Register of the Kentucky Historical Society*, LXVI (April
1968), 97–107.

Although the Scopes trial has a significant place in almost every
general treatment of the evolution controversy, it also has what may be
termed a separate literature of its own. The most detailed study of the
trial is L. Sprague de Camp's *The Great Monkey Trial* (New York:
Doubleday, 1968). A suggestive and highly readable account, Ray Ginger's
Six Days or Forever? Tennessee v. John Thomas Scopes (Boston: Beacon
Press, 1958), probes into the psychological and sociological milieu of the
trial. *D-Days at Dayton: Reflections on the Scopes Trial* (Baton Rouge:
Louisiana State University Press, 1965), edited by Jerry R. Tompkins,
is a symposium by an assortment of individuals who either directly
or indirectly were touched by the "monkey trial." The essays by two
theologians, John Dillenberger and Carlyle Marney, are especially note-
worthy. Although it is not feasible to cite here all historical efforts
devoted to this single event, at least three others deserve mention: Pearl
Kluger, "New Light on the Scopes Trial," (Unpublished M.A. thesis,
Columbia University, 1957); Donald F. Brod, "The Scopes Trial: A
Look at Press Coverage After Forty Years," *Journalism Quarterly*, XLII
(Spring 1965), 219–226; Raymond H. Robison, "The Scopes Trial: A
Case Study in Fundamentalism," (Unpublished M.A. thesis, Pennsyl-
vania State University, 1950).

Studies of various participants in the modernist-fundamentalist
conflict constitute a sizable body of relevant literature. These works
range in scholarly soundness from the detached, gracefully written *Billy
Sunday Was His Real Name* (Chicago: University of Chicago Press,
1955) by William G. McLoughlin to the affectionate *A. C. Dixon:
A Romance in Preaching* (New York: Putnam, 1931) by Helen Dixon.
Hillyer H. Straton, the son of John Roach Straton, has published
several excellent studies which reveal much about his father's role in
the fundamentalist crusade. Among these are his "John Roach Straton: Prophet of Social Righteousness," *Foundations*, V (January 1962),
17–38, and "John Roach Straton: The Great Evolution Debate," *Foundations*, X (April-June 1967), 138–149. No scholarly biography of William Bell Riley, one of the foremost fundamentalist leaders, has yet
been published, but Riley as well as Mordecai F. Ham, Gerald Winrod,
and others who continued their schismatic ministries after the 1920s ap-

pear in Ralph L. Roy's *Apostles of Discord: A Study in Organized Bigotry and Disruption on the Fringes of Protestantism* (Boston: Beacon Press, 1953). The articulate fundamentalist theologian J. Gresham Machen has been the subject of a lengthy two-part article by Dallas M. Roak, published in the *Journal of Presbyterian History* in June and September 1965. Machen's role in the modernist-fundamentalist dispute of the 1920s, as well as his break with the Presbyterian church, has been ably analyzed in Loetscher's *The Broadening Church* cited above, and the story of his Westminster Seminary is chronicled in Alan Kenneth Austin, "The History of Westminster Theological Seminary, 1929–1964," (Unpublished M.A. thesis, East Tennessee State University, 1965). Machen's career is also described in Ned B. Stonehouse, *J. Gresham Machen: A Biographical Memoir* (Grand Rapids: Eerdmans, 1955).

But no other fundamentalist spokesman of the 1920s has attracted the attention of lay historians as has William Jennings Bryan, who was already something of a folk hero before he joined the antievolution crusade. Recent Bryan scholars have gone far toward disentangling the man from the images of him created by a "bad press" in the 1920s and by laudatory biographers shortly after his death in 1925. While historians such as Paul Glad and Paolo Coletta have made substantial contributions to the literature on Bryan's career prior to 1914, the most probing analysis of his last decade is Lawrence Levine, *Defender of the Faith: William Jennings Bryan, 1915–1925* (New York: Oxford University Press, 1965). The repercussions of Bryan's fundamentalist activities on two state university campuses are described in Irvin G. Wyllie, "Bryan, Birge and the Wisconsin Evolution Controversy, 1921–1922," *The Wisconsin Magazine of History*, XXXV (Winter 1951), 294–301, and Samuel Proctor, "William Jennings Bryan and the University of Florida," *Florida Historical Quarterly*, XXXIX (September 1960), 1–15. A useful general description of his crusade against the teaching of evolution is provided by John Edwards, "Bryan's Role in the Evolution Controversy," (Unpublished M.A. thesis, University of Georgia, 1966).

Although studies devoted to the history of education, literary arts, and intellectual life in general during the 1920s are numerous, few deal adequately with the impact of the modernist-fundamentalist disturbance. Richard Hofstadter's *Anti-Intellectualism in American Life*

(New York: Alfred A. Knopf, 1963) advances many tantalizing generalizations about the anti-intellectual stance of the fundamentalists. Several chapters in R. Freeman Butts and Lawrence A. Cremin, *A History of Education in American Culture* (New York: Holt, Rinehart, and Winston, 1953), an unusually able textbook, indicate the dimension of the struggle over the moral tasks of education in the 1920s. Howard K. Beale's detailed *Are American Teachers Free?* (New York: Charles Scribner, 1936) and his *History of Freedom of Teaching in American Schools* (New York: Charles Scribner, 1941) provide a wealth of data regarding pressures exerted upon teachers during the modernist-fundamentalist conflict. Suzanne C. Linder's *William Louis Poteat: Prophet of Progress* (Chapel Hill: University of North Carolina Press, 1966) and Willard B. Gatewood, Jr.'s "Embattled Scholar: Howard W. Odum and the Fundamentalists, 1925–1927," *The Journal of Southern History*, XXXI (November 1965), 375–392, describe the plight of two scholars whose activities aroused the fundamentalists' ire. Of primary significance in most of the studies dealing with the evolution controversy in the various states is the predicament of publicly supported institutions of learning. In addition to such works cited above, Frank McVey, *The Gates Open Slowly: A History of Education in Kentucky* (Lexington: University of Kentucky Press, 1949) and Louis R. Wilson, *The University of North Carolina, 1900–1930: The Making of a Modern University* (Chapel Hill: University of North Carolina Press, 1957) cast considerable light on the plight of two state universities which came under attack by the fundamentalists.

Among a profusion of works related to the literary history of the 1920s one of the most comprehensive is Frederick J. Hoffman, *The Twenties: American Writing in the Postwar Decade* (New York: Viking Press, 1955), which should be supplemented by Alfred Kazin's classic, *On Native Ground: An Interpretation of Modern American Literature* (New York: Reynal and Hitchcock, 1942). Two works by James D. Hart, *The Popular Book: A History of America's Literary Taste* (New York: Oxford University Press, 1950), and "Platitudes of Piety: Religion and the Popular Modern Novel," *The American Quarterly*, VI (Winter 1954), 311–322, are suggestive regarding the extent to which issues involved in the modernist-fundamentalist struggle were reflected in the literature and popular reading of the 1920s. Less pertinent but nonetheless useful in the same connection is James S. Smith, "The

Day of the Popularizers," *South Atlantic Quarterly*, LXII (Spring 1963), 297–309. Walter V. Gavigan's "Religion in Recent Fiction," *The Catholic World*, CXXVI (December 1927) 360–369, provides a useful contemporary assessment of "novels with a religious background" which gained wide popularity in the 1920s. In the absence of a specific work on the relationship of theology and literature during the postwar decade, Amos Wilder's lectures, published as *Theology and American Literature* (Cambridge: Harvard University Press, 1958), and a collection of essays edited by Nathan A. Scott, Jr., and entitled *The New Orpheus* (New York: Sheed and Ward, 1956), offer helpful insights into the nature of that relationship. Austin M. Wright's *The American Short Story in the Twenties* (Chicago: University of Chicago Press, 1961) contains four chapters on morality and moral principles which are especially relevant. Of the several excellent studies of the literary group known as the Fugitives, Alexander Karanikas's *Tillers of a Myth: Southern Agrarians as Social and Literary Critics* (Madison: University of Wisconsin Press, 1966), offers the best treatment of their involvement in "religious polemics."

Finally, a volume which obviously does not belong in the category of secondary literature but nonetheless deserves mention here is Eldred C. Vanderlaan's *Fundamentalism versus Modernism* (New York: H. W. Wilson, 1925), a useful contemporary collection of documents in "The Handbook Series." In addition to a wide assortment of documents relating to the modernist-fundamentalist conflict from 1919 through 1924, this work includes a lengthy and unusually perceptive introductory essay as well as a twenty-four-page bibliography.

Index

Abbott, Lyman, 133
Academic freedom, 35–36, 221, 241–242, 256, 270–275, 280–282
Adams, J. A., 304
Aesculapius, 106
Agassiz, Louis, 343
American Association for the Advancement of Atheism, 16
American Association for the Advancement of Science, 23, 30, 44, 101, 152, 169–170, 260–261
American Association of University Professors: and academic freedom, 35, 222–223, 270, 272, 280–282
American Civil Liberties Union, 332, 340, 359, 416. *See also* Scopes Trial
American Eugenics Society, 171
Ames, Edward Scribner, 15
Amherst College, 162
Anderson, A. C., 303
Anderson, W. B., 306
Anti-Evolution League of America, 19, 125, 154, 237, 323
Aristotle, 105
Arkansas: antievolution legislation in 319–320
Asbury College, 233
Astru, Jean, 122
Atheism, 16, 261, 275, 299, 342, 359
Ayres, Clarence E.: and the folklore of science, 162–168; mentioned, 30, 152

Bacon, Francis, 117
Bailey, Kenneth K., 114
Baker, Alonzo L., 263
Baptist Bible Union, 30, 40
Baptists, 30, 31, 36, 40, 427, 428, 430–431, 433
Barnes, Harry Elmer: and humanism, 44; provokes controversy, 101; and a secular religion, 101–110
Barth, Karl, 45
Barton, Bruce, 373
Bateson, William: views on evolution, 23, 169
Beale, Howard K., 39
Beard, Charles and Mary: on modernism and fundamentalism, 413, 429–432
Begg, James T., 324
Bennett, Hugh T., 291
Bergson, Henri, 193
Berlin, University of, 433
Bewer, Julius, 66
Bible Crusaders of America: objectives of, 243–247; mentioned, 21, 154, 219, 237, 302, 336
Bible League of North America, 347
Biblical scholarship: and linguistics, 69–70; and history, 70–71; and archeology, 71; and comparative religion, 71–72. *See also* Higher criticism
Bimba, Anthony: trial of, 38
Bird, Remsen D., 250

453

Birge, Edward A., 36
Blaisdell, James A., 250
Blanton, Thomas L., 321, 323–325
Blease, Cole, 286, 327–328
Booth, William, 235
Bost, W. T., 159
Bradford, Gamaliel, 373
Brown, Arthur I.: critique of science, 154–156; poem by, 405–407
Brown University, 259, 260
Brown, William Adams: assesses religious controversy, 413, 433–443
Brown, William Montgomery: heresy trial of, 31, 246
Browning, Raymond: poem by, 403–404
Bryan Bible League, 139
Bryan, Mary B., 349
Bryan, William Jennings: quoted, 9, 19; death of, 40, 139, 336; indicts evolution, 134–138; on science, 149–150; on academic freedom, 224; on morality and education, 226–232; in Minnesota, 305; in Tennessee, 331; mentioned, 13, 21, 22, 29, 52, 53, 89, 106, 134, 153, 243, 288, 290, 292, 337, 359, 365, 415, 418, 419, 420, 426, 427, 436, 437. See also Scopes Trial
Bryn Mawr College, 135
Buber, Benjamin C., 311
Buddhism, 261
Buffon, G. L. LeClerc, 142
Burbank, Luther, 148
Burroughs, John, 140
Butler, John Washington, 290
Butler, Nicholas Murray, 286

Calvin, John, 69, 91, 251
Campbell, W. W., 250
Candler, Warren A., 28
Carleton College, 305
Carter, Deck, 333
Carter, Paul, 8, 37, 41–42
Cash, W. J., 20
Cather, Willa: quoted, 3–4; novel by, 373–374
Catholics, 18, 56, 57, 99, 251, 419, 430, 435, 440, 441–442
Chase, Harry W.: opposition to evolution laws, 36, 222, 273–275, 299
Chicago, University of, 334
Christgau, Victor, 307
Christian Science. See Eddy, Mary Baker
Chrysostom, St. John, 68
Clark, Glenn, 435–436
Clark, Walter, 301
Clarke, Edward Young, 30
Clement of Alexandria, 71

Clerk-Maxwell, James, 182
Cobb, Charles, 166
Coffman, Lotus D., 305, 308, 309–310
Colby, Bainbridge, 332
Cole, Glenn Gates, 374
Columbia University, 179, 286
Committee on War and Religious Outlook, 7, 440
Communism, 18, 20, 23–24, 114, 116, 117, 367
Conant, J. E., 219
Confucius, 209
Conklin, Edwin Grant: defense of science, 185–188; mentioned, 30
Connally, Tom, 321–322
"Copec," 440
Copeland, Royal, 320
Copernicus, Nicolaus, 57, 160, 259
Craig, R. J., 290
Crapsey, Algernon, 436
Creelman, Harlan, 66

Darrow, Clarence, 109, 332, 337, 359, 361, 362, 417. See also Scopes Trial
Darwin, Charles, 94, 112–113, 114, 116, 131, 134–135, 147, 165, 172, 187, 192–193, 198–199, 261, 278, 303
Davenport, F. H., 316, 318
Davidson, Donald, 14, 335
Davis, Watson, 20
Day, Frank, 306
Defenders of the Christian Faith, 139
Deism, 409
Denney, Joseph F.: on academic freedom, 270–272. See also American Association of University Professors
Des Moines University, 40
Dever, William E., 37–38
De Vries, Hugo, 114, 199–200
Dewey, John, 44
Dill, C. C., 327, 328
Dinsmore, Charles A.: reconciliation of science and religion, 208–214; mentioned, 150
Dispensationalism, 11
Divorce, 116, 245
Dixon, Amzi C.: antievolution argument of, 117–124; mentioned, 10, 24, 41
Dixon, Thomas, 117
Dodd, T. Hector, 248
Dorsey, George, 109
Drummond, Henry, 133
Duke, V. L., 250

Eddy, Mary Baker, 76, 441
Edison, Thomas A., 148

Edwards, Jonathan, 412
Einstein, Albert, 165, 167, 197, 255, 261
Episcopalians, 31, 419, 436
Ervin, Sam J., 330–331
Evans, Giles, 292–294
Evans, L. Walter, 303
Everett, R. O., 301

Fairchild, Frank M., 30
Family, disintegration of, 20, 117
Faraday, Michael, 181, 182
Farrar, John, 372
Faunce, William H. P.: on control of education, 259–262
Faÿ, Bernard: views of, 411–412
Federal Council of Churches of Christ in America, 51, 440
Ferguson, Charles W., 373
Finney, Charles, 235
Fiske, John, 43, 262
Fitzgerald, F. Scott, 369, 370
Fosdick, Harry Emerson: and evolution, 29–30; quoted, 39–40, 45, 430; on dangers of modernism, 42; changing position of, 44–45; defines modernism, 50; on revelation, 60–65; and modern use of the Bible, 65–73; and science, 72–73; mentioned, 8, 153, 436
Fox, Henry, 35
Franklin, Benjamin, 181
Frederickson, F. O., 305
Freedom Riders, 367
Freud, Sigmund, 414
Fugitives, 14, 335
Fuller, Frank D., 295
Fundamentalists' Federation, 143
Furlow, W. A. S., 297
Fylling, C. J., 316, 317–318

Galen, 106
Galilei, Galileo, 181
Gasper, Louis, 41
Gavigan, Walter V., 373
Geismar, Maxwell, 374
General War Time Commission, 440
Georgia: antievolution bill in, 287, 418
Gill, Harry, 248
Gnosticism, 64–65
Goethe, Johann Wolfgang von, 85, 259
Gore, S. S., 304
Grand View College, 35
Grant, Percy Stickney, 30
Gray, Asa, 187
Gray, James M.: indictment of modernism, 78–80; mentioned, 10, 24, 38, 77

Gray, W. C., 304
Greene, John C., 149

Haeckel, Ernest Heinrich, 125, 142
Haggard, Wallace, 339
Hale, Robert, 312–313
Halfyard, S. F., 316
Hall, G. Stanley, 273
Ham, Mordecai F., 22, 24, 30
Handy, Robert T., 6n, 7
Harrington, Carroll, 10
Hart, James D., 371
Hartt, Rollin L., 11
Harvard University, 189
Harvey, William, 160
Haycraft, Howard, 309
Hays, Arthur Garfield, 332, 333, 360, 364. See also Scopes Trial
Heflin, Thomas, 328–329
Hemingway, Ernest, 369, 370
Heraclitus, 119
Herczeg, Ferenz, 374
Hermelink, Heinrich, 410
Hickman, Frank, S., 310
Hicks, Sue, 339
Higgins, Jim B., 319
Higher criticism, 66, 105, 122, 243
Hill, Lew D., 290, 294–295
Hippocrates, 106
Hodge, Charles, 78
Hoffman, Frederick, 372
Hofstadter, Richard, 6, 20
Hojbierg, C. P., 35
Horden, William, 53
Hough, Sue, 310
Hudson, Winthrop, 9, 37
Humanism, 43–44, 97
Humanist Manifesto, 44
Hume, Alfred, 302
Hunter, George, 332
Huxley, Thomas, 139, 173, 187
Hylan, John F., 219

Immortality, 183–184, 204–205, 212
Institute of World Unity, 189
Interchurch World Movement, 51–52

James, William, 441
Jefferson, Charles E., 51
Jefferson, Thomas, 28, 221
Jews, 59, 99, 105, 208, 419
Johns Hopkins University, 274
Johnson, Albert S., 24
Johnson, Archibald, 88

Johnson, Gerald: and noncombatant Christians, 54, 88–94; mentioned, 25, 353
Jones, Howard Mumford: on the South, 38
Judaism, 167

Kauffman, Reginald W., 373
Kellogg, Vernon: on the limitations of science, 34, 197–207; mentioned, 23, 152
Kent, Frank R., 419
Kentucky: antievolution bill in, 171, 273–279, 415; state university of, 36, 222, 273–279
Kentucky Wesleyan College, 35
Ketcham, John C., 325
Keyser, Leander S., 22
King, T. Benton, 295
Knoles, Tully C., 250
Krutch, Joseph Wood: on the Scopes Trial, 358–367
Ku Klux Klan, 25, 428

La Guardia, Fiorello, 325–326
Lake, Kirsopp, 25, 168, 435
Lamarck, Jean Baptiste, 131, 142, 199
Lawrence, Jerome, 374
Laws, Curtis Lee, 40
League of Nations, 187
Leavitt, John M., 238
Le Conte, Joseph, 127, 131
Lee, Robert E., 374
Le Gallienne, Richard, 3
Leuba, James H., 135, 220, 226, 227–228
Levine, Lawrence: quoted, 21, 134
Lewis, Sinclair, 369, 371
Lilygren, Lloyd E., 307
Linnaeus, Carolus, 190
Lippmann, Walter: on education and fundamentalism, 251–258; mentioned 34, 318
Little, Luther: sermon of, 275; excerpt of novel by, 379–382
Loeb, Jacques, 89
Lowell, James Russell, 418
Lowery, Bill G., 323
Lucretius, 105
Lusk Laws, 5, 326
Luther, Martin, 160
Lutherans, 22, 310
Lyell, Charles, 142
Lynd, Helen, 37
Lynd, Robert, 37

McAlpin, Edwin A., 371
McCann, Alfred W., 28
McCarthyism, 367
MacCartney, Clarence E., 223

McConnell, Francis J., 3–4
Machen, J. Gresham: theology of, 13; and Presbyterian schism, 30; quoted, 148; critique of modernism by, 80–87; mentioned, 23
McLendon, Baxter F., 26
McMillan, R. L., 158
McPherson, Aimee Semple, 38
McVey, Frank L.: opposition to evolution laws, 35, 222, 276–279
Madden, Martin B., 325
Madigan, J. E., 307
Madison, R. L., 300
Maiden, Sheldon, 291
Maine: struggle over evolution in, 311–315
Malone, Dudley Field, 38, 332, 360, 364. See also Scopes Trial
Malthus, Thomas Robert, 120
Manning, William T., 31
Martin, Thomas Theodore: on teaching evolution, 237–242; and the Scopes Trial, 333; mentioned, 13, 19, 237, 302, 323
Massee, Jasper, 10, 18, 30, 38, 77, 114, 119
Mather, Kirtley: defense of science, 189–196; mentioned, 30, 153
Mathews, Shailer: theology of, 15, 16–17; definition of modernism by, 55–60; on science, 149; mentioned, 78
Mencken, Henry L., 162, 333, 360–361, 365, 366, 370
Mendel, Gregor, 114
Mercer University, 35
Merrill, E. D., 314–315
Merrill, William Pierson, 5, 436
Metcalf, Maynard, 30
Metcalf, Zeno P.: evolution debate of, 157–161
Methodists, 31, 80, 419, 428
Millikan, Robert A., 151, 152
Milton, George F., 37
Mims, Edwin, 335–336
Minnesota: fundamentalist crusade in, 74, 143–144, 305–310; state university of, 305, 308
Mississippi: evolution law in, 302–304; state university of, 302
Moody Bible Institute, 24, 38, 77
Moody, Dwight L., 10, 235
More, Louis T., 30
Morison, Samuel Eliot, 419
Morrison, Cameron, 219, 298
Morrison, Henry C., 233–236
Mystics, 88–94 passim

Nathan, George Jean, 370

National Education Association, 34, 222
National Federation of Fundamentalists, 30
National Research Council, 197
Naturalism, 81, 151
Neal, John R., 360
Negroes, 18, 427
Newton, Isaac, 181
Nichol, Francis D., 262
Niebuhr, H. Richard, 37
Niebuhr, Reinhold: theology of, 42–43; quoted, 46; critique by, 95–100; mentioned, 45, 54, 149
Nietzsche, Friedrich: influence of, 23; and Darwin, 114; ideas of, 121–122; and World War I, 140; mentioned, 128, 129
Nixon, Justin W., 33, 42, 43, 44
Norris, J. Frank, 22, 30
North Carolina: evolution bill in, 298–301; state university of, 36, 38, 208, 222, 273, 298
North Carolina Bible League, 143
North Carolina State College, 157
North Dakota: hearing on evolution bill in, 316–318
Northern Baptist Convention, 30

O'Donnell, Catherine, 250
Odum, Howard W., 35, 101
Oemler, Marie, 373
Oklahoma: state university of, 24; evolution law in, 418
Oregon, University of, 273
Osborn, Henry F., 30, 269
Osgood, Phillips, 310
Owen, J. P., 295
Owen, Russell D.: analysis of Scopes Trial, 344–352

Page, Blin W., 311–312
Paine, Thomas, 126
Pantheism, 78, 115, 128, 132
Papini, Giovanni, 373
Park, John A., 158
Parks, Leighton, 8
Pasquet, Désiré, 410
Patterson, Arthur W., 314
Patterson, Robert Leet, 51
Paulin, George, 120
Paulsen, Alice, 441
Peay, Austin, 331
Pharr, Edgar W., 273
Phillips, Wendell, 342
Pierce v. Society of Sisters, 224

Piper, Ellsworth, 312
Plato, 119
Poole, D. Scott, 298
Porter, John W.: antievolution argument, 125–129
Poteat, William L., 30
Potter, Charles F., 130, 349, 353
Pre-millennialism, 11, 41
Presbyterians, 21, 31, 36, 134, 419, 428, 433, 436
Price, George McCready: and the new geology, 23 116; antievolution argument of, 141–142; mentioned, 141, 263
Princeton Theological Seminary, 13, 38
Princeton theology, 11
Princeton University, 185
Psychiatry: and sin, 108–109
Pupin, Michael: on science and religion, 32–33, 179–184; mentioned, 30, 148
Puritanism, 95, 370, 409, 424
Pythagoras, 119

Quartet Music Company, 407

Rader, Paul, 17, 38
Radio Control Bill, 327
Ransom, John Crowe, 13–14, 335
Rappelyea, George, 331–332, 339, 340–341, 359. See also Scopes Trial
Ratcliffe, S. K.: quoted, 410–411; on fundamentalism, 414–423
Raulston, John T., 333, 348–349, 362–363. See also Scopes Trial
Rawlinson, Henry, 69
Red Scare. See Communism
Reed, Clarence, 248
Reinhardt, Aurelia, 250
Reutherdahl, Arvid, 310
Richardson, L. O., 316
Riley, William Bell: crusades of, 18, 143; and millennialism, 41; and Protestant unity, 52; defines fundamentalism, 74–77; evolution debate of, 157–161, 189; and antievolution legislation, 305–310 passim; mentioned, 10, 13, 17, 21, 38, 39, 52, 53, 305, 306
Ritschl, Albrecht, 12, 79–80
Robie, Frederick, 312
Robinson, Fred E., 331, 338, 339, 340
Robinson, James Harvey, 35, 109
Robinson, O. N., 303
Romanes, George, 131, 137
Rood, Paul W., 139
Rosetta Stone, 69

Roy, Henry E., 311, 313–314
Russell, Bertrand, 109

Sacco-Vanzetti Case, 5, 38, 409
St. Olaf College, 310
Sandeen, Ernest R., 10–11
Sanderson, H. F., 303
Santayana, George, 98
Schleiermacher, F. E. D., 12
Schneider, Herbert, 41
Science League of America, 39, 152, 171, 175, 263
Scopes, John T., 257, 331, 338, 359, 360, 362, 414, 416. See also Scopes Trial
Scopes Trial: and the Fugitives, 14, 335; impact of, 40, 224, 335–336; origins of, 338–341; meaning of, 344–352; advertises the South, 353–354; analyzed by Straton, 355–357; J. W. Krutch on, 358–367; mentioned, 5, 34, 36, 37, 197, 286, 289, 331–367 passim, 410, 426, 431
Scott, John F.: short story by, 391–402
Seventh Day Adventist, 176
Sheldon, Charles M., 371
Shelton, John A., 290–291
Shipley, Maynard: activities of, 39, 152, 171, 175; critique of fundamentalism, 175–178; on evolution in public schools, 263–269
Shotwell, James T., 71
Siegfried, André: views of, 412, 424–428
Simonton, C. P., 291, 292
Sims, Cecil, 295
Sims, J. J.: antievolution argument, 139–140
Sinclair, Upton, 25
Slint, John R., 315
Slosson, Preston: poem by, 404–405
Smith, Alfred E., 319
Smith College, 101
Smith, Gerald Birney, 78
Smith, Roy, 310
Snow, C. P., 3
Social Gospel, 4, 7, 10, 28, 42
Socrates, 85
Solberg, S. K., 306
Soper, Edmund D., 113
Spencer, Herbert, 131
Sprowls, Jesse W., 35
Stanford University, 197
Stearns, Harold, 310
Steen, Henry, 307
Stewart, Tom, 348, 350–351

Strachey, John, 411
Straton, John Roach: quoted, 25, 115; antievolution argument of, 130–131; view of the Scopes Trial, 355–357; mentioned, 17, 21, 30, 38, 41, 106, 151
Stribling, T. S.: excerpt from novel by, 375–378; mentioned, 373
Stub, J. A. O., 310
Sturgis, John A., 315
Summers, John William, 321–322
Sunday, Billy: advice to Byran, 342–343; mentioned, 22, 26, 38, 116
Supreme Kingdom, 38

Tate, Allen, 335
Tennessee: state university of, 35; antievolution law in, 45, 75, 290–297, 416, 431. See also Scopes Trial
Tennessee Supreme Court, 334
Textbooks: control of, 244; California investigation of, 248–250; in Mississippi, 304
Theodore of Mopsuestia, 68
Thomson, J. Arthur, 148, 373
Thorpe, George L., 248
Thwing, A. L., 308
Tocqueville, Alexis de, 424
Trice, J. H., 296–297
Turlington, Zebulon V., 298–300

Union Theological Seminary, 60, 433
Union Theological Seminary (Richmond), 226
Union University, 237
Unitarianism, 409, 429
United States Congress: and evolution controversy, 321–329

Vanderbilt University, 14, 60
Van Doren, Carl: short story by, 383–390
Vigness, L. A., 310
Virginia, University of, 251
Volta, Alessandro, 182

Wake Forest College, 30
Wall, E. E., 248
Washburn, George F., 243
Watson, John B., 109
Waugh, Karl T., 250
Weismann, August, 187
Wells, H. G., 86
Wesley, John, 235, 259
Wharton, Edith, 373

Whitfield, Hervey, 296
Wiggam, Albert E.: and the decalogue of science, 171–174; mentioned, 8, 152, 373
Wilbur, Ray L., 250
Williams, Michael, 333
Wisconsin, University of, 21, 36
Wittner, Loren, 323
World War I: and American society, 3–4; and religion, 7, 114; and science, 147–148; education after, 217–225; mentioned, 28, 79, 122, 140, 149, 285

World War II, 45
World's Christian Fundamentals Association: founding of, 17; work of, 18–19; decline of, 39; mentioned, 74, 157, 332
Wright, Austin M., 372
Wright, Harold Bell, 373

Yale Divinity School, 208
Yale University, 433
Young Men's Christian Association, 222, 279